CHANGING

METHODS

CHANGING
METHODS

Feminists Transforming Practice

EDITED BY SANDRA BURT
& LORRAINE CODE

broadview press

Canadian Cataloguing and Publication Data

Burt, Sandra D., 1947- .
Changing methods: feminists transforming practice

Includes bibliographical references.
ISBN 1-55111-033-4

1. Women's studies — Methodology. 2. Feminism — Research — Methodology. 3. Feminist theory.
I. Code, Lorraine. II. Title.

HQ1180.B87 1995   305.42'072   C95-931310-9

Broadview Press
Post Office Box 1243, Peterborough, Ontario, Canada K9J 7H5

in the United States of America:
3576 California Road, Orchard Park, NY 14127

in the United Kingdom:
B.R.A.D. Book Representation & Distribution Ltd., 244A, London Road, Hadleigh, Essex SS7 2 DE

Broadview Press gratefully acknowledges the support of the Canada Council, the Ontario Arts Council, the Ontario Publishing Centre, and the Ministry of National Heritage.

Cover: Michèlle Karch-Ackerman, *Tea Party Dress* (mixed media, 1994).
Photo by Martin Karch-Ackerman. Design by George Kirkpatrick.

PRINTED IN CANADA
5 4 3 2 1 95 96 97

Contents

PREFACE

THIS COLLECTION BRINGS TOGETHER ORIGINAL ESSAYS BY a group of practitioners, researchers, and activists whose work has been shaped by interconnections between feminist process and feminist practice. In planning the book, we invited each contributor to relate in detail, in a concrete way, how a feminist-informed consciousness and feminist political-activist issues have influenced her professional life and/or have had an impact on her methods of conducting research. Furthermore, and integral to the process of producing their contributions, many of the authors sought to understand how their feminism, anti-racism, consciousness of class bias or homophobia, and other such political-social commitments were shaping their analyses of these issues.

This attempt to integrate process and practice culminated in January 1994 in a two-day workshop at York University, where all of the contributors presented early versions of their chapters for commentary and discussion, first by a designated discussant, and then with the assembled group. The workshop enabled us to benefit from one another's insights and criticisms and thus to produce a more integrated book than would otherwise have been possible. The workshop was innovative in breaking the standard pattern of conferences in which academics talk only with other academics: it was an occasion on which feminist participants working from a variety of positions could question one another's taken-for-granted assumptions. In the collection some of Canada's leading feminists offer accounts of their work in ways that explain and strengthen their innovative approaches to it.

Although we have a sense of having participated in a more diverse collaboration than projects of this nature usually achieve, we have no illusions about the extent to which the contributors are "representative" of all Canadian women. We have sought to avoid an assumption that often informs such edited collections, to the effect that inclusiveness can be achieved by the simple addition of a token chapter by one person who is judged "more marginal" than the others, or by introducing an isolated example of otherness. There are obvious ways in which this group is not representative; some of those ways are evident from the list of authors in the table of contents; others are addressed in the texts of the various chapters, both self-critically and in criticisms directed at projects of this kind, in some more explicitly than in others.

Nor does this group pretend to be inclusive to the extent that it "covers" all varieties of feminism, or all women, or even all professional-academic women. It counts, rather, as a preliminary attempt to realize a degree of inclusiveness—more in the issues it engages with than in the identities of its contributors—that could point the way to more elaborated projects that would better demonstrate the heterogeneity of Canadian society.[1] Yet again, the goal of bringing so disparate a group of people together is not to achieve consensus or artificial integration, but to facilitate an exchange that opens new directions for ongoing inquiry. For although most of the contributors to this collection are anglophone, middle-class, white Canadian women, the subject matters they address are neither anglo-centred nor focused primarily on white, urban Canadian female lives.

During the final decades of the twentieth century feminists working in communities and in educational settings have been engaged in challenging established patterns of allowing abstracted, formalized versions of the ideas and experiences of privileged white men to set the standards for social and political behaviour, to establish social policies, and to determine the shape of activist and research projects. Throughout the history of western society, this male reference point has been embedded in a dominant ideology that is implicitly constructed around race, class, gender, and heterosexual privilege. In Canada another privileged point of reference has been geographical location, with Ontario often standing for all of Canada, for all Canadian interests and points of view. Although this collection also originates in Ontario, the contributors disrupt and interrogate pervasive assumptions about centrality and marginality by bringing into their work the concerns of regions and segments of the population that are too often represented as peripheral in more explicitly Ontario-centred writings.

Beginning with a commitment to taking women as a central point of

1   We allude here to Iris Young's concept of the "heterogeneous public" as she elaborates it in her essay "Impartiality and the Civic Public," in Linda Nicholson, ed., *Feminism/Postmodernism* (New York: Routledge, 1990).

reference, Canadian feminists—like feminists throughout the world— have sought to develop ways of bringing the integrity of their own and other women's experiences directly into practical and research contexts, not necessarily treating those experiences as inviolate or sacrosanct, but allowing them to inform their thinking and acting. Feminists are aware that experiences, whether their own or someone else's, rarely speak for themselves; hence they usually require analysis, interpretation. When the inquiry involves speaking for other people or about other people's experiences, there is a tacit consensus among feminists about the responsibility a researcher or writer has to take for the position she occupies, and about her accountability to the persons or groups about or for whom she claims to speak. Questions of expertise and authority are the issues here; and accountability is a central feminist concern, which entails a principled commitment to trying to discover how things are with the people one is studying or working with, in ongoing critical and self-critical, yet respectful, negotiations.

Accountability often manifests itself, too, in a readiness to make sure that people who have participated in the research process as interviewees remain active participants to the extent that the researcher makes her results available, and ensures that they are accessible, to them. Indeed, especially since the 1981 publication of Ann Oakley's work on interviewing women, many researchers have insisted that all such processes should be interactive rather than constructed according to the old subject/object (=interviewer/interviewee) model.[2] Among feminist researchers Oakley's work has produced a growing commitment to contesting and even rejecting the artificial stance of the objective observer. Yet her work has also sometimes generated what Shulamit Reinharz describes as "excessive demands," especially in situations in which the interests of the researcher and the person being interviewed are in conflict, or otherwise incongruent with one another.[3] While Oakley argues that interview encounters necessarily produce a relationship between the researcher and the people she interviews, some theorists have extrapolated from this observation to conclude that researchers and the subjects of their research must become friends. Such a requirement would not only be cumbersome, but could also be coercive in many different ways; and it would eradicate the distance that even this new rapprochement between participants seeks, albeit paradoxically, to maintain.

2   Ann Oakley, "Interviewing Women: A Contradiction in Terms," in Helen Roberts, ed., *Doing Feminist Research* (London: Routledge & Kegan Paul, 1981).

3   Shulamit Reinharz, "Neglected Voices and Excessive Demands in Feminist Research, *Qualitative Sociology* 16, 1 (1993), pp.69-75.

Yet these new and evolving processes are not simple: they resist swift categorizations and neat assumptions about "data" and how they should be read; they are rarely content with single-factor explanations. The strength of their analyses is often apparent in a continuing scepticism about solutions that mask complexities behind crude stereotypes. They are demanding in that they often require researchers and writers to keep numerous strands of inquiry going all at once. Yet when they are successful they avoid the imperialism that, in traditional structures of expertise and authority, often leaves the subjects of study feeling violated because they fail to recognize themselves in the studies of which they are the subjects. Alison Wylie and Lorraine Greaves provide an excellent example of women creating a research instrument that can enable people working with battered women to see and understand their situations as they are for those women, and not as the practitioner imagines they must be, extrapolating from her/his own life. They use this newfound knowledge to transform the ensuing therapeutic practices. Issues of advocacy and expertise figure prominently in their study, as they do in many of the other chapters in this book.

Experientially informed practice and analysis have generally commanded less esteem in the academy and the public world than does work that presents itself as scientific and objective. In consequence, a central problem for feminists is to integrate experiences that are specifically located and structured into a social and research community that tends to make too sharp a distinction between anecdote and evidence and hence relegates first-person experiential data to an area that falls outside the realm of serious scholarly and/or activist debate. The feminist task is further complicated by the problem of how at once to respect and interrogate these experiences. This task has moved "the method question" to the top of many feminist agendas in the 1990s.

Methodological issues take on a special urgency for feminists who recognize the impossibility of maintaining a distinction between process and practice. For example, the process of participating in the Inuit Justice Project, detailed in chapter four, exposes the inability of white Canadian justice principles to address the specific circumstances of Inuit women's lives. Similarly, the process of attempting to use established survey research methods to discover attitudes to social issues and political behaviours (chapter twelve) reveals the inadequacy both of the methods themselves and of the standard ways of interpreting survey findings.

What is particularly innovative about this new process-product rela-tion is that it breaks an old pattern of assuming that if a research tool or method of practice cannot engage with a certain kind of experience or data, there must be something amiss with the experience, or some in-adequacy in the data. Feminists have turned their attention, rather, to wondering—variously, according to the context—whether the fault might lie with the theoretical assumptions or with the methods they have used to approach the issues. The chapters in this book show how a group of Canadian feminists are engaging with these questions.

Our thanks to Michael Harrison for his interest and encouragement throughout this project, to Robert Clarke for careful and sensitive edit-ing, to Barbara Conolly for her work on the production process, and to Ellen Miller for her assistance with the January 1994 workshop. The workshop was made possible by a grant from the Social Sciences and Humanities Research Council of Canada.

LORRAINE CODE

Chapter One: How Do We Know?
Questions of Method in Feminist Practice

FEMINISM AND PHILOSOPHY—KNOWLEDGE QUESTIONS

NON-PHILOSOPHERS TEND TO THINK OF EPISTEMOLOGY— theory of knowledge—as the exclusive concern of one of the most esoteric branches of academic philosophy; hence as a pursuit that is of interest to philosophers alone, with minimal extraphilosophical, practical/activist relevance. And epistemology, together with philosophy of science, is a subdivision of mainstream professional philosophy that remained resistant to feminist intervention long after feminist voices had established themselves within moral-political discourse, in theories of human nature, and in more general critiques of the ingrained misogyny of the philosophical canon.

Reasons for epistemology's declared immunity to feminist critique come from different directions. First, and dominant among such reasons, is a persistent professional and everyday conviction that knowledge is just knowledge; it does not matter whose it is, who has made it, who knows it. The facts, if factual they really are, will prevail. A long tradition of distinguishing between knowledge and "mere opinion" rests, in part, upon granting knowledge a status—and hence a generality, a universal scope—that enables it to transcend the specific experiences of particular knowers. Despite the equivalently universalist and almost as abstract assumptions of traditional moral-political theories, somehow it seems to have been easier for feminist philosophers to insert people, or particularities, into those texts and debates that are, after all, about human actions and social arrangements. Knowledge—facts—are thought to pertain, even if no one knows them.

Second, it may not just be its status as a domain of philosophy that prevented feminists, initially, from venturing onto epistemological territory; for feminist philosophers, too, came to it later than to other "divisions" of the discipline. Reasons for this time lag are more likely to be found in the fact that the epistemologies practised in the professional philosophical mainstream are remarkably impotent when it comes to offering guidance for the knowledge-producing and knowledge-evaluating issues that are urgent within people's lives. Mainstream epistemologies have seemed, somehow, to be irrelevant to knowing the complex situations that feminists have to know; they have seemed to have little practical guidance to offer. It is not easy, for example, to see how knowing medium-sized material objects—a standard epistemologist's exemplar—can translate into situations in which one has to know the power dynamics of a patriarchal social structure or the defining features of sexual assault. Nor do scientific models translate well into psychological research that seeks to analyse the experiential effects of phenomena like systemic racism or rape within marriage, positivistic promises about the unity of science notwithstanding. Nor, again, is it easy to maintain the requisite separation between facts and values when some "facts"—such as the much advertised "harmlessness" to women of the Dalkon Shield—are so clearly the products of power-based knowledge-construction processes. Hence many feminist philosophers have expressed unease with the epistemological options available to them within their chosen academic discipline: an unease out of which, since the early 1980s, innovative feminist critiques and reconstructions of "the epistemological project" have been proliferating.[1]

1   For a representative sampling of feminist philosophical works in epistemology, see Kathleen Lennon and Margaret Whitford, eds., *Knowing the Difference: Feminist Perspectives in Epistemology* (London: Routledge, 1994); Linda Alcoff and Elizabeth Potter, eds., *Feminist Epistemologies* (New York: Routledge, 1993); Louise Antony and Charlotte Witt, eds., *A Mind of One's Own: Feminist Essays on Reason and Objectivity* (Boulder, Col.: Westview Press, 1993); Lorraine Code, *Rhetorical Spaces: Essays on (Gendered) Locations* (New York: Routledge, 1995), and *What Can She Know? Feminist Theory and the Construction of Knowledge* (Ithaca, N.Y.: Cornell University Press, 1991); Jane Duran, *Toward a Feminist Epistemology* (Savage, Md.: Rowman and Littlefield, 1990); Sandra Harding, *The Science Question in Feminism* (Ithaca, N.Y.: Cornell University Press, 1986), and *Whose Science? Whose Knowledge? Thinking from Women's Lives* (Ithaca, N.Y.: Cornell University Press, 1991); Elizabeth Harvey and Kathleen Okruhlik, eds., *Women and Reason* (Ann Arbor: University of Michigan Press,

The dominant epistemologies of modernity, which developed out of the intellectual achievements of the Enlightenment with a later infusion of positivist-empiricist principles, are defined around highly rarefied ideals of objectivity and value-neutrality.[2] Objectivity is conceived as a perfectly detached, neutral, distanced, and disinterested approach to a subject matter that exists in a publicly observable space, separate from knowers/observers and making no personal claims on them. Value-neutrality elaborates the disinterested aspect of objectivity: the conviction that knowers must have no vested interest in the objects of their knowledge; that they have no reasons other than the pursuit of "pure" inquiry to seek knowledge. These ideals are best suited to regulate the knowledge-making of people who believe in the possibility of achieving a "view from nowhere"—of performing what Donna Haraway calls "the god-trick"—that seems to allow them, through the autonomous exercise of their reason, to escape the constraints that location within specific bodies and sets of circumstances impose upon all human knowledge-seeking.[3] Feminists have shown that people who are in positions that enable them to sustain such beliefs, in affluent societies, have overwhelmingly been male, white, able-bodied, heterosexual, and "of a certain maturity" (=neither too young nor too old). Hence feminist epistemologists have exposed the androcentricity and, latterly, the racial, cultural, historical, class, and numerous other "centricities" of the epistemologies of the mainstream Anglo-American traditions.

Androcentricity is the characteristic of being derived from, based upon, and relevant principally to the experiences of men. Yet feminists do not characterize standard epistemologies as androcentred merely because they are man-made; nor do they suggest that all men have had an equal part in their making. They also do not claim that there is a conspiracy to ensure that epistemologies of, by, and for men are granted ascendancy, while "women's ways of knowing" are consciously and consistently suppressed. Rather, feminists have shown that there is a marked coincidence between the ideals and values constitutive of ideal (=white,

1992); Susan Hekman, *Gender and Knowledge: Elements of a Postmodern Feminism* (Boston: Northeastern University Press, 1990); and Lynn Hankinson Nelson, *Who Knows: From Quine to a Feminist Empiricism* (Philadelphia: Temple University Press, 1990).

2   Here I am drawing on my "Taking Subjectivity into Account," in Alcoff and Potter, *Feminist Epistemologies*; reprinted in my *Rhetorical Spaces*.

3   I allude here to the title of Thomas Nagel's book, *A View from Nowhere* (Oxford: Oxford University Press, 1986). Donna Haraway writes about "the god-trick" in her "Situated Knowledges: The Science Question in Feminism and the Privilege of Partial Perspective," in Donna Haraway, *Simians, Cyborgs, and Woman: The Reinvention of Nature* (New York: Routledge, 1991), p.189.

educated, propertied, and heterosexual) masculinity throughout Western philosophical, cultural, and social history, and the values constitutive
of the highest forms of rationality and the most authoritative forms of
knowledge.[4] The psychosocial characteristics that are most commonly
nurtured in affluent white male children in such societies tend to be just
the ones that prepare the men of these dominant social groups for a lifetime of detached, objective control over their circumstances, in a "public" world of work and deliberation; and that give content to stereotypic
conceptions of "what it means to be a man." The regulative ideals that inform theories about conditions for the possibility of knowledge—even
such seemingly incontestable ideals as those of objectivity, autonomy,
and impartiality—resonate with these character traits. And theories of
knowledge, in the main, are androcentric in the sense that these ideals,
which form their core, are distilled out of a generic, abstracted conception of the experiences of this small group of privileged men.

Ideal objectivity and value-neutrality take for granted a homogeneous "human nature," individually and separately realized in each discrete, self-contained person. On such an assumption, knowers are sub-
stitutable for one another in the sense that they can act as "surrogate
knowers" who can put themselves in anyone else's place and know exactly what she or he would know.[5] These ideals erase connections between knowledge and power; hence they lend support to a philosophical
and commonsensical conviction that knowledge properly so called is as
neutral—as politically innocent—as the processes thought to produce
it. Such epistemologies imply that if would-be knowers cannot see
"from nowhere," from an ideal observation position that could be any-
where and everywhere, then they cannot produce knowledge worthy of
the name. Resistance to deviating from a "normal" (=male-derived)
medical model to study women's symptoms separately is just one example that confirms these assumptions. The example attests to a widespread belief that "special-interest groups" cannot be objective, and that

4   The *locus classicus* in feminist philosophy for these arguments is Genevieve Lloyd, *The Man
     of Reason* (Minneapolis: University of Minnesota Press, 1984); 2nd ed., 1993. See also Susan
     Bordo, *The Flight to Objectivity* (Albany, N.Y.: SUNY Press, 1987); and Evelyn Fox Keller,
     Reflections on Gender and Science (New Haven, Conn.: Yale University Press, 1985).

5   I owe the phrase "surrogate knower" to Naomi Scheman, in her paper, "Descartes and Gen-
     der," presented to the conference "Reason, Gender, and the Moderns," University of
     Toronto, February 1990. See Scheman's interesting discussion of the implications of a belief
     in "the interchangeability of authorized knowers" in her "Who Wants to Know? The Episte-
     mological Value of Values," in Joan E. Hartman and Ellen Messer-Davidow, eds., *(En)Gen-
     dering Knowledge: Feminists in Academe* (Knoxville: The University of Tennessee Press,
     1991), pp.181ff; reprinted in Naomi Scheman, *Engenderings: Constructions of Knowledge,
     Authority, and Privilege* (New York: Routledge, 1993).

therefore their experiences and circumstances cannot yield knowledge. So long as women—or Blacks, gays, Native people, the working classes, the disabled, the elderly—are designated "special-interest groups," their concerns do not figure equally on epistemological and political agendas with those of the dominant members of a society. Their lives are not considered to be as worth knowing about; the inequities in their situations not as worth addressing.

For positivist-empiricists, knowers are detached and neutral spectators, and objects of knowledge are separate from them, inert items in knowledge-gathering processes, yielding knowledge best verified by appealing to observational data. Each individual knower is thought to be singly and separately accountable to the evidence, yet the assumption is that *his* cognitive efforts could be replicated by anyone else in the same circumstances. And people seek knowledge so that they can predict, manipulate, and control their environments. It is from the positivist legacy that the fact/value distinction that regulates inquiry also derives. For positivists, expressions of value (such as "abortion is wrong") cannot be verified empirically, for they merely amount to reports of how people feel about the practice in question. Hence they must not be permitted to distort "the facts." Feminist commitments, like anti-racist commitments and gay rights commitments, count within such analyses only as values; hence they cannot be permitted to inspire, govern, or justify the results of research projects. To be a feminist is, in effect, to conduct value-laden research and hence not to be properly objective. Such ideologies sustain the "myth of the neutral man" who is presumed to be able to represent everyone's interests with detached objectivity, in his universally motivated and applicable projects of inquiry. Women, and other "Others," by contrast, are represented as producing only subjective, partial, subjectively interested research.

From a positivistic conception of scientific knowledge comes the dominant ideal of objectivity, together with the tradition of seeing physical science as objective knowing at its best, and its practitioners as knowers par excellence. Positivists and their successors also insist on maintaining a separation between the "context of discovery" and the "context of justification." Hence they can maintain that even though information-gathering (discovery) can be intermingled with the messier details of everyday life, processes of justification can effectively purify the product—the knowledge—from any such taint. Suggestions that human psychology, or socio-cultural-gendered locations, could count among the conditions that shape possibilities of knowing are dismissed as "psychologism," or as concerns that belong merely to the sociology of knowledge. The charge is that although such pursuits might provide anecdotal information, none of them contributes to the real business of epistemology. Such theories make so sharp a distinction between anecdotal information and evidence that it is easy to understand why projects committed to taking experiences seriously cannot easily find entry into their discourse; for experiential accounts are too readily equated with anecdotal evidence.

Moreover, positivists and their successors assume that clear, unequivocal knowledge can only be produced by abstracting the subject/object of study from the confusion of its context—of its location within concrete circumstances. (In chapter 9, Karen Messing amply demonstrates the consequences for women's workplace suffering that such processes of abstraction produce.) In decontextualized research, sanitized examples tend most commonly to be abstracted, whether by chance or by design, from the stylized experiences of the privileged, then to be presented as exemplary of knowledge "in general." Hence the knowledge that epistemologists who base their theories on such examples appeal to is not of concrete or unique aspects of the physical-social world; it is of *instances* rather than particulars. When knowers are depicted as discrete individuals with uniform access to the "stuff" of which this knowledge is made, it is no wonder that the specificities of their experiences—and their specific exclusions from taken-for-granted epistemic "goods"—should disappear in the analytic process.

Here I am representing positivism in its starkest form, because these aspects of its program have "trickled down" to shape the regulative ideals of orthodox epistemology and to inform everyday conceptions of what it means to be objective and to know. These ideals sustain the authoritative status of modern science both in the academy and throughout affluent societies. And they perpetuate its impersonal, assent-demanding status with a rhetoric—"it has been shown," "the facts reveal," "the data indicate"—that effectively erases any suggestion of human participation in the production of knowledge, beyond merely receiving the information in *tabula rasa*-like fashion. Given the spectacular successes of science and science-informed technology, it is no wonder that science appears to offer the best available model for knowledge not just of matters scientific, but of everything anyone might want to know, from what makes a car run to what makes a person happy. It is no wonder that reports introduced by the assertion "Science has proved ..." carry an immediate presumption of truth. Yet scientific and technological successes are inevitably counterbalanced by unforeseen by-products and unexpected environmental and human damage. And despite positivistic disclaimers, feminists have demonstrated that specific values, subjectivities, and social-cultural locations have produced these positivist epistemologies, whose influence is indelibly imprinted on authoritative public knowledge. Hence scientific success is rarely unqualified, and knowledge developed on a scientific model is usually much more ambiguous than its scientific "hard-edged" derivation would suggest.

KNOWLEDGE AND EXPERIENCE

The poverty of mainstream epistemological resources notwithstanding, feminists throughout the second wave of the women's movement have been committed to producing knowledge that can be effective in promoting their theoretical and activist projects. Tacit assumptions about how knowledge can be acquired and validated have informed not only feminist research practices and activist conceptions of what issues are worth pursuing and why, but also feminist endeavours to understand the everyday manifestations of the gender-inflected power and privilege that permeate every society and social group. In working from these assumptions feminists find themselves engaging, often explicitly, with epistemological questions, hence making common cause with feminist philosophers whose interests are primarily epistemological. Questions about what makes knowledge possible, about the research strategies best suited to particular subjects of inquiry, and about discovery and justification, certainty, fallibility, and relativism are central to their discussions, as becomes clear in the chapters of this book. Closely intertwined with these epistemological questions are methodological questions: about methods that can yield knowledge that is reliable, effective, and oppressive neither to women nor to other socially marginalized and disempowered people; about methods that honour feminists' commitments to taking women's experiences seriously; and about methods of addressing differences while retaining a capacity to draw general, even law-like conclusions.

Indeed, feminist commitments to fostering women's emancipation make it imperative for them to *know* the situations and circumstances of women's lives: to know them not just in their surface manifestations, but in their deeper implications and effects. Feminists have to know how to explain the absence of women "both as agents and as subjects of inquiry" throughout received public knowledge.[6] If they are to determine what needs to be criticized, challenged, and/or changed, they have to develop valid, workable analyses of the oppressions and marginalizations from which emancipation must be achieved. They have to be able to articulate informed and practicable strategies for transforming authoritarian knowledge and the social structures that it legitimates and informs, where women still occupy positions of minimal power and authority. To develop such strategies, feminists have to know those structures well enough to reveal their often invisible mechanisms for maintaining hierarchical social arrangements and uneven distributions of the power that knowledge confers.

Producing such good, reliable knowledge should be one of the easiest and most straightforward goals to pursue in the late twentieth century, when physical scientists have developed hitherto unimagined tools and methods for unlocking "the secrets of the universe,"[7] when the achievements of science and technology command unprecedented public respect as the highest accomplishments of human reason, and when there are apparently no limits to what people can know. It would seem to be only a matter of time until, using these scientific methods that have proven so effective, it will be possible to generate an equally impressive explanation of every puzzling phenomenon, whether that phenomenon is natural, psychological, social, or political. Yet many of the research methods modelled on scientific methodology that govern conceptions of what counts as knowledge in the academic mainstream have yielded the consequence that women and other socially disadvantaged groups of people are not only invisible in the data from which conclusions are drawn, but can also find no way of making their experiences count as informed or knowledgeable. Hence the belief persists, at least in the folk

6   I borrow the phrase "agents and subjects of inquiry" from Joan E. Hartman and Ellen Messer-Davidow, "Introduction: A Position Statement," in Hartman and Messer-Davidow, *(En)Gendering Knowledge,* p.2.

7   My reference here is to Evelyn Fox Keller's collection, *Secrets of Life, Secrets of Death: Essays on Language, Gender and Science* (New York: Routledge, 1992).

wisdom, that women have never been able to know very much at all, and that they have only rarely been significant actors in the making of society and history. Nor can women be sure that the knowledge *about* them that is in public circulation will account accurately for their experiences or represent their interests. Moreover, these patterns of incredulity are unevenly distributed within female populations, with the consequence that some women—non-white, working-class, poor, or inarticulate, for example—can claim less public credibility than others.

To illustrate some of these points I offer a reading of a newspaper article that reports an instance of knowledge construction in which gender issues figure both explicitly and implicitly. I take this article as my starting point in order to propose that one productive place for feminist inquiry to begin is in examining actual instances of "local" knowledge claims, situated within the physical or material circumstances of women's lives, as they enter social discourse through publicly circulated documents. Hence I begin with this report partly because of its position in the everyday world, its status as a quotidian epistemological event with a peculiar and by no means atypical impact on women's daily lives: on how they are represented, on how their experiences are interpreted, and on how they come to understand their own experiences as starting points for action. In proceeding thus, I am departing from the more standard philosophical project of producing *a priori* analyses of necessary and sufficient conditions for the acquisition/production of "knowledge in general." I am shifting the focus of my inquiry away from the normative practice of determining what an ideal knower ought to do, and towards a critical analysis of what historically and materially "situated" knowers actually do.[8] I am also intentionally engaging with a source that reports a situation at second hand rather than recording observations at first hand: a source whose credibility needs itself to be assessed, in a communicative process such as people are commonly engaged in, in their everyday knowledge-seeking efforts. The report counts as a point of entry into a debate; an ongoing knowledge-constructing negotiation in which its readers will seek corroboration and interpretation. And indeed, the second "tier" of my analysis will engage with just this issue of interpretation. But I begin in this way to demonstrate that analyses of "knowledge in general" often have to give way to analyses of particular, local moments at which knowledge claims enter everyday

8   The reference, again, is to Haraway's "Situated Knowledges."

lives and conversations, if those analyses are to be effective in explicating and guiding knowledge-producing practices. This conviction that formal, decontextualized abstraction has to be left behind shapes my thinking about the methodological issues I address in the final section of this chapter.

Writing about cardiac medicine in *The Globe and Mail*, Robin Henig describes a heart condition known only as "syndrome X." She reports that patients suffering from a form of angina not readily detected by standard diagnostic procedures are often dismissed by cardiologists as complaining of a pain that is "all in their minds." These patients present themselves in physicians' consulting rooms *knowing* that there is something wrong with them, only to learn that their cardiograms reveal no abnormalities and that, according to their angiograms, their arteries look quite normal. The physicians often assure them that their condition presents no cause for alarm.

Henig claims significance for the fact that two-thirds of these patients are women, quoting associate professor of nursing Kathleen King: "Men often experience what are considered 'textbook' cases of angina and other heart-disease symptoms because the textbooks are written to describe men's symptoms.... You're not going to think of heart disease unless the symptoms fit the classic picture. And the trouble is we don't know what the classic picture for women is."[9] Yet she notes that "a handful of cardiologists" are now paying attention to these "frustrated heart patients," with the result that in the United States a massive clinical trial is under way, with all of its 140,000 subjects women.

Of interest to feminist theorists, not only in medicine but also across the research and intellectual landscape, are the ideological and methodological assumptions that conceal the very absence of female subjects in research that generates standard textbook data; and the processes by which changes in exclusionary research assumptions and methods can be effected. Ideologically, such states of affairs attest to a pervasive and ingrained belief that men (again, white able-bodied men who are neither too old nor too young) are representative of "human nature" and that their experiences, diseases, proclivities, and interests can count as surrogates for the circumstances of all other adult members of the population. With the possible exception of explicitly sex-specific, hence usually reproductive, experiences and phenomena, a common (if tacit) presuppo-

9   Robin Marantz Henig, "Kind Hearts and Coronaries," *The Globe and Mail*, November 20, 1993, p.D8 (reprinted from *The New York Times Magazine*). Kathleen King is identified as associate professor of nursing at the University of Rochester School of Nursing.

sition across the social-scientific disciplines and the research that they inform and that informs them is that studies of (white, adult, usually well-fed) male subjects yield human conclusions. This assumption extends, with variations, across most traditional disciplines and areas of scientific, social-scientific, and humanistic inquiry. Its smooth surface is disrupted in social-scientific studies that focus on specific human groups, but even in such interruptions, silent exclusions frequently occur.

In classical studies, which would appear to be at the furthest remove from medical research, Kathryn Gutzwiller and Ann Michelini maintain that "the ancients themselves could not perceive or discuss the gendered structure of their culture" because they assumed that only male activity was significant: they could not conceive of female activity as worthy of analysis. Gutzwiller and Michelini argue for the necessity of feminist alternatives "not only to correct [masculinist] bias but also to open large areas of potential investigation foreclosed by traditional methodologies."[10] Contributors to this book document similar patterns and practices. Nettie Wiebe shows how the language and ideology of farming in western Canada simply take for granted that "farmer" means "male farmer"—take it so completely as given that the adjective "male" rarely needs to be attached. Nor is the farmer's race or ethnicity commonly named, unless it is other than white and Euro-Christian. Ann Hall demonstrates the androcentricity of sports practices in the academy and the wider society in her analysis of the invisibility of women and gender issues, and of the widespread homophobia, in Canadian sports. Lorraine Greaves reveals how analyses of smoking behaviour and smoking as addiction simply fail to address the issues that prompt women, specifically, to smoke. All of these situations, and others like them, reveal that a crucial first step in developing an adequately sensitive feminist methodology is learning to see what is not there and hear what is not being said. Donna Haraway urges feminists to "become answerable for what we learn how to see."[11] To be thus accountable, feminists have to see what is systematically and systemically screened from view by the most basic assumptions about how people know the world; and they have to understand the power structures that effect these erasures.

Methodologically the cardiac story, like many of the research studies analysed in this book, attests to a pervasive social belief that scientific re-

10   Kathryn J. Gutzwiller and Ann Norris Michelini, "Women and Other Strangers: Feminist Perspectives in Classical Literature," in Hartman and Messer-Davidow, *(En)Gendering Knowledge*, p.66.

11   Haraway, "Situated Knowledges," p.190.

search and "properly scientific" social science research are neutral and
their findings, therefore, are universally valid. They invoke a concomitant assumption that, in contexts such as these, anything that science
does not find to be a fact has no status, no claims to truth. In engaging
critically with these assumptions, it is not enough just to say that medical
(or other) researchers *should* all along have been aware that women's experiences would show up differently; that when women appear in a doctor's office knowing that something is seriously wrong, they *should not*
merely be sent away with instructions to live with their symptoms. These
are hollow "shoulds" when they are uttered in a research context in
which the authority of the textbook and of its interpreters has been established by the best and most refined techniques and instruments, and in
which it is therefore quite reasonable to assume that symptoms that do
not fit the textbook account are aberrant, anomalous. Coming to see a
need to challenge the authority of the textbook, the going wisdom, the
paradigm, or the testing or research practice whose efficacy seems to
have been proven beyond dispute is no simple matter of saying, "They
should have known better." In other words, the presuppositions that
drive such research and the consequent methods of treatment rarely present evidence of a crude conspiracy-theoretical approach, according to
which men are worth studying and women are not. Nor do they always
betray a blatant, overtly articulated sexism, racism, homophobia, or class
bias. If they did, they might be easier to challenge. But the issues are subtler, more complex; and they are as likely to emanate from a *latent* racism, homophobia, sexism, or classism as to be the products of overt
prejudice and discrimination. The problem for emancipation theorists
always is that latent, ingrained bias and prejudgements are even more te-
nacious and more difficult to demonstrate and to counter than blatant
manifestations.

Received theoretical frameworks and the practices they generate create communities of practitioners held together, in part, by their acceptance of certain fundamental principles about how things are and how it
is best to conceive and investigate them. Thinking, still, of Henig's article, it is on the basis of established and tested findings about the nature
of and the most effective treatment for "classic" cardiac problems that
communities of cardiologists agree upon funding and equipment priorities, standard treatment procedures, and the structure and *modus oper-*

andi of caregiving facilities, and make judgements about which "cases" demand intervention and which do not.[12] Assumptions such as these produce and sustain standards of normal practice; and in cardiac medicine in recent decades their successes have been impressive. Such commonality of presuppositions and practices counts, in fact, among the conditions that enable scientific (and social-scientific, and humanistic) research endeavours to achieve impressive results, and hence to gain a public hearing, not just within the academic world, but in wider social-cultural contexts.

Situations like the one Henig reports have their counterparts—analogically, and with varying degrees of disanalogy—in most research projects and academic disciplines that study human beings, and in many other disciplines that do not. The hierarchical patterns of acknowledgement and dismissal that ingrained methodological assumptions produce will manifest themselves variously from one discipline or domain of research to another, where studies are conducted differently and where different subject matters are investigated. And hierarchy is as often patterned along racial, class, ethnic, and economic lines—together or separately—as it is along gendered lines; it occurs both within feminism and without it. But the difficulties of seeing and convincing others to see what is missing—of seeing the invisible and of knowing how to begin making it visible and (where necessary) putting it right—have been constant for feminists throughout the second wave. On a practical level these difficulties are exacerbated, for innovations in research are slow to filter through into public knowledge to the extent that they disrupt entrenched taken-for-granted behaviours.

Henig's story resonates, ideologically and methodologically, well beyond this specific context. Her presentation of syndrome X as a syndrome that has no name recalls the birth of early second wave feminism in a recognition of the need to name, to address, to make visible the "problem that has no name": the "woman" problem, and the sexism that "makes women into cultural, social, and economic non-persons and robs them of their histories and their names."[13] Recurrences and continuing recognitions of these problems have shaped feminist research

12   This description is a very loose interpretation of how, for Thomas Kuhn, a paradigm functions in producing and sustaining "normal science." Here I am leaving aside questions about the boundaries of disciplines, sciences, and paradigms; and consequent arguments about whether there can be more than one paradigm operative within a specific discipline at any one time. See Thomas S. Kuhn, *The Structure of Scientific Revolutions* (Chicago: The University of Chicago Press, 1971).

13   Quoted from the entry "Problem That Has No Name," in Cheris Kramarae and Paula A. Treichler, *A Feminist Dictionary* (London: Pandora Press, 1985), p.358.

since the early 1970s. But *how* can these problems be named? How do they win a place—a salient place—not only as sites of (legitimate) feminist agitation and concern, but also as items on well-funded and publicly acknowledged scientific-social scientific-humanitarian research agendas? In this connection, Henig's comment that a "handful of cardiologists" are prepared, now, to investigate syndrome X is significant. The force of hegemonic presuppositions and paradigms is such that lone dissenting voices have little hope of being heard, let alone of prompting reconstructions of established research agendas. Only when sufficient numbers of dissenting, critiquing, querying voices have been assembled can the momentum of a research project and/or the potential inertia of taken-for-granted assumptions be checked so that it is possible to take these interventions seriously. Clearly, then, it is not enough for women separately and singly to insist on the veracity of "their own" experiences. And yet it is also true that feminist inquiry has a commitment to taking women's experiences very seriously and to attempting to discern what those experiences mean.

Addressing this apparent impasse raises a set of complex questions about testimony and advocacy that have also been central to feminist research and activism since the early 1970s. There is no doubt, within the insider/outsider structures produced by the politics of public knowledge and the esteem accorded to scientific method, that women's voices— "ordinary" women's voices—have not often been heard, and where they have been heard their utterances have often not been taken seriously; and this phenomenon holds, albeit differently, across the many variations of "ordinariness." Women's testimony, by which I mean women's reports of their experiences, is as often discredited as it is acted upon, from their testifying about violence and sexual assault through their experiential accounts of their maladies to their demonstrations of the androcentricity of physics, philosophy, or classical studies.[14] These occurrences, together with Henig's announcement that syndrome X is now gaining a place on some medical agendas, suggest the rather uneasy conclusion that women's (and other non-experts') experiential reports require "expert" advocacy if they are to be heard and received appropriately. This conclusion is an uneasy one, because questions about who can/should speak for whom engage with issues of power and the politics of knowledge that are especially delicate in present-day feminist, and

14   I explore issues of women's testimonial credibility more fully in my "Incredulity, 'Experientialism,' and the Politics of Knowledge," in Code, *Rhetorical Spaces*.

other postcolonial, contexts.

There are many reasons for their delicacy. Not least is the fact of a centuries-long history, in Western societies, of propertied white men speaking for, thinking for, voting for, and making decisions for "their" women, as well as claiming to know women better than women can know themselves. These situations count among the principal features of women's cognitive disempowerment. Patterns of authoritarian expertise still undermine women's agency (by which I mean their possibilities for effective, independent action) across all of the complex domains of highly specialized knowledge and the less complex domains of everyday knowledge, in the late twentieth century, despite the remarkable achievements of women and feminists both within and without the academy.[15] These broad claims about the relative cognitive powers of women and men gloss over patterns that are still more complex, where even in situations in which women are visible and vocal it is always only a few women—usually white, educated, affluent, and mature (but not old) women—who achieve such positions. Hence feminists are just as wary about the issue of how women can speak for one another as they are of men's presumptions to be able to speak on women's behalf.

In the everyday lives even of comfortably situated members of materially replete societies, questions such as those posed by Henig's article are typical of the places where one needs to know responsibly and well, and where standard spectator epistemologies with their disengaged verification/falsification methods are of minimal use. None but a few of such potential knowers will take the route of becoming specialists to the extent that they can corroborate or challenge the reporter. Time alone would prohibit such a course of action for everything one needs to know, and the social division of intellectual/expert labour recognizes this fact in producing—and often exploiting—complex patterns of everyday reliance upon experts and authorities. Yet few, also, will take the reporter merely at her word, assuming that an appearance on the science page of a newspaper confers quasi-scientific credibility. Most healthily sceptical feminist readers will be aware that placing the article thus accords the report an authority that may exceed its warrant, even though they may also value its heuristic, inquiry-generating potential. When *Harvard Women's Health Watch* confirms that research on coronary heart disease has tended to be conducted on middle-aged men, and cor-

15   A now-classic discussion of authorities and experts speaking for women is Barbara Ehrenreich and Deirdre English, *For Her Own Good: 150 Years of the Experts' Advice to Women* (New York: Doubleday, 1978).

roborates the difficulties of distinguishing angina from other chest pain in women, the credibility index of Henig's report rises, even as her rhetorical strategies demand re-evaluation.[16] Knowing—becoming reasonably knowledgeable—thus becomes a matter not of looking to see for oneself, on an elaborated empiricist model, but rather of moving inquiringly within available discourses, sources, conversations, where "knowledge by acquaintance" makes up only the smallest portion of what most people ultimately know with reasonable assurance.[17] Knowledge, in this sense, is truly social knowledge.[18]

This everyday example of a gender-inflected epistemic event is, for the reasons that I have just proposed, more instructive than the older empirical models for thinking about the ordinary knowledge-seeking that permeates people's lives. In this example a would-be knower finds herself face to face *not* with a cup on a table whose presence she needs, propositionally, to record in order to demonstrate her knowledge. Rather, she is confronted with an account that is plainly a human construct, fallible, and in need of corroboration, embedded as it is in webs of expertise, authority, rhetoric, and judgement, which evoke questions about testimony and advocacy. No unilinear verification or falsification approach to such a set of knowledge claims is even possible. And yet many women will need to know how to "take" them. The very typicality of such an example shows that knowledge that is vital to people's lives cannot adequately be understood on a cups-on-tables model. Knowers and knowing are situated in and communally reliant on experiential reports, expert interpretations, and media packaging—rhetorical strategies that can be both mutually informative and mutually obstructive.

Feminists who need to know whether to put their activist energies into campaigning for improvement need to evaluate such events piece by piece. Philosophers—feminist philosophers—trying to put successor epistemologies together in the gaps left open by the incapacity of traditional epistemologies to explicate such ordinary knowledge-seeking need to develop methods and approaches that can address the fact that producing knowledge is less a matter of face-to-face confrontation with

---

16 *Harvard Women's Health Watch* 1, (February 1994).

17 "Knowledge by acquaintance" is Bertrand Russell's expression, in *The Problems of Philosophy* (Oxford: Oxford University Press, [1929] 1959), ch.5. For Russell, knowledge by acquaintance (=direct, observational acquaintance) is the most certain kind of knowledge, far preferable to the derivative "knowledge by description."

18 Here I refer to the title of Helen Longino's book *Science as Social Knowledge* (Princeton, N.J.: Princeton University Press, 1990).

data than of negotiation within an epistemic community,[19] and across media, disciplinary, and other institutional boundaries: of manoeuvring through mazes of experiential, conversational and testimonial deliverances, in which credibility is always an issue. Whereas older epistemologies were modelled on individual encounters with physical objects, many everyday and academic knowing projects are more akin to navigational exercises, to finding one's way across a sea of conflicting textual evidence and testimony. Such challenges may not translate without remainder into every knowledge-seeking project; within natural scientific practice, for example, a practitioner may sometimes be able to assume among "colleagues" a more egalitarian distribution of intellectual stature than people in the everyday world can assume of one another. But feminist epistemologists are wary of the reductive consequences of a universalism that would discredit any methodological claim that could not establish its global scope. Concentration on local knowledge projects moves away from any conviction that if methodological claims are not valid for all possible knowledge projects, then they are valid for none. Hence it recommends piece by piece analyses, which often translate analogically into other situations, and in which disanalogy can be as instructive as analogy.

In inquiries such as those generated by Henig's article, then, the stripped-down image of individual, uniformly perceptive knowers face-to-face with self-announcing and self-explanatory facts gives way to a recognition that knowledge construction is a social-communal affair, and that most would-be items of knowledge are embedded in discourses that are themselves embedded within human interests, structures of power and privilege, uneven credulity, and the pragmatics of placing one's trust to see what it is most reasonable to believe and act upon. Feminists can engage with the cardiac story as another medical tale about the "omission" of women from the data; but more critical readers will also ask which women the new quest for cardiac knowledge will capture in its analyses: will they be appropriately representative of the population with respect to age, race, ethnicity, class, and geography? How, yet again, will one assess the scope of the conclusions? The need to ask these questions does not invalidate Henig's story: it points, rather, to a space she has opened up, and to a continuing need for circumspection in considering and acting upon publicly circulated knowledge claims.

19   For an instructive discussion of epistemic negotiation, see Elizabeth Potter, "Gender and Epistemic Negotiation," in Alcoff and Potter, *Feminist Epistemologies*.

The most convoluted epistemological issues that face feminists of the 1990s are just these: how to tread a path between recognizing that "we" cannot always speak for ourselves and do not always know what is happening with us, yet realizing that others who speak for us or on our behalf or "about" us are as often underinformed, imperialistic, or coercive as they are supportive and empowering?[20] Often we do not understand even "our own" experiences as well as that seemingly sacrosanct expression of ownership implies; and only rarely can we presume to understand exactly how it is for someone else even of our own class, race, sexual orientation, and social group. These issues become exacerbated when feminists claim to speak for others across the complexities of difference, with the consequence that the politics of speaking for, about, and on behalf of other women is one of the most contested areas in present-day feminist activism and research.

In short, questions of advocacy have to be engaged with the greatest of care. Yet despite the need to address them within a principled and well-understood recognition of the potential abuses of advocacy positions, a primary feminist aim still has to be that of ensuring that there are as many women as possible in advocacy positions. I will not be a doctor or a lawyer, but it matters to me that there are good, well-qualified, vocal, and visible feminist/female lawyers, doctors, social workers, and other expert practitioners, or male practitioners whose practice is well informed by a consciousness of feminist issues, who can act as my advocates when I need them and who can advocate on behalf of other, less privileged women.[21] Hence for feminists one of the crucial tasks in the politics of knowledge is to work for continued affirmative action, not for the rather ephemeral goal of producing female "role models," but for reasons of promoting feminist-informed advocacy and a gender-sensitive distribution of intellectual labour, in all of the places where women need to find it.

The advocacy issue is tricky for yet another reason. There is a persist-

20   I discuss these issues at greater length in my "'I Know Just How You Feel': Empathy and the Problem of Epistemic Authority," in Ellen More and Maureen Milligan, eds., *The Empathic Practitioner: Essays on Empathy, Gender, and Medicine* (New Brunswick, N.J.: Rutgers University Press, 1994).

21   Instructive contributions to these issues from within medical practice come from Kirsti Malterud, who set herself the task of investigating "paths toward a broader understanding of the so-called undefined disorders in female patients" and constructed a set of "key questions" to structure clinical encounters with the aim of empowering female patients. See especially her "Strategies for Empowering Women's Voices in the Medical Culture," *Health Care for Women International* 14 (1993), p.368; "Illness and Disease in Female Patients," *Scandinavian Journal of Primary Health Care* 5 (1987); and "Women's Undefined Disorders: A Challenge for Clinical Communication," *Family Practice* 9 (1992).

ent assumption in Western societies, which take for granted a simple empirical basis of knowledge and a picture of individual, self-sufficient knowledge acquisition, that facts are simply self-presenting: hence if a phenomenon such as syndrome X is "real," it will show up. Any researcher/inquirer who is appropriately placed and who follows the approved methods of research will discover precisely the same facts as any other equally scrupulous investigator. The implicit belief is that science is so objective that eventually it will turn up all salient truths—and those it does not turn up are not salient. Even though few theorists of knowledge, and few practising scientists, might subscribe to such a view, it has a forceful public cachet. In consequence, advocacy takes on the aura of a practice that somehow interferes with the objectivity of inquiry: if the facts are self-presenting, there is no need for me to see them through anyone else's eyes. Hence (anecdotally) in a 1993 conference the question arose about whether stories of a patient's personal history, constraints, and concerns could legitimately count as part of the *knowledge* that a physician needed to treat the patient morally/rationally; could reveal relevant information that would not show up in standard case notes. Many participants argued that there was and should be a sharp division between measurable, diagnosable symptoms and context-providing narratives, stories; and the overwhelming presumption was that narratives could not contribute to the investigative process because narrative was bound to be contaminated by its connection with advocacy. A (contestable) dichotomy was presumed between advocacy and "truth" or the "facts," and a clear assumption prevailed to the effect that advocates will, inevitably, obscure and distort truths.[22]

Henig's syndrome X story puts a rather different spin on this issue, as does Karen Messing's work on women's occupational health, and Alison Wylie and Lorraine Greaves's work in the Battered Women's Advocacy Centre. These studies make clear that without advocacy—empirically grounded, but advocacy nonetheless—there would be no breakthroughs. But neither, without advocacy, would alternative readings be possible, such as the one that makes up my second tier. For all of these situations raise issues not just about heart disease, workplace illness, or battery, but about women's oppression much more broadly understood; and if their feminist dimensions are adequately to be understood, they have to be located within contexts much larger than that of

---

22   For an elaboration of the promise of a "storied" epistemology, see my "Voice and Voicelessness: A Modest Proposal," in Janet Kourany, ed., *Philosophy in a Different Voice* (Princeton, N.J.: Princeton University Press, forthcoming), also in my *Rhetorical Spaces*.

separate and distinct female bodies.

Thus Lucy Candib, for example, observes that the problems that Henig analyses need to be reframed and the emphasis shifted to locate this symptom within wider patterns of oppression and victimization. Candib reaffirms the difficulty of diagnosing syndrome X, the invasiveness of the testing procedures, and the reluctance even of feminist-informed practitioners to submit women to excessive and potentially dangerous tests. Yet she cautions against constructing the situation as just another instance of women's erasure from medical research and of their passivity in seeking treatment. Such a reading glosses over "narrative" issues that are integral to the medical diagnosis for practitioners (advocates) sensitive to oppressions and other pervasive power differentials. Anxiety and fear also count among the causes of chest pain, Candib notes, and women can experience chest pain as a result of continual beatings, rapes, and sexual abuse. Candib comments: "These things are so prevalent (15 per cent rape, 25-plus per cent lifetime physical abuse, 30 per cent lifetime past sexual abuse, and so on) that the issue is *not* that women are dismissed as psychosomatic. The issue is that the real oppressions against women that lead us to be more symptomatic and fearful are *not* recognized and thus we are written off."[23] Here it is not a matter of an advocate speaking from within another's experience, imperialistically, but rather of an advocate who has learned to see the hitherto unseen, and who can claim feminist and "public" credibility, reframing received knowledge within a feminist-informed analysis of asymmetrical social structures. Such vigilance for traces of the untold story is central to many feminist research and activist methods.

FEMINIST KNOWLEDGE, FEMINIST METHODS

The interim conclusions that emerge from readings of Henig's report through a feminist lens recall Cheshire Calhoun's analysis, in a moral context, of the requirements of responsibility and reproach that feminists have somehow to negotiate. Calhoun's argument hinges on the concept of an "abnormal moral context" that has a precise epistemological analogue. She writes: "Abnormal moral contexts arise at the frontiers of moral knowledge when a subgroup of society (for instance bioethicists or business ethicists) makes advances in moral knowledge

23   Lucy Candib, personal communication. Lucy Candib is the author of *Medicine and the Family: A Feminist Perspective* (New York: Basic Books, 1995). See also her article "Reconsidering Power in the Clinical Relationship," in More and Milligan, *The Empathic Practitioner*.

faster than they can be disseminated to and assimilated by the general public and subgroups at special moral risk (e.g., physicians and corporate executives)."[24]

Abnormal epistemological contexts, I suggest, are those in which certain extraordinary ways of looking, thinking, and perceiving a problem make it possible for some inquirers to move to the frontiers for example, of medical knowledge, of religious or linguistic studies, of advocacy for children or for battered women. It puts them in a position of having a capacity—and arguably also a responsibility—to advocate for, and ideally *with*, people for whom such knowledge makes a vital difference, who are not in a position to gain acknowledgement by their own unaided efforts.

From these critical reflections there emerges a picture of feminist methods as vigilant methods, dependent on sensitized hearing, seeing, and reading. Feminists who are thus sensitized are often, understandably, reluctant to take on yet another round of educational tasks, instructing the uninformed in what "they" need to do when it has already been so onerous a process learning to see, hear, and read their own environments anew. Yet although feminists may resist this added responsibility, often it turns out that only they are in a position to reproach knowledgeably; hence sometimes there may be no avoiding it. Although no definitive, exhaustive checklist of do's and don'ts can be devised for those who are committed to taking on parts of this labour, some basic recommendations suggest themselves.

(i) First and foremost, androcentred research projects focused primarily or exclusively on (affluent white) men's lives, experiences, symptoms, and actions can no longer presume, before the fact, to yield universal truths. Questions about gender specificity belong within every research project that has any bearing, direct or indirect, on human subjects; and such questions will always require analysis of the intrication of gender with some or all of the other positional variants that I have repeatedly listed in this chapter. As the Biology and Gender Study Group remarks: "We have come to look at feminist critique as we would any other experimental control.... Feminist critique should be part of normative science. Like any control, it seeks to provide critical rigor, and to ignore this critique is to ignore a possible source of error."[25] Gender

24   Cheshire Calhoun, "Responsibility and Reproach," in Cass R. Sunstein, ed., *Feminism and Political Theory* (Chicago: University of Chicago Press, 1990), p.250.

25   The Biology and Gender Study Group, "The Importance of Feminist Critique for Contemporary Cell Biology," in Nancy Tuana, ed., *Feminism and Science* (Bloomington: Indiana University Press, 1989), pp.172-73.

may, in some instances, prove irrelevant to a particular finding or turn out to be a less significant contributor than, say, race or class; but ordinarily its irrelevance can be claimed only after careful investigation. Exceptions might be found in projects that expressly set out to investigate female- or male-specific phenomena, so long as that restriction can be defended on non-sexist and otherwise non-oppressive grounds. (Yet one would have to exclude from such legitimate exceptions research projects such as one I assessed for a university ethics committee, in which an investigator was attempting to discern reasons for girls' academic "underachievement." The design of the project left it open to acting as a self-fulfilling prophesy for the subjects who were to be studied.) These claims have to be refined through a recognition that the men from whose experiences research agendas acquire their androcentric taint are by no means representative of all men, nor are they usually representative of "men in general," if there are such creatures.[26] Hence issues of class, race, age, economics, and other specificities will need equally to be incorporated into the research procedures and/or the ensuing analyses. Postcolonial, post-Enlightenment research needs always to be wary of the arrogance of false universals.

(ii) A feature common to the syndrome X story and to Karen Messing's stories in this book about applying for research funding is the ingrained misogyny that colours responses to women's reports of their symptoms: the idea that women cannot be trusted to know—even to know what is happening to them, what is going on in "their own" bodies. The implication that these women are merely hysterical, implicit in one doctor's comment—"A lot of women live with this all the time—so live with it"[27]—resonates with responses to women throughout the hierarchical structures of authority and expertise that are produced out of the division of intellectual labour in complex scientific societies. Again, that misogyny is not equally distributed: educated, articulate, well-dressed, heterosexual, and not-too-forceful white women, who are not too young or too old or too "pretty," have by far the best chances of being heard in consulting rooms, classrooms, courtrooms, and the offices

---

26   I am thinking here of Elizabeth Spelman's comment: "Those of us who have engaged in it must give up the hunt for the generic woman—the one who is all and only woman, who by some miracle of abstraction has no particular identity in terms of race, class, ethnicity, sexual orientation, language, religion, nationality." In Elizabeth V. Spelman, *Inessential Woman: Problems of Exclusion in Feminist Thought* (Boston: Beacon Press, 1988), p.187. Generic man, and men in general, are equally impossible to find.

27   Henig, "Kind Hearts."

of various bureaucracies throughout the affluent Western world.[28] Nonetheless, Henig reports that women's "great physical and psychological distress" that results from syndrome X has been judged of minimal significance in contrast to the more clearly life-threatening symptoms of other cardiac disorders. The presumption that women are "less prone to heart disease" sets up a kind of feedback loop in which men's cardiac problems go on contributing to the accumulation of medical knowledge, while women's experiences of genuine pain are continually relegated to the insignificant, aberrant margins. Similar results emerge from Messing's studies, and from Greaves's investigations of smoking as an addiction. It is these presuppositions that feminists are increasingly able to detect, and to counter.

(iii) Reclaiming female agency is a central feminist preoccupation that also figures prominently in most of the chapters in this book. A woman Henig interviews says, for example, "If I had been a 34-year-old male I would have definitely been admitted from the emergency room and given a cardiac workup ... but I was too passive." Both normatively and descriptively, passivity has counted as a "natural" female attribute, one that women have been encouraged to cultivate. In matters of knowledge, passivity manifests itself in deference to (commonly male) expertise: hence a woman will rarely insist that, experientially, she knows differently in the face of an expert pronouncement that she cannot possibly be feeling what she says she is. The syndrome X story speaks to the complexity of the need to know well enough to claim knowledgeability in situations in which the division of intellectual labour creates patterns of insider and outsider knowledge, in which the issue is not so much that not everyone can aspire to insider status (although that is probably true), but that not everyone wants to or should have to. And yet a certain level of knowledge-as-information, communally acquired and deliberated, seems not unreasonably to count as a precondition for establishing any sort of credibility, as a complainant or lobbyist.

(iv) Questions about the presumed veracity of women's experience are central here. Feminist activism and feminist research have a common origin in recognitions of the extent to which women's experiences simply have not counted in malestream activities and research endeavours throughout history; and they have a common goal in their commitment to honouring those experiences and making them visible. Yet

---

28   For an interesting study of bureaucratic authority see Kathy E. Ferguson, *The Feminist Case against Bureaucracy* (Philadelphia: Temple University Press, 1984).

feminists are also cognizant of the fact—which governed the consciousness-raising of early second wave feminism—that experience rarely
"speaks for itself," and that experiences are by no means as immediate as
the old empiricist rhetoric implied. Candib's observations about syndrome X attest vividly to this point. Even the most forceful and private
of experiences often needs careful interpretation, especially to reveal its
embeddedness within larger social patterns, hence to make it possible to
see how, indeed, it is mediated by the circumstances of an experiencer's
biographical and social-cultural location.[29] Feminists have therefore to
tread yet another perilous path: between the old tyranny of authoritarian
expertise that discounts women's experiences, much as it discounts the
experiences of other marginalized and oppressed people; and a new tyranny of "experientialism" that claims for first-person experiential utterances an immunity from challenge, interpretation, or debate. Feminist
social scientists are especially wary of the delicacy of these issues;[30] feminists in other areas of inquiry—biographers and biologists, for example—are equally aware of the need to develop an interpretive sensitivity,
able to detect and analyse the effects of constitutive mechanisms of
power in seemingly straightforward experiential reports.

    (v) One of the most salient aspects of the syndrome X story surfaces
in the comments that "physicians are beginning to acknowledge that
what has worked for men might not work for women, and that a
woman's heart may be constitutionally different from a man's" and that
standard diagnostic tests "aren't suited to the problem." Commonly,
not just in medical research but far more generally, when symptoms deviate from the standard, the norm, the "textbook" pattern, the practice
has been to judge those symptoms as aberrant, not classifiable as typical
instances of the phenomenon under investigation. An acknowledgement of the initial plausibility of syndrome X reports requires a
different approach: one that reconsiders the scope and validity of the
texts themselves, that asks about the match between standard testing
procedures and the subjects being studied. Such a revisioning of research practices and techniques contests the assumption that a heart is
just a heart, wherever it is studied, whatever body it inhabits. The rethinking moves away from an "individualism" that treats a heart as an
isolated single organ to a more coherent and integrated approach that

29   In this connection, see Judith Grant, "I Feel Therefore I Am: A Critique of Female Experi-
     ence as the Basis for a Feminist Epistemology," *Women and Politics* 7,3 (1987); and Joan
     Scott, "'Experience,'" in Judith Butler and Joan W. Scott, eds., *Feminists Theorize the Politi-
     cal*, (New York: Routledge, 1992).

30   See, for example, Michaela di Leonardo, "Contingencies of Value in Feminist Anthropol-
     ogy," in Hartman and Messer-Davidow, *(En)Gendering Knowledge*.

studies the heart in a particular body—one whose hormonal composition differs from the male body, whose heart has commonly been the source of medical data; one whose structural specificities demand a different kind of reading to accommodate (for example) the extent to which breast tissue might distort the x-rays; and one whose life circumstances are integral to its physical and mental health, and count among legitimate, "real" causes of dis-ease.

I am not suggesting with these recommendations that non-feminist women and members of other marginalized "kinds" are themselves unable to engage in rational, objective inquiry. Rather, my point is that the methodologies and ideologies that have authoritative status in Western societies generate knowledge that derives from, and hence can explain the experiences and circumstances only of, a small group of scientifically or otherwise institutionally accredited knowledge-makers and their *semblables*. The methods and assumptions that go into producing this knowledge work, often inadvertently, to erase possibilities of addressing specific, yet "different," experiences so that they can yield knowledge or can contest sedimented biases and prejudgements.

The question is whether a specifically feminist methodology would put this situation right: a question that generates a host of subsidiary questions. In articulating responses to it, feminists are caught in a complex tangle of problems. Most late-twentieth-century feminists are (rightly) resistant to simplistic alignments, say of men with objectivist, distanced, positivistic, scientific methods and women with subjectivist, connected, interpretive, non-scientific methods. Few feminists would endorse a wholesale science-bashing that smacks more of ideological excess than of a genuine quest for knowledge. Nor would feminists unanimously opt for the essentialism that identifies quantitative methodologies as male, qualitative ones as female; and positivism as male, "interpretationism" as female. Ruth Hubbard, for example, observes:

> I doubt that women as gendered beings have something new or different to contribute to science, but women as political beings do. One of the most important things we must do is to insist on the political content of science and on its political role.... To the extent that scientists are "neutral" that merely means that they support the existing distribution of interests and power.[31]

31   Ruth Hubbard, "Science, Facts, and Feminism," in Tuana, *Feminism and Science*, p.128.

Lucy Candib's observations corroborate this observation. Even feminists who are wary of the detrimental effects of science and other authoritative knowledge acknowledge and rely upon its (intermittent) successes in producing reasonably reliable diagnostic procedures, statistical analyses, household appliances, and means of transportation. Yet they are also convinced, and on good evidence across a range of disciplines and areas of inquiry, that *feminist* research makes a difference. Hence the "method" question becomes, in effect, a question of how it makes a difference, and what precepts need to be adopted to ensure that it makes a positive one.

Feminists have, in general, abandoned the search for and denied the possibility of a disinterested and dislocated view from nowhere. More subversively of traditional epistemological assumptions, they have contended that most knowledge-producing and knowledge-circulating activity is politically invested, and they have insisted upon the accountability—the epistemic responsibilities—of knowers to their research and everyday communities, not just to the evidence.[32]

Yet my analysis of Henig's story is not meant to discredit or reject traditional epistemological techniques outright. Readers of such a story want to know its empirical basis—to be able to trust that the diagnostic procedures it reports are carried out well enough to confer reasonable reliability on reports about this "syndrome." They want also to know how such a story coheres within systems of public knowledge about hearts and about women; and in seeking answers to these questions they will engage in processes of checking and cross-checking that draw extensively on traditional practices of attending to "the evidence," seeking verification, evaluating falsifying or doubt-producing factors. Lucy Candib adds an interpretive/genealogical dimension to these processes, demonstrating the importance of locating the story within social structures of gendered and other forms of oppression; asking, in effect, how and why evidence achieves its status as evidence, where its persuasiveness comes from, what it excludes.[33] Conclusions such as those that emerge from an interpretive reading of Henig's story are more open-ended than more standard ones, which end in all-or-nothing knowledge claims. Feminist awareness of the historical-locational contingency of such events reinterprets knowledge claims as moments in ongoing—

32   I discuss such responsibilities in my *Epistemic Responsibility* (Hanover, N.H.: University Press of New England, 1987).

33   For an interesting analysis of hermeneutic-interpretive and genealogically informed feminist research, see Kathy A. Ferguson, *The Man Question: Visions of Subjectivity in Feminist Theory* (Berkeley: University of California Press, 1993).

and not necessarily linear—processes of inquiry. Feminist epistemologists are showing, then, that avowedly engaged and political inquiries can yield well-warranted conclusions.

Feminist epistemologists addressing the "method" question have tended to concentrate upon analyzing the nature and positioning of would-be knowers and upon assessing the nature and sources of evidence or data. Some accord more weight to questions of evidence, while others find issues that pertain to the positioning of the knower more salient. In the mid-1980s these divergent emphases prompted some feminists to maintain that there are two distinct ways of addressing the method question, deriving out of two distinct approaches to knowledge production: feminist empiricism and feminist standpoint theory.[34] Very generally speaking, the empiricists direct their primary attention to evidence-gathering and set out to preserve a reasonable respect for a scientific method cleansed of androcentrism, whereas standpoint theorists are concerned more with matters of epistemic positioning and the historical-material conditions of women's experiences; although both sets of issues figure to some extent in each. Feminist thinking about these matters has become subtler and more nuanced in the decade since it first seemed that these two broad theoretical options covered the entire territory, and that varieties of postmodernism could account for most of the anti-epistemological challenges to both. It has become clear that feminist methods are not so easily divided up and categorized. These erstwhile alternatives are not mutually exclusive; nor does either of them offer a single and internally coherent, or a comprehensive and universally applicable, account of feminist knowledge production. Moreover, both are (albeit variously) indebted to postmodern interpretive-genealogical interrogations of even the most seemingly intransigent of traditional epistemological and methodological presuppositions. In the mid-1990s innovative cross-fertilizations across a range of approaches are more common—and more productive—than strict adherence to even a newly emergent methodological orthodoxy can permit. Yet variations on the central insights of empiricist and standpoint feminisms remain integral

34   Sandra Harding's articulation of these distinctions in *The Science Question in Feminism* is commonly cited as the opening into these debates. In the "Introduction: Is There a Feminist Method?" to her edited collection, *Feminism and Methodology* (Bloomington: Indiana University Press, 1987), Harding distinguishes between a research method "a technique for (or way of proceeding in) gathering evidence" and a methodology "a theory and analysis of how research does or should proceed" (pp.2-3). She argues that epistemological questions should not be confused with questions about method or methodology. In my thinking about the "method" question, I have concluded, on the contrary, that these three strands of inquiry are so closely interconnected and mutually informative that there is little to be gained from keeping them separate.

to questions about method. Hence it is worth rehearsing them, briefly, here.

Feminist empiricists argue that, far from being as neutral and objective as they themselves claim, traditional empiricists are caught in the androcentric assumptions that govern their knowledge-producing activities. These feminists believe that an unabashedly value-laden yet rigorous empiricism, informed by feminist ideology, can produce more adequate knowledge than can standard empiricisms ignorant of their complicity in a sex/gender system, because it can enlist the best tools and strategies that an empiricist tradition has developed to discern the manifestations of sexism, racism, and all of the other "isms" that (often silently) contribute to the production of allegedly neutral knowledge.

Thus, for example, in Helen Longino's social empiricism, communities, not individuals, are the primary knowers.[35] Their background assumptions always infuse and shape their cognitive projects and are as epistemologically pertinent as any specific set of knowledge claims. Looking at experiments in genetic research that work from fundamentally different background assumptions, Longino demonstrates the necessity of analyzing processes of discovery as rigorously as processes of justification have traditionally been analysed, in order to understand the assumptions that contribute to the production of knowledge. Her analyses show that theories and observations are always assumption-(=value-) laden; hence they call into question the very possibility of theory-neutral research. Yet they demonstrate the crucial significance of community standards of respect for empirical evidence and of accountable cognitive agency, enacted in collaborative, social contexts. In projects that are compatible with Longino's, especially in their emphasis on the social character of knowledge-making, Lynn Nelson and Jane Duran turn to Quinean "naturalized epistemology" as a resource out of which they—variously—develop neo-empiricist feminist epistemologies, indebted to the impressive achievements of modern empirical and cognitive science.[36] These feminists are united in urging the survival and transformative necessity of producing reliable knowledge of the physical and social world, and in maintaining that women, and other epistemically marginalized people, cannot hope to transform their circumstances hence—to realize emancipatory goals—if their explanations can neither account for the intractable aspects of the world nor engage well with its

35   See Helen Longino, *Science As Social Knowledge.*

36   See Lynn Hankinson Nelson, *Who Knows: From Quine to a Feminist Empiricism*, and Jane Duran, *Toward a Feminist Epistemology.*

malleable, contestable features. Feminists have to devise methods that enable them to achieve some match between knowledge and "reality," even when the reality at issue consists of social productions, such as racism or tolerance, oppression or equality of opportunity. Feminist empiricists claim they can do just that in practising an empiricism that is alert to the operations of gender-specific factors in conceptualizing and conducting any inquiry. Thus, according to Harding, politically informed inquiry can yield a better empiricism, based in a "strong objectivity."[37]

For feminist standpoint theorists, neither orthodox nor feminist empiricists can adequately account for the varied historical and material conditions out of which people produce knowledge.[38] The authoritative, standard-setting knowledge in Western societies is derived from and tested against an abstracted interpretation of the social experiences of a limited segment of the population: white, middle-class, educated men. In consequence, women (like the proletariat of Marxist theory, from which standpoint theorists take their inspiration) are oppressed in marginal, underclass epistemic positions. Just as the subordination of the proletariat to the capitalist class is "naturalized" by the theoretical assumptions of capitalism, so the subordination of women is "naturalized" by the theoretical assumptions of patriarchy. Just as analyses that take the lives of the proletariat as their starting point work to denaturalize these assumptions so too can starting from women's lives work to denaturalize, make strange, the assumptions on which the patriarchal order rests. A feminist standpoint is distinct from a "women's standpoint" because of its achieved feminist consciousness, and hence is more than just another perspective on the world. It is a hard-won product of consciousness-raising and social-political engagement, designed to reveal the false presuppositions that patriarchal hierarchies and androcentred epistemologies are built upon, and to counter the forms of alienation they produce. Starting from the material realities of women's lives and analyzing their oppressions as structural consequences of an unjust social order, standpoint theorists contend that the knowledge that the oppressed have had to acquire just to survive under oppression can become a resource for social transformation.

Neither empiricism nor standpoint theory is without its critics. Some

---

37   Harding uses this phrase to characterize the objectivity of feminist empiricism in *Whose Science? Whose Knowledge? Thinking from Women's Lives*, especially ch.6.

38   See Nancy Hartsock, *Money, Sex, and Power: Toward a Feminist Historical Materialism* (Boston: Northeastern University Press, 1983) for a classic account of feminist standpoint epistemology. See also ch.5 of Harding's *Whose Science? Whose Knowledge?*

theorists suggest, for example, that despite its promise, the feminism of the new empiricism leaves so many traditional assumptions intact that it cannot address the specific, power-saturated circumstances of diversely located knowers, researchers, and activists. Nor can it pose interpretive, politically delicate questions about how evidence comes to count as worthy of that label, and about whose evidence it suppresses in the process. Other critics object that because there is no single, unified feminist position, standpoint theory obliterates differences, and hence fails by its own feminist standards; still others argue that its "locatedness" produces a version of social reality that must be as limited as any other. These problems notwithstanding, the importance of empiricism's commitment to demonstrating the objective reality of gender-specific factors in knowledge-production cannot be gainsaid; nor can standpoint theory's commitment to producing faithful, if often critical, analyses of women's experiences, together with its focus on how oppression is legitimated by hegemonic epistemic values. These criticisms, albeit quite differently, attest to the effects of postmodern critiques of the subject and the object of traditional knowledge-making: critiques that take issue both with the abstract individualism that informs assumptions about who the knower is, and with the conception of knowledge acquisition as disinterested discovery, according to which the object of knowledge is neutrally found, not made.

Caught up as it is in these criss-crossing, mutually informative lines of inquiry and critique, the most viable strategy for feminist research is, evidently, to abandon any quest for one true method, or for a universalism that would replicate the worst excesses of the older, hegemonic theories. At this critical-revisionary juncture an experimental pluralism recommends itself over attempts to establish a new feminist monological theory of knowledge to supplant the old masculinist ones.[39] Feminists have also recognized the promise of empathic and narrative analyses, of qualitative "experiential" research, and of participant, dialogical methods, contending that research that draws on these resources can challenge many of the reductive disciplinary and methodological assumptions that dominate the twentieth-century academy and shape public conceptions of knowledge in the western world. Working with diverse combinations of these methods and techniques, resisting methodological orthodoxy, they have achieved remarkable results in destabi-

---

39   Thus Alison Wylie refers to the need for "some degree of tolerance of methodological and
     theoretical pluralism" in her article, "Why Is There No Archeology of Gender?" in Joan M.
     Gero and Margaret W. Conkey, eds., *Engendering Archaeology: Women and Prehistory* (Oxford: Basil Blackwell, 1991), p.48.

lizing the imperialistic conceptions of knowledge and truth that have governed the research practices of the academy and the knowledge-seeking practices of people in their everyday lives. They have shown that questions of knowledge and method can rarely be answered satisfactorily in abstraction, before the fact. Rather, these questions have to be addressed locally, in piece-by-piece analyses of specific instances of knowledge-making, in which innovative techniques are adduced and tested, and the best of older methods and assumptions are re-evaluated for their residual viability. Any putatively global (interim) conclusions will always have to be assessed for their local pertinence and sensitivity, if we are to ensure that we know responsibly and well.

SUGGESTED READINGS

Linda Alcoff and Elizabeth Potter, eds., *Feminist Epistemologies*. New York: Routledge, 1993.

Louise Antony and Charlotte Witt, eds., *A Mind of One's Own: Feminist Essays on Reason and Objectivity*. Boulder, Colo.: Westview Press, 1993.

Lorraine Code, *Rhetorical Spaces: Essays on (Gendered) Locations*. New York: Routledge, 1995.

Lorraine Code, *What Can She Know? Feminist Theory and the Construction of Knowledge*. Ithaca, N.Y.: Cornell University Press, 1991.

Patricia Hill Collins, *Black Feminist Thought: Knowledge, Consciousness and the Politics of Empowerment*. Boston: Unwin Hyman, 1990.

Jane Duran, *Toward a Feminist Epistemology*. Savage, Md.: Rowman & Littlefield, 1990.

Sandra Harding, *Whose Science? Whose Knowledge? Thinking from Women's Lives*. Ithaca, N.Y.: Cornell University Press, 1991.

Sandra Harding, *The Science Question in Feminism*. Ithaca, N.Y.: Cornell University Press, 1986.

Elizabeth Harvey and Kathleen Okruhlik, eds., *Women and Reason*. Ann Arbor: University of Michigan Press, 1992.

Susan Hekman, *Gender and Knowledge: Elements of a Postmodern Feminism*. Boston: Northeastern University Press, 1990.

Evelyn Fox Keller, *Reflections on Gender and Science*. New Haven, Conn.: Yale University Press, 1985.

Kathleen Lennon and Margaret Whitford, eds., *Knowing the Difference: Feminist Perspectives in Epistemology.* London: Routledge, 1994.

Lynn Hankinson Nelson, *Who Knows. From Quine to a Feminist Empiricism.* Philadelphia: Temple University Press, 1990.

Nancy Tuana, ed., *Feminism and Science.* Bloomington: Indiana University Press, 1989.

Patricia Williams, *The Alchemy of Race and Rights: Diary of a Law Professor.* Cambridge, Mass.: Harvard University Press, 1991.

SUSAN EHRLICH

Chapter Two: Critical Linguistics as Feminist Methodology

ADVOCATES OF NON-SEXIST LANGUAGE REFORM HAVE GEN-
erally assumed that language is not a neutral and transparent means of
representing social realities. Rather, some have argued that a particular
vision of social reality is inscribed in language — a vision of reality that
does not serve all of its speakers equally.

Susan Gal, for example, sees language as serving the interests of the
dominant classes, much like other social institutions and practices;[1] in
the case of sexist language, language can be said to codify an androcentric worldview. The names that a language attaches to events and activities, especially those related to sex and sexuality, often encode a male
perspective. For example, Deborah Cameron discusses terms such as
penetration, fuck, screw, and *lay,* all of which turn heterosexual sex into
something men do to women.[2] (Penetration from a female perspective
would be more appropriately encoded as *enclosure, surrounding,* or *en-
gulfing.*) What becomes clear from "names" such as these is the extent to
which language acts as an ideological filter on the world: language, to
some extent, shapes or constructs our notions of reality rather than la-
belling that reality in any transparent and straightforward way.

---

1   Susan Gal, "Language and Political Economy," *Annual Review of Anthropology* 18 (1989),
    pp.345-67; Susan Gal, "Between Speech and Silence: The Problematics of Research on Lan-
    guage and Gender," in Michaela di Leonardo, ed. *Gender at the Crossroads of Knowledge*
    (Berkeley: University of California Press, 1991), pp.175-203.

2   Deborah Cameron, *Feminism and Linguistic Theory* (London: Macmillan, 1985).

The idea that language determines or in some way influences speakers' perceptions and conceptions of reality underlies much of the current work on women and language and has its origins in the work of two U.S. anthropological linguists, Edward Sapir and Benjamin Whorf.[3] The Sapir-Whorf hypothesis, as it is known within the discipline of linguistics, combines the notions of linguistic relativity and linguistic determinism. According to proponents of linguistic relativity, the grammatical properties of different languages can vary more or less without limit; linguistic determinists hold that the grammatical structure of a particular language has a powerful mediating influence on how a speaker of that language comes to view the world. Taken together, then, the two hypotheses predict that speakers of different languages will perceive the world in radically different ways. For example, Hopi (an Amerindian language investigated by Whorf) distinguishes grammatically between the hypothetical and non-hypothetical nature of an event but not between events occurring in the present or past. Therefore, according to the Sapir-Whorf hypothesis, Hopi speakers have a different conception of time than do speakers of English, because English makes a grammatical distinction between events occurring in the present and the past. For instance, Whorf states:

We dissect nature along lines laid down by our native languages. The categories and types that we isolate from the world of phenomena we do not find there because they stare every observer in the face; on the contrary, the world is presented in a kaleidoscopic flux of impressions which has to be organized by our minds—and this means largely by the linguistic systems in our minds. We cut nature up, organize it into concepts, and ascribe significances as we do, largely because we are parties to an agreement to organize it in this way — an agreement that holds throughout our speech community and is codified in the patterns of our language. The agreement is, of course, an implicit and unstated one, BUT ITS TERMS ARE ABSOLUTELY OBLIGATORY; we cannot talk at all except by subscribing to the organization and classification of data which the agreement decrees.

The fact is very significant for modern science, for it means that no individual is free to describe nature with absolute impartiality

3   See, for example, Mary Daly, *Gyn/Ecology* (Boston: Beacon Press, 1978); Suzette Haden Elgin, *Native Tongue* (New York: DAW Books, 1984); Dale Spender, *Man Made Language* (London: Routledge, 1980).

but is constrained to certain modes of interpretation even while he [sic] thinks himself most free.[4]

While the Sapir-Whorf hypothesis is appealing, the strong version of the hypothesis as articulated here has few adherents today, especially because we now know that speakers of a particular language can make conceptual distinctions that their language appears not to allow. Some Australian Aboriginal languages, for instance, have few words for numbers; the number lexicon may be restricted to general words such as *all*, *many*, and *few*, and to specific words for *one* and *two*. Yet it is not the case that speakers of these languages cannot count beyond two or perform complex numerical operations, as evidenced by their mathematical abilities in second languages such as English.[5] A weaker version of the Sapir-Whorf hypothesis (which has generally come to replace the "strong" version popular in mid-century) suggests that languages predispose speakers to view the world in particular ways, but that such a worldview is not all-determining. In other words, speakers "can see through and around the settings" of their languages, but doing so may require interrogating some of the most basic commonsense assumptions encoded in those languages.[6]

Because individuals and speech communities are, at the least, influenced by the vision(s) of reality that get(s) inscribed in language, it becomes important for feminists to consider the extent to which language encodes a vision of social reality that may not serve the interests of certain groups of women. The tradition of critical linguistics provides a methodology well suited to these goals.[7] Rather than viewing language as a formal system at a level of abstraction that neutralizes social categories and distinctions, critical linguistics assumes that language is inextricably implicated in the socio-political systems and institutions in which it functions. Thus, the motivating principle behind critical linguistics is the investigation of the role of language in the reproduction of dominant

4   Benjamin Lee Whorf, *Language, Thought and Reality: Selected Writings of Benjamin Lee Whorf* (Cambridge, Mass.: MIT Press, 1956), pp.213-14; emphasis in original.

5   David Crystal, *The Cambridge Encyclopedia of Language* (Cambridge: Cambridge University Press, 1987).

6   The phrase comes from M.A.K. Halliday, "Linguistic Function and Literary Style," in Seymour Chatman, ed., *Literary Style: A Symposium* (Oxford: Oxford University Press, 1971), pp.332-33.

7   Critical linguistics references include, for example, Gunther Kress and Robert Hodge, *Language as Ideology* (London: Routledge and Kegan Paul, 1979); Robert Hodge and Gunther Kress, *Social Semiotics* (Oxford: Polity Press, 1988); and Roger Fowler, *Language in the News* (London: Routledge, 1991).

ideologies. By highlighting the insidiousness of linguistic practices in which dominant ideologies are reflected and constructed, critical linguistics has as its ultimate aim the demystification of such social practices.

Indeed, this type of linguistic analysis is critical to the feminist enterprise precisely because the ideological perspectives that languages encode often go unnoticed and are not easily foregrounded by speakers who are predisposed to think about the world in a certain way. For example, Penelope Eckert and Sally McConnell-Ginet talk about the power of dominant groups being sustained by the "naturalizing" of language's ideological perspective as "neutral or 'unmarked,'"—"obscuring its status as one among many perspectives."[8] Naturalization takes place to the extent that speakers are unaware of the power relations and hierarchies influencing their social (including linguistic) behaviour.

This chapter looks at the value of critical linguistics to feminist analysis as a way of elucidating the non-neutrality of language. This kind of linguistic analysis allows us to "see through and around the settings" of our language, allowing for the denaturalizing of sexist and androcentric beliefs and assumptions that are often rationalized as commonsensical in our culture because of their relative "invisibility" in everyday discourse.

THE SOCIAL CONSTRUCTION OF MEANING

In a recent account of the social construction of meaning, McConnell-Ginet suggests some of the mechanisms by which social privilege leads to linguistic privilege.[9] Linguistic forms depend for their full interpretation or meaning on social context, including mutually accessible cultural knowledge. For example, the following sequence of sentences can be interpreted as coherent because readers and listeners have access to general cultural knowledge, including the information that picnic supplies can include beer.

Mary got some picnic supplies out of the car. The beer was warm.

If mutually accessible cultural knowledge is relevant to the process that endows linguistic forms with meaning, the question of whose beliefs and

---

8   Penelope Eckert and Sally McConnell-Ginet, "Think Practically and Look Locally: Language and Gender as Community-based Practice," *Annual Review of Anthropology* 21 (1992), pp.461-90.

9   Sally McConnell-Ginet, "Language and Gender," in Frederick Newmeyer, ed., *Linguistics: The Cambridge Survey*, vol. IV (Cambridge: Cambridge University Press, 1988).

values inform this cultural background knowledge is crucial to a theory of meaning. McConnell-Ginet argues that the cultural knowledge that forms the background for the interpretation of linguistic utterances is not neutral: "Men (and dominant groups generally) can be expected to have made disproportionately large contributions to the generally available background beliefs and values on which speakers and writers rely in their attempts to mean."[10] Research on the linguistic behaviour of North American women and men in mixed-sex conversations has demonstrated that men control conversations in a variety of ways: they take up more air time, they interrupt women more than women interrupt men, and they are more likely than women to have their conversational topics pursued and elaborated upon.[11] This differential access to conversation has implications for those whose perspective on the world constitutes mutually accessible cultural knowledge. Thus McConnell-Ginet argues that the utterance "You think like a woman" functions as an insult in most contexts in our culture, not because all listeners adhere to the proposition that women have questionable intellectual abilities, but because listeners are aware the proposition is prevalent and pervasive within the speech community; that is, it is part of a set of mutually accessible cultural beliefs. Likewise, Muriel Schultz traces the semantic derogation of terms designating women in English, demonstrating that words such as *mistress* and *spinster*, originally positive or neutral in interpretation, have taken on negative meanings in a way unparalleled for words designating men (such as *master, bachelor*).[12] The process that invests linguistic forms with sense or meaning is socially conditioned, often involving sexist (and racist) beliefs and values that are prevalent and pervasive in a culture; for example, that women are sexually wanton, that being single is an undesirable state for women. While a Humpty Dumpty theory of meaning is an attractive one (Humpty Dumpty says to Alice in *Through the Looking Glass*: "When I use a word

10   Ibid., p.91

11   See, for example, Pamela Fishman, "Interaction: The Work Women Do," and Candace West and Don Zimmerman, "Small Insults: A Study of Interruptions in Cross-sex Conversations between Unacquainted Persons," in Barrie Thorne, Cheris Kramarae, and Nancy Henley, eds., *Language, Gender and Society* (Rowley, Mass.: Newbury House, 1983). These generalizations about mixed-sex conversations are subject to qualification. Linguistic features such as interruptions or silence do not necessarily have a unitary function in conversation; that is, interruptions do not always signify power and control, and silence does not always signify lack of power. In addition, a number of contextual factors may affect the correlation of conversation features with gender.

12   Muriel Schultz, "The Semantic Derogation of Women," in Barrie Thorne and Nancy Henley, eds., *Language and Sex: Difference and Dominance (Rowley, Mass.: Newbury House, 1975).*

it means what I choose it to mean, neither more nor less"), we know that meaning is not just a matter of individual will. Indeed, in response to a November 1989 "no means no" rape awareness campaign at Queen's University in Kingston, Ontario, obscene and violent messages appeared in the windows of men's dormitories. Such messages demonstrate the extent to which women's words are not their own: "no means harder," "no means dyke," "no means more beer," "no means 'tie me up.'" That is, a woman will say "no" with sincerity to a man's sexual advances, but the "no" gets filtered through a series of beliefs and attitudes that transform her "direct negative" into an "indirect affirmative": "She is playing hard to get, but of course she really means yes."[13]

In arguing that meanings are socially constructed and constituted, McConnell-Ginet is also saying that challenges to dominant groups' meanings are possible in the context of speech communities that endorse alternative meanings. Because meanings are authorized or codified through the social support of speech communities, alternative linguistic communities have the potential to authorize non-sexist, non-racist, and non-homophobic meanings. Consider the case of gay and lesbian communities reclaiming terms such as *queer* and *dyke* and investing those terms with in-group positive associations. At the least, a feminist critique of language challenges the absolute hegemony of meanings as constituted by racist, sexist, and androcentric social values.

Meanings thus become a site of ideological struggle. Here, I first examine the social construction of meanings associated with terms I call feminist linguistic innovations—such as sexual harassment or date rape. I show how such terms are often redefined and depoliticized in the print media by means of discursive strategies. Second, I show how the phenomenon of sexual harassment is socially constructed in the "talk" of a sexual harassment tribunal. The events in question, characterized as sexual harassment or date rape by the complainants, are similarly redefined and depoliticized in the discursive patterns of this institutional setting. In both cases, I am interested in how language becomes a locus of contestation: dominant ideologies are reproduced and challenged in the discursive practices of both written and spoken texts.

13   Sally McConnell-Ginet, "The Sexual (Re)production of Meaning," in Francine Frank and Paula Treichler, *Language, Gender and Professional Writing* (New York: Modern Language Association, 1989), p.47

MEANING AS A SITE OF STRUGGLE: NON-SEXIST AND FEMINIST LINGUISTIC INNOVATIONS

Feminists have attempted to challenge the absolute hegemony of male-defined meanings and grammar by introducing non-sexist and feminist linguistic innovations into English. Most attempts at linguistic reform have focused on codified instances of sexist language, that is, on those aspects of English that are in some sense intrinsic to its grammatical and lexical structure. For example, by replacing masculine generics (such as *he, man*) with neutral generics (*they, he/she, she*) advocates of non-sexist language reform challenge the claim implicit in the use of masculine generics that men are the typical case of humanity, with women constituting a deviation from this norm. Another instance of feminist linguistic resistance is the coining of new terms to express women's perceptions and experiences, phenomena previously unexpressed in a language encoding a male worldview. Dale Spender and others argue that lexical gaps are not innocent; rather, "when one group holds a monopoly on naming, its bias is embedded in the names it supplies" and the names it doesn't supply.[14] Thus, innovative terms such as *sexism* and *sexual harassment* are significant in that they give a name to the experiences of women. As Gloria Steinem says of these terms, "A few years ago, they were just called life."[15]

While androcentric language clearly reflects and produces sexist social structures and practices, the continuing existence of such structures and practices throws into question the possibility of successful language reform. Because linguistic meanings are, to a large extent, determined by the dominant culture's social values and attitudes—that is, they are socially constructed and constituted—terms initially introduced to be non-sexist, non-racist, or even feminist may (like a woman's response of "no" to a man's sexual advances) lose their intended meanings in the "mouths" and "ears" of a sexist, racist speech community and culture. In what follows, I report on research that I conducted with Ruth King, in which we consider the extent to which language can represent a minority ideological perspective, that is, a non-sexist and feminist one, within the social context of a dominant culture that is primarily sexist. In other words, we consider the fate of non-sexist and feminist linguistic innova-

---

14   Spender, *Man Made Language*, p. 164

15   Gloria Steinem, *Outrageous Acts and Everyday Rebellions* (New York: Holt, Rinehart and Winston, 1983), p.149

tions as they travel through and get integrated into the larger, often sexist, speech community.[16]

Neutral Titles and Generics

While non-sexist language reform has enjoyed a certain degree of success over the last decade (McConnell-Ginet, for example, points out that it is becoming harder and harder to make *he* function generically, given the debates and disputes surrounding the pronoun's so-called generic usage),[17] there are indications that this reform does not always have its intended effect.

For instance, the title Ms was originally popularized by feminists in the 1970s to replace Miss and Mrs and provide a parallel term to Mr in that both Ms and Mr designate gender without indicating marital status. Casey Miller and Kate Swift see the elimination of Mrs and Miss in favour of Ms as a way of allowing women to be seen as people in their own right, rather than in relation to someone else.[18] Unfortunately, while Ms was intended to parallel Mr, considerable evidence suggests that it is not always used or interpreted in this intended way. David Graddol and Joan Swann explain that Ms is not a neutral title for women in Britain, because it sometimes replaces Miss as an indicator of single marital status: "In some contexts it seems to have coalesced with Miss (official forms sometimes distinguish only Mrs. and Ms.)."[19] Similarly, Julia Penelope maintains that speakers in the United States use and interpret Ms as referring to single women who are trying to hide the fact that they are single.[20] These two examples show that the married/single distinction continues to be marked linguistically; only the title signifying single status has changed. In addition, Francine Frank and Paula Treichler cite a directive sent to public information officers in Pennsylvania: "If you use Ms. for a female, please indicate in parentheses after the Ms. whether it's Miss or

16   I draw here from Susan Ehrlich and Ruth King, "Gender-based Language Reform and the Social Construction of Meaning," *Discourse and Society* 3 (1992), pp.151-66; and Susan Ehrlich and Ruth King, "Feminist Meanings and the (De)politicization of the Lexicon," *Language in Society* 23 (1994), pp.59-76.

17   McConnell-Giney, "Sexual (Re)production of Meaning."

18   Casey Miller and Kate Swift, *Words and Women* (Garden City, N.Y.: Doubleday, 1976).

19   David Graddol and Joan Swann, *Gender Voices* (Oxford: Basil Blackwell, 1989), p.97.

20   Julia Penelope, *Speaking Freely: Unlearning the Lies of the Father's Tongue* (Oxford: Pergamon Press, 1990).

it's Miss or Mrs."[21] In a Canadian study of attitudes towards the use of Ms and birthname retention among women, Donna Atkinson found that many of her respondents had a three-way distinction: they used Mrs for married women, Miss for women who had never been married, and Ms for divorced women.[22] What all of these examples demonstrate is the high premium placed on identifying women by their relationship (current or otherwise) to men. In spite of the intended neutrality associated with Ms, it seems to be used and interpreted in ways that maintain the linguistic distinction the title intended to erase.

In a similar way, true generics such as *chairperson* and *spokesperson*, introduced to replace masculine generics such as *chairman* and *spokesman*, seem to have lost their neutrality in that they are often only used for women. Betty Lou Dubois and Isabel Crouch cite announcements of academics changing jobs, taken from the *Chronicle of Higher Education*, demonstrating that a woman is frequently a *chairperson* but a man is a *chairman*.

Margarette P. Eby, *Chairperson* of Humanities at U. of Michigan at Dearborn, to Dean of the College of Humanities and Fine Arts and Professor of Music at U. of Northern Iowa.

David W. Hamilton, Associate Professor of Anatomy at Harvard, to *Chairman* of Anatomy at U. of Minnesota.[23]

As this example reveals, the attempt to replace a masculine generic with a neutral one has been somewhat unsuccessful. Rather than ridding the language of a masculine generic, the introduction of neutral generic forms such as *chairperson* or *chair* has led to a gender-based distinction between forms such as *chairperson* or *chair* (used to designate females) vs. *chairman* (used to designate males). Thus both the title Ms and these true generics are used in ways that maintain distinctions that the terms were intended to eliminate—distinctions clearly important to the speech community in question.

Michael Silverstein considers cases of language reform in which neu-

---

21   Francine Frank and Paula Treichler, *Language, Gender and Professional Writing* (New York: Modern Language Association, 1989), p.218.

22   Donna Atkinson, "Names and Titles: Maiden Name Retention and the Use of Ms.," *Journal of the Atlantic Provinces Linguistic Association* 9 (1987), pp.56-83.

23   Betty Lou Dubois and Isabel Crouch, "Linguistic Disruption: He/She, S/he, He, or She, He/She," in Joyce Penfield, ed., *Women and Language in Transition* (Albany: State University of New York Press, 1987), pp.28-35.

tral terms such as *actor* and *waiter* are advocated as replacements for words with feminine suffixes (with demeaning connotations) such as *actress* and *waitress*.[24] In Silverstein's terms, the category of gender often gets reconstituted in these cases so that a supposedly neutral term like *server* takes on the feminine suffix that the neutral term was intended to eliminate, as in *serveress*. Again, while the terms involved in these oppositions may change (Mrs/Miss to Mrs/Ms, chairman/chairwoman to chairman/chairperson, waiter/waitress to server/serveress), what persists is the linguistic encoding of social distinctions that are clearly of ideological importance to the speech community in question (the married/single distinction among women; the male/female distinction). We thus see the extent to which non-sexist linguistic innovations lose their intended meanings and are appropriated by a sexist speech community.

Feminist Linguistic Innovations

While terms designed to "name" women's experiences (such as *feminism, sexism, sexual harassment, date rape*) pervade our culture, it is not at all clear that their use is consistent with their intended, feminist-influenced, meanings. Ruth King and I identify some of the discursive strategies used systematically by the print media to redefine and depoliticize feminist linguistic innovations.[25] In the process of redefinition, phenomena such as *sexual harassment* and *date rape* are rendered non-existent at best and trivialized and delegitimized at worst. We therefore demonstrate the extent to which these kinds of feminist innovations, like the neutral titles and generics, become appropriated by a sexist speech community, in this case, non-progressive elements of the print media.

REDEFINITION AS OMISSION OR OBSCURING

The first kind of discursive strategy we identify involves the elimination or obscuring of crucial aspects of a term's definition. For instance, the phenomenon of sexual harassment virtually disappears when its distinguishing characteristics are omitted from its description. In an article on sexual harassment in the *National Review*, author Gretchen Morgenson reports on a *Time*/CBS sexual harassment poll in which 38 per cent of

24   Michael Silverstein, "Language and the Culture of Gender: At the Intersection of Structure, Usage, and Ideology," in E. Mertz and R. Parmentier, eds., *Semiotic Mediation* (New York: Academic Press, 1985), pp.219-59.

25   Here I draw from Susan Ehrlich and Ruth King, "Feminist Meanings and the (De)politicization of the Lexicon," *Language in Society* 23 (1994), pp.59-76.

the respondents said that they had been "the object of sexual advances, propositions, or unwanted sexual discussion" with and from men who supervised them or could influence their position at work.[26] However, only 4 per cent of this group actually reported the incidents at the time that they occurred. In attempting to explain the small percentage of formal complaints. Morgenson asks: "Did *Time* offer any explanation for why so few actually reported the incident? Could it be that these women did not report their 'harassment' because they themselves did not regard a sexual advance as harassment?"

Notice the implication here, that without a report of sexual harassment, the harassing behaviour becomes a sexual advance. (Note also the quotation marks around harassment.) Reporting, then, becomes crucial to Morgenson's definition of sexual harassment. This kind of definition ignores the political dimension intrinsic to sexual harassment: specifically, that in the majority of cases women are harassed by male supervisors who have the power to affect the women's position at work. The question of whether to lodge a formal complaint is a complicated one, involving economic and career considerations, among others. To imply that sexual harassment only occurs when it is reported and otherwise is merely a sexual advance is to deny the political aspect of the phenomenon, and it renders the majority of sexual harassment cases non-existent. Indeed, this was one of the tactics used by Republican senators during the 1991 Clarence Thomas/Anita Hill hearings. Thomas, a Republican nominee to the U.S. Supreme Court, was accused of sexual harassment by Hill, a lawyer and his former employee. In an attempt to destroy Hill's credibility, Republican senators pointed to Hill's failure to file a formal complaint of sexual harassment as evidence that she was not, in fact, sexually harassed.

While this example obscures critical aspects of the phenomenon of sexual harassment, another item from *Time* magazine redefines the prototypical case.[27] It comes from a review of the book *Step Forward: Sexual Harassment in the Workplace* by Susan Webb. The book is described as "an accessible sort of Cliffs Notes guide to the topic" and as "refreshingly free of ideology and reproach." The article offers a number of case studies from the book:

26   Gretchen Morgenson, "May I Have the Pleasure..." *National Review*, November 18, 1991, pp.36-41.

27   Janice Castro, "Sexual Harassment: A Guide," *Time* 139 (1992) p.37.

1) You and your boss are single and like each other a lot. You invite him to dinner, and one thing leads to another. Was someone sexually harassed? (No—though it wasn't very smart.)

2) Your boss invites you to a restaurant for dinner and—much to your surprise—spends the evening flirting with you. Just before inviting you to her house for a nightcap, she mentions that promotion you are hoping to get. (You are being sexually harassed. Whether or not you welcome her interest in you, she has implied a connection between the promotion and your response.)

Clearly, these types of examples are meant to help readers differentiate between behaviour that is sexual harassment and behaviour that is not. Significantly, the second case, which *does* constitute sexual harassment, involves a female supervisor and presumably a male employee. (It's difficult to imagine *Time* reporting on lesbian relations.) Thus, what is presented as the *prototypical* case of sexual harassment is a situation in which a female boss is harassing her male employee, a scenario that flies in the face of the overwhelming majority of sexual harassment cases, in which male supervisors or colleagues harass their female employees. This is not to say that women never harass their male employees, but only that this is not a typical case of sexual harassment. Here, however, the emblematic case of sexual harassment is reconfigured as females harassing males. Obscuring critical aspects of sexual harassment through redefinition only succeeds in rendering many of the actual cases non-existent.

REDEFINITION AS EXPANSION

The second kind of discursive strategy is employed consistently with terms such as *sexual harassment, rape,* and *sexual abuse.* It involves expanding the definition of such phenomena beyond reason (exploiting feminists' attempts to expand the definitions of these phenomena) and then imputing this expanded (unreasonable) definition to feminists. The effect of this kind of expansion strategy is to ridicule and trivialize the phenomenon in question. John Taylor quotes the journalist Stephanie Gutmann of *Reason* magazine, who states about date rape: "The real story about campus date rape is not that there's been any significant increase of rape on college campuses, at least of the acquaintance type, but that the word *rape* is being stretched to encompass *any type of sexual interaction.*"[28]

Here Gutmann is presumably referring to feminists' attempts to expand the notion of sexual assault/rape so that it includes more than just sexual intercourse and so that mutual consent becomes a crucial criterion in distinguishing rape from non-rape. Gutmann overstates the case by saying that rape now encompasses "any kind of sexual interaction." Later on in the same article, Taylor misrepresents a feminist revision of the notion of rape imputed to Andrea Parrot: "Any sexual intercourse without mutual desire is a form of rape." Taylor "paraphrases" Parrot— "By the definition of the radical feminists, all sexual encounters that involve any confusion or ambivalence constitute rape"—and quotes Gutmann again: "Ordinary bungled sex—the kind you regret in the morning or even during—is being classified as rape.... Bad or confused feelings after sex becomes someone else's fault."[29]

This same expansion strategy is evident in an article on feminism published in the *National Review*, but this time it is sexual abuse that is redefined. Again, the author plays on feminist attempts to broaden notions such as sexual abuse, rape, and sexual harassment.

> A raised consciousness in this area [feminism] plays with propositions of the form "X per cent of women have experienced sexual interference before the age of Y," where X is a very large number, and Y as low as you care to make it, and "sexual interference" defined so broadly that *it can include hearing an older sibling discuss his/her adolescent sexual experimentation.*[30]

Clearly, women's concern with issues such as date rape and sexual abuse is rendered ludicrous and misguided when date rape can refer to "any kind of sexual interaction" or "ordinary bungled sex" and when sexual abuse is defined as overhearing a sibling refer to sexual experimentation.

---

28   John Taylor, "Are You Politically Correct?" *New York*, January 21, 1991, p.39; emphasis added.

29   Ibid., p.39.

30   Kenneth Minogue, "The Goddess That Failed," *National Review*, November 18, 1991, p.48; emphasis added.

REDEFINITION AS OBLITERATION

Probably the most violent form of redefinition is the complete obliteration of a term's referent. The following examples suggest that phenomena such as date rape and sexual harassment are creations of the feminist imagination.

> For the moment, however, there is agreement on the crime *invented* by Professor MacKinnon—sexual harassment stemming from a hostile work environment. That *invention* is only one aspect of her campaign to protect women from men.

> By campaigning against *the thing called* "date rape," the feminist creates immense hatred and suspicion between men and women, so that the feminist advice to any woman going out on a date is to establish a virtual contract governing what will happen in the course of an evening.

> As with the *hysteria* a few years ago over the sexual abuse of children, endless talk shows, television news stories, and magazine articles have been devoted to date rape, often describing it as "an epidemic."... Much of this discussion starts off with *the claim that* one in four female students is raped by a date.[31]

The emphasized words and phrases all have a similar function: they express the degree to which the writer believes in the truth of the propositions uttered. More specifically, expressions such as *invention, the thing called*, and *the claim that* as ways of referring to date rape and sexual harassment denote the writers' lack of confidence in the existence of such occurrences. (The use of quotation marks also calls into question "date rape" as an event in itself and certainly as "an epidemic.") Once *date rape* and *sexual harassment* become non-existent, the attention paid to the phenomena can be characterized as *hysteria*, with all of the stereotypically female connotations that this word conjures up. Invoking the spectre of "female hysteria" serves to delegitimize even further women's concern with "non-events" such as date rape and sexual harassment.

---

31   Shirley Letwin, "Law and the Unreasonable Woman," *National Review*, November 18, 1991, p.36; Minogue, "The Goddess That Failed," p.48; Taylor, "Are You Politically Correct?" *New York*, January 21, 1991, pp.38-39. All emphases added.

It is perhaps not surprising, given the current "backlash" against feminism documented so well by Susan Faludi, that feminist linguistic innovations would be redefined in ways that trivialize many of the important issues arising from the contemporary women's movement. Faludi comments on the role of language in the feminist backlash: "The backlash has succeeded in framing virtually the whole issue of women's rights in its own language. Just as Reaganism shifted political discourse far to the right and demonized liberalism, so the backlash convinced the public that women's 'liberation' was the true contemporary American scourge—the source of an endless laundry list of personal, social, and economic problems."[32] Because meanings are to a large extent socially constructed, feminist linguistic innovations become endowed with sexist-influenced meanings as they circulate within the broader, often sexist speech community. Just as words such as "no" (in the context of a woman refusing a man's sexual advances) can undergo a kind of "semantic reversal" in a sexist culture, so non-sexist and feminist linguistic innovations can also lose their intended meanings as they get infused with the sexist and androcentric social values of the larger community.[33]

MEANING AS A SITE OF STRUGGLE: SEXUAL HARASSMENT OR
CONSENSUAL SEX?

A study of the interactional patterns of a university sexual harassment tribunal demonstrates how phenomena such as sexual harassment and sexual assault get constructed through "talk." More specifically, the questions asked—and the questions not asked—in this institutional context do ideological work: they construct the events as consensual sex.[34] While the complainants and the tribunal members construct the events in different ways, it is the tribunal members' characterizations of events as consensual sex (rather than as sexual harassment or sexual assault) that dominate the interactions, while those of the complainants are ignored and suppressed. Thus, language again becomes a site of con-

32   Susan Faludi, *Backlash: The Undeclared War against American Women* (New York: Crown Publishers, 1991), p.xviii.

33   See Ehrlich and King, "Feminist Meanings and the (De)politicization of the Lexicon," for examples of similar linguistic mechanisms operative in other kinds of political and ideological disputes. I borrow the term "semantic reversal" from Gill Seidel, "The British New Right's 'Enemy Within': The Antiracists," in Geneva Smitherman-Donaldson and Teun van Dijk, eds., *Discourse and Discrimination* (Detroit: Wayne State University Press, 1988), pp.131-43.

34   The idea that questions accomplish ideological work comes from Sue Fisher, "A Discourse of the Social: Medical Talk/Power Talk/Oppositional Talk," *Discourse and Society* 2 (1991), pp.157-82.

testation: the dominant ideology is reflected, challenged, and reproduced through the linguistic practices of institutional interactions.

The data in this case come from a York University disciplinary tribunal dealing with sexual harassment.[35] York University disciplinary tribunals are university trials open to the university public, operating outside the provincial or federal legal system. At these tribunals members of the university community can be tried for various kinds of misconduct. Each case is heard by three tribunal members who are drawn from a larger pool consisting of university faculty members and students. In this particular case, two charges of sexual harassment had been brought against a male student (the defendant) by two female students (the complainants).

The regulations of York University define sexual harassment as "the unwanted sexual attention of a persistent or abusive nature made by a person who knows or ought reasonably to know that such attention is unwanted." The same individual charged by York University with sexual harassment had also been charged under the Ontario Criminal Code on two counts of sexual assault. Thus, while the defendant's alleged behaviour fell within the category of sexual assault under the Ontario Criminal Code, York University's rules and regulations are such that the university charge laid was sexual harassment.

Both alleged instances of sexual harassment occurred in the women's residence rooms on consecutive nights. Both women had invited the defendant to their rooms, and in both cases he allegedly persisted in sexual behaviour unwanted by the women. Both of the women reported that they were quite clear and insistent that he stop, but their demands were ignored. In one of the cases, another man and woman were present in the residence room during the time of the unwanted sexual behaviour. The woman served as a witness for one of the complainants.

The questions asked by both the defendant's representative and the tribunal members included two themes: (1) the (so-called) "inaction" of the complainants and (2) the deconstruction of the complainants' fear. An examination of these two kinds of questions helps to indicate how both the defendant's representative and two of the tribunal members interpret and construct the events in question as consensual sex.

35   For a more detailed analysis of this case, see Susan Ehrlich and Ruth King, "Consensual Sex or Sexual Harassment: Negotiating Meaning,"Victoria Bergrall, Janice Bing and Alice Freed, eds., *Language and Gender Research: Theory and Method* (London: Longman, forthcoming).

Cross-Examination by the Defendant's Representative

It is perhaps not at all surprising that the questions and statements of the defendant's representative reflect his attempt to construct the events as consensual sex, rather than as sexual harassment or sexual assault. The first step in this discursive strategy involves focusing on the complainant's so-called inaction. In the first example [1] the representative asserts (notice that these utterances are not even in the form of questions) over a couple of turns that if the complainant had *really* been in trouble or been in *real* trouble, surely she would have cried out. Thus the fact that this complainant didn't scream or yell is represented as meaning that she wasn't really in trouble—that is, that sexual harassment or sexual assault did not really take place.

> [1] Q: Why is it that you made no attempt to scream? Can you explain what you mean by 'I really didn't want anybody to know.' If you were in such difficulty, if you felt threatened, if you felt that an assault was taking place, it strikes me as only natural [to cry out] and that help probably was available as that wall was extremely thin.... Could you tell the panel what was in your mind?
>
> A: I was afraid. I was ashamed that I had lost control of the situation. I was embarrassed and above that, I honestly can't tell you why I didn't scream.
>
> Q: I would submit, though I understand your embarrassment, if your story is correct, the fact is that help overrides embarrassment and if you really were in trouble then the only appropriate way to protect yourself was to yell out. Embarrassment would have been the last thing on your mind at the time if you were in real trouble.

In example [2] the representative's questions suggest that the complainant's failure to leave the room, her failure to call the police, and in general her lack of action meant that a sexual assault had not taken place.

> [2] Q: If you were feeling that an assault had taken place why at that point did you simply not leave the room, get dressed, while he

was asleep, leave the building and assuming for the moment that you were embarrassed uh just not go back? Why would you wait for a second assault to take place when he woke up? You had ample opportunity to leave then and call the police. Why did you not call the police?

A: I was in shock. I didn't know what to do. I didn't know what he'd do.

The second step in the construction of these events as consensual sex involves eliminating or minimizing the reasons for the complainant's inaction. That is, if there is no credible justification provided for the complainants' so-called lack of action, their lack of action can only mean that they consented to the sexual activity. In response to the numerous questions posed by both the defendant's representative and the tribunal members regarding the complainants' "inaction," the complainants generally responded by making comments about how frightened they were, and how frightening the defendant was, that night. For example: "I know it was dumb of me to invite let Tom stay in my bed but in residence everyone's like your brother and you don't imagine that that could happen. I've definitely learned from this but I didn't yell—I didn't do anything.... Marg and Bob weren't going to help me. If he hits me they're not going to stop him and the door was locked. He's a scary guy.... I didn't want to get hit. I didn't want to get raped but I didn't want to get hit."[36]

Example [3] illustrates an attempt on the part of the defendant's representative to deconstruct or minimize the complainant's fear of the defendant. The second part of constructing these events as consensual sex involves eliminating the justification for the complainant's inaction.

[3] Q: You also say here [in your testimony] that I thought I had offended him. And it strikes me that women who feel threatened are not likely to worry about whether or not they offend the person who is in the process of threatening them.... So I guess my question is if you're worried about offending him, were you feeling threatened at that point? Because your testimony implies you were feeling threatened at that point and yet you say that you didn't want to offend him.

---

36   The names of the tribunal participants have been changed.

Here the defendant's representative points to an ostensible contradiction: feeling that you don't want to offend someone and at the same time feeling threatened by that person. Given this apparent contradiction he calls into question the complainant's feelings of fear. These comments attempt to eradicate the complainant's feelings of fear and, therefore, eradicate the justification for the complainant's inaction. With the justification for inaction eradicated, the inaction is represented as meaning that the sex was consensual.

Tribunal Members' Questions of Complainants and their Witnesses

Although it might not be surprising that the defendant's representative would have as his explicit goal the construction of these events as consensual sex, and not sexual harassment or sexual assault, what is perhaps more surprising is that the tribunal members' questions follow the same themes in their cross-examination of the complainants: (1) the so-called "inaction" of the complainants and the witness and (2) the deconstruction of these individuals' fear of the defendant.

The tribunal members—in this case two faculty members and a graduate student—constitute a supposedly neutral body, ultimately responsible for deciding on the guilt or innocence and the penalty (if any) imposed on the defendant. Interestingly, one of the tribunal members prefaced her questioning of the two complainants and the witness with a lengthy statement asserting the neutrality of her questions. But in fact, two of the tribunal members (the two professors, male and female), like the defendant's representative, also manage to construct and define the events as consensual sex through their questioning. The so-called inaction of the complainants and witness was a particular concern of one of the tribunal members, who asked numerous questions about the women's options.

[4] Q: I realize you were under certain stress but in your story I heard the men left the room twice on two different occasions. And you and Marg were alone in the room. What might have been your *option*? I see an *option*. It may not have occurred to you but I simply want to explore that *option* with you. Uh, did it occur to you that you could lock the room so that they may not return to

your room?

A: It did, but it didn't. Now it does. I mean looking back. Everyone was telling me nothing's going on. Don't worry about it. Forget about it. When your friends are telling you nothing's going on, you start to question—maybe nothing is going on. I just, I couldn't think.

Q: It didn't occur to you that Marg or you, I mean I understand you were under stress.... Was Marg also intimidated by Mr. A.?

This tribunal member, while producing several interrogative sentences, is not, for the most part, asking information-gathering questions. Rather, her utterances function as assertions: *You had other options. You should have locked the door. It should have occurred to you to lock the door.* Compare her utterances in example [4] with those of the defendant's representative in [1], who was much bolder about producing utterances that were assertions in both their form and function. Notice that both the defendant's representative and the tribunal member are either directly or indirectly asserting what these women should have or could have done.

While questioning the witness for the complainant, the tribunal member again discusses the witness's options.

[5.] Q: In spite of Jenny telling you that he was trying things that she didn't want, were you ... I don't know how to phrase ... Did you feel you had some *options* to do something for Jenny?

A: Well, I wanted to do something for her but I didn't know what to do. I was afraid that if I said anything to Tom or tried to do anything that he would hurt me or hurt Jenny for trying to stop it. And everything was happening so fast. I didn't even think about knocking on the neighbour's door or anything.

[6.] Q: I mean that evening did you ever feel you knew Bob enough to get him involved because I think you were intimidated?

A: Yeah, I was close enough with Bob to ...

Q: ...to tell him: "Get up and do something. I hear some noises."
Or you didn't feel that there was anything really going on. I don't
want to put words in your mouth. Tell me how you felt.

A: towards Bob?

Q: What *options* you might have had to tell Bob something?

A: When I asked Bob to talk to Jenny was the only thing I could
think of—to get someone to tell Tom to stop it. I thought Bob and
Tom are friends. He'll listen to Bob but they didn't get the opportunity. I kind of think that Bob is very much influenced by Tom....
I think he's scared of Tom. I think Tom is a very intimidating person. He scares a lot of people—the way he talks.

In example [5], the tribunal member has difficulty forming her question,
as indicated by a couple of false starts and her admission about not
knowing how to phrase the question, perhaps because what she really
wants is not to ask but to assert that the witness should have done something to help Jenny. In example [6], the tribunal member explicitly
states what the witness could have/should have said to Bob to provoke
him into action and then says that she does not want to put words into
the witness's mouth. This repeated emphasis on the women's so-called
"options" in examples [4] to [6] functions to highlight their inaction:
they didn't lock the door, Marg didn't help Jenny, Marg didn't get Bob
to do something. And by focusing on the women's lack of action in spite
of the "options," the events begin to get constructed as the result of
choices the women made. After all, options—and this is the word used
consistently by this tribunal member—imply choices. The women are
represented as having had options: they simply did not choose the best
options. In other words, the women are represented as having exercised
some agency in or even as having chosen to engage in the sexual activities. In a much more subtle way, then, this tribunal member is also raising the possibility that the women engaged in consensual sex; or, in the
case of the witness, that she was a witness to consensual sex.

The most frequent response to the questions concerning the complainants' lack of action in spite of "options" was an indication of fear. We see this in both [5] and [6]. After the complainants'/witnesses' expressions of fear (and these occurred numerous times during the testimony and questioning), the tribunal members usually followed with questions attempting to deconstruct the cause or source of the fear.

> [7.]Q: In your statement, I think, twice, you mention "he was sounding very angry" and "I was scared" and I was wondering if you could elaborate on what you mean by that? What was he saying that you found scary? If you remember anything specific or whether it was an impression.

> A: It was just rough. It was mostly ... He just ... It was demanding. I didn't feel like I had any more choice. And whatever he said was no longer a request. It was a demand.

> Q: So, in your statement when you say he said "I paid for dinner and you invited me up so what did you expect"—that was something you perceived as demanding and rough. It wasn't like a joking comment in your mind.

> A: No, it wasn't a joke at all.

> Q: Did he raise his voice? Or was it just very emphatic?

> A: No, he didn't raise his voice but it was very blunt, very ...

Here the tribunal member tries to get at the precise causes of the complainant's fear. What was it about the defendant that was frightening? Was it his tone of voice? There is also a suggestion that some of the defendant's frightening comments might have been jokes. In a line of questioning following directly from example [6], the same tribunal member asks:

> [8.] Q: Could you explain that? Because we've heard that twice and in your story the only time you mention about being scared of

Tom was with the eavesdropping incident—that he was very scary. He was insisting that you tell him. Were there other things that he did or is it general demeanour? What do you mean by he's very scary?

A: He's ... the way he.... It seems to me if his way—It's either his way or no way. The way he was talking to Bob like even his friend Bob when I asked Bob to come to the bathroom, Tom said "No, don't go." And Bob hesitated not to go which sort of led me to believe that Bob was scared of Tom and maybe Bob knows a history of Tom.

Q: Well, let's just stick to what you know. The two times in that evening that you found Tom scary would be the eavesdropping incident and with Bob how insistent he was about Bob. You saw a side of him that scared you. Anything else than those two things.

A: No.

Here the questioner again tries to isolate the precise aspects of the defendant or the defendant's behaviour that were frightening to the witness. These attempts to assist so precisely and specifically the causes of the women's fear have the effect of reducing or minimizing their fear—notice especially the use of *only* in the first question of example [8]. It was not sufficient for the women to simply report that the defendant "was a very scary guy." Through this tribunal member's questioning and his attempts to break down the women's fear into its component parts, the women's fear begins to be attributed to specific incidents or specific aspects of the defendant's behaviour. In the last part of example [8], the tribunal member cuts the witness off and rephrases her comments about her fear of the defendant. What began with the witness's general comments about how intimidating the defendant was gets transformed into the witness feeling frightened only twice over the course of the events. The attempt to deconstruct the witness's fear has the effect of minimizing and reducing it.

Again, the minimizing and reducing of the complainants' fear eliminate the complainants' justification for their so-called inaction. This two-part discursive strategy functions to construct and define the events in question as consensual sex, not as sexual harassment or sexual assault: first, the women's inaction is established; second, the justification for the inaction is eliminated or minimized; conclusion, if there is no justification for the inaction, then the inaction means that the sexual activity was consensual. In the case of the defendant's representative, this discursive strategy is quite explicit and conscious; in the case of the tribunal members it operates in a more subtle, less conscious manner, perhaps, but the same strategy is operative.

Negotiating Meanings

The questions asked by the defendant's representative and the tribunal members function to characterize or construct the events in question in a particular way. This is not to say, however, that the complainants subscribe to this same characterization or interpretation of the events. In example [7], for instance, we see the complainant, Kelly, commenting on her perceived lack of choice during the events and the fact that Tom's utterances were demands, not requests. Indeed, throughout the hearing, the complainants and their witness provided an alternative interpretation of the events—as sexual harassment or sexual assault. The question that arises, then, is the extent to which there was a struggle over the meaning or interpretation of these events, and, if so, whose meanings prevailed?

Research on both courtroom discourse and doctor-patient discourse has highlighted the power of the questioners in these settings (the lawyers or judges, the doctors) to control interactions. Anne Graffam Walker, for example, in her research on courtroom discourse, discusses interviews with witnesses who "report a feeling of frustration at being denied the right to tell their stories their own way and complain of the lack of being in control."[37] Sue Fisher compares a doctor-patient interaction to a nurse-practitioner-patient interaction and shows how the doctor, much more than the nurse-practitioner, interrupts and questions the patient in a way that allows "a very limited exchange of information and leaves the way open for his [the doctor's] own assumptions to structure subsequent exchanges."[38] The nurse-practitioner, on the other hand, uses open-ended, probing questions to maximize the patient's voice and to hear how she constructs her life.

---

[37]   Anne Graffam Walker, "Linguistic Manipulation, Power and the Legal Setting," in Leah Kedar, ed., *Power through Discourse* (Norwood, N.J.: Ablex, 1987), p.79.

[38]   Fisher, "Discourse of the Social," p.162.

In our example [8], the tribunal member cuts off Marg's speculations about the relationship between Bob and Tom by saying, "Well, let's just stick to what you know." What begins as Marg's general comments about how frightening and intimidating Tom is gets transformed, through the tribunal member's series of questions, into a case of Marg feeling frightened *only twice* over the course of the events. It seems, then, that the tribunal member's method of questioning has resulted in assumptions that structure how Marg's fear gets talked about. This example is typical of how the tribunal members' assumptions and concerns prevail in these interactions because of the control that comes with the questioner's role.

As Walker says of lawyers or judges who are legally sanctioned to question witnesses: "Choice belongs to the examiner, who because of *his* socially and legally sanctioned role ... has the right to present, characterize, limit and otherwise direct the flow of testimony. It is in the hands of the questioner that the real power lies."[39]

Outcome of the Tribunal

In the university's submission to the tribunal members (a thirty-five-page written document), the university's legal counsel argued that "Mr. A. has fallen substantially below the standards of [the university] community in respect to his behaviour towards the complainants" and "that he be sanctioned accordingly."[40] In a letter to the tribunal very early in the process, the two complainants requested that the university apply the harshest penalty possible, that is, expulsion from the university. Indeed, in submissions on sanctions to the panel, the university's legal counsel also recommended that the defendant be expelled from the university.

In their written decision the tribunal members accepted that the defendant was guilty of some unwanted sexual aggression; however, they continued to minimize and discredit (as two of the tribunal members did during the trial) the complainants' feelings of fear: "Both complainants testified that they were deeply frightened by Mr. A.; whereas their actions seemed to undercut this claim. For example, both complainants remained in the room with Mr. A. after the sexual activity had finished and he had fallen asleep.... It seems somewhat inconsistent to assert fear

39 Walker, "Linguistic Manipulation, Power and the Legal Setting," p.79; emphasis added.

40 York University Discipline Tribunal, *Submissions to the Panel on Behalf of the University*, York University, 1993, p.33.

on the one hand and on the other hand to be comfortable enough to fall asleep alongside the feared individual."[41] By discrediting the women's feelings of fear, the tribunal's decision again focuses on the women's behaviour and raises the possibility that the women's "inaction" or "lack of resistance" was curious, perhaps unjustified. While deeming Mr A's behaviour as falling "below the standard of conduct we must expect for all members of the University community,"[42] the tribunal did not accept the university legal counsel's recommendation regarding sanctions. Expulsion from the university was judged to be unjustified: "Mr. A. was clearly insensitive and disrespectful to the complainants and this insensitivity led to harm; however I do believe that Mr. A. will be far more careful, caring and sensitive in the future. Considering that we do not find that he poses a threat, it is our view that if there is any institution in which Mr. A. can be sensitized to the need for respecting the sexual autonomy of women, it would be in a university setting. Rustication would be counter-productive to the educational mission which must be part and parcel of the University's disciplinary process."[43]

Thus, the decision allowed the defendant to continue his studies, but barred his access to various parts of the university, including its dormitories. We would suggest that such a penalty is lenient for two convictions of sexual harassment or acquaintance rape, but at the same time it is entirely consistent with the interactional patterns of the adjudication process, which served to construct the events as consensual sex.

Kimberle Crenshaw points to the androcentric character of legal definitions of rape, focusing specifically on the notion of consent.[44] Historically, the requirement of "utmost resistance" was a necessary criterion for the crime of rape; that is, if a woman did not resist a man's sexual advances to the "utmost," then rape did not occur. While the criterion of "utmost resistance" is not currently encoded in criminal definitions of rape, Crenshaw notes that a similar concept is operative in the adjudication of rape and sexual harassment cases. In such inquiries, attention tends to be focused much more on the woman's behaviour and character than on the man's. Thus, whether or not androcentric

41   *In the Matter of —————— Reasons for Judgement of the University Discipline Tribunal,* York University, 1994, p.18.

42   Ibid., p.22.

43   Ibid., p.37.

44   Kimberle Crenshaw, "Whose Story Is It Anyway: Feminist and Antiracist Appropriations of Anita Hill," in Toni Morrison, ed., *Race-ing, Justice, En-gendering Power* (New York: Pantheon Books, 1992).

definitions of sexual harassment or rape are actually encoded in law, the interpretation and characterization of events in such cases are "overwhelmingly directed toward interrogating and discrediting the woman's character on behalf of maintaining a considerable range of sexual prerogatives for men."[45]

What we see manifested in the interactional patterns of this disciplinary tribunal reflects and reproduces the privilege that legal adjudication often bestows upon men. By continuing to focus on the women's "options," the defendant's representative and the tribunal members raise the possibility that the "utmost resistance" standard had not been met, that is, that acquaintance rape had not taken place. (It is noteworthy that the same tribunal member who spoke continually about the complainants' "options" does not, when questioning the defendant, focus on the "options" available to him—that is, to adhere to the women's wishes.) By minimizing and invalidating the complainant's feelings of fear (in both the interaction and the tribunal's written decision), the defendant's representative and the tribunal members fail to acknowledge that women's submission to men's sexual aggression often occurs in the context of potential violence and injury.

CONCLUSION

Because no use of language is truly neutral and value-free, the aim of critical linguistics is to expose linguistic practices that are implicated in the maintenance and reproduction of dominant ideologies. As we've seen, language can become a site of ideological struggle. Dominant ideologies are not only reproduced in the discursive practices of spoken and written texts, but also challenged. Indeed, because meanings are to a large extent socially constructed, words or terms at the heart of political and ideological disputes typically develop diverse meanings and representations within a culture.

Non-sexist and feminist linguistic innovations, while challenging the hegemony of androcentric meanings and grammar, are at the same time being co-opted by the very structures they are meant to subvert. Likewise, the phenomena of sexual harassment and sexual assault can be constructed through "talk" in diverse ways. In the sexual harassment tribunal the questions asked accomplish ideological work, the events are

45   Ibid., p.409.

constructed discursively as consensual sex, and this interpretation pre-
vails (in spite of the complainants' alternative characterization of
events) due to the control that accompanies questioners in institutional
settings. In other words, the interactional patterns in this sexual harassment tribunal reproduce the pre-existing power relations. More generally, linguistic analysis can elucidate the non-neutrality of language, denaturalizing the somewhat invisible hierarchies and power relations
embedded in our linguistic practices.[46]

SUGGESTED READINGS

Deborah Cameron, ed., *The Feminist Critique of Language*. London: Routledge,
    1990.
Deborah Cameron, *Feminism and Linguistic Theory*. 2nd ed. New York: St. Mar-
    tin's Press, 1992.
Jennifer Coates and Deborah Cameron, eds., *Women in Their Speech Communi-
    ties*. Essex, England: Longman, 1988.
Penelope Eckert Sally McConnell-Ginet, "Think Practically and Look Locally:
    Language and Gender as Community-based Practice," *Annual Review of An-
    thropology* 21 (1992), pp.461-90.
Suzette Haden Elgin, *Native Tongue*. New York: DAW Books, 1984.
Frank, Francine and Paula A. Treichler, *Language, Gender and Professional
    Writing*. New York: Modern Language Association, 1989.
David Graddol and Joan Swann, *Gender Voices*. Oxford: Basil Blackwell, 1989.
Ruth King, *Talking Gender*. Toronto: Copp Clark, 1991.
Cheris Kramarae and Paula A. Treichler, *A Feminist Dictionary*. London: Pan-
    dora Press, 1985.
Cheris Kramarae, *Women and Men Speaking*. Rowley, Mass: Newbury House,
    1981.
Sally McConnell-Ginet, Ruth Borker, and Nelly Furman, eds., *Women and Lan-
    guage in Literature and Society*. New York: Praeger, 1980.
Sally McConnell-Ginet, "Language and Gender," in Frederick Newmeyer, ed.,
    Linguistics: The Cambridge Survey, vol. IV. Cambridge: Cambridge Univer-
    sity Press, 1988.
Sally McConnell-Ginet, "The Sexual (Re)production of Meaning," in Francine
    Frank and Paula Treichler, eds., *Language, Gender and Professional Writing*.
    New York: Modern Language Association, 1989.

46   I thank Lorraine Code and Sandra Burt for comments on previous versions of this paper.
     Some of the research I report on here by Ehrlich and King was supported, in part, by a Regu-
     lar Research Grant from the Social Sciences and Humanities Research Council of Canada,
     Grant #410-94-1506.

Casey Miller and Kate Swift, *Words and Women*. Garden City, N.Y.: Doubleday, 1976.

Julia Penelope, *Speaking Freely: Unlearning the Lies of the Fathers' Tongues*. Oxford: Pergamon Press, 1990.

Susan Philips and Susan Steele, and Christine Tanz, eds., *Language, Gender and Sex in Comparative Perspective*. Cambridge: Cambridge University Press, 1987.

Dale Spender, *Man Made Language*. London: Routledge, 1980.

Barrie Thorne, Cheris Kramarae, and Nancy Henley, eds., *Language, Gender and Society*. Rowley, Mass.: Newbury House, 1983.

RANDI R. WARNE

Chapter Three: Further Reflections on the "Unacknowledged Quarantine": Feminism and Religious Studies

WRITING IN 1992, CANADIAN HISTORIAN RUTH BROUWER lamented the exclusion of the study of religion from Canadian women's history. Noting the number of U.S. works "highlighting the centrality of religion in women's lives," Brouwer made a strong assertion: that "Most of the best-known historians of Canadian women have appeared uninterested in or uneasy with the topic of religion. A few have been perceptively hostile to the subject."[1] Brouwer took her title from a review of a 1987 collection of articles, *Disciplines of Faith: Studies in Religion, Politics, and Patriarchy* produced by the History Workshop Centre for Social History in England. In that review, according to Brouwer, Deborah Valenze "rejoiced that 'under the banner of socialist and feminist collaboration,' a work had at last been produced that allowed social historians of religion in Britain to move out of the 'unacknowledged quarantine' in which they had been labouring and 'into the blissful sunshine of public recognition.'"[2]

My experience as a feminist scholar in religious studies with specific interests in methodology, social ethics, and turn-of-the-century feminist

1 Ruth Compton Brouwer, "Transcending the 'Unacknowledged Quarantine': Putting Religion into English-Canadian Women's History," *Journal of Canadian Studies* 27, 3 (Fall 1992), p.47. Brouwer's article was originally given as a paper at a joint session of the Canadian Historical Association and the Canadian Society for Studies in Religion, Kingston, Ont., June 1991.

2 Ibid.

social activism confirms Brouwer's assessment. In my own work I have
thus found myself "between two stools." Feminist scholarship in religious studies (if less so, in recent years, work on women per se) has been
accorded the same resistance and attempts at marginalization by the
mainstream that feminist scholarship has received in other academic
disciplines. Yet I have found that academic interest in religion is considered equally suspect by many Canadian feminist scholars.[3] It has been
my contention for the past two decades that religious studies suffers
when its scholarship is not gender-critical. But feminist scholarship is
also diminished when it dismisses religion as a legitimate subject of critical study, particularly when it uses historical judgements in generating
its theoretical base.

I therefore have two aims in this chapter. My primary task will be to
explore the impact of feminism on Canadian religious studies, with
regard to both methods and the existential state of the discipline. Then I
will turn to what I see to be some of the consequences of the marginalization of religious studies in Canadian feminist scholarship. In both instances I will draw from my own experience in doing work on Canadian
feminist and religious activist Nellie McClung. The objections to and
barriers placed in the way of my pursuing McClung as a subject of doctoral research illuminate the methodological dilemmas a feminist
scholar of religion may encounter—as well as the political battles inevitably attendant upon challenging dominant intellectual constructions
(materially embodied in senior male professors with power).

In contemporary Canada my work raises questions of another kind,
in that I take as my interpretive focus McClung's religion, understood
constructively, and without privileging the analytical pivot of race. In
describing my focus on religion, I will refer to what Australian feminist
historian Judith Allen has called the "cycle of identification and repudia-
tion" that has been a feature of feminist scholarship worldwide.[4] Ultimately it is my hope that the "unacknowledged quarantine" that informs the study of both women and religion will be lifted, to the benefit
of both feminist and religious studies scholarship. To that end, I will try

---

3   Australian feminist Penelope Magee argues that this disposition holds for feminist scholar-
    ship in general. Observing that "religious ideas are seen as anomalous or difficult to ap-
    proach from the viewpoint of much feminist theory and practice," she draws from postmod-
    ernist analysis to illustrate "the real difficulty experienced with leaving a fundamental binary
    opposition (sacred/profane) unquestioned in general feminist discourse." Penelope Magee,
    "Disputing the Sacred: Some Theoretical Approaches to Gender and Religion," in Ursula
    King, ed., New Perspectives on Gender and Religion (Oxford: Basil Blackwell, forthcoming).

4   Judith Allen, "Contextualizing Late Nineteenth Century Feminism: Problems and Compari-
    sons," Journal of the Canadian Historical Association 1,1 (1991), pp.17-36.

to make the territory of the academic study of religion somewhat more familiar in the course of describing the impact of feminism upon it.

RELIGIOUS STUDIES AS AN ACADEMIC DISCIPLINE

In brief, religious studies is the academic, secular (non-confessional) study of religion as a complex phenomenon of human culture.[5] It comprises aspects of sociology, psychology, philosophy, ritual practice, artistic expression, studies of claims about ultimacy and meaning, and concrete expressions of values embodied in ethical systems, worldviews, and ways of life. While the modern critical study of religion dates itself from the Enlightenment, *Religionswissenschaft* (translated "science" or "history of religions") usually finds its origins in mid-nineteenth-century Europe, with F. Max Muller's plea for the critical, *scientific* study of all religious traditions, Christianity included.[6] The nineteenth-century impulse for "objective" and "value-free" study (its imperialist, racist, hierarchical, and evolutionary manifestations notwithstanding) has deeply marked the development of religious studies as a discipline, figuring centrally in discussions of method to the present day. It has also informed its interdisciplinarity. Drawing freely on the rich explosion of theories about human nature and culture in anthropology, psychology, and sociology from the century's turn, at least one stream of the "scientific study of religion" upheld the ideal of rationality and scholarly detachment, which alone could guarantee discovering "the truth." Textual, philological studies joined these other points of entry in the understanding of religious cultures, providing a multifaceted array of options for the scholar interested in religion.[7]

Yet from the outset *Religionswissenschaft* was also shaped by another agenda. True to its origins in philosophy and theology, the phenomenological approach to the study of religion has deeply influenced the

5   For a good basic introduction, see Harold E. Remus et al., "Religion as an Academic Discipline," in Charles H. Lippy and Peter W. Williams, eds., *Encyclopaedia of the American Religious Experience: Studies of Traditions and Movements*, vol. III (New York: Charles Scribner's Sons, 1988).

6   F. Max Muller, "Plea for a Science of Religion," in Jacques Waardenburg, ed., *Classical Approaches to the Study of Religion: Aims, Methods and Theories of Research* (The Hague: Mouton and Co., 1973), pp.86-89. For a concise overview of the study of religion, see William Paden, *Religious Worlds* (Boston: Beacon Press, 1988), ch.1-2. The term *Religionswissenschaft*, and the problems of definition that attend it, are hotly debated in the field.

7   The philological branch of religious studies scholarship analyses sacred scriptures in terms of internal literary and linguistic structures and, more importantly, as a resource for historical, philosophical, and cultural analysis.

discipline as it is currently practised.[8] Phenomenologists see both experience and the understanding (*Verstehen*) grounded in and by it as essential preconditions for any informed commentary on religion.[9] Some
scholars charge that this strategy is actually a covert plea for specific religious *faith*; that to talk about "the Sacred" implies a *real* object beyond
any human experience so designated.[10] The debate about methods, and
about the desirability of (or inherent disqualification by) having religious faith for the study of religion, continues to rage in religious studies,
with no small amount of intensity. Usually this debate is construed
around the relationship between theology and religious studies.[11] However, its implications for feminist engagements with the academic study
of religion are obvious, given the centrality of questions of "scientific
neutrality" (also "the neutrality of expertise"), the place of experience in
generating reliable knowledge, and the role of values in feminist scholarship.

Currently, as Allan Andrews argues, the academic study of religion
admits three main methodological approaches: normative, social-scientific and, humanistic.[12] The first includes explicitly theological ap-

8   The phenomenology of religion is the attempt to turn to "the things themselves," without im-
     posing an overlay of expectation, conviction, or other forms of prejudgement on the objects
     or experiences studied. This critical suspension of disbelief, it is held, allows "the Sacred" to
     manifest itself for engagement; only then can its universal structures be discerned and a relig-
     ious culture be truly understood.

9   The classic in the field is Rudolph Otto's *The Idea of the Holy* (Oxford: Oxford University
     Press, 1931). Otto informs readers at the outset that if they have not had the experience of
     "the numinous" they should read no further, because they will not be capable of under-
     standing what he has to say.

10   Perhaps the scholar most taken to task for implying a real status to "the Sacred" is Mircea
     Eliade, a prolific scholar whose final contribution to the field was the massive *Encyclopaedia
     of Religion*, edited by him and published shortly after his death in 1986. Eliade was part of the
     so-called "Chicago School," whose influence on religious studies has been enormous.

11   A key Canadian figure in this debate is Don Wiebe, ironically a professor of theology at Trin-
     ity College, an Anglican institution affiliated with the University of Toronto. He is also well
     known on the international scene. Wiebe has written extensively, and with increasing inten-
     sity, about the "incommensurability" of theology and religious studies. Only the latter, in
     Wiebe's view, belongs in the university, and then only if it is purged of its "closet theologi-
     ans." For a succinct example of Wiebe's position, see his influential article, "The Failure of
     Nerve in the Academic Study of Religion," *Studies in Religion/Sciences Religieuses* 13, 4 (Fall
     1984), pp.401-22. Wiebe's work continues to provoke lively, ongoing debated, albeit exclu-
     sive of feminist or postmodernist perspectives. Wiebe dismissed both feminism and post-
     modernism as "relativism" at a session devoted to his work at the Kingston Learned Societies
     meetings in 1991.

12   Allan A. Andrews, "The Status of the Field: Normative, Humanistic and Social Scientific Ap-
     proaches to the Academic Study of Religion," CSSR *Bulletin* 22, 4 (November 1992), pp.101-5.

proaches, as well as those such as transpersonal psychology or "the perennial philosophy," which either seek or presume to know the nature of "ultimate reality" beyond human existence. The social-scientific approach, in contrast, "takes as its subject matter data on religious behaviour, that is, empirically observable and, ideally, quantifiable facts about what religious people think and do."[13] The "humanistic" approach (also known as "comparative religion"):

> sees as its principal strength and value that it ... seeks to understand the religious dimension, *qua* religious dimension, of human existence both in particular instances and in general. It does not, like the normative approach, critique the religious claims of others, nor like the social scientific approach, subordinate the religious dimension of behaviour and culture to other factors. Comparative religion uniquely sees the religious dimension of human life to be *equally*—no more, no less—important as life's other facets.[14]

Andrews acknowledges that the comparative approach (in which different religious traditions are studied for both similarities and differences, from a multiplicity of perspectives) has perceived weaknesses, including the fact that "it is not possible to be totally objective, to entirely 'bracket out' presuppositions and judgements, nor to completely understand other human beings, especially those of distant times or different cultures." Nevertheless, he believes that acknowledging these limits allows the comparative or humanistic approach to assess its findings more realistically, and that this is a strength. Remarkably, given their very different agendas, normative, social-scientific and, humanistic approaches to the study of religion tend to co-exist productively and relatively peacefully in religious studies departments across the United States and Canada. This may be due in part to their small size and often marginalized status, hence an unwillingness to jeopardize their existence through self-destructive infighting. (There are of course some colourful counterexamples to this generalization.) Whatever the reason, the one underlying feature of religious studies departments that serves as a unifying factor across other forms of difference is their overwhelming maleness.

13   Ibid., p.102.

14   Ibid., p.103.

In keeping with this reality, Andrew's article completely omits any mention of feminism as an analytical or methodological tool in the study of religion. While it may be argued that one article does not exhaust the field, the omission stands as an indicator of the status of gender-critical scholarship in methodological discussions, at least as they are currently entertained in the mainstream.[15]

THE IMPACT OF FEMINISM ON RELIGIOUS STUDIES

The academic study of religion is curiously placed, in that it does not take place only in the secular academy. Theological colleges and seminaries too have attended critically to the subject matter of religion, albeit with different ultimate aims. The seminary context is, oddly enough, of pivotal importance for understanding the impact of feminism on religious studies. Although at least some of the methodological approaches of religious studies affirm the importance of personal experience in understanding, historically the "experiencers" doing the understanding have been male. The received cultural gender script that separates male and female into "masculine" and "feminine" qualities, valorizing the former and subordinating the latter, has been unproblematic for these scholars. Insofar as the experience of the scholars confirms received categories, the categories themselves have gained greater credence, setting up a cycle of mutual confirmation that accords the status of "objectivity" to the data. Within the scientific paradigm as such there is no place to critique the gender script;[16] nor, given the gender uniformity of the experiencing subjects, has the gender specificity of their perspective been visible to those more open to the role of subjectivity. Thus the secular academic study of religion has proceeded until relatively recently within a masculinized world, and it has produced scholarship to match.

Ironically, critical feminist scholarship on religion first came to the fore in Christian seminaries, for a number of different reasons. It is often felt that "the church" is the most repressive of cultural institutions on gender issues, and it is certainly true that historically it has proved to be a prime repository for ideas and practices that justify the subordination of women. At the same time, Christian tradition, and the Biblical heri-

15   A recently published program for the Midwest Region meetings of the American Academy of Religion supports this point. While there were four full sections of papers on "Women's Studies" (more, for example, than either "Religion and Science" or "Philosophy and Theology of Religion"), none of the three "Methodology" sections dealt with gender.

16   Sandra Harding also makes this point in "Rethinking Standpoint Epistemology: What is 'Strong Objectivity'?" in Linda Alcoff and Elizabeth Potter, eds., *Feminist Epistemologies* (New York: Routledge, 1993), p.49-82.

tage of which it is a part, has within it a countervailing trend that affirms—the overwhelming dictates of its common social practice to the contrary—within women as well as in men the *imago dei*, or image of God. There are thus resources within the tradition that can be called upon to advance women's full inclusion and equal status with men in various arenas of human activity, not just as a "human right" but as a divinely ordered imperative.[17]

As the 1960s unfolded, the overall liberalization of religious culture and an increasing demand for and access to higher education meant that more and more women found it possible to attend seminary. The result for patriarchal stability was catastrophic. Women began to question their doctrinally articulated subordination, and did so informed by close textual and theological studies that called the tradition to public and scholarly account.[18] The call for the ordination of women was an especially lively debate, illustrating the many barriers, formal and informal, to women wishing to fulfil what they felt to be their god-given calling, as well as the demands of simple justice. By the end of the 1970s there was a virtual explosion of literature on women and religion, due in no small measure to the efforts of women to retrieve their theological traditions from what they understood to be a religiously illegitimate patriarchalism.

In 1960, for instance, Valerie Saiving published "The Human Situation: A Feminine View."[19] The piece argues a position that feminist scholars now take as axiomatic, namely that gender makes a difference in how men and women experience the world; that theories of "man" have been constructed out of male experience alone, so much so that the term "man" is in fact a false generic, and that where women have been

17   The twofold dynamic of religion—as both support and potential transformer of the status quo—is axiomatic to the field and dates back to at least Max Weber (1864-1920). In the popular mind, however, only the conservative dynamic of supporter tends to be acknowledged. The complexity and contradictions of women's status within religious culture are a primary locus of inquiry for feminist scholars of religion.

18   The importance of mounting such challenges from within religious tradition, and on a scholarly base, was well understood by feminist activists of the nineteenth century. Elizabeth Cady Stanton, author of *The Woman's Bible* (New York: Arno Press, 1974, originally published in 1895 and 1898), is a well-known example, although her adolescent expertise as a Greek scholar is less familiar. Katharine Bushnell was another textual scholar who in *God's Word for Women* (1916, 1921, 1923, 1930; rpt. North Colling, N.Y.: Ray Munson, 1975) urged women to read the Bible in its original languages to protect them from the male-serving interpretations offered them from the pulpit. For an excellent treatment of Bushnell, see historian Diane Hallman's article "Katharine C. Bushnell: Her Word to Women—Research in Progress," *Atlantis* 16, 2, pp. 64-75.

19   Valerie Saiving, "The Human Situation: A Feminine View," in Carol P. Christ and Judith Plaskow, eds., *Womanspirit Rising: A Feminist Reader in Religion* (San Francisco: Harper and Row, 1979), pp.25-42.

included, their placement tends towards subordination, if not denigra-
tion. Saiving challenges the supposed "universality" of theological for-
mulations of human nature on these grounds. She suggests that if there
is an "original sin," it manifests itself differently in women than in men,
so that while "pride" makes sense as the fundamental moral deforma-
tion of men, it is self-abnegation that obscures the *imago dei* in women.
In brief, men make too much of themselves, while women make too little.[20] Saiving's article presents conclusions strikingly similar to those of
Carol Gilligan, drawn over twenty years later. Gilligan's work is problematic both in itself and in its applications, and I do not wish to suggest
uncritical support for it here.[21] What is important is Saiving's explicit
appeal to "feminine" experience as a privileged vantage point from
which to judge allegedly universal theorizing. This is a rudimentary
point for feminist scholarship, but it is one in the main that has not yet
been taken by religious studies. It has, however, been widely incorporated in theological circles.

The privileging of the vantage point of the marginalized and oppressed came to the fore in the work of Catholic theologian and patristics scholar Rosemary Radford Ruether. Ruether found her political origins in two questions: anti-Semitism and the legacy of the Holocaust,
and liberation theology, first proclaimed at Medellín, Colombia, in 1968.
A prolific editor and writer, she has produced several important collections and texts for feminist scholarship on religion, including the
groundbreaking *Religion and Sexism*, published in 1974.[22] Her publications illustrate the general trajectory of the field: first, documentation of
the tradition and the sexist, exclusionary treatment of women within it;
then an affirmation of women's agency within historical context; an exploration of the historical complexity and multitraditioned character of

20   There is a logical link between this shift of theological perspective and feminist activism. If
     self-abnegation is the epitome of sin, then women have to learn to value themselves and as-
     sert themselves more. Social structures that impede this process therefore need to be
     changed, because they are in violation of "God's intent for Creation."

21   Carol Gilligan, *In a Different Voice* (Cambridge, Mass.: Harvard University Press, 1982). Gilli-
     gan suggests that the moral task for men is to consider others as legitimate objects of moral
     concern, while for women the task is to consider themselves as such. For critiques, see for ex-
     ample the various discussions in Marsha Hanen and Kai Nielsen, eds., *Science, Morality and
     Feminist Theory* (Calgary: University of Calgary Press, 1987) and Eva Feder Kittay and Diana
     T. Meyers, eds., *Women and Moral Theory* (Totowa, N.J.: Rowman and Littlefield, 1987). A
     key concern with Gilligan's work is the extent to which it assumes an essentialist notion of
     gender.

22   Rosemary Radford Ruether, ed., *Religion and Sexism: Images of Women in Jewish and Chris-
     tian Tradition* (New York: Simon and Schuster, 1974).

women's religious experience; a focus on language, and her most recent work on ecological concerns and spirituality.[23] Her extremely critical reading of Christian tradition notwithstanding, over the last twenty years Ruether has continued to place herself within Catholic tradition, claiming her position as a "radical Orthodoxy" that identifies patriarchal power within the church as a manifestation of men's "original sin" of the will to dominate.

A similar concern for material culture and the establishment of just relations within it underlies the work of Protestant feminist ethicist Beverly Harrison, whose articles "The Power of Anger in the Work of Love" and "Misogyny and Homophobia" remain classics in the field.[24] Other scholars have turned their attention to Christian scripture, arguing for attention to the "silenced" voices of women and a revisioning of tradition in light of that understanding.[25]

A second generation has now joined the first, pushing boundaries even further through treating subjects such as wifebeating and incest, "divine child abuse," the erotic, "selfhood" and "difference."[26] The sub-

23   Rosemary Ruether and Eleanor McLaughlin, eds., *Women of Spirit: Female Leadership in Jewish and Christian Traditions* (New York: Simon and Schuster, 1979); Ruether and Rosemary Skinner Keller, eds., *Women and Religion in America*, 3 vols. (San Francisco: Harper and Row, 1981, 1983, 1986); Rosemary Radford Ruether, *Sexism and God-Talk: Toward a Feminist Theology* (Boston: Beacon Press, 1983); and Ruether, *Gaia and God: An Ecofeminist Theology of Earth Healing* (San Francisco: Harper, 1992).

24   In Beverly Wildung Harrison, *Making the Connections: Essays in Feminist Social Ethics*, ed. Carol S. Robb (Boston: Beacon, 1985). See also Harrison, *Our Right to Choose: Toward a New Ethic of Abortion* (Boston: Beacon, 1983). Harrison has been a member of the multiracial Mud Flower collective, whose book *God's Fierce Whimsy: Christian Feminism and Theological Education* (New York: Pilgrim Press, 1985) engages with both passion and clarity issues of class, economic exploitation, racism, and heterosexism. For further challenges to heterosexist theology, see Carter Heyward, *Touching Our Strength: The Erotic as Power and the Love of God* (San Francisco: Harper and Row, 1989).

25   For example, see Elizabeth Schussler Fiorenza, *In Memory of Her: A Feminist Theological Reconstruction of Christian Origins* (New York: Crossroad, 1983). Fiorenza advocates the extension of a "hermeneutics of suspicion" to the reality claims of the dominant, and a "hermeneutics of generosity" to the reality claims of the oppressed. See also Phyllis Trible, *Texts of Terror* (Philadelphia: Fortress, 1984).

26   Ann Taves, *Households of Faith* (Bloomington: Indiana University Press, 1989); Joanne Carlson Brown and Carole R. Bohn, eds., *Christianity, Patriarchy and Abuse: A Feminist Critique* (New York: The Pilgrim Press, 1989); Rita Nakashima Brock, *Journeys by Heart: A Christology of Erotic Power* (New York: Crossroad, 1988), with a chapter on "The Feminist Redemption of Christ"; Catherine Keller, *From a Broken Web: Separation, Sexism and Self* (Boston: Beacon, 1986); and Marilyn J. Legge, *The Grace of Difference: A Canadian Feminist Theological Ethic* (Atlanta: Scholars Press, 1992). Legge was a student of Beverly Harrison's at Union.

ject of racism and its legacies is producing scholarship that is particularly vibrant, challenging and theoretically sophisticated.[27]

Pushing the boundaries has sometimes meant that theologically
based feminist scholars of religion have found themselves outside of tradition entirely. This became quickly true for Mary Daly, widely known
within the feminist critical community for her "meta-ethical," outra-
geously redefinitional, poetic, visionary, and lexicographical "voyages"
such as *Gyn/Ecology*, *Pure Lust*, and *Websters' New Intergalactic
Wickedary*.[28] Initially her position was quite reformist. Inspired by liberalism, she combined Paul Tillich, process thought and the Thomism of
her Catholic upbringing in an invitation to embody the promise of Vati-
can II in revised gender roles.[29] By 1973 she had repudiated her critical
but optimistic assessment to call for "castration" of all "phallocracies" in
Beyond God the Father.[30] Daly's later work builds on this position and
indeed makes it seem moderate. Her sustained critique of all traditional
religion as irrevocably patriarchal has been challenged by some as ahis-
torical and totalizing, just as her post-Thomistic philosophizing is seen
as insensitive to issues of class and race.[31] Nevertheless, Daly's hyperin-

27   In addition to *God's Fierce Whimsy*, see especially Katie Geneva Cannon, *Black Womanist
      Ethics* (Atlanta: Scholars Press, 1988); also Emilie M. Townes, "To Be Called Beloved:
      Womanist Ontology in PostModern Refraction," and Katie G. Cannon and Kristine A.
      Culp, "Appropriation and Reciprocity in the Doing of Feminist and Womanist Ethics," in
      Society of Christian Ethics, *Annual*, 1993.

28   Mary Daly, *Gyn/Ecology: The Metaethics of Radical Feminism* (Boston: Beacon, 1978);
      Websters' New Intergalactic Wickedary of the English Language, conjured by Mary Daly in
      Cahoots with Jane Caputi (Boston: Beacon, 1987).

29   Mary Daly, *The Church and the Second Sex* (New York: Harper and Row, 1968); also publish-
      ed with a "Feminist Postchristian Introduction by the Author" by Harper Colophon in 1975.
      Daly makes a practice of retrospectively casting her positions in self re-creation; see *Outer-
      course: The Be-Dazzling Voyage: Containing Recollections from my Logbook of a Radical
      Feminist Philosopher (be-ing an account of my time/space travels and ideas—then, again,
      now, and how)* (San Francisco: Harper, 1992). Paul Tillich was a Christian existentialist who
      fled Hitler's Germany to become a leading Protestant theologian on the U.S. scene in the
      1950s and 1960s. One of his best known books is *The Courage to Be* (New Haven, Conn.: Yale
      University Press, 1952). Process theology also came to the fore in the 1960s. Building on the
      foundation laid by philosopher Alfred North Whitehead, process theologians emphasized
      the elements of change, growth, uncertainty, and relativity in human life, and conceived of
      God in like fashion as "Creative Process."

30   Mary Daly, *Beyond God the Father: Toward a Philosophy of Women's Liberation* (Boston:
      Beacon, 1973).

31   With typical Dalyesque style, she states, "*Patriarchy is itself the prevailing religion of the entire
      planet*, and its essential message is necrophilia. All of the so-called religions legitimating pa-
      triarchy are mere sects subsumed under its vast umbrella/canopy." *Gyn/Ecology*, p.39. For a
      critique, see Audre Lorde, "An Open Letter to Mary Daly," in *Sister Outsider* (Trumansburg,
      N.Y.: The Crossing Press, 1984), pp.66-71.

tellectual yet lyrically accessible "re-speaking" of the world has had both profound appeal and a lasting significance in her analyses of the power of naming.[32]

What unites all of this scholarship is its grounding in and affirmation of women's experience (whatever that might be, or might mean) and its rejection of the disembodied, acontextual voice of "truth," whether it is alleged to be found in history, scripture, or tradition, or in philosophy, doctrine, or systematics. Feminist scholars of religious studies share this commitment and identification. Indeed, some collections of articles on women and religion do not distinguish between theological and religious studies' treatments of the subject matter.[33] Both the reconstruction of existing tradition and the creation of new traditions are put forward as options, suggesting that these studies are of some practical as well as intellectual significance. Indeed, it was in these early explorations and critiques of tradition that the now burgeoning area of female spirituality, especially Goddess worship, first came to the fore.[34]

One of the first feminist scholars who forayed into this area was Carol Christ. In contrast to the theological frameworks employed by other scholars (systematics for Saiving, textual and historical studies for Ruether, philosophy for Daly, and ethics for Harrison), Christ approached her subject from the perspective of religious studies, looking through the lens of symbol. In "Why Women Need the Goddess: Phenomenological, Psychological, and Political Reflections," Christ recasts anthropologist Clifford Geertz's well-known definition of religion as a cultural system in feminist terms, arguing: "Religions centred on the worship of a male God create 'moods' and 'motivations' that keep women in a state of psychological dependence on men and male authority while at the same time legitimating the *political* and *social* authority

---

32   Daly challenged methods in the patriarchal academy early and explicitly: "It should be noted that the god Method is in fact a subordinate deity, serving Higher Powers. These are social and cultural institutions whose survival depends upon the classification of disruptive and disturbing information as nondata. Under patriarchy, Method has wiped out women's questions so totally that even women have not been able to hear and formulate our own questions to meet our own experiences. Women have been unable even to experience our own experience." *Beyond God the Father*, pp.11-12.

33   See, for example, *Womanspirit Rising*; also, Nancy Auer Falk and Rita M. Gross, eds., *Unspoken Worlds: Women's Religious Lives* (Belmont, Cal.: Wadsworth: 1989).

34   Carol Christ, "Why Women Need the Goddess: Phenomenological, Psychological, and Political Reflections," Carol P. Christ and Judith Plaskow, eds., *Womanspirit Rising: A Feminist Reader in Religion* (San Francisco: Harper and Row, 1979), p.275. See Clifford W. Geertz, "Religion as a Cultural System," *The Interpretation of Cultures* (New York: Basic Books, 1973), pp.87-125.

of fathers and sons in the institutions of society." She asserts that since "Goddess symbolism undergirds and legitimates the concerns of the women's movement, much as God symbolism in Christianity under-girded the interests of men in patriarchy," women need to develop a *thealogy* in which the theological emphasis on explanation is replaced by a more intuitive and experiential woman-centred emphasis on sym-bol.[35] In her most recent work, *Laughter of Aphrodite*, Christ develops these themes further.[36] Other less academically centred names associ-ated with this approach are Merlin Stone, Zsuzsanna E. Budapest, and Starhawk, a self-proclaimed witch. Riane Eisler's *The Chalice and the Blade* provides a historically revisionist account of these contemporary concerns grounded in an ancient, prepatriarchal past.[37]

Over the last thirty years, feminist studies in religion have generated a tremendous body of literature, a significant portion of which continues to emerge out of a religiously committed context.[38] It would seem rea-sonable that this literature would begin to figure in the methodological debates now taking place in religious studies, but in my experience this has not yet happened in any depth on the Canadian scene, for a number of reasons. First, the debate has been so deeply shaped by the question of objectivity, understood as "scientific" and in contradistinction to theo-logical commitment, that feminist concerns have barely been acknow-ledged, much less engaged.[39] This exclusion has been reinforced by the

35   Christ, "Why Women Need the Goddess," pp.276,279. Naomi Goldenberg also advocates thealogy over theology, but from an atheistic, depth-psychology base. See Naomi Golden-berg, *Changing of the Gods: Feminism and the End of Traditional Religions* (Boston: Beacon, 1979). Goldenberg was a former advocate of Freudian, then Jungian, thought who has re-cently turned her attentions to the British school of psychoanalysis and Melanie Klein. Gold-enberg, *Returning Words to Flesh: Feminism, Psychoanalysis and the Resurrection of the Body* (Boston: Beacon, 1990).

36   Carol Christ, *Laughter of Aphrodite: Reflections on a Journey to the Goddess* (San Francisco: Harper and Row, 1987).

37   See Merlin Stone, *Ancient Mirrors of Womanhood: A Treasury of Goddess and Heroine Lore from Around the World* (Boston: Beacon, 1979); Z. Budapest, "Self-Blessing Ritual," in *Womanspirit Rising*, pp.269-72; Starhawk, *The Spiral Dance* (San Francisco: Harper and Row, 1979) and *Truth or Dare* (San Francisco: Harper and Row, 1987); and Riane Eisler, *The Chalice and the Blade: Our History, Our Future* (San Francisco: Harper, 1987). Eisler retains the dualism characteristic of Western culture, but reverses the traditional valorization to ad-vocate a "partnership" model that is ostensibly more characteristic of "women's culture."

38   Much contemporary work on Goddess religion is grounded in such religious commitment.

39   As Don Wiebe graphically stated regarding the desirability of "objectivity": "We may never be able to construct a wholly value-free study of any subject matter ...[but] that a completely aseptic condition can never be obtained in the operating room is not reason for surgery to be done in the sewer." Quoted in Francis Schussler Fiorenza, "A Response to Don Wiebe," CSSR *Bulletin*, 23, 1 (February 1994), p.8.

history of the development of religious studies departments. The reality is that many religious studies departments in Canada find their origins in faculties of theology, and that current and former priests and ministers make up a sizeable portion of their senior professorate.[40] Where there is concern for a distinctive "religious studies" identity, an extensive effort is made to distance the enterprise from any hint of involvement with confessional studies. The Christian/post-Christian focus of the bulk of feminist work on religion thus renders it doubly suspect, both because it is "committed" scholarship and because of the nature of the commitment implied.[41]

The most troublesome aspect of feminist commitment for the mainstream is not its connection, if any, to Christianity, but its commitment to the critique and transformation of patriarchy. This concern manifests itself in two areas for male scholars of religion, one scholarly and one personal. The academic study of religion, whether in religious studies departments or in the enterprise of *Religionswissenschaft*, has been carried out almost exclusively by men. This androcentrism has meant that the bulk of theory pertaining to religion has tended overwhelmingly to reinforce the culturally received gender script of male-defined female difference and inferiority.[42] Even when gender is not central to the theory or perspective espoused, the exclusion of women from the theory

40 Some faculties, such as those at Queen's and McGill, are integrated. Others, like the University of Toronto, where I did my graduate work, hold themselves at a greater distance from the theological schools on campus. Debate on the proper relationship of religious studies and theology has been lively within both formats. In my own experience, I found that religious studies' concern to distinguish itself from theology made it difficult for me to pursue non-confessional studies in Christianity. (One of the consequences of this concern was over-prescription of requirements. For example. I sat five four-hour exams for my doctoral comprehensives. My most minor exam was on the social-scientific study of religion, in which I was examined on Marx, Weber, Durkheim, Freud, Jung, and Eriksson. Given the issues of "legitimacy" involved, in no exam did I answer a question on women.)

41 This interest in women's place in and relation to Christianity is a logical outcome of feminists' concern to critique Western patriarchal culture and does not necessarily signal confessional intent.

42 A classic example is the case of initiation rites. Mircea Eliade, perhaps the key figure in the phenomenological school, has written extensively on this subject. Throughout, he assumes an innate connection with nature in women, which renders them unsuited for initiation. Yet it is through this process that "man" (understood with considerable slippage in both gender-specific and generic ways) is made "human." That "man" is a social construct itself needing exploration is never considered, because it is completely plausible to Eliade that where men are *made*, women just *are*. Mircea Eliade, *Birth and Rebirth: The Religious Meanings of Initiation in Human Culture*, trans. Willard R. Trask (New York: Harper and Bros., 1958). For a feminist critique of this ubiquitous view, see Sherry Ortner, "Is Female to Male as Nature is to Culture?" in Michelle Zimbalist Rosaldo and Louise Lamphere, eds., *Woman, Culture, and Society* (Stanford: Stanford University Press), 1974.

base is still an issue. Male scholars who admit feminist critique to the discipline thus run the very real risk of hearing that "everything they know is wrong"—or, at best, severely partial and limited.[43]

The challenge feminists pose to male scholarly authority also has a personal dimension. As an increasing number of volumes attest, the academy is a "boy's club" or male fraternity that is in the main un-friendly and at times overtly hostile to women.[44] Where religious as well as cultural values support the segregation of women from men, the ex-clusion of women from intellectual work, and the subordination of women in marriage to husbands in the home, the situation for women can be grim indeed.[45] The hiring patterns cited in *Religious Studies in Ontario: A State-of-the-Art-Review* illustrate this overall assessment:

YEARS	FEMALE	MALE
1955-59	0	5
1960-64	1	19
1965-69	5	51
1970-74	2	52
1975-79	4	23
1980-84	3	16
1985-87	4	5
TOTALS	19 (10%)	171 (90%)

43   The challenge may be particularly unsettling for those for whom the main source of tension in "the human [sic] condition" is "anxiety over finitude." See Saiving, "Human Condition." The existentialist, psychoanalytic, and neo-orthodox frameworks most marked by this un-derstanding enjoyed major popularity in the 1950s and 1960s, when a considerable number of the current faculty in religious studies received their training.

44   See Nadya Aisenberg and Mona Harrington, *Women of Academe: Outsiders in the Sacred Grove* (n.p.g.: University of Massachussetts, 1989); Resa Dudovitz, *Women in Academe* (Ox-ford: Pergamon, 1984); for a Canadian example see Paula Caplan, *Lifting a Ton of Feathers: A Woman's Guide to Surviving in the Academic World* (Toronto: University of Toronto Press, 1993). Caplan's book contains an excellent bibliography.

45   That religious beliefs of male faculty can play a role in how female colleagues are treated is not, of course, a situation unique to religious studies.

Harold Remus, William Closson James, and Daniel Fraikin also note, "Among all the fields in the humanities, religious studies continues to have among the fewest number of women enrolled in, and graduating from, doctoral programs."[46]

Given this landscape, it is not surprising that women (and even more so, feminist) scholars of religion should feel some sense of dislocation. Karen McCarthy Brown astutely describes the situation from her own religious studies experience: "Because academic women are workers in a system that, not only is not designed for us, but at times is positively antagonistic to us, we cannot operate in that system in a simple and direct way. All our communications, like all our perceptions are mixed. Understood sympathetically, this can be seen as the inevitable result of having to speak in an idiom unsuited to what we have to say."[47] McCarthy Brown's experience was certainly my own.

FEMINISM AND RELIGIOUS STUDIES: PLAYING OUT THE IMPLICATIONS

When I came to religious studies as an undergraduate English major in the early 1970s, I was motivated by two interests: the quest for meaning in literature, and nineteenth-century explorations of atheism. Neither philosophy's then fascination with logical positivism nor English studies' focus on literary structure addressed my concerns. In religious studies I found a multidisciplinary openness to questions of meaning and their material and symbolic cultural manifestations that was absent in more established disciplines. Consistent with the time, these questions were entertained in exclusively masculine language—"Man" and "his dilemma of meaning," for instance. When a term like "the human condition" came into play, it clearly referred to a *male* condition—concerned with issues of agency, authenticity, and the ever-present "anxiety

---

46   Harold Remus, William Closson James, and Daniel Fraikin, *Religious Studies: A State-of-the-Art Review* (Waterloo, Ont.: Wilfrid Laurier University Press, 1992), pp.149-50. Ontario has the highest percentage of religious studies programs and faculty in English Canada. The proportion of total male faculty (90 per cent) is close to the figures for history (90 per cent) and philosophy (92 per cent) in Ontario. While some might be tempted to argue that the proportion of hiring women to men shifted significantly in 1985-87, promising longer-term changes in the field, the overall number of hirings decreased dramatically from twenty-seven (1975-79) to nineteen (1980-84) to nine. Current economic realities make increased hirings unlikely, much less hirings of women in sufficient numbers to change the existing gender balance in religious studies departments.

47   Karen McCarthy Brown, "Heretics and Pagans: Women in the Academic World," in David G. Jones, ed., *Public and Private Ethics: Tensions Between Conscience and Institutional Responsibility* (New York: The Edwin Mellen Press, 1978), p.285.

over finitude." Phenomenological studies reinforced the invisibility of my experience, for although they attended to "universal" categories that included "the masculine" and "the feminine," that dichotomy was understood in terms that were at best romantic, if not staunchly traditionalist. Nor did women figure in concrete studies of religious tradition.[48] The precariousness of my position was brought home to me in a class in which a male professor stated that the subordination of women over the millennia was not an injustice, but a necessary precondition for the individuation of the consciousness of "modern man." By 1974 I was self-consciously identifying myself as a feminist, a description that would have horrified me only two years earlier.

I carried my search for an authentic voice, now articulated specifically around the invisibility of women's experience in religious studies, to graduate school at the University of Toronto in 1976. Here too women were absent as a subject of study. Questions arising out of the specificity of female experience were received with bemused puzzlement, if not outright hostility. Most telling for my future studies, traditional constructions of gender dichotomy in the courses that I took towards my masters degree in philosophy of religion were brought forward as simple statements of ineluctable fact. The only respite from this overwhelming masculinism came from the growing body of literature in feminist theology. I ended up with a master's thesis on Rosemary Ruether and Mary Daly, and a strong commitment to study the material conditions of women's exclusion in the dominant constructions of culture and their methodological manifestation in the academy.[49]

The brief history of my first dissertation topic illustrates one of the barriers to feminist scholarship in religious studies—a barrier related to Christianity's prior dominance in Western culture. I was originally interested in the women of the eighteenth-century *salons*, and the fluidity with which they moved through and away from their Jewish heritage. I soon came up against the reality that the only person competent to supervise me in this area, while unarguably brilliant, was religiously conservative and uninterested in the feminist questions I would be bringing

48   This continues to have a certain irony, as the majority of the world's religious practitioners were and are women. Furthermore, the normal basis for the exclusion of women, that is, their lack of position as clerical leaders, should not matter for phenomenology, which is concerned with (allegedly) universal categories of religious experience.

49   Carol Christ has argued that theological schools are often more welcoming of feminist work than religious studies because they accept the importance of commitment in academic work. Christ, "Toward a Paradigm Shift in the Academy and in Religious Studies," *The Impact of Feminist Research in the Academy* (Bloomington: Indiana University Press, 1987), p.64. In keeping with Christ's analysis, the supervisor for my master's thesis was a noted left-wing Catholic theologian, Gregory Baum.

to the study. Within religious studies, scholars of non-Christian traditions may feel a special responsibility to convey the nature and integrity
of those traditions in a way that respects the tradition's own cultural understanding. Feminism can seem like just one more westernizing
influence, a judgement compounded by the high profile of Christian
feminism in the study of women and religion.[50]

My eventual decision to do my thesis on Canadian feminist and social activist Nellie McClung illustrates another point made by McCarthy
Brown in "Heretics and Pagans." Brown notes that women in the academy face the challenge of having to find an area not only in which they
can speak authoritatively, but also in which they are perceived and accepted as doing so. One practical consequence of marginalization, then,
is women's development of an "expertise of the margins." That was certainly my experience. Despite every effort to locate myself within an area
perceived as central in religious studies (Jewish/Christian relations; the
impact of the Enlightenment on religion; anything written in German), I
found myself with a thesis subject who was Canadian, Christian, historical, "popular"—and feminist.

The difficulties of undertaking this work soon became apparent. The
first problem was that McClung was an anomalous figure for religious
studies methodologies. She just did not fit the available categories. As a
laywoman involved in social activism, she provided neither the systematically developed body of ideas nor a familiarly articulated "theology"
that would allow her to be scrutinized within the normative framework
described by Andrews. Nor, as a single female figure, was she particularly amenable to social-scientific investigation (although the director of
my graduate program, himself a sociologist of religion, did suggest that I
write my dissertation on how McClung fit within Weber's theory of
"charisma"). The comparative approach was only slightly more congenial, allowing for the specificity of focus on an individual, but generally
requiring comparison with other traditions or persons with a similar religious role. Since my interest was in the interrelation of McClung's religion, feminism, and social activism, largely as mediated through her
literature, it seemed unlikely that I would find a comparable figure who
would be useful for that task. That the intended study was historical presented further problems. Canadian religious history was either taught in
seminaries as church history (hence a problem for religious studies

50   See the discussions in Yvonne Yazbeck Haddad, "Islam, Women and Revolution in Twenti-
      eth-Century Arab Thought," and William R. Darrow, "Woman's Place and the Place of
      Women in the Iranian Revolution," in Haddad and Ellison Banks Findly, eds., *Women, Re-
      ligion and Social Change* (Albany: State University of New York, 1985), pp.275-306 and
      pp.306-20.

boundary maintenance), or in the secular academy (where the prevailing disciplinary assumption was that history was to be pursued "objectively," unconditioned by agendas and personal convictions.)[51] Neither environment was particularly inviting for an interdisciplinary study of religiously based feminist social activism.

Since religious studies did not provide ready methodological resources, I turned to what had been done on McClung in other disciplines. What I found when I conducted my research in the mid-1980s was a literature that was truncated and often dismissive. In theology she had been the subject of an admittedly poor masters of divinity thesis, as well as a useful but non-academic text intended as a study guide for United Church women. The "scrapbook biography" put together by Candace Savage, while balanced and in the main sensitive in presentation, was similarly non-academic in intent. Literary scholars tended to dismiss McClung as a quaint example of a bygone era, and the didactic character of her subject matter as an impediment to, rather than the substance and primary reason for, her writing.

While historians proved more varied in their treatments, they were no more adequate. Mainstream history limited McClung's significance to those issues seen as important by traditional historians, that is, events in the political and legislative spheres. McClung's involvement in temperance and suffrage campaigns was therefore acknowledged, as was her participation in the Persons case of 1929, but the character of her feminism and her religious and literary activities were left unexplored. The materials dealing with Canadian religious history noted McClung's role in the ordination debate and superficially linked her with the widespread Christian movement for reform known as the Social Gospel, but they engaged neither her feminism nor the resulting difference of her reform agenda from male social gospellers. Feminist historical materials on McClung were even more problematic, marked by interpretive frameworks that judged McClung exclusively in relation to contemporary political agendas and issues. While other, less "presentist" materials

---

51   The first thesis committee set for me included such a "secular" historian who informed me that I could never "get away" with doing this thesis in history because historians have to attend to the *facts*, not just what they want to see. My second committee, while overall congenial in composition, was primarily made up of sociologists with very little idea of the interdisciplinary feminist work I was trying to do. After several years out of the program, I returned with a completed thesis and a committee was struck to examine me. Its composition (my supervisor, a social ethicist; a theologian; two feminist historians; a feminist literary scholar; a scholar in religion and Canadian society) reflected the subject and approach of the thesis, which in 1988 became the first dissertation in religious studies at the University of Toronto to pass "as it stands."

eventually began to surface, feminist scholarship proved no more free from limiting presuppositions regarding women and religion than was scholarship in religious studies.[52]

I was faced with a serious problem: a figure who in her lifetime was internationally known and widely loved, deeply religious, extremely liberal in perspective, considered by many a social radical and who for years had been an important literary figure on the Canadian scene. I had no doubt that had she been male she would have been the subject of intense and detailed study. What was it her contemporaries saw that current scholars did not?

I eventually wrote a dissertation focusing on McClung's literary writings—her humorous, homely tales of didactic intent—held in creative tension with the explicitly political speeches and essays collected in the 1915 volume *In Times Like These*.[53] Reasoning that McClung was writing for a broad popular audience, I tried to attend to explicit messages about gender roles, political observations, and religious understanding as conveyed through conventional literary forms. My task, as I saw it, was to try to make visible an integrated, intelligible human being whose actions had had a significant impact on the larger Canadian scene; my task was first and foremost a task of *recovery*.[54] And it was through McClung's religion—her broad, integrating vision of life as informed by her historical context and expressed through her literature and social activism—that a whole person began to become visible.

What is the relevance of all of this for "the impact of feminism on religious studies"? First, some reflections on method: blindness to gender in traditional approaches and closure on the question of religion in

52   For a discussion of these problems, see Randi R. Warne, *Literature as Pulpit: The Christian Social Activism of Nellie L. McClung* (Waterloo, Ont.: Wilfrid Laurier University Press, 1993), pp.4-9 and *passim*.

53   Reprinted in 1972 by University of Toronto Press, with a "Scholarly Introduction" by Veronica Strong-Boag, this is currently the most well-known and widely distributed work by and on McClung. Most contemporary feminist criticisms of McClung seem to be grounded in this text, read acontextually, and in Strong-Boag's introduction. Strong-Boag has revised the deep presentism of her earlier account in "Ever a Crusader," in V. Strong-Boag and Anita Clair Fellman, eds., *Rethinking Canada: The Promise of Women's History* (Toronto: Copp Clark Pitman, 1986), pp.178-90. Interestingly, *In Times Like These* was not considered a particularly important part of McClung's corpus during her lifetime. On her own writing, McClung stated: "I hope I have been a crusader, and I would be very proud to think that I had even remotely approached the grandeur of a Sunday School hymn. I have never worried about my art. I have written as clearly as I could, never idly or dishonestly, and if some of my stories are sermons in disguise, my earnest hope is that the disguise did not obscure the sermon." Nellie L. McClung, *The Stream Runs Fast* (Toronto: Thomas Allen, 1945), p.69.

54   This task of "recovery" or "retrieval" is central to much of the work of feminist historians. See Gerda Lerner, *The Majority Finds Its Past* (Oxford: Oxford University Press, 1979).

feminist ones meant having to find an almost "pre-theoretical" entry point to the subject for the kind of integrative recovery work that I was trying to do.[55] My questions were very basic: "What did McClung say? How was it received? What was the most adequate way to make sense of her life and work?" To that end I read and reread everything McClung wrote, including her personal papers, to try and get a sense of the "world" in which she lived.[56] This strategy of discerning religious "worlds" in fact derived from my religious studies training. It is a long established rule in comparative studies that religious systems cannot be understood solely in relation to one facet. All aspects of the tradition— ritual, beliefs, social and institutional organization, religious experience, theology, scriptures, and social positioning—need to be explored to understand what is going on in any adequate way.[57] Taking McClung's written texts as my basis for exploring her "world," I sought to provide an alternate reading of her life and work that would shift attention from theory to narrative and from abstract ideas to cultural systems. In so doing I hoped to provide some antidote to the prescriptive abridgements that marked so much of the treatment of her elsewhere.

It was also essential to bring feminist insight to this task. Women's worlds are not culturally normative. Despite McClung's facility with political activism and speechmaking, she still had to negotiate the contradictions of gender in creating herself as an effective public figure. Since by all reports she was outstandingly successful at that task, I sought to determine why that was so. Undoubtedly, McClung's oratorial gifts and charismatic personality were factors, as was her innate ability to "tell a

55   For an attempt to address the "undertheorized" character of women's history, see Joan Wallach Scott's influential article, "Gender: A Useful Category of Historical Analysis," republished in her *Gender and the Politics of History* (New York: Columbia University Press, 1988). For an attempt to theorize women's history within the contemporary Canadian scene see Ruth Roach Pierson, "Experience, Difference, Dominance and Voice in the Writing of Canadian Women's History," in Karen Offen, Ruth Roach Pierson, and Jane Rendall, eds., *Writing Women's History: International Perspectives* (Bloomington: Indiana University Press, 1991), pp.79-106.

56   McClung's personal papers, comprising eleven shelf-feet of material, are held at the Provincial Archives of British Columbia in Victoria, B.C.

57   William Paden lists twelve ways in which the notion of "world" is important for religion. His final point, that "interpretations of religion are themselves products of worlds," is especially important for evaluating feminist treatments of religious subjects. Paden, *Religious Worlds*, pp.53-58. Specifically, Canadian feminist scholarship has emerged from a fiercely secular, anti-institutional context that sees religion as the embodiment of repression, as well as the source of myriad other evils, of which racism is one. In focusing on an accurate depiction of McClung's religion, my work on McClung underestimated the depth of conviction on this point, and the importance of foregrounding race in contemporary feminist discussion.

good story" that her readers would recognize and identify with.[58] She made good use of that skill, employing conventional literary genres like romantic melodrama to convey an unconventional content of feminist analysis. She also drew significantly from other feminist discussions of the time. Serendipitously, I found evidence in McClung's personal papers and published writings that established significant links between her work and that of U.S. social theorist Charlotte Perkins Gilman.[59] Making that connection helped position McClung within a particular intellectual landscape and highlighted the shaping given her views by her religion, experience, and wit, and it gave background to the specific claims made by McClung in *In Times Like These*.

Equally important to the study was the realization that prejudice distorts discourse. Again, Karen McCarthy Brown provided a useful illustration with regard to women in academic life:

It is a stunning blow when we realize the tools of the trade—this language loaded with metaphors of sports and war—changes fairytale-fashion from singing sword to witch's pointed hat when a woman appropriates it. This was brought home to me with great clarity when, as a graduate student, I heard two professors debate

58 Some contemporary feminists, such as Arun Mukherjee (see her chapter in this book), take issue with McClung for the way she "constructs woman," believing it to be exclusionary and even "racist." It is true that McClung wrote from her own experience, that of a rural, prairie, Scots-Irish second-generation immigrant. She was unaware of the full extent of her white-skin privilege, as are those who share such privilege now. See Peggy McIntosh, "White Privilege and Male Privilege: A Personal Account of Coming to See Correspondences Through Work in Women's Studies, " in Margaret L. Anderson and Patricia Hill Collins, eds., *Race, Class, and Gender: An Anthology*, 2nd ed. (Belmont, Cal.: Wadsworth, 1995). Contrary to current feminist practice, McClung also often spoke of "women" as a single definable group in her political speeches, because it was on this basis (being female) that women were excluded from full participation and equal treatment in the public sphere. Yet her novels and stories bear witness to McClung's not always successful struggles with resolving the contradictions of her deep liberalism. See especially Nellie L. McClung, "Red and White," in *All We Like Sheep and Other Stories* (Toronto: Thomas Allen, 1926), pp.128-75. It is important to distinguish between what Gloria Yamato in "Something About the Subject Makes It Hard to Name," in *Race, Class, and Gender*, pp.71-5 calls "unaware/unintentional racism," which I would argue characterizes McClung, and more invidious forms of racism based on subordination of others, which can arguably be found, for instance, in Emily Murphy or Charlotte Perkins Gilman. That such distinctions have not been made owes much, in my view, to widespread feminist assumptions about the "necessarily" negative effects of religious faith—bigotry, narrowness, and conservatism—which make the charge of racism plausible and further substantiation with textual and historical evidence beside the point.

59 Especially Charlotte Perkins Gilman, *The Man-Made World; or, Our Androcentric Culture*, first published in 1911 (New York: Source Book Press, 1970). For a discussion of the connections and differences between McClung and Gilman, see Warne, *Literature as Pulpit*, pp.144-54.

in a department colloquium. One began his response to the other's presentation with: 'Now, if my learned opponent had actually read any of the books we are discussing today...' The rules of male bonding allow for that message to be sent out and received with at least the appearance of great good humor among men, but when I tried to think how that line would sound if delivered by me or any other woman, I knew it kept coming out somewhere between a bitch and a whine.[60]

McClung, no less than contemporary feminists, was working in an environment that marginalized and twisted women's speech. To offset this, she appropriated dominant modes such as melodrama in her literature and the rhetorical strategies of the pulpit in her public speaking to help give her purchase in the public world.[61] However, to analyse only her actions in isolation from the context and conversations in which she was enmeshed was to provide a one-sided and distorted view of her world. I therefore undertook a detailed study of McClung's anti-feminist context, focusing on a literary opponent (Stephen Leacock), a political nemesis (Sir Rodmond Roblin), and a representative of anti-feminist thought in general.[62] Exploration of this material helped further contextualize McClung's feminism and provided important insight into the usefulness of humour in combatting prejudice against women.[63]

My study of McClung highlighted the importance of problematizing precisely those commonplaces that seem most self-evident. From my experience and my training, I had learned to critique culturally received constructions of both gender and religion, and I therefore had some places to engage the existing literature. I also had to learn to problema-

60   McCarthy Brown, "Heretics and Pagans," p.285.

61   That preaching was an important strategy employed by women otherwise silenced is argued by Christine L. Krueger, *The Reader's RepentAnce: Women Preachers, Women Writers, and Nineteenth-Century Social Discourse* (Chicago: University of Chicago Press, 1992). That McClung was aware of the futility of rational argument in an environment of heightened prejudice, see *In Times Like These*, p.57: "After one has listened to all these arguments and has contracted clergyman's sore throat talking back, it is a real relief to meet the people who say flatly and without reason: "You can't have it—no—I won't argue—but inasmuch as I can prevent it—you will never vote! So there!"

62   Sir Almroth Wright, *An Unexpurgated Case Against Woman Suffrage* (New York: Paul Hoeber, 1913). Wright was an internationally known pioneer of vaccine immunology. His "proof" of the mental, moral, and physical inferiority of women is notable for its impeccable use of scientific method. For a full discussion, see Warne, *Literature as Pulpit*, ch. 3.

63   For a contemporary treatment, see Regina Barreca, "'They Used to Call Me Snow White, but I Drifted ...' Women's Strategic Use of Humor" (New York: Viking, 1991).

tize the centrality of "formal ideas" and to see how political effectiveness can depend less on logical coherence than on facility of expression. Too, I needed to relearn how to read the surface meanings of narratives—not what authors were "really" trying to say (the "hidden meaning" only a sophisticated and well-trained scholar might discern), but what they in fact said. Focusing exclusively on the former can in fact be a silencing strategy, as anyone who has ever been subject to "friendly" impromptu psychoanalysing can well attest. I tried to produce an integrated study of McClung's religion, feminism, and social activism that would help readers understand why McClung saw and acted in the world in the way she did. In my view she has been enhanced, not diminished, as a subject for serious critical study by this move from caricature and stereotype to human being.

EXCURSUS: FEMINISTS AND RELIGION

One of the puzzling realities I encountered in doing this work on McClung was the "dis-ease" and even hostility that mention of her religion caused in feminist colleagues. Their remarks were customarily linked with the most unusual comments, about their own unhappy religious upbringings, nervous questions about my own presumed religious vocation, or general damnations of religion for "causing wars." What I found most troubling was the immediate closure on conversation that followed. Religion was not a subject to be discussed, it seemed, or, if spoken of at all, not positively and certainly not in depth. Ruth Brouwer's piece on the "unacknowledged quarantine" was confirmation, if not entirely welcome, that my experience was not idiosyncratic.

This situation has obvious and immediate import for the study of women and religion, as well as for feminist scholarship as a whole. Feminists reject the study of religion for at least three reasons.[64] First, as cultural institutions, religions have embodied and reflected patriarchal dominance, explicitly prescribing women's social roles and agency. Moreover, they have justified women's subordination by claiming that their views reflect the aims and structures of an ultimate (presumably spiritual) reality that is beyond the realm of common human judgement. Neither of these moves is congenial in the secular, broadly liberal and rationalist culture within which we currently live. A second factor is

---

64   See also Randi R. Warne, "Religious Studies and Women's Studies: Resonances, Reactions and Future Possibilities," in Klaus Klostermaier and Larry Hurtado, eds., *Religious Studies: Issues, Prospects and Proposals* (Atlanta: Scholars Press, 1991), pp.347-60.

that many women have had negative personal experiences of religion, which inform their rejection of it as a subject worthy of scholarly inquiry. Given the role played by experience in feminist analysis, this is not a meaningless quibble. Unfortunately, there is a tendency to consider only negative experiences as accurate, and all positive ones, by definition, as a kind of patriarchally induced false consciousness. Judgements such as these pose serious problems for scholars interested in both women and religion, because work that attempts to be more nuanced is sometimes read as betrayal, or as patriarchal co-optation. Finally, disregard for religion as a worthy object of continued study issues from the fact that much feminist theory is deeply indebted to Marxist analysis, which has a particularly narrow "read" on religion as a tool of capitalist oppression.

Yet religion is a complex cultural phenomenon. It both maintains the status quo and generates dynamics to change it. It may be patriarchal and "start wars," but so do governments, and few would suggest that politics is an illegitimate subject of study for feminists. As a building block of culture it has defined and shaped most women's lives through time.[65] To understand women, especially those outside of our own secular Western contemporary culture, it would seem that we need to study the relation of women and religion with some skill.

Consider the following analogy. Most people reading this chapter will have driven a car. Even more will have ridden in a vehicle driven by an internal combustion engine. We all know that there are problems associated with driving cars: they have led to the creation of suburbs, people who drive them get into accidents, and most importantly, they cause horrendous pollution. We know all of this, but we (most of us) continue to drive cars and ride the bus, though we sometimes try, where physically and geographically possible, to ride bicycles and walk. Even so, the world we live in is organized in so many particulars around the ease of mobility and patterns of life set by this technology that we continue to participate in that world most of the time.

Given everything we know about the damage caused by vehicles powered by internal combustion engines, it is not hard to imagine the outrage of the denizens of some car-free future society towards all of us twentieth-century, car-driven dupes. They could accuse us of knowing what the problems were and doing very little about it. They could point

---

65   This is a social and historical observation, not a normative claim.

out how we organized our whole existences around this mode of transportation, designing our cities for its needs rather than those of the larger global community. And they could dismiss all our attempts to explain the positive contributions of internal combustion vehicles to our lives as self-serving rationalization. Even now we can understand these assessments, and agree with much of what is said. But would it be reasonable for this future society to dismiss the multidimensional role of internal combustion vehicles in creating twentieth-century culture because they do not approve of such vehicles themselves? Yet this is what happens with religion. To make this point is not to argue either for pollution or for—or against—religious affiliation.[66] Rather, it is to illustrate the fact that prior closure does not help in our attempts to understand human life fully. This is particularly true in the case of women, because the features of our lives are often hidden from immediate public view.

Judith Allen argues persuasively against the imposition of contemporary political and social agendas on the experience of women of the past. She further cautions against exclusively national studies, asserting that these will lead inevitably to a parochialism and inwardness that serve no one well. Writing from a position of identification, whether of nation or politics or in rejection of religion, is understandable, given the centrality of experience in most feminist analysis. However, Allen reminds us:

> Identification may not be, however, the best way to write the history of feminism.... It would be a great pity if the inward-looking quality of some feminist analysis, of which this identification/repudiation dualism is symptomatic, consigned historians of feminism to a pattern of endlessly reinterpreting its past largely in the light of current preoccupations.... It is now time for historians of feminism to seek a broader context, to recognize parochialism for what it is—a major obstacle and limitation that must be overcome.[67]

The disregard of contemporary mainstream feminists for religion as a legitimate subject of analysis could be usefully reconsidered in light of this observation.

---

66 I would argue that religion is in fact a much more multifaceted, complex, and morally ambiguous phenomenon than this analogy would suggest.

67 Allen, "Contextualizing Late-Nineteenth Century Feminism," p.28.

FEMINISM AND RELIGIOUS STUDIES: THE CONTEMPORARY
CANADIAN SCENE

The status and future possibilities for feminism and religious studies in
Canada are mixed. Like most academic disciplines, religious studies is
starting to feel the impact of postmodernism on its dominant constructions. Emerging and mid-career scholars fluent in this new language are
beginning to recast some traditional methodological configurations as
well as to produce scholarship informed by postmodernist sensibili-
ties.[68] A recently initiated journal, *Method and Theory in the Study of Religion*, has provided a specific focus for the discussion of methodological
issues, although it has not yet placed feminist concerns in the foreground. Still, the journal has made space for the presentation of alternative approaches to religion that are more congenial in general to feminist
engagement.[69] These developments bode well for disciplinary transformation in the future.

Feminism has also had a noticeable effect on scholarship in more traditional modes. Graeme MacQueen's article in the discipline's main
journal, *Studies in Religion/Sciences Religieuses*, challenges the "universalist" categories of Mircea Eliade's phenomenological approach not for
reifying "the Sacred" but for their classist, racist, and sexist assumptions.
"*Whose* Sacred History? Reflections on Myth and Dominance" is an important reminder of the contribution made to all scholarship by the insights of feminist critique.[70]

68   For example, Dawne McCance, "Projecting a Future for Feminist Religious Criticism," in
     Klostermaier and Hurtado, *Religious Studies*, pp.381-407. Also Morny Joy, "Levinas:
     Alterity, the Feminine and Women—A Meditation," *Religious Studies/Sciences
     Religieuses* 22, 4 (1994), pp.463-86. The whole of this volume of *SR* is devoted to the
     theme of postmodernism.

69   See Jeppe Sinding Jensen, "Is Phenomenology of Religion Possible? On the Ideas of a Hu-
     man and Social Science of Religion," *Method and Theory in the Study of Religion* 5, 2, pp.109-
     33. For an exception to the usual avoidance of feminist concerns, see an article by Russell
     McCutcheon on feminist revisions of "God-talk, 'Naming the Unnameable?' Theological
     Language and the Academic Study of Religion," *Method and Theory in the Study of Religion*
     2, 2, (1990), pp.213-29, with responses in volume 3,1 (1991) by J. Shannon Clarkson and
     Pamela J. Milne. *Method and Theory in the Study of Religion*, originally produced out of the
     Graduate Centre for Religious Studies, University of Toronto, is now published in Berlin by
     Walter de Gruyter & Co..

70   Graeme MacQueen, "*Whose* Sacred History? Reflections on Myth and Dominance," *Studies
     in Religion/Sciences Religieuses* 17, 2 (1988), pp.143-57. MacQueen notes (p.153) of one textual
     practice: "The male editor, in equating the cultures of males with culture in general, is dem-
     onstrating 'the masculinist usurpation of universality' and is actively (although probably un-
     consciously) collaborating with males of other cultures in the process of naming that ensures
     the subordination of women."

The insights of feminist analysis have also had an impact on the use of inclusive language in religious studies. Long the bane of scholars sensitive to questions of accuracy, androcentric language was officially repudiated by the then-editor of *Studies in Religion/Sciences Religieuses*, Tom Sinclair-Faulkner. His elegant announcement of the journal's official inclusive language policy is a model of gentility, rising above the often bitter debate that preceded the decision: "Those who are not moved by moral, political or scholarly commitment to endorse our policy of inclusive language will, no doubt, be brought by simple courtesy to recognize that many of their colleagues are in fact offended by language which is sexist. And none of us wish to offend unwittingly."[71]

Greater inclusiveness in both language and perspective is now also being seen in some of the textbooks available for university teachers in the discipline. For example, Huston Smith's classic *The Religions of Man* has now become *The World's Religions*.[72] "Humanity" and "humankind" are starting to replace "man" as a common term, and one of the most popular introductions to the field even has a special section on women and religion that not only attempts to use inclusive language but also alerts students to the problem of women's subordination within religious systems.[73]

These changes to the field are laudable and constructive. Unfortunately they have been undercut by the desperate hiring situation in Canadian religious studies departments in the early 1990s. Current realities well serve those who wish to be seen to be "progressive" but who actually oppose significant change in departmental gender balances, because there are no jobs to be had by anyone, male or female. This further limits the transformative impact of feminism on the discipline, by excluding younger male scholars whose own work is in conversation with feminist analysis.

Economic constraints also threaten the existence of religious studies departments. In Alberta, for example, the severe government cuts of 1993-94 resulted in the closure of the Department of Religious Studies at the University of Lethbridge and led to the merging of religious studies at the University of Alberta with comparative literature and film studies. While this new configuration holds positive promise for scholarly congeniality and creativity, others may not be so lucky. Religious studies as

71   Tom Sinclair-Faulkner, *Studies in Religion/Sciences Religieuses* 18, 1 (1989), p.4.

72   Huston Smith, *The World's Religions* (San Francisco: Harper, 1991). The text was originally published as *The Religions of Man* in 1958.

73   Robert S. Ellwood, *Introducing Religion: From Inside and Out*, 3rd ed. (Englewood Cliffs,

an academic enterprise is not widely appreciated, and its position is therefore vulnerable.

Somewhat offsetting the total grimness of this picture is the strong representation of feminist scholars of religion on the executives of the discipline's main scholarly societies and organs. The current executive of the Canadian Society for Studies in Religion, for example, has four women members (including myself) out of eleven, all strong feminists. The male members of the executive are either tolerant of or conversant with feminist analysis, which has contributed to a significant repositioning of scholarship on women and religion in the Society's annual meetings.[74] The public availability and high profile thus accorded scholarship on women serve as important signals to entering scholars and encourage those who in past generations were discouraged in their efforts to produce gender-critical work. A new publication series on women and religion has also been established by the Canadian Corporation for Studies in Religion, with an editorial board composed of leading feminist francophone and anglophone scholars in the field.[75] These positive changes would not have come about without the continued and concerted efforts of feminists in religious studies; however, they have also received the support of key male colleagues in the field.[76] Their support may be called upon increasingly in the future as a disintegrating university system tries to survive by sacrificing its most marginalized members.

CONCLUSION

As an intellectual movement and as a social reality, religious studies has been changed by feminism. The changes are neither fully integrated nor irreversible. The anticipated reconfigurations of academic life, which include a normalization of part-time or temporary positions, a two-tiered faculty system of "research scholars" and lower status "university teach-

74   This is a far cry from when I gave my first paper for the CSSR in 1983. Typically, it was the first session the morning after the society's banquet and grouped papers on Tibetan Buddhism, Jungian psychology, and my own work on early twentieth-century Canadian religious activism. It is a measure of our current status that for the 1994 Learned Societies conference the society planned a major panel on the status of women in the discipline, including scholars from graduate school through to the most senior ranks.

75   This umbrella organization includes the Canadian Society for Studies in Religion, the Canadian Theological society, the Canadian Society for the Study of Patristics, the Canadian Society of Biblical Studies, and the Canadian Society for Church History.

76   Good examples are the past two presidents of the Canadian Society for Studies in Religion, Martin Rumscheidt and Jacques Goulet, and the former editor-in-chief of *Studies in Religion*, Tom Sinclair-Faulkner.

ers," and the self-financing of institutions all bode extremely ill for feminist scholarship and for academic women in general.

Constructive efforts have been made to incorporate feminist work and workers into mainstream organizations. At the same time feminist scholars of religion are working to make links with feminist scholars and scholarship in other disciplinary sites, while—albeit in fewer numbers—feminist scholars like Brouwer make links with those of us whose main focus of study is religion. All of this is to our mutual benefit as scholars, social analysts, and (for those who share this agenda as well) agents of social change. Even more because of the constraints facing all of us who labour in the academic vineyard, these connections need to be acknowledged and enhanced. It is time for the quarantine to be lifted and a healthy body brought out into the light of day.

SUGGESTED READINGS

Barbara Hilkert Andolsen, Christine E. Gudorf, and Mary D. Pellauer, *Women's Consciousness/Women's Conscience*. San Francisco: Harper and Row, 1985.

Joanne Carlson Brown and Carole Bohn, eds., *Christianity, Patriarchy and Abuse*. New York: The Pilgrim Press, 1989.

Carol Christ and Judith Plaskow, eds., *Womanspirit Rising*. San Francisco: Harper and Row, 1979.

Paula Cooey et al., eds., *After Patriarchy: Feminist Transformation of the World's Religions*. Maryknoll: Orbis Books, 1991.

Eva Dargyay and Morny Joy, eds., *Plotting the Path Forward*. Waterloo, Ont.: Wilfrid Laurier University Press, forthcoming.

Nancy Auer Falk and Rita Gross, eds. *Unspoken Worlds: Women's Religious Lives*. Belmont, Cal.: Wadsworth, 1989.

Yvonne Yazbeck Haddad and Ellison Banks Findly, eds., *Women, Religion and Social Change*. Albany: State University of New York Press, 1985.

Ann Loades, ed., *Feminist Theology: A Reader*. Louisville, Ky.: Westminster/John Knox, 1990.

Judith Plaskow and Carol Christ, eds., *Weaving the Visions: New Patterns of Feminist Spirituality*, San Francisco: Harper, 1989.

Rosemary Ruether, ed., *Religion and Sexism*. New York: Simon and Schuster, 1974.

Arvind Sharma, ed., *Women in World Religions*. Albany: State University of New York Press, 1987.

LINDA ARCHIBALD AND MARY CRNKOVICH

Chapter Four: Intimate Outsiders: Feminist Research in a Cross-Cultural Environment

WHITE FEMINISTS WORKING OUTSIDE OF THEIR OWN CULTURE face certain ethical and methodological challenges. In the case of this chapter, the moment we began writing we were confronted with the contradictions inherent in our location as members of the dominant society attempting to write about our work with women from a minority culture in a way that does not exploit the knowledge they share with us. We have attempted to do this by focusing on our own experience of the research process; that is, the experiences of two southern, white feminists, each of whom has a long history of working with Inuit organizations, but neither of whom has lived in the north or has plans to do so[1]. Very clearly, this chapter reflects our views, ideas, and experiences, and not those of Inuit women.

The first contradiction arose shortly after we conceived the idea for this chapter. A one-page outline we prepared brought invitations to present the paper (at that point unwritten) to two conferences, one in Canada and the other in Australia. In other words, the fact that we were even considering writing this paper opened up the possibility of being publicly acknowledged as experts of some sort. Yet our approach is based on a belief that expertise is not embedded in the researchers but, rather, that it resides among the women we work with, the people who rightly "own"

---

1 There are approximately 36,000 Inuit living in Canada, half of whom are female. Until the 1960s, most Inuit lived a traditional way of life on the land. Today, Inuit live primarily in communities scattered throughout the north and eastern Northwest Territories and along the northern coasts of Quebec and Labrador.

the problem being studied, the research process and products, and any action resulting from the research. The search for a way of writing about our work that does not lead to donning the mantle of expertise has been challenging.

The second contradiction pertains to scholarly writing. Working with women who speak a different language made us aware of the extent to which a working knowledge of English (or French) is necessary to obtain funding for projects and have your ideas heard in the public policy arena in Canada. While Inuit women take pride in the fact that their language thrives in the north, the rest of Canada sees their inability to speak English or French as a weakness or a problem: literacy, for example, is measured by the ability to read and write English or French, not Inuktitut. The specialized language of scholarship, which is the language of most research studies, adds another layer to the hierarchy of knowledge: first there is competence in English or French, then there is scholarly expertise. In writing this chapter, we have tried to use the English language as a tool for communication rather than alienation, and since the target audience is primarily southern (university students), we have probably succeeded. We are uncomfortably aware, however, that our language and style of writing may be inaccessible to many Inuit women. In fact, this chapter would require substantial rewriting as well as translation into Inuktitut if it were to be distributed in the north.

To illustrate some of the methodologies we believe are necessary for researchers who work outside of their own culture, we describe a research project undertaken for Pauktuutit, a non-profit organization representing Canadian Inuit women. We also discuss feminist research and how the writing of one woman—Maria Mies—provided us with the theoretical background necessary for understanding that our approach to research is both rooted in and the result of our feminism. Our methodologies, however, are based on certain assumptions we bring to our work.

ASSUMPTIONS

Our first assumption is that feminism must be inclusive. Before we began working with Inuit, our experiences were limited primarily to working and studying within dominant cultural structures occupied mainly by women and men who were also white Euro-Canadians. Working with women who speak a different language and approach issues and problems from a very different perspective—one rooted in their culture, traditions, and life experiences, just as our own is—can be very revealing. We discovered that western feminism makes a great deal of sense to women of a certain class and race, raised in particular nations and regions during a particular period of time. We are all products of our generation, culture, gender, race, education, environment, and economic background. Working closely with women from entirely different backgrounds leads to respect for difference as opposed to a search for universality, and we have come to recognize that feminism must be flexible, expanding, inclusive, and capable of incorporating this respect for difference in theory and in practice. This has led us back to basics, back not only to an understanding of feminism as a validation of women's diverse realities, experiences, knowledge, histories, and worldviews, but also to an acknowledgement of the striking commonalities as well as differences among women.

Within feminist research it is widely recognized that feminist theory is not merely "a pursuit of a true analysis of social life but the pursuit of consciousness, which in turn becomes a form of political practice."[2] Accordingly, feminist research challenges many assumptions about the purpose and goals of traditional research. At the heart of feminist research is a recognition of women's oppression and a commitment to work towards the alleviation of the conditions of that oppression.[3] Our second assumption, then, is that research should take place because it is required as part of a strategy to address a particular problem, concern, or situation; thus it is action-oriented and political in nature as well as intent.

The premise that research is part of a process for change is a reflection of where this research originates. We are researchers located within an organization (Pauktuutit) with research goals defined by the women represented (although often modified by the funding source). Within this type of institutional infrastructure it is a given that research is conducted for the purpose of changing the status quo, usually in response to

2   Catherine MacKinnon, "Feminism, Marxism, Method and the State: An Agenda for Theory," *Signs* 7,3 (Spring 1982), p.543.

3   In Patricia Maguire's work, *Doing Participatory Research: A Feminist Approach* (Amherst, Mass.: The Centre for International Education, 1987), she refers to feminism as "a worldwide movement for the redistribution of power." She says feminism incorporates a belief that women are oppressed and exploited, a commitment to uncover and understand what causes and sustains oppression, and a commitment to work to end all forms of oppression, whether based on gender, class, race, or culture.

specific issues or concerns raised by Inuit women at their annual meetings. For example, concerns over racial and gender bias in the justice system can lead to research aimed at changing that system or creating an alternative system; or the desire to document traditional midwifery practices includes the goal of changing the health-care system to provide Inuit women with culturally appropriate birthing options and more control over childbirth. Research is not undertaken simply for the purpose of acquiring knowledge; and the follow-up work resulting from the research is as essential as the research itself.

Working within an organization with clearly articulated goals provides a structure that is often lacking in the academic realm and that is hostile to the concept of academic freedom. The resolutions of the annual general meetings and Board of Directors meetings of Pauktuutit determine the type of research to be undertaken. Researchers within the organization do not have the freedom to do research outside of the issues defined by the membership. We view the limitations placed upon us as a result of this structure as beneficial.

Our final assumption is that "research" here refers to a specific model that is community-based and includes a process that is participatory and action-oriented. Discussions of community-based research most often refer to three models: action research, participatory research, and participatory action research.[4] People involved in participatory or action research focus on a combined goal of consciousness-raising and action aimed at social-political change. However, none of these approaches en-

---

4   In her "Action Research: A New Sociological Approach in Developing Countries," in *The IDRC Reports* 13,3 (1984), p.25, Nellie Stromquist explains: "Action research seeks social transformation. This emphasis leads action-research to examine problems that affect disadvantaged social groups and makes the researched become advocates of their interests.... Actual experience with action research indicated that it can take various forms. The involvement of community people varies from project to project and does not always occur at all key stages of the research process. Also it appears that the action component of action-research is not always immediate."
     On the other end of the continuum is "participatory research," which may not always be action-oriented or undertaken for the purpose of taking action and making change. Rather it tends to emphasize the aspect of community participation in the research process: A publication by the International Research Development Council, *Participatory Research in IDRC: Working Paper* (Ottawa: International Research Development Council, September 1988), p.9, states: "Participatory research in principle accords individuals who must live with or resolve the issue under study joint ownership of the research projects. The researched in other words, become themselves the researchers." Jan Barnsley and Dianne Ellis combine participatory research and action research to come up with a research process referred to as "participatory action research." They explain that it is "the systematic collection and analysis of information for the purpose of taking action and making change.... We emphasize both research for the purpose of making change and community participation in the process." Jan Barnsley and Dianne Ellis, *Research for Change: Participatory Action Research for Community Groups* (Vancouver: Women's Research Centre, 1992), p.9.

sures that full control of the research process and products resides with the community involved in the study. In fact, the distinction among these approaches becomes blurred when we determine where, in the larger process of change, the research takes place and who actually controls it. Our approach to research assumes a version of a participatory and action-oriented model in which the control at all stages is rooted in the community/organization/women involved in the study, and not with the researchers.

PAUKTUUTIT AND THE LABRADOR JUSTICE PROJECT

Pauktuutit, the national organization representing Inuit women in Canada, has its office in Ottawa, but has maintained strong community roots and support for one significant reason: it derives its mandate and seeks its instruction and direction from Inuit women in the communities. The views it expresses, the research it undertakes, and the policy reforms it advocates are called for by women from the communities through resolutions passed at annual general meetings of the organization. Over the past ten years, resolutions have been passed on issues ranging from economic development and the need for child-care programs to family violence[5] and child sexual abuse.

The annual general meetings have become a gathering place where women discuss and share painful and sensitive issues, their personal histories and experiences. These discussions of personal problems in a public forum have resulted in a wide range of public education initiatives around issues of family violence, sexual assault, and child sexual abuse. In turn, these initiatives have led to further discussions focusing on the inadequacy of the justice system in responding to the problems. Over the years, Inuit women attending Pauktuutit's annual general meetings have passed resolutions calling on all levels of the justice system, including police, courts, crown lawyers, and justices of the peace, to denounce family violence, sexual assault, and child sexual abuse as serious crimes and to ensure that their decisions reflect the seriousness of the offence.[6]

5   The term "family violence" is used in the North to describe violence against women and children. While the majority of abusers are male, there is a reluctance to label the violence suffered by women as "male violence" or "violence against women."

6   It is evident from the resolutions passed at annual general meetings and minutes of the meetings that issues of violence against women and children in the family and the treatment of women as victims of violence have emerged as priority concerns among the women represented by Pauktuutit.

In response to the resolutions addressing the need to take action on these issues, in 1992 Pauktuutit sought and received funding from the federal Department of Justice to design and undertake a project addressing issues regarding Inuit women and the justice system.[7] As part of the Justice Project, delegates to the 1993 annual meeting met in regional groups (Baffin, Keewatin, Kitikmeot, Western Arctic, Nunavik [Northern Quebec], and Labrador regions) to review and respond to issues raised in fictitious scenarios, highlighting problems such as sexual assault, child sexual abuse, and child custody. The women were asked to assume that Canadian laws no longer applied and that they had the power to create their own laws—they could, in fact, use any means to resolve these problems. This exercise was an attempt to explore alternatives to the existing justice system, alternatives reflecting the real-life experiences of Inuit women. The objective was to use the material generated and any follow-up work as a starting point for developing a policy paper on alternatives to the justice system.[8]

As requested, each group responded to the scenario given to it and reported back with suggestions for dealing with the problems. The information gathered seemed to form a good start for the project. But later, in a discussion unrelated to the Justice presentation, one of the delegates from Labrador began to speak about her personal experiences of family violence. She told the group about the recent murder of her daughter and how the RCMP (Royal Canadian Mounted Police), despite what they later said, did nothing to save her daughter. She spoke of the failure of the police to take threats to her daughter's safety seriously. She told the group that she had requested an inquiry into the actions of the RCMP relating to her daughter's death. She had yet to hear whether or not an inquiry would be held, and she was seeking support from Pauktuutit to lobby the police to conduct an inquiry.

Before the meeting ended, the Labrador women met again. They shared their grief about this incident and spoke of their own experiences and concerns about the failure of the police to respond to family violence. This led to further discussions between the women and Pauktuu-

---

7   One of the functions of the Aboriginal Justice Directorate is financially to assist organizations like Pauktuutit to develop policy papers on issues concerning justice and Aboriginal peoples.

8   As a non-profit organization, Pauktuutit was dependent upon federal financing to undertake the necessary documentation and related research on justice issues raised at its AGMs. This dependency resulted in Pauktuutit having to negotiate and compromise on the "deliverables" of the project. In the funding contract with the department, Pauktuutit was required to prepare a policy paper on justice issues and the responses of Inuit women regarding the justice system in Inuit communities in Canada.

tit about the steps to be taken next. They decided it was important to document what had happened leading up to and following the death of the woman's daughter.

Pauktuutit prepared a report in collaboration with the victim's mother and other women in her home community. The report identified serious concerns regarding the RCMP's failure in Labrador to respond to violence against women. While it was primarily a report on one specific incident, it also documented other incidents of police neglect. The report was submitted to the RCMP, the provincial minister of justice, and the federal solicitor general. In a letter accompanying the report, Pauktuutit requested a meeting with the RCMP to discuss the matter further.

The Justice Project included funds to cover the costs of holding workshops in Labrador and the other regions of the north. Originally these workshops were intended to provide follow-up to the annual general meeting by developing, in greater detail, the alternative approaches to justice raised by the women in their regional groups. The Labrador group decided that rather than develop options for a policy paper their regional workshop would focus on what could be done to follow up on the report they had helped to prepare. It became obvious that the focus of attention was now on the issue of policing and, in particular, the police response to violence against women. The workshop was scheduled to coincide with an RCMP conference in Goose Bay, Labrador; and Pauktuutit made a request to present the results of the workshop at this conference.

By the end of the four-day workshop, which took place in September 1993, the women had developed an "action plan" to deal with the inadequate policing services they had experienced. They presented this plan to the RCMP. In response, the RCMP officials agreed to outline immediate, short-term, and long-term recommendations they were prepared to implement. The RCMP also indicated that they would identify which aspects of the plan they would not be able to implement, and why.

While awaiting the RCMP response to the action plan, Pauktuutit received a letter from the RCMP outlining their reaction to the report on the murder of the Labrador woman. In the letter the RCMP suggested that the allegations of police unresponsiveness were unsubstantiated and that the police had done everything possible in the case. They stated

that reported rates of violence were not sufficiently high to warrant sta-
tioning permanent police officers in the community, something the
women had explicitly recommended. They also suggested that the community was "apathetic" and failed to report crimes. To decide how to respond to the RCMP letter, Pauktuutit organized a conference call with
the Inuit women who had participated in the regional workshop and
other women in the communities who wanted to participate (the core
group was expanding).

In the action plan developed at the regional workshop, the women
had identified the need to undertake their own study of the rate of violence in the three Labrador Inuit communities that had no permanent
policing. This need was raised again during the conference call, and, in
light of the RCMP position, the participants decided to proceed with
their own study as soon as possible. They hoped to demonstrate the un-
reliability of police data with respect to violence in those communities,
and then use this information to argue for better and more police protection there. The women were confident that their study would reveal
that RCMP data on violence in the communities were flawed in two respects: women were not reporting all violent incidents, and the RCMP
were not recording all telephone calls made regarding violent incidents.
The study would also examine the reasons for under-reporting, because
the women were sure that community apathy was not the problem.[9]

ISSUES WE FACE IN THE LABRADOR JUSTICE PROJECT

As non-Inuit researchers working with Inuit women, we have had to
deal with a number of important issues.

For instance, as white women raised in the dominant culture, we are
frequently expected to perform the role of "translator" or "intermediary" between Inuit women and the public policy officials they deal with.
Although we are members of the dominant society, our knowledge
about Inuit women, their culture, and their lives is "valuable" to the government officials who have the power to make the changes the Inuit
women are seeking. This is probably a matter of being more comfortable
conversing with people who share the same first language and a similar
culture, but it can have the effect of undermining the Inuit women present and increasing the status of the white researcher.

9   The "Non-reported Rate of Crime Study" was completed in March 1995.

This did not happen during the meeting with the RCMP when the Labrador women presented their action plan, in part because the researcher made a conscious decision not to be drawn in, even when questions were addressed to her, and partly because the Labrador women were so clearly committed to presenting the plan they had worked so hard to produce. In our writing, however, we do attempt to translate recommendations and strategies into policy papers and reports that officials from our own culture can understand and support. Yet there is still a danger that the role of intermediary or translator can be seen as, and become, the role of a "representative" of the organization. An outsider who crosses this line and sees herself as a "representative" is, in our view, exploiting her relationship with the women with whom she shares her research work.

While we are usually at a disadvantage in working with women whose first and sometimes only language is Inuktitut, we do have one clear advantage: at no time can we presume to speak on behalf of Inuit women. At meetings, conferences, and workshops, and often during private conversations, we can only understand the discussions because of the presence of Inuktitut-English interpreters. This interpretation process is a constant reminder that we are outsiders, that no matter how good, bad, or indifferent our work is, we will not have to live with the consequences of decisions based on our work. This sometimes leads to situations in which we advocate for changes that we personally do not support; and for the most part we are comfortable with this. As members of the dominant society, we face the challenge as researchers within Pauktuutit of employing our power and privilege in a way that is positive and does not exploit the Inuit women whom we work with and who share our work. This includes those instances in which we might personally prefer the adoption of a different position or strategy.

There is a further dimension to the language issue. Researchers working with women who speak a different language are entirely dependent upon them for conducting the research. Two options are available to a researcher in this situation: working with an interpreter, or depending on the women to conduct research in their own communities. In our view the second option is always preferable.

MIES'S GUIDELINES AND THEIR APPLICATION

European feminist Maria Mies suggests that feminist research should be part of a process that supports the development of a reciprocal relationship between the researcher and those being researched. This relationship would be one in which researcher and researched learn from and partially identify with each other. This is a significant departure from scientific researchers in the Western tradition, who typically maintain a distance from the research objects in an attempt to gain an "objective" view of reality.

We discovered Mies's work after the Labrador justice project was under way, while we were in the initial stage of writing this chapter. It was exciting to find an approach so appropriate to our work: in effect, our practice had found a theory. Mies's thesis is that when women begin to change their situations of exploitation and oppression, these changes will have consequences for the research areas, theories, concepts, and methodologies of studies that focus on women's issues. In the following pages we outline Mies's seven postulates of feminist research and discuss their relationship to the Labrador justice project. We are particularly interested in examining the possibilities available for researchers attempting to be part of progressive, feminist research projects involving people from cultures different from their own.

PARTIAL IDENTIFICATION AND DOUBLE CONSCIOUSNESS

Mies rejects the claim that it is possible to be objective and value-free in social-scientific research. She proposes replacing objective or "spectator knowledge" with "conscious partiality," which is achieved through partial identification with those being studied. Conscious partiality views research "objects" (in our case, Inuit women) as part of a bigger social whole, and also views the researcher (white feminists) in this way. In a second article, Mies expands on the notion of partial identification, making clear that it is not total identification, which would be impossible except in situations in which only "like studies like." Rather, it involves developing a double-consciousness in which we begin to see both ourselves and each other as we exist in the material world. This is the best explanation we have found of our experience of working with Inuit women. Over time we have gained an intimate knowledge of the issues facing Inuit women, identifying, as women, with many of them, yet always being aware of our differences. Many of these differences are based on our cultural backgrounds, but others are rooted in the fact that we are members of the dominant society, a society that has perpetuated racism and inequality in its treatment of Inuit.

The development of double-consciousness, or the process of being able to observe oneself from the outside, is integral to Mies's approach. She explains: "The outside in this case is not, however, some imaginary reality, but rather the real, living woman who is looking at me, trying to understand me, posing unusual questions."[10] In interactions among women of radically different backgrounds—Mies refers to Third World and First World women—this process, if reciprocal, is a key component of a new methodological approach to feminist research.

We believe it is as essential for members of a dominant group to gain a double-consciousness as it is for those who are oppressed. Mies describes how double-consciousness on the part of the researcher is not only a "methodological and political opportunity," but also a "necessity."

> The postulate of truth itself makes it necessary that those areas of the female existence which so far were repressed and socially "invisible" be brought into the full daylight of scientific analysis. In order to make this possible, feminist women must deliberately and courageously integrate their repressed, unconscious female subjectivity, i.e., their own experience of oppression and discrimination into their research process.[11]

Even though we have been working within an organization that has a clear agenda to ensure that Inuit women are included in the efforts to reform the justice system, as outsiders working on this initiative we work consciously and directly with the women involved. A researcher cannot be a "spectator." Our double-consciousness enables us to understand where we and the women we are working with fit into the bigger social

---

10   Maria Mies, "Women's Research or Feminist Research? The Debate Surrounding Feminist Science and Methodology," in Judith Cook and Mary Margaret Fonow, eds., *Beyond Methodology: Feminist Scholarship as Lived Research* (Bloomington and Indianapolis: Indiana University Press, 1991), p.79.

11   Maria Mies, "Towards a Methodology for Feminist Research", in Gloria Bowles and Renate Duelli Klein, eds., *Theories of Women's Studies* (London and New York: Routledge, 1983), p.121.

whole. As women, we all know oppression and our oppressors. As white women in a racist society, we have access to power that is not shared by the Inuit women we work with.[12] At the same time, as cultural outsiders, we lack the knowledge these women have and the ability to communicate with them in their language.

As researchers we must also be aware of the hierarchy of knowledge, its social construct, and the fact that different skills and knowledge are valued in different societies and during different times. Western scientific knowledge is not inherently more valuable than other forms of knowledge, yet there is little recognition of this fact. When the federal government decided that all Inuit women should give birth in hospitals, medical evacuations to southern hospitals became commonplace. Few people in government even considered asking, "Is an Inuk woman better off giving birth under medical care in a hospital hundreds of miles away from her home and family, or in her home community attended by a traditional midwife who knows her family and personal history and speaks her language?" While the answer to this question is debatable, Pauktuutit president Martha Flaherty has pointed out that the debate is too often "premised on a disrespect for our history and for the knowledge and skills which many of our elders still possess."[13]

For a researcher, part of developing a double-consciousness is being able to look at one's own historical and cultural biases and not presume that what one takes for granted—for example, the high value placed on formal education or access to medical technology—is universally accepted.

VIEW FROM BELOW

Double-consciousness, including an awareness of differences and the power derived from these differences, becomes more apparent the closer the researcher is to the researched. The researcher should abandon the "spectator" knowledge approach and reject a hierarchical relationship between researcher and researched. Mies suggests replacing the traditional "view from the top" approach to research with a "view from be-

---

12 The ability to pursue education at the university level is still greatly dependent on one's class, economic resources, geographic region, and cultural and family values. Western values support a hierarchy of knowledge whereby those with higher levels of education are more deserving of respect and high income jobs than those with lower educational attainment (except that gender and race can also lower status).

13 Pauktuutit, "Brief to the Royal Commission on Aboriginal Peoples." Unpublished 1993 document on file with Pauktuutit.

low." She states, "This is the necessary consequence of the demands of conscious partiality and reciprocity."[14] According to Mies, this demand for a systematic view from below has both a scientific and ethical-political dimension. It is the ethical-political dimension we want to explore further here.

The experience of the Labrador workshop would support Mies's position that the "view from below" promotes a more collaborative relationship between the researcher and researched. The researcher was constantly aware that she should not assume a position greater than that of a technical resource person. In previous meetings, the researcher noted that her skills as a lawyer tended to be accorded inappropriately high status. This was no doubt due, in part, to the socialization of the local women and the value placed on legal skills by the dominant culture. This response also reflected a lot of the women's past experience with researchers who fly into the community to do their studies. In those instances, Inuit women were interviewed and questioned, confined to the role of research "objects," and the researchers did little to dismantle the status accorded to them in this hierarchical relationship.

This raises the ethical dimension to this approach. Working with women in the communities, the researcher must be prepared to give up control over decisions about the research process, as well as the data acquired. In the case of Labrador, the Pauktuutit researcher was expected to give up control over decisions to the women in Labrador. Other researchers, not located within the organization, are left with the choice and discretion to give up this control of the research process.

When the researcher is committed to the "view from below" perspective, she supports a process that empowers women, provides the opportunity for the women to self-identify and build important networks. In the Justice Project, the "view from below" approach has encouraged the development of new networks across the North that have begun to replace the existing network between women in isolated northern communities and Pauktuutit's Ottawa office. The Labrador women have provided role models for other Inuit women across Canada: they were the first regional group involved in the Justice Project to hold their own workshop and initiate action, so women in other regions are turning to them for advice. This alone is significant and valuable for empowering and uniting Inuit women since they are so geographically isolated. The

14   Mies, "Towards a Methodology for Feminist Research," pp.123.

view from below also involves working directly with "ordinary" women, who are not necessarily the elected community leaders; and building networks among these women further empowers them. The realignment of the north-south network to one stretching across the north serves to limit the role of the researchers. The Ottawa-based researcher is not the primary or only source of information, and therefore her role is truly limited to that of a legal technician. Without such a realignment, the Ottawa-based researcher can become the link between the regions and may be in a position to inform members of the groups about what is happening in other regions and, at the same time, retain considerable control and power over the process and its outcome.

RESEARCH TIED TO POLITICAL ACTION

Although research is part of a larger political strategy for change, it can rarely initiate such change. Mies's third postulate or guideline is that research must be an integral part of "actions, movements, and struggles for women's emancipation."[15]

The research undertaken by Pauktuutit—with its strong grassroots support and guided by resolutions passed each year at its annual general meeting—is to further the causes of the Inuit women's movement, including reform of the justice system. The research process must be flexible enough to allow the Inuit women involved to control the project. In the Labrador project, the decision to abandon the policy paper on alternative approaches to the administration of justice and focus instead on policing reflects the position taken by the Inuit women. The decision to change the focus of the Labrador project was intended to ensure that the women living in Labrador would have the opportunity to direct the research project to address their needs.[16] Because Pauktuutit, the Inuit women's movement, is responsive to its membership, this flexibility was possible and necessary.

INTEGRATION OF THEORY AND PRACTICE

For her fourth guideline, Mies proposes that practice and theory cannot be separated in research. She applies her motto, "If you want to know a

15   Ibid, p.124.

16   With this approach, requirements and expectations of the funding source were recognized to be secondary and not a limiting factor on addressing the needs of the women.

thing, you must change it,"[17] to the study of women and proposes, "We have to start fighting against women's exploitation and oppression in order to be able to understand the extent, the dimensions, the forms and causes of this patriarchal system."[18] In Labrador the fight for police protection led Inuit women to acknowledge the extent of violence in their lives, the extent of police resistance to providing them with protection, and the gender and racial biases implicit in the police response.

Mies also speaks about disruptions in normalcy, such as a crisis, as creating the conditions in which oppressive or exploitive relationships are recognized: in Labrador, the ongoing violence that ultimately resulted in the death of one woman at the hands of her abusive partner was an unfortunate but precipitating event. This woman's death forced many women to realize the extent to which violence had become part of their "normal life." Their need to talk about this issue with other women was evident.

COLLECTIVIZATION OF WOMEN'S CONSCIOUSNESS

In her fifth, sixth, and seventh postulates, Mies shows how collective involvement in and ownership of the research process can contribute to a deeper understanding of oppression and, through this, a reclaiming of lost voices and forgotten histories. She suggests that a group approach to problem-solving, starting with individual experiences that are shared and documented, is "not only therapeutic but is the basis for collective women's consciousness and a starting point for emancipatory action."[19]

The Labrador workshop provided an opportunity for consciousness-raising, and from it group members began to acquire the tools they needed to become researchers themselves. The outsider-researcher only provided specific information on technical matters. If the violent death of one woman in Labrador was what Mies would call the rupture point for many of the women who came to be involved in the Labrador Justice Project, the workshop was the point at which a sense of collective consciousness and a desire to take action in response to the death of the woman became most evident.

Meeting and working as a group mobilized the women and strengthened their connections to each other. The presentation made to the RCMP following the workshop was carried out by women who had little

17   Mies, "Towards a Methodology for Feminist Research," p.125.

18   Ibid, p.125.

19   Ibid, p.132.

previous experience in public speaking. They spoke forcefully and pas-
sionately about the work completed in the workshop, presented the action plan they had prepared, and called upon the RCMP to join them to
implement it. The women began to take this newly acquired knowledge
and apply it. As a result, they strengthened their advocacy skills and became directly involved in negotiating changes to an inadequate policing
system. This process also helped the women develop confidence so that
they, rather than an outside "expert," represented Labrador women in
negotiations with the RCMP.

In addition, completing and distributing the report on the violence
against and murder of one woman provided the women with a documented account of experiences they had lived through or were personally familiar with. It was perhaps the first time that many of the women
learned that the feelings about death and the violence they experienced
in their own lives were shared by many others. Similarly, the group
workshop provided the women with a opportunity to share their histories around violence as well as their responses to these problems as a
group. The workshop proceedings were written up each evening by the
researcher and reviewed by the women the following day, followed by a
discussion of the type of action required. This exercise laid the ground-
work for developing an "action plan" to address the inadequate police
response to violence against women in their communities.

BEYOND MIES

Collectively, Mies's postulates form the basis for an argument that feminist researchers working in social and cultural environments different
from their own must be cautious about the exploitive nature of their relationship with those being researched. If we look beyond Mies's postulates, relying again on our experience within the Pauktuutit organization, we can see one further issue to consider: the need for follow-up.

Some researchers argue that once the research has been undertaken,
it is up to the community to decide to act upon the findings. Under a
participatory research model, the community's immediate and personal
identification with the research is said to encourage them to take direct
action. In other words, it is only after they have acquired the knowledge
that they are able to act. We would argue that action cannot be viewed as

a separate phase of a research project but must be ongoing and woven into the project. In the Labrador Justice Project, the research stage was just beginning when the women participated in a variety of actions aimed at changing adverse conditions. These actions include developing a plan, presenting it to the RCMP, and working towards implementing portions of it, specifically the research component. All of this took place as part of the research process.

Recognizing that action is essential, a related issue arises as to whether a separate follow-up phase is required in order to take action; and if it is, researchers, as active participants in a community project, must be committed to participating in it. In the initial stages of a research project it is often difficult to determine what form the follow-up will take, but presenting the community with a research report is clearly not enough. Too often, researchers gather their data and then leave the research site. While studies may be published in an academic journal, no one in the community has access to the research results. If they are to be accessible, studies must be made available in a form and a language that the people involved can easily understand.

Universities may be appropriate sites for theoretical and archival work in support of various movements, but if the community is not in control of the research process, the participation of academics and other "outsiders" in community-based research must be seriously and cautiously considered. In all cases, it is essential that the results of research, including historical and theoretical work, must somehow be incorporated into women's knowledge base at the community (or movement) level. It is difficult to imagine how this incorporation can be accomplished if the women are not intricately involved in the process from the beginning. Moreover, action cannot be relegated to a separate, follow-up phase of the research project, but should be integrated throughout.

THE NEED FOR AN ETHICAL STANCE

We argue that the constraints on our freedom as researchers imposed by the organizational structure of Pauktuutit, as well as our ethics as feminists committed to social and political change, create boundaries that have a positive impact on our research methodologies. Researchers must take responsibility for the research methods they use, as well as for the assumptions that underlie their work. Rules or guidelines are one way of making these assumptions and methodologies clear to everyone involved in the research process. For us, Mies's guidelines provide a framework that allows us to reflect on our role as feminist researchers working outside our own culture and enables us to refine our practice. This approach is essential when the researcher is part of the dominant culture and the researched are not.

Research within a women's organization is intended to be for and by the women that the organization represents, and the links with the community are very different from those established by outside researchers. Researchers working in Aboriginal communities usually find it necessary to demonstrate to funders that some level of community support exists before a project goes ahead. Getting letters of support from people and organizations in the community is entirely different in nature from having the community search for researchers who have the skills and tools to conduct the research they need. For example, an Aboriginal women's group applying for funds to start up an innovative family violence program may have to gather information citing the levels of family violence in their community. Research conducted for this purpose is qualitatively different from the efforts of an outside researcher pursuing her interest in examining the problem of family violence in Aboriginal communities. The first is aimed at responding to a problem that women know exists, the second at understanding the problem and its extent. Understanding may be useful—it can lead to developing responses that work—but if it is not initiated by women in the community, if it is not connected to a movement for change, it remains merely academic.

CONCLUSION

Among women of radically different backgrounds and life experiences, the link between "us" and "them" may be our identities as women. In our work with Inuit women, our double-consciousness allows us to understand oppression and dominance, albeit in a different way than Inuit women do. For example, Inuit political organizations, including Pauktuutit, have focused on Inuit survival in the face of the dominance of another culture and society. Inuit survival incorporates issues related to land, language, culture, values, traditions, and economies.

Historically, the family has been crucial for Inuit survival. Inuit women and men criticized Pauktuutit's initial attempts to address problems such as wife battering and child sexual abuse on the grounds that these attempts could threaten the family and, therefore, Inuit cultural survival. Pauktuutit persisted in addressing these issues, but the approaches developed were very different from those taken in southern Canada—and different from what we, as southern feminists, might advocate. In Pauktuutit's work, Inuit-ness does not necessarily take precedence over woman-ness, or vice-versa, because Inuit women are both.

Thus, a western feminist approach with gender as the starting point of understanding oppression and inequality may not be relevant to the lives of women who confront inequalities on many levels. What we, as white feminists, perceive as links among women may prove to be weak when tested in an environment in which feminists with Euro-Canadian cultural and social influences are in the minority. Yet white middle-class women dominate feminist movement[20] in Canada. Double-consciousness could be a useful tool for women within feminist movement, because it provides a way for them to stand back and assess their relative power and privilege in relation to and *with* women of different economic backgrounds, cultures, races, abilities, and ages. Being dialectical and reciprocal in nature, it could provide all the women involved with opportunities to learn from and teach each other and to change. White middle-class women involved in feminist movement need to go beyond a theoretical understanding of race and class in the analysis of oppression; feminism itself must change.

In discussing our work in a cross-cultural environment, we have implied that ethics (including the assumptions underlying our work) and research methods, like theory and action, must be intertwined. To be consistent, our chosen methodologies must clearly reflect our ethics, and when they do not the contradictions can point to areas that require change. Feminist movement in North America is in the midst of dealing with just such a situation. Bell hooks, in a published conversation with Mary Childers, points to a contradiction in feminism's current preoccupation with issues of race. She notes that women who have challenged feminist theory for being too exclusive have remained marginalized, while the movement itself has incorporated the language of inclusion:

20   In the article co-authored with Mary Childers, bell hooks says "I drop the definite article rather than speaking of 'the' feminist movement. When we do not have a definite article, we are saying that feminist movement can be located in multiple places, in multiple languages and experiences." Mary Childers and bell hooks, "A Conversation about Race and Class," in Marianne Hirsch and Evelyn Fox Keller, eds., *Conflicts in Feminism* (New York: Routledge, 1990), p.68.

A lot of black women I know feel that it is one of the tragic ironies
that we forced recognition of quote "race" and "racism" and now
a lot of white women are appropriating this discussion to serve
opportunistic ends, to serve the projection of themselves as politically correct, cool, or to engage in a kind of sterile discourse that is
not connected to behavioral change.[21]

Feminism and feminist theory depend entirely upon women's experiences to find expression. Working with Inuit women has taught us, as
white feminist researchers, to be cautious, to be aware of the ability of
feminist theory and practice to overlook fundamental aspects of inequality that go beyond gender. In a similar way, the experiences and the
writings of Aboriginal women and women of colour have challenged
white feminists with the need for flexibility and the need to continually
revisit and rework their feminist theories and practice. For many
women, gender may be a central factor in their inequality but not the
primary or only factor. Other significant factors have to be taken into account.

Feminist theory must be drawn from the diversity of women's experiences, in a way that does not "appropriate the discussion to serve opportunistic ends" and does not generalize from the experiences of a homogeneous group of white women. To that end, feminist research that
contributes to the development of theory must be similarly rooted in diversity, and control of the research process should remain outside of the
mainstream.

21   Childers and hooks, "A Conversation about Race and Class", p.69.

SUGGESTED READINGS

Jan Barnsley and Dianne Ellis, *Research for Change: Participatory Action Research for Community Groups* Vancouver: Women's Research Centre, 1992.

Gloria Bowles and Renate Duelli Klein, eds., *Theories of Women's Studies*. New York, Routledge, 1983.

Judith Cook and Mary Margaret Fonow, eds., *Beyond Methodology: Feminist Scholarship as Lived Research* Bloomington and Indianapolis: Indiana University Press, 1991.

Mary Crnkovich, ed., *Gossip: A Spoken History of Women in the North*. Ottawa: Canadian Arctic Resources Committee, 1990.

Lena Dominelli, *Anti-racist Social Work: A Challenge for White Practitioners and Educators*. London: Macmillan Press, 1988.

bell hooks, *Yearnings: Race, Gender and Cultural Politics* Toronto: Between the Lines, 1990.

Rosemarie Kuptana, *No More Secrets*. Ottawa: Pauktuutit, 1991.

Pauktuutit, *The Inuit Way: A Guide to Inuit Culture*. Ottawa, 1990.

Pauktuutit, *Arnait: The Views of Inuit Women on Contemporary Issues*. Ottawa, 1991.

Pauktuutit, *Naalatsiarlutit: A Presentation of Artwork by Northern Artists on Spousal Abuse*. Ottawa, 1992.

Pauktuutit, *Taimaninuit: An Introduction to Basic Counselling Skills*. Ottawa, 1993.

ARUN P. MUKHERJEE

Chapter Five: Reading Race in Women's Writing

Ever since I became conscious that my reading or, rather, my interpretations of the texts I read differed from what my professors at school and the eminent critics' writings in the library were saying, I have puzzled about the mysterious process that is called reading. When I went to graduate school, it was the author's intention that determined what the correct, or closest, interpretation was. Or, if that wasn't available, then we had to follow the directions taken by the eminent critics. My own responses, based on what I would call a gut sense of natural justice, were disallowed by the overall climate of the profession. So I wondered why the critical work on a book ignored things that seemed the most important to me, things such as poverty or social inequality, political vision, engagement with local realities, and racist or anti-racist perspectives of the text (I wasn't, of course, considering gender as a separate category at this stage).

Basically, it was the writer's moral passion, or what one might call social consciousness, that engaged me most deeply in literary texts. And yet, the critical analyses that I was taught to produce and the models I was asked to read seldom engaged with such aspects of the texts. Indeed, to pay attention to such things was pejoratively called "sociological," and we were amply warned not to produce any analyses that smacked of such tendencies. As students of literature, our job was to pay attention to the texture of language, to tropes and figures of speech, to symbols and imagery, and to form and structure. Yes, it was permitted to speak of the characters in the text, but only in terms of their passage from innocence to experience or in terms of their personal relationships.

Many of us went through graduate school with a split consciousness. I felt a strange disjunction between my gut responses to a text and the "proper" language I had to use to produce an analysis acceptable to my professor so I could get a good grade and remain in graduate school. I and some of my other contemporaries went through graduate school always a little uneasy about whether we had spotted a text's key symbols and images and whether we had figured out its underlying structure. To my utter mortification, I never could figure out the preferred response on my own. I made up for my shortcomings by finding out what the eminent critic or reviewer had said about the text.

It is hard to pinpoint that transformative moment when I found my own voice and was no longer afraid of authority. It happened some time during the writing of my Ph.D. thesis, with the help of two Marxist critics: Raymond Williams and Kenneth Burke. Yes, they were male and white and not at all astute on race and gender. But during the twenty-year siege that was my education in literary analysis, they were the only two voices of dissent, unsanctioned by the academy, that gave me the permission to think about literature as a comment on human life in all its ramifications.

So my professional radicalization did not come about through feminism. It was already formed when I encountered feminist literary theory. And while it was exhilarating to read Kate Millett's *Sexual Politics*, mainly because of her disrespect for the rules of academic decorum, I also felt quite uncomfortable with her text's lapses into xenophobia.[1] I feel that way about most feminist literary theory. Its project of "recovering" and interpreting women's writing has often rubbed me the wrong way. Shaped as my consciousness is by the fact of having been born a non-white British subject, anti-colonial, anti-imperial, and anti-racist struggles are of utmost importance to me, and any feminism that ignores these realities is of no use to me.

I have been teaching women's studies courses now for at least ten years, only the last three as a tenure-stream faculty member. During this period I taught many canonical women's texts that upset me because of

1   Arun Mukherjee, "A House Divided: Women of Colour and American Feminist Theory." in Constance Backhouse and David H. Flaherty, eds., *Challenging Times: The Women's Movement in Canada and the United States*. (Montreal and Kingston: McGill-Queen's University Press, 1992), pp.165-74.

their attitudes to such things as colonialism, racism, and classism. While texts such as Aphra Behn's *Oroonoko*, Charlotte Brontë's *Jane Eyre*, Charlotte Perkins Gilman's *Herland*, Kate Chopin's *The Awakening*, Nellie McClung's *In Times Like These*, and Margaret Atwood's *The Handmaid's Tale* alienate me as a non-white woman reader because of how they diminish non-white people's humanity, and while I can testify to similar responses from many of my students and acquaintances, both white and non-white, I feel dispirited that new work continues to be produced on these and other women writers that continues to ignore the question of the "isms."

This overlooking on the part of white feminist critics of the wounding aspects of these texts for non-white readers, and the celebration of these works, create a gulf between us. Why, I ask, every time I come across yet another paean about one of these books, can they not see the "isms" embedded in the text that I and some other readers see?

This is the epistemological problem we face in literary studies. Now that we have emancipated ourselves from the stultifying vocabularies of universalist humanism, we have moved towards a free-for-all pluralism in which all readings have equal value, supposedly. We have not developed criteria that would help us discriminate between readings. Of course we do choose between readings based on our individual response to the critic's style and ideological framework. But we have not developed ground rules for this choosing. I believe that we need to do that.

The way things are right now, I believe that we feminists operate as two solitudes. This feeling has been with me since I first encountered the fact that the texts I found utterly demeaning to my and other Third World people's humanity were being taught and written about as feminist classics. I will have to narrate this discovery as an anecdote.

I came to York University in 1985 on a Contractually Limited Appointment in the Humanities division. One of the courses I was hired to teach was "Images of America." One of the texts being taught on it was Charlotte Perkins Gilman's *Herland*. The senior colleague who was explaining the course to me asked me what I thought of this book. When I said that I had never heard of it, he told me enthusiastically that it was a recently "recovered" feminist classic and that its radical analysis of women's condition would blow my mind, given the fact that it was written in 1915.

I began reading the book with great enthusiasm, but halfway into it I recoiled in horror as the text wiped out all the non-white women in order to create the racially pure utopia of herland. Hadn't, I wondered, my senior colleague noticed this textual genocide? The following year I had to teach *Herland* on the women's studies core course "On Women." After I lectured, one of the teaching assistants told me that she had never read any critical work on the text that spoke of its racism and thanked me for bringing it out. She had failed to spot it herself, she said, because "We constantly commit the error of using 'women' when we really mean 'white women.'" And so when the text focused only on white women, it had not seemed unusual to her.

Reading and teaching *Herland* was a watershed for me. I went on to do more work on the text and the general problem of racism in white feminist literary theory. I scoured the feminist responses to these "recovered" texts that were being published at a prodigious rate as essays in journals and as books, and I found nothing that was not in the celebratory mode.

I went on to write about this yawning gulf between my reading of these texts and those by prominent feminist literary theorists. But a paper I presented at a major feminist conference and that was published in the proceedings elicited this response from a reviewer, Janet Mancini Billson:

> Mukherjee would have us disavow the early white feminists, whom we have only just discovered, because they colluded with "racist and imperialist forces of the time." This seems like a very tall order. If we investigate the values of most historical figures who lived prior to last week, of colour or white, we will find racist biases, homophobia, and ethnocentrism. Shall we discard them all and spin, rootlessly, in the wind of history? Or take their values into account, then ferret out what we can learn from them as sisters under the skin? We will lose the battle if we don't find ways of living together in the trenches.[2]

Of course I had never demanded that we do not read these women who, I said, "colluded with the racist and imperialist forces of the time." I had demanded that they not be written about and taught in the tone of

---

2   Janet Mancini Billson, "'Challenging Times': Complexities of Feminism and the Women's Movement," *Canadian Review of American Studies*, Special Issue, Part II, 1992, p.323.

breathless celebration that they have been accorded. Billson's review, as well as plenty of work that continues to be published on writers like Gilman, Chopin, and McClung, once again underlines for me how wide the gulf of misunderstanding is between those who find racism in women's writing objectionable and those who do not notice it.

I use that expression, "do not notice it," deliberately, for it may be possible that these theorists did not see it in the text when they produced their emancipatory reading of it. Perhaps they would change their readings if it were shown to them that there were problems like embedded racism in the text? It seems that inability to "see" the racism in the text is the problem faced by some feminist readers. At least that is the impression I get from Greta Nemiroff's comment: "I have never been aware of racism in the few McClung works I have read. I would appreciate some elucidation on this point, as well as a more detailed account of how the history of feminism in Canada has been internally shaped by racist ideology, as [Marianna] Valverde argued."[3] While Nemiroff's language suggests that she does finds racism to be an objectionable presence and that she will change her mind about McClung once someone has shown how McClung is problematic—an attitude I can live with a little more comfortably than the one shown by Billson—I am still puzzled by her not being able to see the exclusionary aspects of McClung's texts.

This is an epistemological problem. How do I show Nemiroff what I see in the text? Is there a methodology we can develop that will allow readers like Nemiroff to spot racism or other "isms" in a text? After already doing work on uncovering racist subtexts in works deemed as feminist "classics,"[4] I would find it boring to continue to produce studies of individual texts contesting the dominant versions of feminist analysis that overlook racism.

But to develop such a methodology, we will have to have a discussion about the feminist understandings of literature and the literary institution. I feel that such a discussion has not taken place. Feminists have produced individual readings of women's writing that have focused on these women's exclusion from the canon, on the writers of these texts as oppressed women because they could not give unfettered attention to their creativity, on the female characters of these texts as epitomizing the oppression of women in the patriarchal society, and on the possibly

3   Greta Hofmann Nemiroff, "That Which Divides Us: That Which Unites Us," in Backhouse and Flaherty, *Challenging Times*, p.279.

4   See Mukherjee, "A House Divided"; and "Right Out of 'Herstory': Racism in Charlotte Perkins Gilman's *Herland* and Feminist Literary Theory." in Himani Bannerji, ed., *Returning the Gaze: Essays on Racism, Feminism and Politics* (Toronto: Sister Vision, 1993), pp.131-43.

"feminine" qualities of women's writing. Feminists working on "theory" have been writing about the construction of the "subject" in terms borrowed from French feminism.

Neither of these approaches, whether that of reading and writing of individual texts or producing theory, has been concerned about placing literature in the overall feminist project: that of demanding and working for a better world in which all human beings will be equal, regardless of their gender and other attributes such as race, class, sexual preference, ethnicity, religion, and nationality. That is certainly how I conceive of the feminist project.

Placing literature within the larger feminist project would mean that feminist critics interpret and evaluate writing in terms of its values. Feminists do produce a value-oriented criticism when they pay attention to gender in literary texts, and they have been criticized for it. However, for me, they have not gone far enough. In fact, they have exacerbated my problem because where I find racism and classism, they find value.

Let me give an example. Kate Chopin's *The Awakening* is one of those "recovered" women's texts that holds an important place in the feminist canon. First published in 1899, it was criticized for its "immorality" and barred from libraries and bookstores. It is now taught extensively in both American literature and women's studies courses. While I have no objection to the text being chosen for teaching, I do have grave problems with how it has been interpreted.

Sandra M. Gilbert has written a thirty-one-page introduction to the Penguin edition, the text most often used for classroom purposes.[5] In the "Introduction," Gilbert tells us that *The Awakening* can be read "as a book-length vindication of the rights of women" (p.8). Later on, she claims that both "author and character alike became representative late-nineteenth-century figures; even more dramatically, they became representative *women* of the *fin de siècle*" (p.12). Gilbert also suggests that texts like *Jane Eyre* and *The Awakening* should be read as depicting "the troubled female consciousness itself" (p.15). We are encouraged to read *The Awakening* as "the female struggle for identity" (p.18), as "the struggle for autonomy that she [Chopin] imagines would have engaged any nineteenth century woman who experienced such a fantastic transformation" (p.29). This entire "Introduction" focuses on Edna Pontellier,

5   Sandra M. Gilbert, "Introduction: The Second Coming of Aphrodite," in *The Awakening and Selected Stories by Kate Chopin*, (Harmondsworth, England: Penguin Books, 1983).

the white heroine of the novel, and it is her life of "domestic entrap-
ment," as the wife of Leonce Pontellier, a well-to-do businessman of
New Orleans, that the critic sees as the universal condition of women.
Although the text is full of references to "quadroon," "black," and
"darkie" servants who look after Edna Pontellier's children and household, the critic does not see them. They remain as inconsequential for
her as they are for the author of the text. Chopin refers to them as part of
the furniture. She refers to "the quadroon," for instance, as giving the
children their bath or putting them to bed. She neither gives words to
nor describes the character. Chopin describes the black servants by their
function and their colour: they cook, sweep, receive guests, provide
child care, and work on the plantation. But they are given neither names
nor voice.

I am not going to read a book that focuses only on the white bour-
geois housewife's experience and denies voice and name to her black
domestic workers as a text that is about "female consciousness." And
any critic who ignores the portrayal of black servants in the text as
"quadroon" and "darkie" and foists it on us as a text about "the female
oppression" is doing a disservice to the feminist project.

I do not see that pointing out Chopin's collusion with the "racist and
imperialist forces of the time" is "a tall order." In fact Gilbert clearly
wrote her "Introduction" after a lot of study. She places it in the context
of literature being produced at the time in Europe and the United States.
However, not one of the texts she mentions is written by a non-white.
And although she informs us that Chopin was a Confederate, she does
not examine the meaning of such an allegiance. She does not examine
Chopin's plantation-owning family, its role in the Civil War and the
war's aftermath, and the overall social and political context of the postbellum outhern United States that the novel is set in. Thus the critic uses
history selectively.

So what I am demanding is that social and political context be
brought to bear on our interpretation of texts. I do not see why this is "a
tall order." After all, the critic *is* going outside the text and supplying a
lot of historical information. The question is what kind of historical information is being supplied and what is being suppressed.

I can only puzzle over why Sandra Gilbert cannot see the deep en-
trenchment of the text in the racist ideologies of the American South in

postbellum America. However, her reading is certainly very powerful insofar as she has been chosen to write the "Introduction" of the Penguin edition and thus influence the young readers' responses.

We in the profession of teaching literature need to work out a feminist literary theory that will be more responsive to the problem of determining value. And racism, certainly, is not the only "ism" that needs to be looked at. For instance, my second-year students did not feel that Edna Pontellier could be called oppressed when she had so many servants to take care of the domestic drudgery. In fact, they felt that she was "spoiled." Now that is a very different kind of reading from Gilbert's "poor oppressed Edna" who represents every woman. I hear a number of such responses in my classroom about almost every "oppressed" heroine in the feminist canon.

Feminist literary theory has wandered far away from the feminist emancipatory project. Its practitioners address their postmodern, deconstructionist language only to the insider. Even now, in my late forties and spending a lot of time trying to understand the "hot" theorists even when they knock out my cerebral cortex, I am often at a loss to understand this language. A lay reader can, therefore, have no hope. We really need to think about what has happened to feminist literary theory: what questions it is debating and why. It is certainly not engaging with issues that concern me as a non-white woman living in racist North American society.

What I want from feminist analysts is an acknowledgement of my "hurt." Racist texts diminish non-white people's humanity. Yet to prove that a text *is* racist, I am somehow asked to prove that its racist content is *in* the text and not in my head. Contemporary theories of reading that speak of the endless play of the signifier or the indeterminacy or multiple meanings disallow the possibility that I and other non-white readers can communicate our hurt. If all attempts at making meaning are permitted, then there is no way of discriminating between them.

Of course, in real life, people do make up their minds about what interpretations they are going to give their allegiance to. And whatever these theories tell me, I do read texts my own way and I do discriminate between good and bad ones. Only, I put them in those two slots on the basis of how they appeal to my moral sense, a basis that has not been considered worthy of theoretical discussion.

Perhaps that is so because there has been a strong tendency to consider literary works as automatically moral. Literature, supposedly, makes us better human beings by providing us access to the intimate details of other people's lives. Such statements are harder to come across these days, although one can still see them in introductions to anthologies. In any case, it seems to me that the feminist critics who celebrate the canonical works I have mentioned must find them moral. Otherwise they would not praise or endorse them. In their work they do use moral criteria, without explicitly spelling them out, when they point out the strategies these writers adopt to speak out against the oppression of women.

The question simply boils down to this: the texts endorsed by eminent white feminist literary critics as emancipatory do *not* only not seem emancipatory to me and several other non-white women readers, but in fact they also hurt us. As Frank Lentricchia says, "We need to know that what is therapeutic or prophylactic for some is poison for others; that the literary cannot free itself from this double effect."[6]

I think we need to talk about why I and many other readers receive as "poison" what is propagated as "therapeutic" or "emancipatory" by white feminist critics such as Elaine Showalter, Sandra Gilbert, and Susan Gubar. I do not think we can get around this yawning gap between our interpretations by devising better methodologies. Instead, opening up a dialogue about our disagreements might be the answer.

6   Frank Lentricchia, *Criticism and Social Change* (Chicago: Chicago University Press, 1985).

NETTIE WIEBE

Chapter Six: Farm Women: Cultivating Hope and Sowing Change

CANADIAN FEMINISM OWES MUCH TO THE RICH LEGACY OF struggle and thought inherited from the pioneer women who courageously worked for a better life on the farm, lobbied for the right to vote, and fought endlessly against the adversities of nature.

However, despite a long and illustrious history of struggle, agrarian feminists, like their urban counterparts, have not yet dislodged or transformed the patriarchal structures that characterize their society.[1] The agricultural sector, from the family farm to the corporate agribusiness domain, remains a deeply patriarchal system. So although the current context of farming women is in many ways vastly different from that of those brave foremothers, some striking similarities remain. For contemporary agrarian feminists, many of the issues and attitudes from the earlier part of the twentieth century are all too familiar.

As part of a small and declining farm population that is grappling with hard economic times and the increasing industrialization of food production, farm women in the 1990s face a complex array of challenges. Their position remains largely invisible, their farm work unremunerated, and, indeed, their status as legitimate "farmers" unrecognized.

---

1   The term "agrarian feminist" as used here includes both "equal rights" and "social" feminism. Agrarian feminism holds that women are not inferior to men and must be treated as
    equals. But it recognizes that there are differences in the situation of women and men that
    stem from social constructions of gender culturally and historically rooted in the agricultural
    community and that disadvantage farm women and undermine their status as autonomous
    persons. For a more detailed discussion of the usages of "agrarian feminism" see Georgina
    Taylor, "'A Splendid Field Before Us': Violet McNaughton and the Development of Agrarian
    Feminism in Canada, 1909 to 1926," *Prairie Forum*, forthcoming.

Like their urban counterparts, rural women must deal with the general range of gender issues that characterize our society. These include violence against women, wage disparity, and lack of representation in public institutions. A number of issues, such as education, child care, health care, and other social services are of concern to all Canadian women but have a particular impact on women living in the countryside. Some issues are unique to farm women, such as the ownership of land and the division of labour and income on the family farm.

In this discussion of feminist methodologies as practised by farm women, I will concentrate on issues that are either particular to farm women or have a specific content for these women because of the rural context. The rapid industrialization of food production during the second half of the twentieth century has changed farm work, women's work, and farm women's lives. To understand how farm women analyse, interpret, and react to issues, we must first understand something about the context from which they view these issues.

The working reality of farm women includes not only the work they do but also how this work is described, counted, and valued. But a history of leaving farm women's work uncounted, discounted, and undervalued inhibits attempts to collect accurate data using standard methods such as census data and random sample surveys although, as we will see, farm women have organized themselves to overcome this problem.

The working reality of women on their farms is also informed by the social and institutional structures that govern agriculture in the larger context. Government departments of agriculture and mainstream farm organizations reflect and reinforce the male dominance of this sector. Not only are there very few women in official decision-making roles, but farm women's work and needs have rarely been included in the programmes and agendas of these agricultural agencies. Farm women have dealt with this exclusion in a variety of ways, sometimes working within existing organizations, sometimes creating new ones. These efforts have led to varying views on what needs are being met, as well as conflicts between ways of organizing to meet those needs.

My conclusions on the question of organization and effective methodology are shaped to some extent by my own experiences as a farm girl, farm woman, and agrarian activist. I served as the Women's President of the National Farmers Union from 1988 to 1994. This period of working locally, nationally, and internationally in a leadership position from within a so-called "mainstream" farm organization to improve the situation of farm women strengthened my own feminist commitment to work towards greater equality and justice for all women. But the particular circumstances and issues that had to be confronted also forced me to re-examine and adapt my feminist methodology to fit the sometimes complex mix of demands that seem to pit feminist priorities and women's needs against the needs of their own family farms, or that create conflict between loyalty to one's own organization and the necessity of working with a broad range of organizations to achieve common ends. The long history of the agrarian feminist struggle gave me a sense of the depth of the issues—and of the necessity for tenacity coupled with patience.

In the course of my work as a farm leader, I became increasingly conscious of how very significant the backdrop of male dominance in agriculture is for farm women. Like a painter who slowly assimilates the knowledge that the apparent discolouration of the strokes from her paintbrush are in fact caused by the dark tone of the canvas she is working on, I continue to discover historical and contextual background that influences the issues that farm women identify as important, as well as how we work on them—or even whether it is possible to identify farm women's issues at all and to identify oneself as a farm woman.

Many of the issues that are important to farm women are the same ones that are important to women in other sectors.[2] However, because the contemporary women's movement, reflecting the general population, is predominantly urban-based, the particular perspectives of farm women on those shared issues are seldom articulated and analysed. Nor are the issues unique to farm women given much public attention. I hope that the concrete examples and first-hand experiential knowledge presented in this chapter will help women who work in other sectors to draw useful parallels with issues facing this small minority of women. This discussion may also serve as encouragement to feminists everywhere by demonstrating how a largely unnamed agrarian feminism, adapting feminist strategies to a unique context, continues to flourish in rural Canada.

---

2   The other chapters in this book deal with issues that are also relevant to farm women, especially the discussions on child care by Kris Colwell, women and violence by Alison Wylie and Lorraine Greaves, workplace safety by Karen Messing, and working with women in marginalized communities by Linda Archibald and Mary Crnkovich.

FARM WOMEN: THE CONTEXT

Although the industrialization of food production began before the turn
of the century, the rapid move from horsepower to tractor power after
World War II revolutionized farming. As machine power replaced animal and human energy, the traditional "mixed farm" gave way to more
specialized on-farm production.[3] This shift has had, and continues to
have, a profound effect on the kind of work required in farming and on
the gender dynamics within the farm family. It has also changed the face
of the farming community as a whole.

The most obvious social effect of the technical revolution in farming
has been a dramatic demographic shift. Canada has gone from having a
predominantly rural and farming population at the turn of the century
to having an overwhelmingly urban population.[4] Industrialization has
made it possible for fewer farmers to work much bigger farms. This
trend towards fewer, larger farms continues. The 1991 Agriculture Census of Canada revealed that farm people make up only 3.2 per cent of the
Canadian population.[5]

The most obvious manifestation of the decline in farm numbers is
that there are fewer neighbours and those that remain live farther away.
Not only are there fewer people within communities, but also whole
communities have disappeared. Rural Canada is dotted with the empty
remnants of what used to be thriving, well-populated villages. For farm
women, whose roles have always included generating and maintaining
community life, rural depopulation has forced them to adapt in a great
many ways. They face a growing challenge: weaving the intricate, multifaceted tapestry that is "community" with fewer and fewer threads.

Although improved communications, especially the telephone, make
it possible to talk to ever more distant "neighbours," telephone conversation is only a partial replacement for the in-person visiting within
neighbourhoods that was the custom in most rural communities. The
isolation, which has always been a factor in farm women's lives, is aggra-
vated by the sparser rural populations. Although modern transportation

---

3   A mixed farm includes the raising of a variety of both plants and animals rather than concen-
    trating on animal husbandry only, as is the practice on most modern commercial chicken op-
    erations, for example, or growing only grains or only horticultural crops. Traditionally, the
    mixed farm included cattle, hogs, and chickens, as well as crops and a vegetable garden.

4   See Tables A67-69 in M.C. Urquhart and K.A.H. Buckley, *Historical Statistics of Canada*, 2nd
    ed. (Toronto: Macmillan, 1965).

5   Statistics Canada, *Agriculture Census*, 1991.

and communications are a definite advantage, they do not entirely relieve that isolation.[6]

Not only are there far fewer farm women in the countryside today, but the women who do remain in farming communities are less likely to be related to each other. As the farms enlarge and the economics of farming deteriorate, it is more difficult for extended families or single families to farm together on one farmstead or even in one area. Farmsteads that used to provide livelihoods for two and three generations of the farm family simultaneously, and to require the labour of many family members, are now frequently operated by single, nuclear families. For farm women, this means that the extended familial support system of kinswomen, often including a mother-in-law, if not a mother, is no longer there.

The most apparent consequence of the rural depopulation on the lives of country women, however, has been a concentration or centralization in the rural service infrastructure. Although this is most noticeable in the prairies, where the distances between settlements are greater, farming communities across Canada have suffered the loss of public institutions and services. Small country schools have been consolidated into larger town schools. Thousands of village post offices have disappeared.[7] Rural hospitals, churches, libraries, and other services are becoming scarcer.

Service delivery to rural areas is usually comparatively more costly than urban service delivery because of the added distances. Because there are fewer and fewer users of the services it becomes ever more expensive per client to maintain the service infrastructure. The emphasis on lowering public costs and being "more efficient" that has characterized much of government policy since the 1980s has meant an increasing emphasis on using cost/benefit analysis to evaluate public services. The use of standard cost/benefit measurements involves an assessment of the cost of service delivery per individual client, with "efficiency" defined as the lowest cost at which that service can be delivered. Critics frequently cite the higher cost per user in rural areas to justify the closing of the rural facilities that have been judged to be "less efficient" using these measurements.

6   Nanci Langford and Nora Keating, "Social Isolation and Alberta Farm Women," in K. Storrie, ed., *Women: Isolation and Bonding—The Ecology of Gender* (Toronto: Methuen, 1987). For a description of the isolation farm women suffered in previous decades, see Georgina Taylor, "'Should I Drown Myself Now or Later?' The Isolation of Rural Women in Saskatchewan and Their Participation in the Homemakers' Clubs, the Farm Movement and the Co-operative Commonwealth Federation 1910-1967," also in Storrie, *Women*.

7   Rural Dignity statistics as reported in Terry Pugh, "Closing Rural Post Offices," *Briarpatch*, July/August 1988, pp.14-18. A reprieve on the closure of rural post offices was declared in February 1994. See *The Western Producer*, February 24, 1994, p.4.

This logic of economic efficiency has serious consequences for farm families. It means that instead of attending a nearby school, most farm children spend many hours a week on school buses. Just going to get the mail and groceries entails a long trip. Going to doctors, dentists, libraries, or church requires a lot of planning and travel time. Because farm women continue to take primary responsibility for the life of the domicile, the loss of local services has a major impact on their lives and work. The inconvenience, expense, and added travelling time that the loss of infrastructure presents as a cost to farm women has not even been measured, let alone calculated into the cost/benefit analysis.

Fewer people and lower farm incomes also make other economic activity in rural areas less viable. As small businesses in the towns and villages fail, and as governments close institutions, vital off-farm jobs are harder to find.

THE WORKING REALITY

The industrialization of agriculture has sharpened the on-farm division of labour between men and women. The high demand for manual labour in food production before mechanization meant that women took full part in most kinds of farm work. Women were usually responsible for small-animal production (chickens, pigs, sheep) as well as for the dairy and working in the fields.[8] With the introduction of more machinery in the 1940s and 1950s, women were initially excluded from some of the "productive" activities as men took over the roles of driving tractors, threshing machines and operating other equipment.

Although farm life seldom offered women the possibility of remaining exclusively in the home like some of their urban, middle-class, single-income family counterparts, the first decades of rapid industrialization (from the 1940s to the late 1970s) released women from doing field work on many farms. Industrialization was necessarily accompanied by capitalization, however, which increased the bookkeeping and accounting functions on farms. These tasks have always fallen predominantly to farm women.

By the 1980s, the economic position of many family farms had worsened significantly so that there was less money for hired help. This, among other factors, has led to an increase in the amount of farm work

8   Marjorie Cohen, "The Decline of Women in Canadian Dairying," in Susan Mann Trofimenkoff and Alison Prentice, eds., *The Neglected Majority*, 2 (Toronto: McClelland and Stewart, 1985) p.73.

("outside chores") women are performing on many farms. A greater demand for women to do the farm work has also arisen because an increasing number of farm men have taken off-farm jobs to compensate for farm income shortages.

Even when they are not required to take part in the daily farming chores, farm women have always served as a residual labour force to be called on during peak farming seasons. In grain and horticultural operations, women's farm work increases during planting and harvesting. Women involved in animal husbandry work more hours, more evenly distributed throughout the year, than do those who live on grain or horticultural operations.[9]

Although there is no accurate account of the amount of farm work done by women, from the data available it is obvious that women do a major share of the work on Canadian farms. The first attempt to quantify the contribution of farm women through a survey done by the National Farmers Union in 1982 revealed that women did an average of twenty-seven hours of farm work per week, which represented 16 per cent of all farm work.[10] At the time of the survey women, together with their children, performed four times as much farm work as hired help did.

Like women everywhere, farm women also do almost all of the household work. With most farm homes now modernized, the amount of housework, about fifty hours a week on average, is not unlike that performed by other women.[11] However, the inconvenience of having to go further for goods and services adds time and stress to the domestic workload. Women in farm families, like women elsewhere, also take primary responsibility for the nurture and care of children.

A significant change in the workload of farm women has been the addition of yet another job to the double day. As farm incomes decline, it has become increasingly common and necessary for farm families to search out off-farm income. In 1971, 18.9 per cent of farm women held

9   See Pam Smith, "What Lies within and behind the Statistics?" in *Growing Strong: Women in Agriculture* (Ottawa: Canadian Advisory Council on the Status of Women, 1987), pp.171-73; and Pam Smith, "Murdoch's, Becker's and Sorochan's Challenge: Thinking Again about the Roles of Women in Primary Agriculture," in G.S. Basran and D.A. Hay, eds., *The Political Economy of Agriculture in Western Canada* (Toronto: Garamond, 1988).

10   Susan Koski, *Employment Practices of Farm Women* (Saskatoon: National Farmers Union, 1982). See also Nettie Wiebe, *Weaving New Ways: Farm Women Organizing* (Saskatoon: National Farmers Union, 1987).

11   Jean Wilson, "What Is a Farm Wife Worth?" *Alberta Rural Development Studies*, Series A, Edmonton: 1976. See also Pam Smith, "On and Off the Farm: Trends in Farm Women's Work across Canada and in the Provinces: 1971, 1981 and 1986," in *Broadening Our Horizons: Canadian Farm Women in Decision-Making*, conference proceedings (Ottawa: Canadian Federation of Agriculture, 1991), Table 9,10.

off-farm jobs. By 1981 this number had climbed to 33.6 per cent and in 1986 more than 40 per cent reported a non-agricultural occupation.[12]

Farm women hold many of the off-farm jobs in part because they are not the "primary operator" on most family farms and hence can be spared more easily from the farm work. They are also more likely to be better educated and have professional training than their spouses, which enhances their ability to obtain off-farm employment.[13] An obvious and urgent issue for farm women with young families is the need for child-care services in rural communities, to be used both when parents are away from the farm doing off-farm jobs and when they are working on the farm with dangerous equipment.

The addition of the off-farm job to their work day has had a major impact on the lives of farm women. It has extended their work days to include yet another range of responsibilities. As a consequence, many farm women put in a triple work day.[14] This is reflected in the number of hours that they work during a week. For a farm woman an average work week, which includes domestic work, farm work, and off-farm work, consists of 95 to 103 hours.[15] Although the off-farm work adds to the workload, it also expands the opportunities for a greater variety of work. This is an important advantage for all those farm women who have other professions or career interests. Also important is the fact that off-farm work results in a paycheque for farm women—unlike their farm work. Many farm families depend on that salary to meet household expenses. Farm women spend most of the money they earn on the family or invest it in the farm.

UNCOUNTED AND DISCOUNTED

Although it is a gender-neutral term, "farmer" has almost exclusively male connotations in the English language. Most of the material on agriculture makes reference to "the farmer, *he*" or speaks of "the farmer and *his* sons." The images that come to mind when farmers are referred to are most often

12   Pam Smith, "'Not Enough Hours, Our Accountant Tells Me': Trends in Children's, Women's and Men's Involvement in Canadian Agriculture," *Canadian Journal of Agricultural Economics*, vol.33 (June 1986), p.187. Pam Smith and Ray D. Bollman, "Integration of Canadian Farm and Off-Farm Markets and the Off-Farm Work of Farm Women, Men, and Children," in Basran and Hay, *Political Economy of Agriculture*, pp.185ff.

13   Smith, "What Lies within and behind the Statistics?" pp.143-44.

14   Nettie Wiebe, "Farm Women: The Triple Day," *NeWest Review* December/January 1989.

15   Wiebe, *Weaving New Ways*, p.26; Faye Davis, *The Social, Economic and Legal Equality of Saskatchewan Farm Women* (Saskatoon: Legal Education Action Fund, 1989). The statistics gathered include many older women who no longer have as many child-care duties and are less likely to have off-farm jobs. Hence the number of work hours per week is probably considerably higher for younger farm women.

images of men in overalls and/or on tractors. Reading articles on farming or watching farm advertisements on television serves to reinforce the predominant impression that farming is a male profession.

The exclusive male connotation of the title "farmer" is so pervasive that farm women themselves seldom appropriate it. When they do so they usually qualify the term in a way that draws attention to fact that the "farmer" being discussed is female. The more common way of naming that sector of farming people who are women is to refer to them as "farm wives." This title serves to imply that their status as farm people is definitely a function of their marital status. Other terms, such as "farmerette," have found even less favour, for obvious reasons.

The problem of including women under the rubric of "farmers" extends beyond the language although the language symbolizes and continues to reinforce the exclusion of women from recognition as farmers. Almost all (98 per cent) Canadian farms are family farms. Because virtually all families include women, it is safe to assume that about half the adults living on farms are women. But, as elsewhere, women's identity here is simply submerged in the general language of "family" without trace of their particular role in, or contribution to, the farming unit.[16]

Until 1991 there was no way for farm women to be counted officially as farmers unless they were sole operators of the farm or able to displace their spouses in claiming that title on the Census Canada form.[17] Statistics Canada defines a farm operator as "the person responsible for the day-to-day decisions made in the agricultural operation of this holding." With only one space for the "farm operator" to be named, the census recorded the vast majority of farms as having male operators. Women could name only one occupation, and those who held off-farm jobs usually reported that. Some listed agriculture as their occupation, but many were simply relegated to the "unoccupied" category. A Statistics Canada press release in 1988 notes, "On the Prairies, only a quarter of married women living on farms reported no occupation. In the other provinces, this was up to a third."[18] If a survey frames its questions in a certain way, women who work incredibly long hours end up listing themselves as "unoccupied."

16   Max Hedley, "Normal Expectations: Rural Women without Property," *Resources in Feminist Research* 11,1 (1982), pp.15-16; Smith, "Murdoch's, Becker's and Sorochan's Challenge," pp.168-71.

17   For a thorough, critical discussion of how statistics on farm women are gathered and what is missing, see Smith, "What Lies within and behind the Statistics?" Note the discussion on under-reporting, pp.130-54.

18   Statistics Canada, Press Release, December 5, 1988, reporting on the 1986 census.

The official statistics that have rendered farm women invisible are only one part of the larger picture that leaves out farm women. The importance of being overlooked in the official count, however, is that it not only reflects the general bias against accepting women as farmers but also reinforces their exclusion from the profession insofar as policies are formulated on the basis of those statistics.

The 1991 Statistics Canada Census on Agriculture incorporated a welcome change by allowing several farm operators to be listed. This new way of counting revealed that in 1991, 26 per cent of Canadian farm operators were women.[19] Although this was widely regarded as a great increase in the numbers of women farmers, it signals a bigger change in the methods of gathering information than in the actual situation. Even with improved data-gathering, the current statistics are still probably highly inaccurate. Given the deep-seated patriarchy that characterizes agriculture, methods of gathering data on the work of farm women have a major bearing on what kind of data will be collected. Not only does our language make it difficult for farm women to name themselves as farmers, but also our culture and history make it difficult for farm women to regard themselves as legitimate claimants to that title. Despite their long history of farming, women have received very little recognition or credit and virtually no remuneration for that activity.[20] They are seldom the owners of the land or the animals that they take care of. Industry, government, and financial representatives often insist on dealing with their male counterparts. Most farm women are familiar with the experience of having a farm industry salesman come to the door and ask, "Is the boss home?" They are systematically overlooked as spokespersons or representatives in agriculture. Individual women find it difficult to resist internalizing the view and status accorded them by the society they live in.

Given this background, it could be expected that even to begin to capture the reality of this work the methods of collecting information on the work and lives of farm women would have to go beyond the standard, impersonal questionnaire. Indeed, when farm women are asked to name or assess their work, their own responses reflect the general discounting of that work. Their first response is frequently to back away from the title of "farmer." "I don't really farm, George is the farmer. I just help along sometimes." One telling survey in eastern Ontario asked a small group of farm women what percentage of the on-farm work they

19   Statistics Canada, Census in Agriculture, *The Daily*, November 17, 1992.

20   Norma Taylor, "All This for Three and a Half a Day," in Gwen Matheson, ed., *Women in the Canadian Mosaic* (Toronto: Peter Martin Associates, 1976).

did, as well as how frequently they participated in farm work. Most said they were doing a minor share of the farm work. But in further questioning some who had "said they did virtually no on-farm work were found to be doing regular field and barn chores—some regularly milked cows or cared for farm animals, others regularly harvested crops, plowed, disked and cultivated, all but one did the farm books as well as their household work."[21] For the most part the women surveyed valued their labour on the farm as worth less than $5,000 a year.

In general, very little reliable data has been gathered on the work of contemporary farm women. But in a culture in which to be uncounted is to be discounted, this leaves farm women at a distinct disadvantage in arguing for equality and justice for themselves. Hence the importance of accurately quantifying the work and conditions of farm women.

Agrarian feminists have long recognized the importance, as well as the difficulty, of documenting and quantifying women's work both in and outside the home. As early as 1920 the Women's Section of the United Farmers of Manitoba began collecting data by conducting a survey of forty-eight farm homes. Two years later, in 1923, the Women Grain Growers of Saskatchewan expanded the survey and then followed it up with a mailed survey.[22]

The first national attempt by farm women to quantify their own work was undertaken by the women of the National Farmers Union in 1980. Recognizing how farm women depreciate and underestimate their own work when they find themselves in an impersonal question/answer position, the women of the NFU carefully designed a process to try to change this situation. Teams of farm women were trained in conducting interviews and women's meetings in such a way as to involve the interviewers and interviewees in an interactive process. All of the participants in the process had a stake in the information being gathered and were themselves contributors to that information. In group and team discussions at kitchen tables and in more formal meetings, farm women worked together to describe and give measure to the amount and kinds of work they did. They drew diagrams, told stories, compared experiences, and supported the speaking of their own reality. The whole process of quan-

21   Susan Watkins, "What Are You Worth? A Study of the Economic Contribution of Eastern Ontario Farm Women to the Family Farm Enterprise," *Women for the Survival of Agriculture*, Winchester, Ont. 1985.

22   Veronica Strong-Boag, "Pulling in Double Harness or Hauling a Double Load: Women, Work and Feminism on the Canadian Prairie," *Journal of Canadian Studies* 21,3 (1986), p.37; Mary Kinnear, "'Do You Want Your Daughter to Marry a Farmer?': Women's Work on the Farm, 1922," in Donald Akenson, ed., *Papers in Rural History*, vol.VI (Gananoque, Ont.: Longdale, 1988).

tifying the workload and experience was done as much as possible in an environment in which women could feel safe in departing from the public perceptions of what they did, how much of it, and of what importance, to articulate their own assessments. More limited subsequent surveys have reiterated most of the findings, supporting the efficacy of the method.[23] Unfortunately, the information is in need of updating because the circumstances and work on farms have changed considerably since the report was produced in 1982.

Women's failure to be publicly recognized and valued as farmers is grounded in, and reinforced by, the patriarchal patterns of land ownership in this country.[24] The publicly instituted regulations that distributed homesteads to males solidified the control over land in men's hands. Only in exceptional cases could pioneering women in the west become the owners of land farmed by their families.[25] Those early patrilineal patterns of ownership and inheritance continue to hold sway, making it much more likely that farm land will be deeded to sons than to daughters.

Although there has been some ameliorating legislation to protect farm women, their ownership position remains minor. In the prairies, legislative changes to give farm women some protection against eviction from their farms were gradually introduced by each of the provincial governments before the 1920s.[26] The Matrimonial Property Acts passed in most provinces during the 1970s improved the legal claims of farm women to at least part of the farm upon the dissolution of marriages. But two decades later few women actually have their names on land titles. Land ownership remains primarily a male prerogative.

23   See Wiebe, *Weaving New Ways*, pp.21, 26, 70, for several such comparisons.

24   Smith, "Murdoch's, Becker's and Sorochan's Challenge," p.171, notes land ownership as first among the four factors that are "impediments to the recognition of women's contributions to agriculture. The underlying structural factor of unequal ownership is one, which finds its expression in the other three: patriarchal attitudes within the family and larger community; women's attitudes towards themselves as individuals and towards other women and in our 'scholarship' on this topic."

25   For a discussion of the early struggle of women to gain access to land in western Canada that was being distributed free of charge by the government of Canada in order to lure settlers into the west, see Susan Jackel's Introduction to a new edition of *Wheat and Women* (Toronto: University of Toronto Press, 1979; originally published 1914). The Dominion Lands Act, 1872, provided that "every person who is the sole head of a family and males over age 18" could apply for the free 160-acre homestead. Women who were widowed, divorced, or, in exceptional cases, deserted, might qualify but rarely succeeded in being granted title to homestead land.

26   In Alberta the 1915 "Alberta Married Women's Home Protection Act" gave a wife the right to prevent any transaction involving her homesite. (This was slightly revised but not significantly changed with the 1917 "Alberta Dower Act.") The Manitoba "Dower Act," 1918, and the Saskatchewan "Devolution of Estates Act," 1919, gave married women some limited claim to their homesites.

Increased public discussion of farm women's status, coupled with a more general awareness of gender equality issues, appears to have created for farm women the impression or belief that they have achieved equal partnership on the farm. Whereas 45 per cent of the farm women surveyed in 1991 claimed to be "partners" in their farming operations, only 9 per cent of family farms have partnership agreements or incorporation documents.[27]

It is not surprising, then, that there is a long list of issues that agrarian feminists see as critical. The list includes equality of status within the industry as whole and on the family farm itself; recognition of, and adequate remuneration for, the work they perform; and an improved infrastructure, including flexible and appropriate rural child-care services. Agrarian feminists share many concerns with their urban counterparts, such as equal pay for work of equal value, an end to violence against women, and a myriad of other oppressions experienced by women in our society.

THE OFFICIAL DECISION-MAKING STRUCTURES

The "agricultural industry," as modern industrialized food production is often referred to, is male dominated at all decision-making levels. At the corporate level, agribusiness firms are as securely in the hands of men as are corporations in other sectors. Government agriculture departments are virtually bereft of women in senior or policy-making positions. The federal department, Agriculture Canada, has no women in senior positions in the policy branch, although it did establish a Status of Women Unit 1981. The unit was renamed the Farm Women's Bureau in 1986, and part of its mandate is the inclusion of farm women in consultations on policy issues in agriculture. It consists of a director and a policy analyst who administer a small programming fund and seek to liaise between farm women's organizations and policy advisors. Given its small size and resources, the Farm Women's Bureau can only provide a muted, tentative female voice in agriculture policy-making within the Department of Agriculture as a whole.[28]

27   Frances Shaver, in a Farm Women's Bureau research paper, "Farm Women and Agriculture: An Overview of Issues," January 1991, p.6. Pam Smith puts the figures at 6 per cent partnerships in 1971 and 19 per cent in 1981. These include "written and unwritten" partnerships, however, and given the various data collection methods, the statistics may reflect the impression women have of their ownership status rather than their actual legal claim.

28   Despite its limited resources, the Farm Women's Bureau has been very useful for organized farm women in providing research, information, interorganizational consultations, and government contacts, as well as some financial support for specific projects and meetings.

Provincial agriculture departments, with the exception of the province of Quebec, have no provisions for including farm women in policy-
making processes. The government of Quebec has established a funded
programme and action plan to improve the status of women in agriculture.[29] It has also sent the description of its endeavours to other provincial agriculture departments, with no discernible results to date.

A faltering farm economy has resulted in a need for off-farm income
on many farms. Because farm women earn a good deal of that income,
both governments and financial institutions have included more women
in discussions of how farm finances must be managed, debt payments
met, or, in many cases, the "rural transition" achieved. Women who
were never before included in planning and financial decisions now find
themselves meeting with bankers when their farm accounts are in ar-
rears.

The spate of farm management training courses initiated by the provincial and federal governments in response to the farm financial crisis
of the 1980s included a series of courses specifically designed for farming
couples. These "Farming to Win" courses worked from the premise that
farm families needed to set goals and make financial plans that took account of both the husband's and the wife's strengths and earning poten-
tials.[30]

It is not a new phenomenon that women make advances towards the
goal of equality during hard times, when "equality" is interpreted as the
chance to occupy spaces and perform functions previously reserved for
men. Much as women temporarily filled in in the shortage of labour
during World War II, gaining a momentary foothold in the industrial labour force, earning their own wages and a greater measure of independence and equality, farm women today are making progress towards
gaining a foothold because their earning power is needed. The blessing
is not unmixed. A woman whose family farm was in a financial crisis
commented, "It's *his* farm, it's *our* debt, and it's *my* fault."

Farm women continue to have difficulty arranging financial credit and
being treated by bankers and businesses as independent, autonomous
adults. As in other sectors, achieving this status is not a simple matter of
changing openly sexist policies. If woman are to gain a place as legitimate
farmers, many of the current underlying assumptions influencing the interpretation of policy in these institutions will have to be changed.

29   "The Policies of the Ministère de L'Agriculture des Pêcheries et de Alimentation to Improve
      the Status of Women in Agriculture: 1992-95," Government of Quebec, 1992.

30   The standard target group for these more inclusive initiatives is heterosexual farming cou-
      ples. To date no programmes or information are targeted to include either lesbian couples or
      sole women operators.

The farm organizations that influence agricultural policy and provide a wide range of services and functions for agricultural producers are almost entirely male. Most of the approximately 450 farm organizations in Canada have no women in executive positions. Although many have some form of electoral or democratic procedures in place for selecting leadership, these processes only rarely succeed in putting women on boards of directors or delegate bodies. Those that are formed to pursue specific economic goals or farm business interests, such as marketing boards or commodity groups, are even less likely to have women participants than the general farm organizations that have broader mandates or purposes.[31]

Despite the long history of activist farm women, the "mainstream" farm organizations continue to reinforce the view that farmers are men and important decisions in agriculture should appropriately be left to men. Not only does the predominantly male leadership reinforce this, but the membership of most of these organizations is also mostly male. In many cases, only one vote is allowed per farm and the "primary operator" is the voting member. In others, where individual memberships and votes are permitted, women seldom join, leaving membership to their spouses. Not surprisingly, farm organization meetings are most often gatherings of men only.

Historically, the progressive farm movement[32] was influenced to begin changing this male-only make-up by introducing women's positions into its structure. Women's struggle to gain entry met with some success when the Saskatchewan Grain Growers' Association, Women's Section, was formed in 1914. The prairie farm women of Alberta and Manitoba formed such sections in their provincial organizations in 1915; Ontario followed in 1918. These women's sections gave women a place within the bigger organization rather than relegating them to segregated auxiliary organizations.[33]

31   For statistics on women in leadership positions in various Canadian farm organizations, see Lynne Nieman's presentation to "Broadening Our Horizons: Canadian Farm Women in Decision Making," conference proceedings (Ottawa: Canadian Federation of Agriculture, 1991); and Smith, "What Lies within and behind the Statistics?" pp.183-91.

32   I am using the term "progressive" as a positive, evaluative term to denote positions valuing broader social and cultural goals as well as economic interests. The term has a socialist connotation insofar as it captures the view that egalitarianism and justice must include diminishing the structural and social factors that lead to the inequality of people's power to make decisions in areas that affect them.

33   Georgina Taylor describes some of the choices between segregation or integration facing women who strove to participate in farm politics earlier in this century in "Should I Drown Myself Now or Later?" pp.88-92.

Currently, the only mainstream farm organization that ensures women's representation at the executive level is the National Farmers Union.[34] Following in the tradition of the prairie unions that amalgamated to form part of it, the National Farmers Union reserves elected positions for women, both to ensure that there will always be women at the decision-making level of the organization and to encourage the participation of women through special women's programming.

The usefulness of these affirmative action positions within the National Farmers Union continues to be questioned both within the organization and elsewhere.[35] The most frequent challenges are based on the argument that women's positions are both divisive and no longer necessary because women already enjoy equality within the organization. Actual experience does not support this argument. Women hold official positions at all levels of the farmers' union but are not close to achieving equal representation or influence at any of these levels. This is especially apparent at the local levels, where overall member participation is low and very few women attend any local meetings at all. About a third of the participants at the annual national meetings are women.

In broad outline, there are three options open to farm women who want to take part in the organized, public discussion of their industry. They have the option of seeking to work within the male-dominated agricultural organizations with no special reference to, or recognition of, their gender. A second alternative is to form separate women's organizations in which women form the entire leadership and build their own agenda. The third option is to seek constitutional guarantees for the participation of women within the decision-making structures of farm organizations. Farm women have used all of these strategies.

FARM WOMEN ORGANIZING

The agrarian feminist movement has deep historical roots in rural Canada. The early landmark battles over the right to vote and the claim to legal status as persons are a recorded and well-known part of that move-

---

34 Women have occasionally gained leadership positions in other farm organizations. Recent examples include Bridget Pyke, who served several terms as president of the Ontario Federation of Agriculture, and Marlene Cowling, second vice-president of the Keystone Agricultural Producers for two terms. The Canadian Federation of Agriculture changed the previous observer status of the two women's representatives on its board of directors to voting status in 1992.

35 For a discussion of the internal NFU debate on this issue see Wiebe, *Weaving New Ways*, pp.8-14. A brief description of the role of women in several of Canada's large farm organizations is given in "Broadening Our Horizons," pp.8-9.

ment. Less well known are farm women's struggles for better living conditions, better health care, and birth control. For example, under the leadership of Violet McNaughton, Sophia Dixon, and others, Saskatchewan women advocated for legalized birth control and socialized health care throughout the 1920s and 1930s. Their campaign for better healthcare services, begun in 1914, led eventually to the implementation of medicare, first in Saskatchewan (1962) and later in Canada (1967).

The struggle to make birth control legal and available was equally lengthy. After fomenting public discussion on the issue throughout the 1920s, the women successfully spearheaded a resolution through the United Farmers of Canada, Saskatchewan Section, asking to have birth-control clinics attached to hospitals. This innovation would have required changes to the Criminal Code, which made dissemination of birth-control information a punishable offence. However, the resolution was rescinded a year later, apparently in preparation for the formation of the Farmer/Labour party (CCF) in 1933.[36] Birth control was not legalized in Canada until 1969.

The farm women's movement did not evaporate in the years between the pre-World War II period and the 1960s. As with the women's movement in general, the apparent lull in activism reflected changing conditions and situations for women.[37] For farm women, the rapid industrialization of food production promised improved living conditions and better incomes. Nevertheless, farm women of the progressive farm movement continued to maintain their organized sections within the provincial farm unions throughout that period, and they succeeded in retaining affirmative action positions when these organizations amalgamated to form the National Farmers Union in 1969.

By the 1970s it was becoming apparent to many farm women who were not involved in farm organizations that better farm incomes did not necessarily translate into a better position for themselves on the family farm. Although conditions in general were much better as rural areas acquired modern utilities and services, women's overall position remained unchanged relative to their male counterparts. They were still working on the farm without any recognition or remuneration for their work; and they were still economically dependent on the farm while being left out of decision-making both on the public-policy level and on many of their own farms. They remained a subsidiary, unpaid labour

---

36   Conversations with Sophia Dixon.

37   See Naomi Black, "The Canadian Women's Movement: The Second Wave," in Sandra Burt, Lorraine Code and Lindsay Dorney, eds., *Changing Patterns: Women in Canada*, 2nd ed. (Toronto: McClelland & Stewart, 1993), pp.151-76 (see especially pp.153-56).

force with virtually no ownership position.

Increased mobility and communications helped to bring urban discussions about women's liberation into the rural consciousness. Although the second wave of the women's movement was essentially urban-based, its ripples were felt in the countryside.

Another factor that may have contributed to a growing gender consciousness, especially among younger farm women, is that many of them were themselves urban transplants, and they brought their urban values and expectations with them.[38] The influence of the feminist movement from urban Canada has continued to be strong as more farm women spend more of their time at jobs in towns and cities.

Several high-profile legal cases in the 1970s also served to heighten awareness among farm women about their own position. In the most widely publicized of these, *Murdock vs. Murdock* (1975), a woman who had made some of the initial investment in the farm and worked alongside her husband for several decades as well as taking responsibility for the domestic workload was found, upon dissolution of the marriage, to have no rights to any of the property acquired. The case was so patently unjust that even those with a high tolerance for injustice to women were repelled. This and other cases highlighted the need for better matrimonial property acts.The case also focused the attention of farm women on their vulnerability. Organized farm women took an active hand in drafting new matrimonial property legislation and used the issue to raise issues of gender equality on the farm.

A description from Jean Leahy, the Women's President of the National Farmers Union (1975-80), captures the grassroots consciousness-raising and practical activism this issue evoked.

> I took office in 1975, International Women's Year. I hadn't really thought alot about whether or not I was a feminist. I knew that women should be able to have property, they should have their names on it, they should have their own bank accounts but along came IWY and we were the women in charge of the NFU. Provinces started to change their Matrimonial Property Acts and we had to know the legislation in each province. We had workshops everywhere to talk about what the legislation should be—workshops with men and women. Sometimes they were pretty tense be-

---

38   Adjustment to farm life and complaints about the inequalities on the farm remain the grist
     for amusing anecdotes and serious discussions. See, for example, the popular and amusing
     booklet, *The Farmer Takes a Wife*, by Gisele Ireland (Chelsey, Ont.: Concerned Farm
     Women, 1983), or comments from Donna Lunn (Ontario Farm Women's Network) to the
     Senate Standing Committee on Agriculture and Forestry, March 2, 1993.

cause all of a sudden the men started thinking "Now this woman wants some of MY property". But also some really good things happened and I'll never forget one fellow who said "you know until this legislation was proposed and we had to think about matrimonial property I just assumed that my wife owned half of everything. Now I know legally she has nothing." And he was really exasperated by it. Both men and women were unaware of these things.[39]

The 1980s was a period of vigorous reorganization among farm women. Small local organizations sprang up where women gathered together to share their experiences and press for recognition of their contribution and better treatment. Some of these organizations, such as Concerned Farm Women, Women for the Survival of Agriculture, and Women in Support of Agriculture, formed chapters in several locations in Ontario, Alberta, and Prince Edward Island. These organizations have several characteristics in common.[40]

First, they are women's organizations that segregate women from the mainstream male-dominated farm organizations for the purpose of gaining greater recognition for farm women. Membership in these organizations may be open to men but they remain women's organizations. They deliberately separate women into their own organizations so that women can gain recognition and have organized input into organizations. However, they do not engage in critical analysis of the mainstream farm organizations, whose mandate is to give organized farmers input into agricultural policy, for failing to include the participation of women like themselves. Instead, they look for education and leadership training that will help them gain entry into these mainstream agricultural organizations.

Second, they do not view themselves as modern off-shoots of the earlier Homemakers or the old-line organizations such as the Women's Institutes.[41] Their emphasis is on the professional status of farm women as equal partners in their industry rather than on the "softer" social-gath-

39   Quoted in Wiebe, *Weaving New Ways*, p.43.

40   There are, of course, differences in emphases and approaches among these various organizations. For example, Women for the Survival of Agriculture denotes itself as feminist, whereas Concerned Farm Women eschews that description.

41   See Ella Haley, "Getting Our Act Together: The Ontario Farm Women's Movement," in Jeri Dawn Wine and Janice L. Ristock, eds., *Women and Social Change* (Toronto: James Lorimer, 1991), pp.169-83; and Pauline Rankin, "The Politicization of Ontario Farm Women," in Linda Kealey and Joan Sangster, eds., *Beyond the Vote: Canadian Women and Politics* (Toronto: University of Toronto Press, 1989), pp.309-32.

ering and community service orientation of the Women's Institutes or the Cercle des Fermières in Quebec.

Unfortunately, the low status of farm women in their industry is not just due to the decision-makers' shortage of information and education about their work and worth. Men in the industry enjoy the economic advantages and privileges that come from having the crucial support of a large body of unpaid and unrecognized labour without having to share the control and decision-making prerogatives with that group. So the surveys and information pamphlets detailing women's agricultural work may have raised the profile of Canadian farm women in various quarters, but they have not been entirely efficacious in bringing about the structural and cultural changes sought by agrarian feminists.

The difficulty of persuading the male-run farm organizations to give equal place and power to women can be circumvented by the creation of farm women's organizations. However, because farm women frequently find it hard to identify themselves as legitimate practitioners of their own trade, they are not easily drawn into any organization, even a women's organization, built on that identity.

These factors, coupled with the large amounts of energy, commitment, and finances necessary to build and maintain any organization, have made it difficult to sustain many of the new farm women's groups. Some, such as Concerned Farm Women, have disbanded altogether, while others have combined with provincial farm women's networks.[42]

Although rural women have the same range of ideological differences as their urban counterparts, their organizations made a conscious attempt to meet in a national forum in 1980. The first national farm women's conference was organized with input from all of the major organizations and it succeeded in drawing participants from across Canada. Despite amicable relations, attempts to amalgamate all of the organizations into a single network/organization that would be the "voice of all Canadian farm women" were unsuccessful.

The conflict at the fourth Canadian Farm Women's Conference (Saint John, N.B., November 1989), where delegates pushed forward the formation of a new national farm women's organization, served to highlight the ideological and political differences that separated the various groups.[43] The oldest of the organizations represented, the Federated Women's Institute of Canada, has a long history of drawing rural

42   The end of Concerned Farm Women is reported in "Seven Year Fight for Family Farms Collapses," *The Toronto Star*, February 17, 1989. Haley describes the movement of Ontario-based farm women's organizations into networks in "Getting Our Act Together," pp.181-83.

43   "Baptized in Fire," *The Western Producer*, November 23, 1989. "Farm Women's Conference, 1989," *Country Guide*, January 1990.

women together for support, education, social life, and community service. Their wider rural women's constituency encompasses more small-town and village women than farming women. Their status and financial security were threatened by the formation of a national farm women's group, which was also to receive core funding from the Department of Agriculture. Women of the National Farmers Union also opposed the formation of an all-encompassing farm women's organization, again because such an organization would compete for scarce government project funding. The women of the Farmers Union saw this as the resurfacing of the age-old problem of public funding being used to support women's organizations that would undermine the voice of those who engaged in socialist feminist analysis and activism.[44]

But the funding dispute was only a symptom of deeper differences. The Canadian Farm Women's Network, which emerged out of the conference, is at best a liberal-feminist organization with no public admission of feminism at all.[45] It continues to be committed to gaining "recognition" for farm women and entry into the current decision-making structures in agriculture by raising the profile of farm women.[46] In contrast, the women of the National Farmers Union lean more towards socialist feminism, challenging the structures within which agricultural decisions are made as well as the male domination of the industry as a whole, from the farmstead to the ministry.

To be seen as making progress on the participation of women in mainstream farm organizations, the federal agriculture ministry prevailed upon the Canadian Federation of Agriculture, a large umbrella farm organization, to host a conference on this question in 1990. The original conference name, "Barriers to Participation," was changed to "Broadening Our Horizons," which avoided having to confront the issue of women's participation as a structural one.

The conference discussion was instructive. Although many speakers lamented the fact that women were vastly under-represented in farm organizations, there was little support for or interest in the affirmative ac-

44   L.J. Wilson, "Educating the Saskatchewan Farmer: The Educational Work of the Saskatchewan Grain Growers' Association," *Saskatchewan History*, Winter 1978, p.27. Note that the Women's Institutes, and the Homemakers before them, have always been subsidized by governments.

45   For a good discussion of the various strands of feminism, see Lorraine Code, "Feminist Theory," in Burt, Code, and Dorney, *Changing Patterns*. The apt description of liberal feminism includes their assumption that "the structures themselves need no modifications beyond those that would automatically come about if women were included on an equal basis with men" (p.37).

46   See, for example, the Canadian Farm Women's Network 1993 conference discussion reported in "Women Urged to Join Mainstream Groups," *The Western Producer*, December 19, 1993, p.52.

tion model of the National Farmers Union. Women continued to argue that leadership must be based on merit and that the lack of women in key positions was obviously a comment on their ability, knowledge, and/or commitment. The conference also discussed women's lack of time and money and their responsibility for domestic and child-care duties, but with little analysis of why these conditions function to exclude women particularly, rather than excluding all members of the farm family equally. Nor was any consensus reached on whether farm organizations themselves were structured in such a way as to bar women from full participation.

A similar question about the absence of women in farm organizations at a workshop of the Alberta Farm Women's Conference (Red Deer, October 1989) progressed through a series of stages of understanding. The first response to the question "Why are women not equal in farm organizations?" met with denial and an adamant "We *are* equal if we think of ourselves as equal." The reality of representation could not be denied, however, so personal self-blame came next. "We are not self-confident enough," or "We don't work hard enough or take the time to participate." This analysis could only be sustained until more self-examination had been done. Then individual husbands were named as the real barriers "George won't let her go to meetings." Eventually, after George and Roger and Don had been flagged, a larger picture emerged. It was not just individual husbands here and there who seemed to intervene, but rather a whole social structure or process of socialization that made it seem improper or impossible for women to participate in those organizations. The conclusion that the structures themselves were hostile to women's equality and full participation within them was not reached happily.[47]

WAYS OF WORKING

Like women everywhere, farm women frequently have difficulty recognizing and acknowledging their own expertise. The value of their work, their skills, and their experience are discounted or underrated when they are compared with the more technical production expertise claimed by farm men. Although more women are becoming the primary operators of farms, and there is an increasing number of women graduating from

47   From the author's notes of the workshop.

colleges of agriculture, technical expertise continues to be predominantly male; and the public voice of agriculture is almost entirely male.

This problem is being dealt with in several ways, and the methods of approaching it reveal a good deal about the underlying analysis. Those who subscribe to the view that women lack the necessary knowledge to be confident about their expertise in agriculture adopt a strategy of educating women about the issues. The best way of getting the real information on the issues is obviously to engage the real experts. It is not uncommon to find that seminars or conferences organized by farm women's groups have programmes filled by male speakers. For example, in the recent conference organized to celebrate its tenth anniversary, the Alberta Women in Support of Agriculture Association featured eight men and one woman as presenters.[48] This practice continues to reinforce the message that agricultural expertise is male expertise.

In contrast, progressive agrarian feminists work to build expertise and self-confidence among farm women by affirming women's knowledge, and by sharing that knowledge. Women's meetings in the National Farmers Union usually feature a man to lead a discussion or make a presentation only when a woman cannot be found to do the job. This strategy is designed not only to affirm the expertise of women but also to challenge the whole notion of what kind of knowledge is most valuable or what constitutes real expertise in farming.

The question of what constitutes a genuine and important farm issue is a complex topic for farm women's organizations. There is a good deal of tension between the view that so-called "women's issues" are less important than the "real farm issues" (product marketing, commodity production, and pricing) and the contention that women have no choice but to work on women's issues such as child care, gender equality, and community services. The women who adopt the prevailing evaluation that places women's concerns, the so-called "social issues," secondary to the economic issues object that to deal with women's issues will leave them out of the important decisions in agriculture.[49]

Attempts to resolve this conflict often include the argument that there really are no "women's issues" per se, only family issues. After all, children are the responsibility of the whole family, and hence child care, for example, cannot be said to be a women's issue only. The truth in this

48 Alberta Women in Support of Agriculture Association, "Farming Beyond 2000" conference brochure, High River, Alberta, November 5-6, 1993.

49 Canadian Farm Women's Network conference-goers were advised to get "involved with a farm lobby group because some women's groups don't deal with hard enough issues. 'Women's farm groups are good but it's hard to move to the big stuff.'" "Women Urged to Join Mainstream Groups," The Western Producer, December 19, 1993.

argument does not overcome the reality that it is women who have primary responsibility for child care and that women are therefore faced
with the necessity of doing something about it.

Farm women activists can be tempted to stay with the social or
women's issues because there is more likely to be agreement on the
needs and solutions in that sphere. The current trend towards interorganizational consultations and even joint projects between the various
farm women's organizations seems to demonstrate this. The national
networking conferences of the 1980s, which dealt more with general
farm policy issues, resulted in few concrete agreements, while the first
national conference on rural child care, which had delegates from all the
major farm women's organizations in Canada, passed a unanimous
resolution on rural child care.[50]

There is a complex integration between the economic and social elements everywhere in society. This is especially true for women on family
farms, where the workplace and the domicile are combined. Unlike the
waged worker, whose economic activity can be separated at least superficially from private, domestic life, work life and domestic life are so
closely bound together on most family farms that it is difficult to sort out
where the business ends and the private life begins. It is this complex
and inseparable integration of the work, lives, and economic fate of the
men and women who make up family farm units that persuades many
contemporary agrarian feminists, including myself, to continue to work
within the structure of a mainstream organization instead of building
separate farm women's organizations.

The "women's work" within the progressive farm movement has always been to broaden the agenda beyond "the price of barley" to include
women's, familial, social, and environmental issues.[51] However, work
within such an organization requires double duty from women. To hold
their place as credible spokespersons for the organization they must, of
course, keep abreast of the "price of barley" issues. But to work as
women within the organization they must also encourage the participation of other women. This requires special programming, which becomes an added workload.

To facilitate this work, the women of the National Farmers Union
have developed various organizing tools and strategies. The tools in-

50   Proceedings of the National Conference on Farm Women's Employment, November 1992;
     available from the Fédération des Agricultrices du Québec, Montreal.

51   See the Policy Manual of the National Farmers Union, 1994.

clude resource kits for organizing, information pamphlets, cookbooks, and poems. The strategies are those of women working together for justice and equality everywhere: collective, community-based work on shared agendas that speak to the experiences and values of women. They include social and cultural elements: songs, stories, poetry, and games.

The immense workload and particular circumstances of farm women make it necessary to acknowledge and come to grips with the balance between their private lives and their public purposes.[52] Farm women are adapting feminist analysis and strategies in order to make progress in understanding and changing the position of women in farming, rather than just to cope with the traditional disadvantages. With a changing context over time, agrarian feminists have had to adapt their working strategies, moving to more conference calls instead of neighbourhood meetings, for example, or using radio spots as well as pamphlets and letters. They continue to search for better ways of working with each other and with their urban counterparts on issues of common concern. Although the methods have to be modified to accommodate a changed context, the deeply rooted aspirations of gaining their rightful place as respected, remunerated, autonomous persons in the farming community remain firmly in place.

52   See the Proceedings of the National Farmers Union Women's Planning Workshop, Bruno, Sask., November 4-7, 1993, available from the National Farmers Union, Saskatoon, Sask.

SUGGESTED READINGS

Canadian Advisory Council on the Status of Women, *Growing Strong: Women in Agriculture*. Ottawa: Canadian Advisory Council on the Status of Women, 1987.

Ella Haley, "Getting Our Act Together: The Ontario Farm Women's Movement," in Jeri Dawn Wine and Janice L. Ristock, eds., *Women and Social Change*. Toronto: Lorimer, 1991.

Molly McGhee, *The Changing Scene: Women in Rural Life*. Toronto: Ontario Ministry of Agriculture and Food, 1983.

Pauline Rankin, "The Politicization of Ontario Farm Women," in Linda Kealy and Joan Sangster, eds., *Beyond the Vote: Canadian Women and Politics*. Toronto: University of Toronto Press, 1989.

Pam Smith, "Murdoch's, Becker's and Sorochan's Challenge: Thinking Again About the Roles of Women in Primary Agriculture," in G.S. Basran and David A. Hay, eds., *The Political Economy of Agriculture in Western Canada*. Toronto: Garamond, 1988.

Pam Smith, "'Not Enough Hours, Our Accountant Tells Me': Trends in Children's, Women's and Men's Involvement in Canadian Agriculture," *Canadian Journal of Agricultural Economics* 33, (1986).

Georgina Taylor, "'A Splendid Field Before Us': Violet McNaughton and the Development of Agrarian Feminism in Canada, 1909 to 1926," *Prairie Forum*, publication pending.

Georgina Taylor, "'Should I Drown Myself Now or Later?' The Isolation of Rural Women in Saskatchewan and Their Participation the Homemakers' Clubs, the Farm Movement and the Co-operative Commonwealth Federation 1910-1967," in Kathleen Storrie, ed., *Women: Isolation and Bonding—The Ecology of Gender*. Toronto: Methuen, 1987.

Wiebe, Nettie, *Weaving New Ways: Farm Women Organizing*. Saskatoon: National Farmers Union, 1987.

KRISTIN COLWELL

Chapter Seven: Child Care: A Community Issue

MY THOUGHTS ABOUT YOUNG FAMILIES IN THE 1990S HAVE prompted me to examine the connections that might be developed among feminists, the child-care community, and parents. The nature of the relationship between child caregivers and parents is obvious; the connection to feminism is less obvious. As a feminist early childhood education (ECE) instructor at a community college, I am interested in how these different groups share common ground. One of my goals here is to examine the areas of contact and overlap among child caregivers and feminists.[1]

Feminism is a perspective on social arrangements that seeks not just to promote equity, but also to legitimize women's ways of being.[2] Women who care for children, women who advocate on behalf of child care, or women who explore and reveal the structure of women's lives all have important, if differing, perspectives on the social web of community life. Yet frequently the isolation of one group from another precludes the formation of allegiances and prevents healthy cross-fertilization. What is needed, I think, is a dialogue on a kind of collaboration that can support women who care about children and about women.

I identify myself foremost as an advocate for children. My feminism is linked to this advocacy because I believe that, as Shulamit Reinharz puts it, "feminist research aims to create social change,"[3] and that child

---

1   I would like to acknowledge the invaluable support given me by Pat Wright throughout the writing of the chapter.

2   Shulamit Reinharz, *Feminist Methods in Social Research* (New York: Oxford University Press, 1992), p.240.

3   Reinharz, *Feminist Methods*, p.240.

care, like education, can be seen as the cradle of social change. Because "the family" has changed to the extent that most parents require child care outside of the home, the primary responsibility for children's daily experiences, and thus for their healthy development, is spread among unrelated adults more frequently than had been the practice in recent times in western societies. My advocacy rests on the conviction that in child care all acts make a difference whether they are acts done or left undone and that the cumulative impact of child care will be positive or harmful for society as a whole. Indifferent care has an immediate, dulling effect, which in the long term can undermine healthy development in children. The quality of the care is always an indication of what the caregiver, whoever that person is, considers to be the worth of children in any society.

Changes in Canadian society in the second half of the twentieth century have had profound repercussions for families. Daily lives are now far more complex than they were at the beginning of the century. New challenges have emerged that have not yet been fully met. One such challenge, of special pertinence for parents, is to ensure that good quality care is readily available for children in an era of dual-parent labour-force participation and single-parent families; an era when the nuclear family's pattern of stay-at-home mother, wage-earning father, and dependent children is no longer the norm. In fact, the middle-class nuclear family is a recent and short-lived phenomenon in the history of family arrangements, and many researchers consider it to be an unnatural phenomenon.[4] As Betty Friedan argued in 1963, middle-class women who work in the home lead stunted lives when they are confined to repetitious, trivial activities, even though they have an economic security that is envied by less affluent women, and despite the comfort of "normality" that their situation seems to offer.

In this chapter I explore developments in child care and examine the impact of feminism on early childhood education, in particular with a view to considering public provisions for flexibility and for the development of good citizenship. I consider how, in recent decades, Canadian adults have been finding diverse ways to conduct their daily lives. While traditional patterns and expectations dictated family structure in the past, there are now what Craig McKie calls "multiple normalcies of family life."[5]

4   For a discussion of the economic boom of the 1950s, during which single-family suburban housing and the ideology of the middle-class, white, heterosexual family mushroomed, see Stephanie Coontz, *The Way We Never Were* (New York: Basic Books, 1992), ch.2.

5   Craig McKie, "Demographic Changes and Quality-of-Life," in *Family Security in Insecure Times* (Ottawa: Canadian Council on Social Development, Publications, 1993), p.118.

THE PRESENT STATUS OF CHILD CARE IN CANADA

Census statistics indicate that the majority of Canadian children, many from before their first birthday, are experiencing care outside the home.[6] The greatest number of these children are in arrangements that their parents have made privately with a babysitter or a relative. Only 15 per cent of children under five are enroled in licensed child-care centres. Before- and after-school care for children from six to twelve years old reflects similar trends, with the smallest number (3.8 per cent) attending supervised, licensed programs.[7] Everywhere in Canada parental preference for centre-based care is documented by long waiting lists. However, even when spaces are available, many parents cannot afford the fees and must therefore turn to the unregulated sector. Many parents, especially of the middle classes, believe that the care provided by a day-care facility is more educational and offers their children opportunities to develop social skills and make friends. Day-care environments that score high on rating scales are shown to have positive effects on children's development.[8] Many parents speak gratefully about their experi-

---

6   Definitions of child-care terminology in Canada:

- *Nanny:* typically a trained caregiver who comes to or boards in the home of the child.

- *Babysitter/Childminder:* an untrained person who comes to the home of a child when called— an irregular arrangement.

- *Home-Care Provider:* a person, untrained or trained, who takes in children in her own home.

- *Home-Care Agency:* an agency that provides administrative and support services to women who look after children in their own homes. The number and combination of ages of children are regulated, the agency and/or the homes may be licensed.

- *Nursery School:* a half-day licensed program of social and cognitive enrichment for pre-schoolers. Some portion of staff is trained in early childhood education (ECE).

- *Day care:* care provided in a licensed centre for infants, toddlers, or preschool children during parents' working hours, primarily 8 a.m. to 6 p.m. Some centres are able to accommodate ill children or shift work. The majority of staff has training in ECE.

- *Family Resource Centre:* a community facility for parents, caregivers, ECE students, that provides information, programming, and toy lending, as well as drop-in programs, evening courses, library, consulting, and neighbourhood networking.

7   "Focus on Child Care," Centre for International Statistics, Canadian Council on Social Development, *Newsletter* 2 (July 1993).

8   Assessment through ECERS: the Early Childhood Environmental Rating Scale, a tool developed by Thelma Harms and Richard Clifford, Teachers College Press, New York, 1980, and

ences when their children attend or have attended centres providing high quality care. Non-profit, co-operative centres require active parent participation on boards or committees, thereby providing parents with opportunities to get to know the staffs and gain insights into the centres' practices. Small centres, those with thirty children or fewer and good adult-to-child ratios, can be highly responsive to children's needs and often see their role as an extension of a particular kind of home environment, one that can give the kinds of supports that stabilize family life. But there is also evidence in Canada of mediocre and poor care. Sometimes this is the result of large, impersonal facilities ill suited to group care, or because the staff behaviour suggests not so much professionalism as "just performing a job."[9] Early childhood educators face the challenge of how to make the best possible care more widely available and affordable.

The media in Canada periodically disclose unacceptable incidents in a day-care centre or home, thus shaking public confidence in institutionalized child care. More frequently parents, child-care advocates, and some employers agitate for affordable, high-quality day care that can accommodate the most frequently arising emergencies. Day-care policies have been on the public agenda several times in recent years in Canada. Hopes for more child-care spaces of consistently high quality have been raised only to be shattered when political wrangling marginalizes and eventually dismisses the child-care issue.[10]

used extensively in Canada, is widely accepted as giving reliable indication of strengths and weaknesses in child-care programs. See, for instance, E. Schliecker, D.R. White, and E. Jacobs, "Predicting Pre-school Language Comprehension from SES, Family Structure and Daycare Quality," *Research Bulletins 7*, 002 (Montreal: Concordia University, Centre for Research in Human Development, 1988).

9   The variability across Canada with respect to teacher-child ratios, group size, and the maximum number of children permitted in a centre is documented and summarized most recently in Rosemary Young, *Introduction to Early Childhood Education*, Canadian edition (Scarborough, Ont.: Nelson Canada, 1994), pp.111-13.

10   In 1984 two major national investigations of child care were launched. The Liberal government commissioned the *Report of the Task Force on Childcare*, by Katie Cooke et al. (Ottawa: Supply & Services Canada, 1986). This was followed by the Conservative government's Report of the Special Committee on Child Care, *Sharing the Responsibility* (Ottawa: Queen's Printer, 1987). The Cooke Report laid out a plan by which child care would become a government-funded service by the year 2001. The Conservative Childcare Act, Bill C144, based on the 1987 report, proposed a system of child tax credits and redistributed the cancelled Canada Assistance Plan provisions under this bill. Opposition from child-care advocates was vehement. Ministers were shuffled to other cabinet posts, and finally in 1992, shortly before the Tories lost the election, Benoit Bouchard, then Conservative Minister for Health and Welfare, announced that "day care is a dead issue." In contrast to this, Ontario's NDP government began to make serious attempts to improve child care through salary-enhancement programs and particularly child-care reform.

The urgent need for manageable arrangements for children of work-ing parents has not been addressed adequately in government, industry, or the business community. After nearly a century of child-development research, no federal government has been able to see its way to formulat-ing a national child-care policy. The considerable knowledge and under-standing that have found their way into college textbooks and journals, and the expertise and vision that have accumulated in the writings of child-care advocates have not had a commensurate impact on the quality of daily care. Insights gained from research findings too frequently elude the attention of child-care staff because the immediate reality of provid-ing for the health and safety of the children and ensuring an appropriate flow of suitable activities leaves little time for reading and reflecting.[11] Yet studies of the kind pursued by many feminists in the social sciences are pertinent and potentially beneficial to the practice of child care.

From time to time the federal government has attempted, through programmes such as the Child Care Initiatives Fund, Better Beginnings, and Brighter Futures, to influence the direction of child care. The chan-nelling of funds to hard-to-serve child populations and areas of the country has been one thrust; funding studies, publications, and national child-care conferences has been another. While communities have re-sponded with enthusiasm to innovative programs, funding is always for a limited time, and in economically depressed areas, where no other lo-cal support is available, the initiatives are frequently forced to close when federal money ends. A national child-care policy would change this piecemeal approach. Coherence could come from the adoption of a uniform vision of child care for the whole country, with regional vari-ations built in. As it is, child-care policies, like many other arrangements that fall under provincial jurisdiction, are cost-shared with the federal government and municipalities through the Canada Assistance Plan (CAP, about $290 million a year). The combined expenditures of CAP and special funds for identified projects could carry stipulations for na-tional policies. After all, "What is being purchased is the child(ren)'s daily environment for months, even years an environment that will in-variably affect children's development."[12]

11   While paid time for planning and preparation is not a specific item in the report *Caring for a Living: A Study on Wages and Working Conditions in Canadian Child Care* (a joint project of the Canadian Child Care Federation and the Canadian Day Care Advocacy Association, re-search conducted by Karyo Communications, 1992), it appears as a staff concern under "Negative Aspects of Working in the Child Care Field," Appendix B, p.167.

12   Edward F. Zigler and Johanna Freedman, "Psychological-Developmental Implications of Current Patterns of Early Child Care," in Shahla S. Chehrazi, ed., *Psycho-Social Issues in Day Care*, (Washington: American Psychiatric Press, 1990), p.5.

REGULATED CHILD CARE

In short, Canada has no national child-care policy with any strong sense of vision and direction. Instead the provinces and territories have jurisdiction over both the scope and quality of child care through the enactment of specific regulations for day-care centres and home-based care. These regulations set the minimum acceptable standards for operating a centre. They define child/adult ratios considered to be safe and stipulate the requirements that centres must meet to receive and maintain a license. They stipulate provisions relating to children's care and education, such as space, health and safety, furniture, equipment, and programming. They outline the auspice and resulting organizational structure whether it is a non-profit board, private ownership, or a larger institution (church, college, industry) that operates the centre, along with guidelines for staff management, qualifications, record-keeping, and financial accountability. There is considerable variance from province to province on specific requirements and enforcement.[13] British Columbia, for instance, has had a Day Care Act since 1937; while the Northwest Territories first legislated child care in 1988.

In each provincial and territorial ministry, child-care advisors/consultants have responsibility for annual licensing-inspection visits, which include a review of all physical, educational, health, and administrative requirements. Given the proliferation of centres and home-care agencies in Canada since the 1970s, as well as the fiscal restraints imposed on ministries, these inspectors are often able to identify only gross contraventions of child-care regulations. Not only are there significant variations across the country with respect to minimum acceptable standards for group child care, but there are also discrepancies of standards within each province between urban and rural communities. A fundamental issue arises when these standards are applied to First Nations and Inuit communities. Those communities have endorsed child care as an essential support to rebuilding their communities and rightly identified childrearing practices as a means of passing on the traditional ways. They sometimes see regulations, externally imposed, as a threat to those traditions. Native caregivers and families see government standards of child care as one more manifestation of Euro-Canadian attitudes, a view

13   Variances in requirements across the country indicate, for example, that infant/staff ratios in
      most provinces are 3:1; in Nova Scotia it is 7:1. Maximum centre size can be fifty children
      (P.E.I.) and ninety in Saskatchewan. Maximum fine for a first licensing offence can be $300
      in Saskatchewan; $500 in P.E.I. and Newfoundland; $2,000 in Ontario; and no fines in other
      provinces. Sylvia Fanjoy, "Another Look at Child Care in Canada," *Interaction* (Canadian
      Child Care Federation) 7,3, (Fall 1993), p.24.

clearly expressed in the *Report of the National Inquiry into First Nations Child Care*:

> For First Nations children, government policies have been doubly detrimental because of cultural conflicts and differences. Subliminal, residual, archaic, colonialist roots are buried in all policies specific to native people. These underlying concepts have become so insidiously institutionalized as to be unrecognizable by the policy makers.... Our most basic recommendations are for immediate funding of community-controlled native child-care as part of the healing process.[14]

The creation of a national child-care policy would have to recognize regional, economic, and cultural diversities across the country. It would set expectations for the integration of social and health services to children and families. Without adequate leadership from the federal government, child care of a consistently high quality will elude us, and child poverty will deepen not only among our Native population, but also in all regions of the country.

HOME CHILD CARE

In the informal child-care sector there is no legislated third-party involvement. The child's parents make a private arrangement with the primary caregiver, who could be a friend, stranger, or relative looking after children in her/his own home. This caregiver does not have to meet any official standards, although private caregivers who choose to register with a licensed home-care agency are screened, visited periodically, and may have access to the agency's collection of toys and equipment.

Private home care seems to be the child care of choice. Children in informal care arrangements account for 80 per cent of all child care used by parents in Canada. The most obvious reason for this is the perceived intimacy of a home environment located in the family's neighbourhood and able to provide personal, loving attention for small children. The service usually involves a lower number of children and a range of ages, possibly providing care for several children from the same family.[15] It means also that parents whose employment requires shiftwork can ne-

14   *Report of the National Inquiry into First Nations Child Care*, unedited draft, Assembly of
      First Nations, Ottawa, July 1989, p.vii.

15   Most provinces stipulate child/adult ratios for home care. In Ontario, for example, it is 1:5,
      including the woman's own children.

gotiate hours of care to suit their schedules. Finally, lower fees make this form of care attractive.

Then again, "the element of the unknown" can make home care less desirable for many parents.[16] For example, the parents have to take on faith that their children are well cared for, kept clean, and given nutritious meals, that the caregiver provides a range of good activities, including outdoor play involving vigorous physical activity, that safety is a prominent concern for the caregiver, and that the children experience guidance rather than discipline and punishment. Beyond their control are the use of television, the presence of cigarette smoke, the physical and mental health of the provider, and the pattern of visitors to the home. Of equal concern for many parents is the issue of how to balance their values and attitudes towards childrearing and education with the possibly different values and attitudes of the caregiver.[17]

Home care can be a very positive experience for child and parents. The arrangements have led to lasting friendships between parents and caregivers,[18] and the consistency of care can be valuable, especially for infants and toddlers. But parents are likely to know little about or have no control over many facets of the child's daily experiences.

Government support of informal care grew in part out of a policy position: that for very young children, a single consistent caregiver in a home was preferable to the larger day-care centre environment. Policymakers also assumed that home care was a more reliable provision. In too many cases, however, the opposite has proven to be the case, with the result that the instability of caregiving arrangements has come to represent a serious problem. In an Alberta study, agency co-ordinators reported an annual turnover rate of caregivers of 51 per cent. In 97 per cent of cases, individual caregiver arrangements between a single provider and a child lasted less than two years.[19]

Other findings have emerged from Canadian research addressing questions relating to children's development in formal and informal

16   Laura Johnson and Janice Dineen, *The Kin Trade: The Daycare Crisis in Canada* (Toronto: McGraw-Hill Ryerson, 1981), p.21.

17   Parents may have similar concerns about staff in child-care centres; however, the larger number of children and the constant presence of several adult caregivers have the potential of exposing children to diverse values and attitudes.

18   Hillel Goelman and Alan R. Pence, "The Victoria and Vancouver Research Projects," in Isabel M. Doxey, ed., *Child Care and Education: Canadian Dimensions* (Toronto: Nelson Canada, 1990), p.272.

19   Annette LaGrange and Malcolm Read, "Those Who Care: A Report on Approved Family Day Home Providers in Alberta" (August 1990), *Focus* 1 (October 1993), Canadian Child Care Federation, p.9.

child care. Using children's language skills as an indicator of caregiver-child interactions, Hillel Goelman and Alan Pence found in British Columbia:

Children in unlicensed family child-care scored significantly lower on tests of language development than did children in licensed family child care.

Both the amount of caregiver training and level of maternal education affected the children's test scores.

Children from low-resource family backgrounds (for example, single-parent families, or families where parents had low levels of income, occupational status, and education) were found to be disproportionately represented in low-quality family child-care homes.

Low-quality family child-care homes were over-represented in the unlicensed family child-care sample.[20]

Similar conclusions had surfaced in a 1981 Toronto study, *The Kin Trade*. Most parents surveyed stated a preference for centre-based care for their children because they thought it provided an organized programme, that the caregivers had training, and that it would benefit their children more than a babysitter.[21]

The provincial response in the 1980s to pressures for more accessible child care in Ontario, Saskatchewan, and British Columbia, for instance, was to stimulate a variety of support services to home caregivers. The governments made available funds for information and referral networks, drop-in resource centres for caregivers and the children they care for, and toy libraries.[22] In 1987 in Ontario this mandate was extended to "family resource centres serving parents directly, as well as providing support to informal care and licensed programmes. They can also be the local community focus for child care services as a whole."[23] Provincial

20   Goelman and Pence, "Victoria and Vancouver Research Projects," p.273.

21   Johnson and Dineen, *The Kin Trade*, pp.27-29.

22   "Day Care Policy: Background Paper," Ministry of Community and Social Services, Ontario, 1981, p.62.

23   "New Directions," *Child Care*, Ministry of Community and Social Services, Ontario, 1987, p.13.

initiatives in Ontario have resulted in the flourishing of family and child resource centres, which offer a diverse range of programmes in response to local needs and conditions. Of the 1,700 or so family resource programmes in all of Canada, over 400 are located in Ontario.[24] Significantly, the conception of resource centres was not, as Irene Kyle notes, based on "an interest in prevention or the promotion of child development, per se." Instead, it came "out of concerns for the quality of care being provided in unsupervised (informal) child care arrangements." Kyle points out: "While the need for additional public child care services was increasingly being documented, the government of the day was unwilling to deal directly with these problems. The introduction of initiatives to develop child care support programs was seen as one way to avoid (and contain) the larger costs of expanding and maintaining the licensed child care system."[25]

Not surprisingly, then, the child-care field has a diversity of standards and variations in programs, and governments have been reluctant to become involved. The history of child care in Canada is rooted in settlement houses and crèches, in welfare, rather than in education. Until the 1960s child care carried the stigma of social assistance.[26] Day care was for children whose families were labelled poor or "dysfunctional." Ironically, it was the Second World War—but for its duration only—that raised the image of day care. During that period, when the labour of women from all walks of life was required in industry, the government funded day-care centres. Since the 1960s, in response to a growing economy and, more recently, out of economic necessity, increasing numbers of women have again joined the labour force. Now the need for child care is seen as a personal choice; and access to child care, based on recognition of the mother's contribution to the economy, is not yet deemed an entitlement.

Regardless of whether the child care is in a centre or the home of a caregiver, one principal effect of the arrangements is that children are more or less invisible throughout the day. For many adults with older children and, it seems, particularly for politicians, this is an "out of sight,

24   Alla Ivask, Annual Executive Director's Report 1993-94, Canadian Association of Toy Libraries and Parent Resource Centres, June 1994.

25   Irene J. Kyle, "Towards an Understanding of Best Practices in Family Resource Programs," rev. ed., prepared for TLRC Canada, now the Canadian Association of Family Resource Programs (Ottawa, August 1993), p.11.

26   For a concise history see: Patricia Vandebelt Schulz, "Day Care in Canada: 1850-1962," in *Good Day Care, Fighting For It, Getting It, Keeping It* Kathleen Gallagher Ross, ed., (Toronto: The Women's Educational Press, 1978).

out of mind" phenomenon. In essence, much of the larger community absolves itself from questioning or examining the adequacy or appropriateness of the experiences of children under the age of five. The cost of this care, if it were to come, like education, out of the public purse, is one major reason. Many people subscribe to the view that access to birth control gives parents and especially women the choice of whether or not to raise children; and they conclude that women therefore can and must take financial responsibility for their decision.

"Our children deserve the care of all Canadians. We owe this to them not only because they are ours, but because they are the expression of our hope for the future," states the opening of the Final Report of the Special Committee on Child Care (1987) to the Canadian Parliament.[27] Such rhetoric has a familiar ring. However, when child-care policies appear on a federal agenda, they tend to become a political onion that is stripped, layer by layer, of those provisions that would make stable, affordable child care available to all Canadians who need it.[28] At the heart of this debate is the role of the family, conceived by some as an autonomous unit, by others as the primary social component of the community. The autonomous family is thought to maintain its integrity by taking responsibility for itself and the well-being of its members. It is financially independent. Those who subscribe to this view see day care as the personal choice of parents and, again, especially of the mother; and therefore think that it should be privately arranged with no involvement from the state. Child-tax benefits, as introduced by the Conservative government under Mulroney, were designed to support this kind of unregulated "open market" for child care.

Contrasted with this conception of the autonomous family is the notion of social solidarity, enacted in the Scandinavian countries as well as France and Germany. In this notion the family is the core of the community, contributing to and benefiting from inclusive social service provisions. Child care becomes an essential component, available and publicly funded as part of the social provisions and used by parents as they need it. In Canada these two ideologies co-exist uncomfortably side by side and fuel the child-care debate, with public opinion tending more commonly to support the autonomous side that leaves each parent-child unit responsible for itself.

The issues surrounding child care are complex and the debate heated.

27 *Sharing the Responsibility*, Final Report of the Special Committee on Child Care (Ottawa: Queen's Printer: March 1987).

28 Linda McQuaig, "Canada's Social Programs Under Attack," *The Toronto Star*, November 11, 1992.

The recession that began in the 1980s and inaugurated high levels of unemployment in Canada has intensified this debate. In the mid-1990s
there is fear that social programmes may be reduced or phased out, leaving many people, including young parents, dangerously vulnerable.
Families under stress without resources to turn to are not able to maintain healthy environments for small children; or so it would seem. Yet a
longitudinal study begun in Nova Scotia in 1978 of some seven hundred
mothers and their children is providing valuable insights and shattering
negative myths about unmarried mothers. Significant among the many
findings is that most mothers, whether married or not, require intermittent (less than two to three years) family benefits, and only 3 per cent receive assistance for nine years or more. Nonetheless, even mothers who
are employed live in or close to poverty, with 53 per cent of the unmarried and 18 per cent of the married mothers living below the poverty
line.[29] Contrary to common belief, however, unmarried mothers had
fewer children (1.55), compared to mothers who had been married from
the outset of the study (2.40). The report makes clear that unmarried,
poorly educated women are the least well off and usually cannot expect
to attain job security and a standard of living comparable with older
married women.[30]

However, the concern that prompted this study—that the babies born
to teenage mothers who were keeping them would not develop properly—has not been confirmed. The researchers state: "The dedication
and consideration of the mothers for the well-being of their children is
impressive."[31] This is not to say that all the children developed equally
well. The factors that appear to have the greatest effect on well-being are
the education and age of the mothers when the first child is born, regardless of the mother's marital status. These findings are particularly significant in that they strengthen the hands of school boards that are locating child-care centres within high schools to retain students who become
parents and to encourage mothers to return to school and complete their
diplomas.

Awareness in schools of social work and departments of social services of the existence of multiple stresses on families has contributed to
current discussions about the fate of the Canadian family. *Family Security in Insecure Times*, a collection of essays published by the Canadian

29   *Mothers and Children: One Decade Later*, a follow-up study to "Vulnerable Mothers, Vulner-
     able Children" (Halifax: Nova Scotia Department of Community Services, 1991), p.244.

30   Ibid., p.245.

31   Ibid., p.234.

Council on Social Development, the Council's newsletter, *Focus on Child Care*, works published by the Vanier Institute, and articles in the national press have contributed valuable information to this discussion. These voices speak firmly in support of adequate social programmes for young families, arguing that a society that fails to invest in its children runs the risk of creating a cycle of dysfunction. With specific reference to the disadvantages and hardships experienced by poor families, lone mothers, and teen-parents, they review the literature on health and stimulation in early childhood, linking positive early experiences to later competence. "There is some evidence that a significant part of the high school dropout phenomenon is set in place before children enter the school system."[32] Given the accumulating evidence, it is not difficult to define a vital role for high quality child care and neighbourhood family resource centres to see families through stressful economic and social times.

CHILDREN

This century has witnessed radical transformations in family life in the Western world. Before industrialization and the growth of cities, old and young people in most social classes often shared living space and worked jointly to maintain the household. In some instances infants were provided with the special care essential to their survival. As their dependency decreased, surviving children were expected to become helpful and useful. In the process of assisting in their parents' labour, children learned about the social order in which they lived. Life for children in the middle and lower classes may have been harsh and narrow, but it provided them with a rightful place. Church, work, family status, and expectations as well as social and gender roles unfolded in a communal environment to which children had easy access.

Industrialization not only removed many labouring families from the country into cities but also transferred many workers away from labour within or close to the home. Work became segregated and more specifically gendered as men found employment in factories and industry. Fewer middle-class and working-class women produced most of the clothing and grew food for their families. Skills associated with self-sufficiency, indigenous to an agrarian way of life, were displaced by factory production. Paid labour became specialized, diversified, invisible, and

32   Daniel P. Keating and J. Fraser Mustard, "Social Economic Factors and Human Development," in *Family Security in Insecure Times* (Ottawa: Canadian Council on Social Development Publications, 1993), p.96.

most often only available to men, although working-class women held jobs both as domestics and in mills and factories. As urbanization progressed, the labour of most middle-class married women was increasingly confined to the home, and childraising became exclusively their responsibility. Children tended to be equally present and exposed to housework, but over time, in two-parent families, the gendered division of labour that clearly identified the father as the breadwinner and the mother as one of his dependents encouraged boys to resist and scorn domestic work while girls were socialized to be willing helpers.[33] The role of housewife, narrow in its sphere of influence, dependent in its economics, clashed with the world described to children in the tales and stories read to them and that they later read for themselves. Books like *Robinson Crusoe* or *The Jungle Book*, action-packed and romantic, provided the visions of what boys might become if they were daring, if they resisted and broke the ties to their mothers and their homes. At the same time *Little Women* had equally clear messages for girls to domesticate their spirit and prepare themselves to tend the hearth.

For adult women, male influence over what was and still is nostalgically considered their domain manifested itself in a growing "industry" of male expert advice. In fact, the experts' advice to women at once glorified and sentimentalized the woman in her home and provided a stream of instructions and injunctions on what she must do to do it right. The impact of "expert advice" has cast doubt and confusion where once people might have acted from certainty and conviction.[34] Nowhere is this uncertainty more evident than when women have babies and raise children. Only since the work of feminists has challenged the sanctity of male scientific knowledge and campaigned for a re-valuation of lived experience has there been hope of claiming the power and validity of personal knowledge.[35] Today no family or woman's magazine is without its advice column, attesting both to a preoccupation with childraising and to the insecurities that surround parenting.[36] Most young mothers are

33   Jane Roland Martin, *The Schoolhome* (Cambridge, Mass.: Harvard University Press, 1992), p.47.

34   This phenomenon is richly documented in Barbara Ehrenreich and Deirdre English, *For Her Own Good, 150 Years of the Experts' Advice to Women* (New York: Anchor Press/Doubleday, 1978).

35   For a full discussion of the disempowerment of women's experiences see Lorraine Code, *What Can She Know?* (Ithaca, N.Y.: Cornell University Press, 1991), especially ch.5,6.

36   Elly Singer, *Child Care and the Psychology of Development* (London: Routledge, 1992), p.8. Berry Brazleton, Stanley Greenspan, Lilian Katz, Bernice Weissbourne, Penelope Leach, and many others contribute columns about child-care issues to the popular press in magazines like *Parents, Redbook,* and *Canadian Living.*

no longer within easy reach of relatives, and for many of them advertising and the popular press, or even the local library, provide the best available information.

In the mid-nineteenth century childhood came to be identified as a specific phase within the human lifespan.[37] Along with the designation of ages and stages of childhood (infant, toddler, preschooler, and so on), each developmental phase has been characterized by specific needs and sensitivities.[38] Equally influential has been the growing field of child study, which has provided information and speculation about the psychology of development. This knowledge has fostered a growing conviction that children require protection from the adult world. Yet at the same time psychological observations of children indicated that stimulation could enhance development. The creation of safe environments, which simultaneously promote children's social and cognitive development, was manifested in the 1950s and 1960s as nursery schools. They were replaced in the 1960s in many provinces by publicly funded kindergartens. More recently, all-day care in both formal, licensed centres and informal arrangements, responding more to parental need, have tended to create a special world for children that insulates but also isolates them and their caregivers from the rest of the community. Jane Roland Martin raises a serious concern when she points out that throughout the day the home is empty and no longer able to be the main source of domestic and moral education for children.[39] This current reality heightens the need for high quality child care that attempts to provide children with a broad range of socializing experiences.

THE CHILD-CARE WORLD

At present in the world of child care it is primarily young adults, usually not related to the children, who create the daily environment.[40] The in-

---

37   Philippe Aries, *Centuries of Childhood, a Social History of Family Life*, trans. Robert Baldick (New York: Alfred Knopf, 1962); J.H. Plumb, "The Great Change in Children," *Horizon* 13,1 (Winter 1971).

38   Children came to be the subject of study and research only at the beginning of the twentieth century. In Canada Dr. W. Blatz founded what is now the Institute of Child Study at the University of Toronto in 1926 with a grant from the Rockefeller Foundation.

39   Martin, *Schoolhome*, pp.30-31.

40   Some 58 per cent of the staff in centre-based care are thirty years old or younger, a fact indicating something about the energy required to work with young children but also, more specifically, the lack in most centres of a pay scale that honours years of experience. *Caring for a Living*, p.xxi.

terests, preoccupations, and preferences of these workers tend to shape the choice and range of activities in the centre and to mould patterns of personal interactions. This situation makes the transmission of preferences and biases almost inevitable. Of special concern for feminists is the fact that in the myriad daily interactions with children, educators often resort to quick, gut reactions, many of which attest to ingrained assumptions about boys being more important or deserving or requiring more attention than girls. As a teacher and observer in day-care centres since 1968, I have seen ample evidence of how gender stereotypes are sustained. Trained, experienced, well-meaning staff are likely to resort to guidance techniques that ensure the smooth flow of activities, and they frequently rely, quite unconsciously, on stereotypical interactions. A striking example, which resonates with Susan Ehrlich's discussion of socially constructed linguistics (chapter two), is the case of a staff member commenting on how helpful or kind Jane is to another child, while remarking on Bob's new shoes. Jane will be rewarded for looking after others, but Bob has the chance to tell the teacher all about the adventure of going to the mall to buy shoes.

Studies remind us that "global differences" continue to structure young children's play environments according to gendered lines.[41] Traditional gender differences and sexist assumptions are strengthened in adults' toy selection for children, in media presentations, and in sex-stereotyped advertising of toys. As children grow older they tend to choose toys and play that echo and reinforce these early experiences. One group of authors hypothesizes:

> Infants who are encouraged and reinforced to play with dolls and child's furniture, or sports equipment and tools will be more likely to choose these objects when they are given a choice. They are familiar with these objects and know what can be done with them. They have also learned that these objects are appropriate for them, and for children of their own gender.[42]

Caregiver values and attitudes form the "hidden curriculum" in child-care programmes and day-care homes. Yes, there are blocks and trucks, but what is the "acceptable" level of noisy play, and who is allowed to be noisier? It is not uncommon during group times to observe

41   A. Pomerleau, D. Bolduc, G. Malcuit, L. Cossette, "Pink or Blue: Environmental Gender Stereotypes in the First 2 Years of Life," *Sex Roles* 22,5/6 (1990), p.365.

42   Pomerleau et al., "Pink or Blue," p.366.

a member of staff giving full attention to a fidgeting boy while insisting that she will only call on those to answer questions who sit quietly. Many school-age observations also comment on the amount of time and attention given to boys as compared to girls. Boys "dominate the physical space of the classroom ... and the teacher's time too, so that girls have less opportunity to assert themselves and their learning."[43]

The hidden curriculum in group care is shaped to a great extent by the activities that a caregiver thinks are appropriate for all, some, or none of the children, and by the activities that she enjoys planning and supervising. Toys for boys and toys for girls are distinguished by the skills and ideas they promote. Construction materials (blocks, Lego, sand, playdough, clay) explore the physical world. They are predictable, and they invite testing. They demand discipline and careful work, and they present a challenge of experimentation and problem-solving. Children who play with these materials learn ingenuity and tend to find interesting solutions on their own. Play with dolls and dress-ups, or dramatic house play, re-creates a different aspect of the world of adults. It explores the social and emotional environments in which there are no laws of nature. It focuses on the players and how accurately they have observed adults' ways, how sensitively they can read cues, and how well they are able to reproduce what they know.[44] Each area of learning is important for development; it is vital that girls and boys participate equally and freely in each. Good programmes for children promote a balance of activities free of gender, racial, and other constraining expectations.

On the playground, where adult involvement tends to be more supervisory than interactive, boys are commonly trusted to test their endurance/strength, while girls are cautioned to be careful and often encouraged to take the teacher's hand. Yet in neither body size nor strength is there a statistically significant difference between boys and girls at this age. On one occasion, when a boy cut his cheek in a fall, the teacher's comment, when band-aids and comfort had been applied, was that "the scar would give his face character." When I looked puzzled she suggested, "I'd worry a lot more if it were one of our girls." Protecting, inhibiting, and proscribing girls' activities are still strong urges among caregivers, and will have noticeable inhibiting effects in later life for girls

43   Anti-Sexist Working Party, "'Look, Jane, Look': Anti-Sexist Initiatives in Primary Schools," in Gaby Weiner, ed., *Just a Bunch of Girls* (Milton Keynes, England: Open University Press, 1985), p.136. Both the frequency and content of teacher-student contact favours boys, as documented in several studies by David and Myra Sadker, "Sexism in the Classroom: From Grade School to Graduate School," *Phi Delta Kappa* 68 (1986).

44   Jeanne H. Block, "Differential Promises Arising from Differential Socialization of the Sexes: Some Conjectures," *Child Development*, 1983, p.54.

(as Ann Hall discusses in chapter ten). Making girls feel unable and compliant, urging them to cultivate their appearance, and restricting their activities are bound to limit their chances to master gross motor skills, develop agility, and feel alive and comfortable in their skin.

Efforts on the part of caregivers and educators to challenge stereotypes are in constant danger of erasure by the daily influence of television, which instils in children a craving for the toys featured in the programs. The deregulating of children's television programming in the United States during the Reagan presidency allowed toy manufacturers free rein to advertise their products in the guise of TV entertainment. In consequence, play has changed from more imaginative, self-initiated fun to the re-enacting of what the children have seen on the TV show. Children who watch these programs come to believe that they cannot play without the featured toys.[45] The pressures on parents to keep them supplied with all that the TV show demands or suggests are incessant: "The trends of the sixties and seventies towards helping children expand their gender roles beyond narrow stereotypes in play, toys, and child-rearing practices, in general, have been replaced by a toy and play culture which is more gender-specific than ever."[46]

Stereotyping is alive and thriving in most parts of North American society. It is constantly reinforced in the commercial world, where clothing and toys bear unmistakeable cues as to who the consumers are, for whom they are being marketed. Television reinforces in crude as well as subtle ways ideas about who will compete in the real world of action, what a child must do to be desirable. And as more adults become preoccupied with surviving a slumping economy, the energy to demand greater integrity from manufacturers and to monitor and fight sexism in the media may be displaced by more immediate concerns like retaining a job or paying the bills.

Gender-discriminating attitudes and behaviours are subtle, usually only semi-conscious, and deeply entrenched. "Prejudices are passed on as indisputable truths in childhood and are never again questioned," suggests author Elena Belotti.[47] Feminist pedagogy set out to challenge

45   I am indebted to Robert Clarke for alerting me to Steve Kline's *Out of the Garden: Toys and Children's Culture in the Age of TV Marketing* (Toronto: Garamond Press, 1993), which supports these findings.

46   Nancy Carlsson-Paige and Diane E. Levin, *Who's Calling the Shots? How to Respond Effectively to Children's Fascination with War Play and War Toys* (Philadelphia: New Society Publishers, 1990), p.90.

47   Elena Belotti, *Little Girls* (London: Writers and Readers Publishing Co-operative, 1975), p.21.

those prejudices and has been, in some places, remarkably effective.[48] Yet becoming conscious of one's racist, sexist inheritance requires determined, continuous effort and a willingness to change. None of us would wish to be racist, sexist, or gender-biased, yet awareness of implicit prejudices or preferences in words and actions requires us all to be constantly on our toes and to be well schooled for detection. This is no easy task, and in an early childhood educator's short one or two years of college training it is difficult to make significant inroads on long-held beliefs. As Selma Greenberg notes, and my experience of ECE teaching bears her out: "The potential impact of teacher education institutions on sexism in the schools is very limited, at best. There is ample reason to believe that what students learn during their training has only a minor effect on their subsequent work.... Most of their socialization into the teaching profession occurs once they are employed."[49]

This child-care world is staffed primarily by women (98 per cent),[50] which means that children are steeped in an environment in which traditional women's ways are often pre-eminent, women's values predominate, and women's preferences prevail. The importance of ongoing feminist, anti-racist, and anti-sexist consciousness-raising in such environments cannot be overestimated.

WOMEN, PARENTS, MOTHERS

In the late twentieth century most women anticipate working in the labour force for most of their adult lives. Yet when they become mothers they find themselves caught in a spectrum of conflicting social expectations that commonly relegate full responsibility for infant and child care to them. Traditional Canadian attitudes see women in the home caring for children (or the elderly) and performing domestic chores. It is only in the last third of the twentieth century that women's contribution in "caring for non-earning members of society (young, old, disabled, unemployed)" has begun to be valued for the "vital economic role" it plays in Canadian society.[51]

When biology is invoked as the determinant of "woman's role," conventional ideology is clearly very much alive. Warnings from traditional

48 See, for example, Patti Lather's discussion in *Getting Smart: Feminist Research and Pedagogy with/in the Postmodern* (New York: Routledge, 1991).

49 Selma Greenberg, "Preschool and the Politics of Sexism," in Barbara Sprung, ed., *Perspectives on Non-Sexist Early Childhood Education* (New York: Teachers College Press, 1978), p.58.

50 *Caring for a Living*, p.xxi.

51 Susan McDaniel, "Women and Family Security in Canada," in *Family Security in Insecure Times* (Ottawa: Canadian Council on Social Development Publications, 1993), p.167.

psychoanalysts that children will become disturbed, deviant, or perhaps even criminal if mothers do not commit to their nurturing attest to the tenacity of these older convictions, as blame for children's failures is laid at their mothers' feet.[52] This still-prevalent line of reasoning assumes a symbiosis between mothers and their offspring, which yields the result that when mothers—especially middle-class mothers have—to work or decide to return to work, it is still often suggested that they are "choosing" to pursue their own fulfilment at the expense of their children's well-being.[53] There is no doubt that a strong attachment between children and their mothers plays a vital role in children's development. Yet changing social arrangements require us to ask how exclusive this relationship must be and to reassess its positive and negative aspects.

Traditional gender-role expectations generate complex conflicts for mothers of young children. Social disapproval of women who have children who will be raised mostly by others is still prevalent, even in the 1990s, as mothers' active participation in the public world of work is questioned, frowned upon, and often condemned, even as it is clear that this is rarely a simple matter of choice. Women's reproductive labour, which contributes to the survival and nurturance of the species, is taken for granted and denied public esteem. The concerns that women raise that most impinge on their daily lives are often ignored by employers and sometimes their own partners in favour of promoting the roles they are expected to play.[54] For example, the difficulties of finding reliable child care are held to be an issue for the mother, not for her partner (if she has one) or for her employer, yet male partners and employers may each ignore the challenges of settling a child into care in favour of workplace or domestic demands.

When women and men are equal participants in the labour market, the lack of support systems, which this participation requires, becomes painfully obvious to women. As Daniel P. Keating and J. Fraser Mustard observe, "Labour market policies that do not recognise the extensive demands placed on families with young children, combined with the dearth of good, affordable childcare, create a situation in which ade-

52   "Prolonged deprivation of the young child, of maternal care may have grave and far-reaching effects on his character and so on the whole of his future life." John Bowlby, *Maternal Care and Mental Health*, as quoted in Bob Mullan, *Are Mothers Really Necessary?* (New York: Weidenfeld & Nicolson, 1987), p.32. See also Sara Ruddick, *Maternal Thinking, Toward a Politics of Peace*, (Boston: Beacon Press, 1989), p.29.

53   Singer, *Child Care and the Psychology of Development*, p.1.

54   McDaniel, "Women and Family Security," p.164.

quate nurturing of the next generation cannot be assured."[55] In fact, labour policies conspire against working women. Many women experience the current Canadian policy of maternity leave allowance of seventeen weeks of paid leave as far too short to enable them to adjust to and integrate a new child into their lives. Most workplace structures and employment practices lack the range of options that might enable women and men to better balance working and family life. Job-sharing, part-time pay with benefits, flexible hours, or preferential shifts are some of the options that would reflect employer consideration of parental needs. Such arrangements are only just beginning to be considered in the Canadian workplace, more as a result of increasing automation or redundancy than parents' needs. If it continues to be evident that such practices make for greater productivity and stability at work, one might anticipate an increase in these kinds of arrangements.

EARLY CHILDHOOD EDUCATION ISSUES

Early childhood educators who train students to work in child-care centres are aware of the pivotal position that day care has in providing support for families. The invisible work of child care that middle-class mothers did in their homes, that upper-class mothers frequently handed over to a nanny, nursery maid, or governess, and that for working-class women was solved mostly through the aid of relatives or babysitters, is now in the hands of young women who may or may not have completed a one- or two-year diploma in ECE. Instructors of early childhood education programmes are prominent among child-care advocates promoting greater awareness of the informal sector of child care, which is so prevalent in Canada. Their concerns are twofold. The quality of daily care and education of the children is a primary concern, but the status of the caregiver and the quality of her working life are equally an issue.

Caregivers who make private child-care arrangements with parents may experience much stress and little financial reward. Throughout the day, constant vigilance of the children is required, and when the needs of the parents' various schedules are accommodated this care may stretch over more than an eight-hour day. The demands of maintaining a home life in a space that doubles, throughout the week, as the work environment can create conflict for family members and the caregiver.

55   Keating and Mustard, "Social Economic Factors and Human Development," p.88.

There is also the perception that some parents and certainly the general public are oblivious to the demands of this job. These conditions may not be consistent with job satisfaction,[56] and the children being cared for may lose out because the good intentions of the caregiver are eroded by the daily stresses of providing that care.

The fact is that poor quality care has a depressing impact on children's potential at a time in their lives when a rich, warm environment would allow them to blossom. An overburdened caregiver can set demands for order that restrict active play; worse, a caregiver's uncaring attitude will take its toll in limiting children's concerns for each other and generally create an abrasive environment. Such environments have been associated with poor language development and do little to build self-esteem. Equally harmful is the long-term effect of making children unco-operative and resistant. Excessive use of television can be one resort that discourages children from their own play. A poor selection of toys can frustrate children's manipulative and imaginative development. The extent to which these toys and the caregiver guidance are sex-stereotypical will discourage girls and boys from moving freely among available activities.

The findings accumulated in Canada, the United States, and Britain leave no doubt that poor quality care, whether in a centre or a home, has a pervasive and lasting impact. Gillian Doherty's review of these findings states:

> There is a substantial body of research which demonstrates the immediate and long-term benefits of special highly resourced child care programs for children from low socioeconomic backgrounds and/or at environmental risk.... However, there is disturbing evidence from the United States and from England that the reverse is not true. A stable middle-class family with parents who have high school or higher education does not appear able to compensate for poor quality child care, at least for children in full-time attendance.[57]

This is a particularly disturbing finding because Doherty's work of reviewing research literature has also established that low-income families frequently make inferior child-care arrangements for their children.[58]

---

56   Gillian Doherty, *Quality Matters in Child Care* (Huntsville, Ont.: Jesmond Publishing, 1991), p.69.

57   Ibid., p.4.

58   Ibid., p.6.

Certainly enrolment in correspondence courses indicates that some caregivers take measures to educate themselves on the developmental needs of young children and endeavour to provide a range of suitable toys and experiences. In areas that have a family resource centre, the regular attendance of caregivers with their charges indicates the value they place on this facility. Often caregivers make use of the book and toy library, and many take part in discussion groups and courses. In some places informal networking has resulted in the founding of home provider associations. This kind of growth of commitment to the work that home-caregivers do is likely to support their self-esteem as well as benefit the children.[59] However, in most parts of this country such resource centres have not yet been established, and informal caregivers may need to rely entirely on their own skills or take advantage of courses through correspondence or long-distance education, a lonely and quite costly undertaking.

A brief look at the wages and working conditions of caregivers in licensed centres provides further clues about the extent to which private caregivers are undervalued. Their colleagues, 65 per cent of whom have postsecondary credentials in early childhood education (ECE), earn an average hourly wage of $9.60. As the principal researcher of the national study *Caring for a Living*, conducted between November 1990 and August 1992, points out, "The average wage for a warehouse worker, a job requiring less skill, less education, less experience and certainly less responsibility is 58% more."[60] Mean wages of child-care workers across Canada indicate that Newfoundland is at the lowest level, with $12,000 per annum, and the Northwest Territories are at the peak, with $23,750. The majority of staff work in non-profit or commercially operated centres and earn respectively 38 per cent and 72 per cent less than those in municipal centres.[61]

The ownership of the centre also has a significant impact on staff benefits and working conditions. The three types of operations—municipal, non-profit, and commercial—have variable provisions for staff, with unionized and municipal centres providing better benefits. However, municipal centres are only found in Ontario and Alberta, and unions represent only one in five staff members. Non-profit groups lag somewhat behind the municipal sector, and commercial operations

59   The Canadian Association of Family Resource Programs (formerly TLRC, the Canadian Association of Toy Libraries and Parent Resource Centres) currently has a listing for 1,700 resource facilities across Canada.

60   *Caring for a Living*, p.xvii.

61   Ibid., p.xix.

generally offer the poorest working conditions and benefits. Here are three examples of conditions for municipal, non-profit, and commercial operations, respectively: retirement/pension plan (98 per cent, 34 per cent, 24 per cent); staff room (96 per cent, 65 per cent, 59 per cent); and written contracts (42 per cent, 45 per cent, 18 per cent). The only benefit provided by 39 per cent of commercial centres is reduced fees for parent employees (12 per cent, 23 per cent, 39 per cent).[62]

Not surprisingly, the primary reason given for staff turnover (national average 26 per cent) is low wages. Low pay and little public recognition are the two factors that drive trained early childhood educators from the field. "The opportunity to turn the job into a career is limited, many trained and experienced staff leave the field at a time when they have the most to offer. Because of low wages and poor conditions of work, child care is a young woman's profession, and the lack of opportunity for recognition and advancement keeps it that way."[63]

What is surprising in the survey results is that despite these disappointing conditions, 62 per cent of child-care staff say they would choose the field again. The main reason cited is the opportunity to work with colleagues as a member of a team and to make a positive contribution to children's lives. The greatest cause for discontent is the same: working within a non-functioning team, with the starkest complaint coming from staff in the Northwest Territories. This may be a reflection of the fact that Alberta, the Yukon, and the Northwest Territories require no formal qualifications to work in child care.[64] One could theorize that satisfying working conditions are linked positively to professional performance.

CHILD CARE AND FEMINISM

The daily reality is that the majority of women with children pay other women for their child-care services. Perhaps because the work of mothers who stay home to care for their children is not remunerated, women who provide child care are among the lowest paid professionals in this country, even when these caregivers have college diplomas in early childhood education. The shocking claim "day-care staffers—rated as

62   Ibid, p.56.

63   Ibid., p.153.

64   Ibid., p.35.

the lowest paid of all professional workers" appeared in my local paper in November 1993.[65]

The undervalued and underpaid status of child care is a source of discomfort to some feminists. Some middle-class women see their "liberation" in terms of self-fulfilment arising from meaningful employment; others know the desperate need to run or contribute to the household. When child care is required to enable women to work outside the home, paying another woman becomes the solution. Domestic help, child-caregivers, and nannies are virtually all female. Feminists recognize the paradox inherent in securing their working status by passing over to another woman what is publicly considered their private responsibility. They understand that this work is everywhere undervalued, that its appropriately valued costs would be totally unaffordable. For the moment the real contribution and work of a primary caregiver, whether the mother, a sitter, or day-care staff, remain unacknowledged and undervalued. Many child-care staff realize that their labour subsidizes working families. However, many women who choose to become caregivers do not see themselves as having "marketable skills," but as "doing what comes naturally."[66] And society's unwillingness to confront the social significance of childraising relegates children to invisible places until they are old enough to "learn properly."

For middle-class feminists, who are often not the sole financial supporters of their children, there are other reasons why the issue of child care is particularly troubling. On the one hand the desire or need to work outside the home, to have the personal and financial rewards of employment, represents an articulated goal. On the other, becoming a parent, realizing one's traditional role as woman and mother, can also be a passionate choice. While children are small, these two goals seem to be mutually exclusive for many mothers. When a woman decides to stay at home after the birth of her child, there is a hard reality to face. As Joanna Dean writes:

> The effects of staying at home to care for children, whether full- or part-time, are enormous and often under-estimated. The woman who drops out of the labour force for five years to raise a family loses not only the income from those years, but also her seniority,

65   Bill Hutchison, "Economy Hits Day-Care Centres Hard," *The Whig-Standard* (Kingston, Ont.), November 15, 1993.

66   Selma Greenberg, "Preschool and the Politics of Sexism," in Barbara Sprung, ed., *Perspectives on Non-Sexist Early Childhood Education* (New York: Teachers College Press, 1978), p.53.

her pension, and most important, her place in the work force. The years she misses are crucial ones for job advancement, and most women never catch up. Taken over a lifetime, the cost of this setback can run into hundreds of thousands of dollars. Personal costs are even more difficult to calculate. Women who are isolated in the home all day and financially and emotionally dependent on one man lose self-esteem and the confidence they had while in the work force.[67]

For feminists a central concern in their work, as in their lives, is the question of values. We know about the hard work and the relentless soul-searching that are needed to identify and challenge the inequities of a patriarchal society. We know and continue to struggle with our personal pasts, with restrictions and expectations absorbed from our upbringings. Many of us cherish the positions we have gained in the wider world. We know the effort and vigilance required to promote opportunities for other women. However, if these hard-won gains are to have some hope of becoming the accepted status, then as mothers, and as feminists, we need to be cognizant of the environment provided for children. When children spend their days with a babysitter or the staff in a child-care centre, with people the mother hardly knows, can she assume that the caregivers are aware of and sympathetic to the aims of the women's movement? Have the caregivers thought about or been taught about stereotyping or sexist and racist issues? A central question for feminists seeking child care needs to be: are the caregivers likely to share my values and concerns?

Parent(s) and caregivers jointly determine what children learn. For this reason alone, issues of value and stereotypical practices in child care cannot be ignored. Because very young children are not yet able to reflect on what they experience, they simply absorb the values, attitudes, gender ideology, and orientation of those around them. They accept as right and good what adults say and do and extrapolate from their personal contact what these adults think is important or worthwhile. Under these circumstances, consistent adults, congruent caregiving practices, and compatible messages to the child are critical. For infants and toddlers, in particular, consistent loving care is important, because such experiences support their desire to learn, to become a part of this world.

67   Joanna Dean, "Mothers Are Women," in Geraldine Finn, ed., *Limited Edition, Voices of Women, Voices of Feminism* (Halifax: Fernwood Publishing, 1993), p.18.

When there is a significant discrepancy between parents and caregivers in how they behave and interpret the world to children, in how they promote acceptable behaviour for each gender, children can become confused. Research confirms this discrepancy: "The existing evidence suggests that families and early childhood programs constitute different social environments for children in terms of childrearing values, behavioral expectations, and patterns of adult-child interactions."[68] While it is desirable that children, as they grow up, become flexible and adaptable to changing circumstances, in the preschool years, for infants and for toddlers, consistency in experiences seems to support their healthy development.

Whether women are stay-at-home mothers or work with children in an official or private capacity, it cannot be assumed that they are all equally well prepared or suited to care for children. Indeed, some of them would become happier people if they were involved in work that made fewer personal demands. The myth that girls are good with children often arises out of years of babysitting as young teenagers, taking on responsibilities that thwart their opportunities to discover other interests. The narrow range of girls' out-of-school experiences throughout their teen years often leads guidance counsellors to suggest more of the same: child care as a career. Yet for some girls smouldering, often unconscious, resentments about expectations to meet others' needs are carried into the child-care situation and become part of the environment surrounding little children. The ways in which their lives have been stereotyped, their own potential truncated, are bound to have deleterious effects on children in their care, or on babies born to them.

It is worth noting that stereotypes in the Inuit culture of the Canadian Arctic can have similar and equally confining effects on girls. It is typical among Inuit for childraising to be a communal responsibility, with women taking primary control. Frequently young girls, older sisters, or cousins are kept from school to mind younger children.[69] While these girls are then involved in stereotypical women's work, they gain a secure identity practising and passing on traditional ways of socializing young children. But the resulting lack of formal education becomes an impediment to their ability to join the labour force and bars the way into better paying, challenging jobs, which tend to be filled by southern Canadians

68   Douglas R. Powell, *Families and Early Childhood Programs*, NAEYC Research Monograph of the National Association for the Education of Young Children, vol.3, Washington, D.C., 1989, p.32.

69   Information from the Bureau of Statistics of the Government of the Northwest Territories indicates for 1991 a population of 11,385 in the Baffin Region; of those, 6,540 were under the age of twenty-five. The high-school graduation list in 1993 included twenty-three names.

who migrate to the Arctic.[70] The present pattern of early childbearing among Inuit girls creates a cycle of poverty and undereducation that perpetuates economic disadvantage. The birth rate among Inuit is one of the highest in the world, yet the Arctic is not an environment that can support a rapidly growing population. These trends have prompted women's groups like Pauktuutit to work towards creating greater options for women and to encourage children to complete their schooling, to pursue the development of day care in Inuit communities.

As long as society holds only individual women responsible for childrearing there is a risk that these responsibilities will be fulfilled at children's expense. Working mothers and fathers have limited time to parent their children, yet few men see it as a task of critical importance to which they could devote their lives. In the child-care field only two per cent of staff are males.[71] Certainly, low wages contribute to this underrepresentation, as does the lack of prestige enjoyed by the child-care profession. It is also possible, as bell hooks suggests, that some women may not wish to relinquish this area of "power and control."[72] Policies that would force women to stay at home are highly undesirable, and so too is an economic situation that forces them back to work when they and their children are not yet ready for this separation. Yet a shift towards paying women who care for children a living wage will require vastly different social arrangements from those we now have. Like schools, day care needs to be funded at all levels of government. Care for children under five will need to include a wide range of options that reflects the diversity in the community; and, more important, child care needs to be much more collaborative with parents than schools are.

Loren Lind and Susan Prentice pursue a compelling line of argument for the development of a national day-care system that is publicly funded, of high quality, non-profit, non-compulsory, and universally accessible: a system of community child care—"care of, for, and by the community." They see it as a way to build community "and of the community itself making the critical decisions about that care." They rightly insist on parental involvement, so that at every level the users (children and parents) and beneficiaries (community and country) can help to shape the system.[73]

70   During a two-year period (1988-90) in which I worked at Arctic College in Iqaluit a combined staff of some thirty-five instructors and administrators included only two Inuit.

71   *Caring for a Living*, p.xxi.

72   bell hooks, *Feminist Theory: From Margin to Center* (Boston: South End Press, 1984), p.138.

73   Loren Lind and Susan Prentice, *Their Rightful Place: An Essay on Children, Families and Childcare in Canada*, Monograph Series G (Toronto: Our Schools/Our Selves, February 1992), p.118.

The role of fathers, when they are present in their children's lives, is worth examining, not just to promote the sharing of domestic chores, but also to promote opportunities through which men can discover the pleasures of parenting. In her chapter on "Revolutionary Parenting," bell hooks makes the point that "men will not share equally in parenting until they are taught, ideally from childhood on, that fatherhood has the same meaning and significance as motherhood."[74] More recently in Newfoundland, for example, where the fisheries have closed off employment for many, fathers have had parenting thrust on them. For instance, one young father of twenty-month-old twins became unemployed and, with some apprehension—after all, he said, he didn't know "anything about this"—took over the child care. He was surprised at his enjoyment. "I am amazed at what I learn and how rewarding it is!" He also confessed that it was hard work. In the current economic climate many men are becoming "house-husbands," with unforeseen and positive implications. A more equitable division of labour, a loosening of stereotypical roles, is slowly taking place. In two-sex, two-parent families, joint participation can extend to more communal forms of childrearing, activities that take children and adults into the neighbourhood. The involvement of fathers in child-care responsibilities not only is an equitable move, but also exposes children to a wider range of adult relationships.

Yet the welfare of children is still by no means a prominent issue on feminist agendas.[75] In the child-care community, which has grown from many regional into several national associations, the concerns and demands are clear: a national child-care policy, financial support for day care, more stringent staffing requirements and higher standards of care, and better salaries, working conditions, and status. The concerns also address the inconsistent quality of care that children receive within some licensed centres, in day-care homes, and from untrained, "invisible" caregivers. National, provincial, territorial, and local professional organizations advocate on behalf of child care throughout Canada. Yet members of these groups are often isolated: 84 per cent of child-care

---

74   hooks, *Feminist Theory*, p.137.

75   A survey of topics presented at women's conferences indicates that child care is not seen as a public, communal issue. For example, in the 948 presentations at the Third International, Interdisciplinary Congress on Women, Dublin, 1987, eight sessions addressed child care, preschool children's issues specifically. Also, in the Proceedings of the 1990 Canadian Women's Studies Association Conference there is no mention of child-care issues. In the seven most recent conferences held by CRIAW (Canadian Research Institute for the Advancement of Women), children or child care appears only once.

staff surveyed believe that they are not respected by the general public.[76] It would seem that an allegiance between the child-care community and feminists could raise the profile of a mutual concern to make the private domain public. Such connections are being explored.

Good child care can take many forms, but a central issue is always a respectful acceptance of the child and a genuine facilitation of what will be of benefit to children. Good feminist research similarly promotes respect for women's individual voices and aims to improve women's lives.[77] Any work that brings women from academia and child care together in creating community directions for children's care, which sheds light on sexist, racist, and classist practices, would serve children well. It would have a lasting impact on the community.

As a feminist whose training and mothering took place in prefeminist times, I find myself often balancing conflicting values. My awareness that children are resilient gives way to the knowledge of their vulnerability. My desire for better opportunities for women, including women who work in early childhood education, also means that more children will be in communal care from infancy on. The urgency to provide nurturing childhood experiences is dampened by the knowledge of public resistance to providing adequate resources. How to balance and resolve these conflicting demands seems to be at the root of women's and children's lives. Finding the key and tipping the scale in the direction of children's needs are matters of critical importance.

77   Reinharz, *Feminist Methods*, p.4.

SUGGESTED READINGS

Carol Baines, Patricia Evans, Sheila Neysmith, eds., *Women Caring: Feminist Perspectives on Social Welfare*. Toronto: McClelland & Stewart, 1991.

Lyda Beardsley, *Good Day, Bad Day: A Child's Experience Of Child Care*. New York: Teachers College Press, Columbia University, 1990.

Mary Georgina Boulton, *On Being a Mother: A Study of Women with Pre-school Children*. London: Tavistock Publications, 1983.

Nancy Carllson-Paige and Diana E. Levin, *The War Play Dilemma: Balancing Needs and Values in the Early Childhood Classroom*. New York: Teachers College Press, 1987.

Nancy Carllson-Paige and Diana E. Levin, *Who's Calling the Shots? How to Respond Effectively to Children's Fascination with War Play and War Toys*. Philadelphia: New Society Publishers, 1990.

Gillian Doherty, *Quality Matters in Child Care*. Huntsville, Ont.: Jesmond Publishing, 1991.

Isabel Doxey, ed., *Child Care and Education: Canadian Dimensions*. Scarborough, Ont.: Nelson Canada, 1990.

Stephen Kline, *Out of the Garden: Toys and Children's Culture in the Age of TV Marketing*. Toronto: Garamond Press, 1993.

Fredelle Maynard, *The Child Care Crisis: The Thinking Parent's Guide to Daycare*. Markham, Ont.: Penguin Books, 1985.

Jane Roland Martin, *The Schoolhome*. Cambridge, Mass.: Harvard University Press, 1992.

Deborah A. Phillips, ed., *Quality in Child Care: What Does The Research Tell Us?* Washington, D.C.: Research Monographs of the National Association for the Education of Young Children, vol.1, 1987.

Valerie Polakow, *Lives on the Edge*. Chicago: University of Chicago Press, 1993.

Elly Singer, *Child Care and the Psychology of Development*. London and New York: Routledge, 1992.

Valerie Polakow Suransky, *The Erosion of Childhood*. Chicago: University of Chicago Press, 1982.

Nancy Boyd Webb, *Preschool Children with Working Parents: An Analysis of Attachment Relationships*. London: University Press of America, 1984.

LORRAINE GREAVES

Chapter Eight: Women & Health: A Feminist Perspective on Tobacco Control

WOMEN'S SMOKING IS OFTEN CONSIDERED SIMPLY A HEALTH problem, when it is actually a complex political issue. The marketing and promotion of tobacco to women, girls, and specific populations are not only part of a deliberate plan to create addicted markets, but the use of smoking by and its meaning to such groups are also related to life experience.

While working within the violence against women's movement, and observing many shelters and centres for abused women, I noticed that both abused women and the workers smoked a great deal. Until recently shelters had few policies and restrictions on smoking because many people connected to shelters often considered changes in smoking behaviour to be a low priority for abused women and their helpers. This is also a common attitude in social service agencies, mental health services, and agencies for low-income people.

Nevertheless, I began to wonder about the connections between smoking and abuse, oppression, and sexism, and how addiction to tobacco fitted into the lives of the women. Traditional research in smoking offered little insight into this question. It became obvious that investigation of this issue demanded a new theoretical and methodological orientation. The first level of inquiry into this question concentrates on gender, but race and class are equally important variables.

The political nature of this research cannot be ignored. The meaning of tobacco smoking is fraught with socio-cultural interpretations that change over time, and the political economy of tobacco marketing and production is a matter of capitalist exploitation and the deliberate creation of addicted markets. Key to these global strategies is the ongoing targeting of women and minorities in both developed and developing countries by a few massive (and diversified) transnational tobacco companies. Consequently, the task of understanding the issues surrounding smoking for women and girls is a political as well as a health issue.

The "tobacco control movement" is a term that describes the global coalition of health groups, governments, and advocacy organizations devoted to eradicating tobacco use in the world. Canada is a prominent leader among countries involved in this movement. While this coalition has been relatively powerful in certain circumstances, it has also been narrow in its focus. Until very recently it paid little attention to the specific issues surrounding women and minorities, assuming that a generic approach to smoking (that is, androcentric) was adequate.

Research on the links between inequality and smoking and the use of more qualitative methods are the goals of the few feminists working within this movement. In this context, the International Network of Women Against Tobacco (INWAT), a global activist group, works within the movement to widen the prevailing understanding of the issues connected to tobacco use and their solutions. This means many things: political action, research, encouragement of women's leadership, program development for women and girls, and lobbying. In research it often means a clear departure from the traditional approach of massive quantitative studies, investigating questions derived from adherence to a medical model. This chapter describes one such approach: its purpose, its method, and its implications for responding to the trends of women's smoking.

Smoking is the leading cause of death of Canadian women. Each year in this country, about fifteen thousand women die of smoking-related causes[1] — or one every thirty-five minutes.

However, this women's issue has received less attention than it merits. The tobacco-control movement has dealt with the issue of smoking, not

---

1   Regarding these rates and others, please see: *The Background Paper on Women and Tobacco*, Health Canada, Ottawa, 1990; and *Taking Control: An Action Handbook on Women and Tobacco*, Canadian Council on Smoking and Health, Ottawa, 1989.

women's smoking. The women's health movement has seen it as an issue much lower in priority than other more clearly "female-specific" health issues, such as reproductive health, abortion, and breast cancer. The policy and program developers in government have generally overlooked gender-specific qualities of smoking behaviour (as well as issues of class and race) in developing tobacco-control legislation and regulation.

Despite growing research on the female-specific effects of smoking, such as links with cervical and breast cancer, osteoporosis, and menstrual, menopausal, and pregnancy irregularities, women's and girls' smoking is still not widely seen as a women's issue. The task of uncovering the full effect of smoking on the female body is incomplete. A gender-sensitive perspective in smoking and health research has emerged only in the last few years and will take some time to permeate health promotion and policy development.

Although ultimately the health effects of smoking are the main concern, economic, social, psychological, and cultural aspects of women's smoking are also important. The feminist approach to understanding tobacco use is holistic and interdisciplinary, developing the links between these aspects and the health effects.

TRENDS IN WOMEN'S SMOKING IN CANADA

Although the overall rates of tobacco consumption have declined in the last twenty-five years, the steadiest and greatest decline has been in the male smoking rate. It has fallen by over 25 per cent over the past twenty-five years (54 to 26 per cent), while the female rate has declined by only 2 per cent (28 to 26 per cent).[2] Among teen girls, for the first time in history, the rate of smoking is higher than that of their male counterparts (20 per cent compared to 12 per cent for fifteen- to nineteen-year-olds).[3] There is also a trend towards more older women smoking than before, in part because more women smokers are moving through the population. Finally, the high rates of First Nations girls' and women's smoking stand out as a serious problem in Canada and in the world.[4]

These trends are typical of several other industrialized countries.

2   *The Canadian Labour Force Survey* (1966), Statistics Canada, and *General Social Survey* (1991), Statistics Canada.

3   *General Social Survey* (1990), and *The Canadian Labour Force Survey* (1991).

4   For example, high rates of smoking are found among Dene (62 per cent), Metis (62 per cent) and Inuit (73 per cent) girls in the Northwest Territories, where their rates are higher than non-Native girls (44 per cent). For more detail, see W. Millar, *Tobacco Use by Youth in the Canadian Arctic*, Health and Welfare Canada, 1989.

Women's and girls' smoking rates in developed countries have appeared particularly resistant to general control measures, and Aboriginal peoples' smoking rates in several countries (such as Australia and New Zealand) are also extremely high.

Women began to smoke in great numbers later than men. Consequently, it is to be expected that their rates of smoking and morbidity and mortality will peak later than men's.[5] Despite this, the slower rate of decline between male and female rates is disturbing, as is the potentially troublesome rate of teen girls' smoking. Possibly smoking in Canada in future will become primarily a female activity.[6] It is already associated with social class.[7] However, the possibilities for preventing further development of these patterns may be increased if research, policy, and programming become gender-sensitive, and if relevant, effective interventions are created.

The cultural history of women's smoking is an important dimension of this problem. Women's smoking behaviour has always been interpreted and influenced by social, political, and economic interests. Prior to the 1920s in Canada smoking was associated with prostitution. Women's smoking was actively proscribed until the 1920s, when it was redefined as a daring, liberating behaviour. By 1928 the tobacco industry had produced the first advertisement explicitly directed at women.

The ensuing decades brought differing cultural definitions of women's smoking. In the 1930s, smoking was associated with glamorous and sophisticated Hollywood stars and promoted as a fashionable, classy behaviour. By 1940 it was being portrayed as androgynous, in keeping with the industrious wartime image of women catapulted into the non-traditional workforce. After the war smoking was portrayed as romantic, (hetero)sexual and companionate, in keeping with the dominant trend of women reverting to domesticity.

By the 1950s, as the first health concerns about smoking were just beginning to emerge, the image of smoking for women was shifted to em-

5   In 1992, 5,200 died of breast cancer and 5,000 died of lung cancer in Canada, according to the Canadian Centre for Health Information, Statistics Canada. The current lung cancer mortality reflects twenty years of development in women who began to smoking in the 1970s. Hence, this rate will rise in the years to come.

6   In 1991, according to the *General Social Survey*, there were equal proportions of smokers among men and women in Canada. As there are more women in the population, there are about fifty thousand more women than men smoking in Canada.

7   For example, according to the *Health Promotion Survey* of 1990, unemployed women smoke at the rate of 42 per cent, and employed women at 31 per cent. According to the *General Social Survey* of 1991, university-educated women smoke at the lowest rate (18 per cent) of all groups of women.

phasize several features of the newly developed "feminine" cigarette: long, light, and filtered. These cigarettes developed the special market of women's cigarettes, still a focus of marketing today.

By the 1960s and 1970s, women's smoking was associated with feminism, equality, and liberation. The famous Virginia Slims advertisements, still used, featuring the slogan "You've Come A Long Way, Baby!" emerged during this period. By the 1970s and 1980s smoking for women was associated with sexual risk, sexual excitement, athleticism, and heterosexual companionship, but advertising was also introducing several themes of all-female sociability. By the late 1980s advertisers were searching for positive imagery of a habit that had fallen into a minority activity in North America and had become associated with oppressed groups that had few choices. The theme of "choice" was exploited by the marketers and advertisers to promote cigarettes to women, encouraging women to resist authority and keep "choosing" to smoke.

Although the advertisers, marketers, and promoters of cigarettes have taken a women-specific approach since 1928, researchers and program- and policy-makers in tobacco control have only recently seen the value of this perspective.

TRADITIONAL RESPONSES TO WOMEN'S SMOKING

Before the 1920s, opposition to cigarettes was firmly on the agenda of the Canadian and U.S. maternal feminist movements, which saw both tobacco and alcohol as instruments of women's oppression. Although the campaigns were morally based, they were adamant that the use of both of these substances contributed to the oppression of women and children, at least indirectly.

The tobacco issue disappeared from the agenda of the women's movement during the First World War, as the North American tobacco industry, in concert with government, redefined cigarette smoking as patriotic. The political economy of tobacco and the powerful influence of the tobacco industry were, and still are, a primary force in defining tobacco policies. Developed and developing countries alike become dependent and committed to protecting the interests of the tobacco industry.

Apart from this historical opposition, women's smoking has been socially acceptable in Canada. As a health problem, only two aspects of

women's smoking—pregnancy complications and facial wrinkles—
merited mention by the programmers in tobacco control until the mid-
1980s. This limited and sexist view of women's smoking was not unique
to Canada, as many countries similarly restricted their approaches.

The concentration on pregnancy complications indicates that the
only important aspect of women's smoking was considered to be its
effect on fetal health. The issue of the supposed facial wrinkling caused
by smoking illustrated a similar sexist assumption that women's visual
beauty was compromised by smoking, which was also something to
merit intervention. As a result, during the 1970s and 1980s several campaigns in various countries were designed to end smoking by pregnant
women and to convince female smokers that they were threatened with
diminished looks.[8]

The pregnancy campaigns were in the "uterine tradition,"[9] stressing
the reproductive value of women. Bobbie Jacobson describes these campaigns as seeing women's health as important insofar as women are "re-
ceptacles for future generations."[10] The facial wrinkles campaign is consistent with the "beauty culture" formulation of attitudes to women's
bodies and health, in which ideal female beauty is defined as eternally
youthful.[11] This blend of ageism and sexism renders the facial wrinkle
campaigns as particularly unacceptable.

In *The Beauty Myth* Naomi Wolf states, "Our society *does* reward
beauty on the outside over health on the inside,"[12] and therefore women
are "right" when they smoke to lose weight. This desire is one exploited
by tobacco marketers and uncritiqued by traditional tobacco-control
programmers. Only after feminist critique of these interventions in re-

8   Some examples include the 1984 "Pretty Face" campaign in Western Australia featuring the
     theme of facial wrinkling, and a New South Wales "Quit for Life" campaign featuring a
     woman with a tracheotomy due cancer of the larynx, a rarely seen smoking-related disease of
     relatively little importance being featured in a dramatic, horror-based campaign. In the
     United States, a Cancer Society campaign featuring a fetus smoking was roundly condemned
     by the women's movement, which perceived it as an anti-choice conspiracy. In the United
     Kingdom the "Faggash Lil" campaign became famous for stressing only women's superficial
     beauty as an issue. Another example of retrogressive campaigning was the 1987 New South
     Wales Anti-Cancer Council of 1987, which said "Women are supposed to be smart" and con-
     cluded that those who smoked were anything but. This reinforcement of individualized
     blame drew complaints about its guilt-producing potential.

9   J. Matthews, "Building the Body Beautiful: The Femininity of Modernity," in *Australian
     Feminist Studies* 5 (Summer, 1987), pp.14-17.

10   B. Jacobson, *Beating the Ladykillers* (London: Pluto Press, 1986), p.125.

11   See Matthews, "Building the Body Beautiful," pp.24-31.

12   Naomi Wolf, *The Beauty Myth* (New York: Vintage Books, 1990), p.230.

cent years has there been any serious attempt to make the value of women's health, for its own sake, central to the tobacco cessation and prevention message.

TOBACCO RESEARCH

In the background of these programs, tobacco research usually followed a traditional, medical, large-scale model. Much research was (and still is) dependent upon medical clinical trials and large-scale household surveys to establish further health effects of smoking, rates of smoking, or the effectiveness of large-scale prevention programs. While these activities are useful and necessary for the identification of important research areas, they can pay little attention to the psychosocial issues and subjective interpretations of smoking behaviour. Innovative, qualitative feminist research is intended to address these aspects of smoking behaviour. Indeed, bringing feminist methods to bear on smoking research creates several changes.

First, research becomes gender sensitive and, in fact, deliberately directed at women and girls. Research becomes *for* women; that is, the results of the project are translated into useful information and action. The researcher becomes located on an equal plane as the research participant, and the knowledge and wisdom of the woman smoker become important. There is more chance that the research is interdisciplinary, involving perspectives on several aspects of women's lives.

The study described here incorporates all of these characteristics. The research question was, "What does smoking mean to women smokers?" Thirty-five women smokers, some of them abused women residents in shelters and some self-identified feminists, were asked to discuss aspects of this question in open-ended interviews. These interviews were done in light of a central unresolved question in developing a feminist theory of smoking (indeed, of addiction): "Is smoking a passive response to inequality and oppression, or is it an act of resistance to patriarchal oppression?" No hypothesis was set out to be proven, and no differences were predicted between the two groups; rather, themes were expected to emerge from the research to guide both theory development and program and policy initiatives.

Unstructured interviews ranged from one to four hours and included these questions:

1. Can you recall your first cigarette?
2. What do you like about smoking?
3. What do you dislike about smoking?
4. When and where do you smoke?
5. What changes in your smoking patterns have taken place over the years?
6. Do you ever smoke in place of doing or saying something else?
7. Have you ever thought of quitting?
8. Have you ever quit? In what circumstances?
9. How do you feel about smoking? What does it mean to you?
10. Can you visualize yourself as a non-smoker? What would your life have to be like?

The study was aimed at constructing theory from the data generated in the conversational interviews, "guided by the principle of emerging theory," and aimed at "detecting and reconstructing those generalizations inherent in the intersubjectively performed 'social construction of reality' of the life-world."[13]

The results of the study can be used in several ways. First, they may make a contribution to the development of a theory of women's smoking. Second, the results are pertinent to the development of woman-positive and woman-sensitive prevention and cessation programming. Third, the results can be used to improve policy measures with respect to their effect on female smokers. Most importantly, women, and specifically women who smoke, may acquire insights into smoking behaviour.

CHANGING METHODS

Attempting to understand why women continue and girls start to smoke in an era of smoking's diminishing popularity and intense social proscription requires this type of qualitative methodology. Traditional survey and large-trial research on smoking has pinpointed trends of concern and the general effectiveness of broad-based interventions. Such

13   J. Matthews, *Interactionism in Sociology: Theoretical Basis and Methodological Implications* (Singapore: The Institute of Southeast Asian Studies, 1981), p.24.

research has also informed the development of macropolicies designed
to affect the availability and control of tobacco, such as tobacco taxation
policy, or legislation regarding packaging or sales. While such policies
do have an effect on overall consumption, and clearly have had an effect
on some women, they have usually been conceived with little knowledge
of the meaning of women's smoking. In addition, such research and the
policy and programming that it underpins have often been androcentric, ignoring the female reality and, worse, assuming the total relevance
of the male reality.[14]

Ironically, most qualitative research on subjective interpretations of
smoking has been done in secret by tobacco companies in order to improve and focus their brand development. This information has probably been a crucial factor in the development of some highly successful
advertising and marketing directions over the past several decades.

CHANGING DATA

The interview material was taped and transcribed and then analysed to
identify emerging themes. The five main themes that emerged indicated
a number of meanings attributed to smoking:

1. Smoking as a means of organizing social relationships

> *Michelle:* I tend to say to the kids, "Just let Mommy have this
> smoke in peace" ... it's something like it's my time
> that I've put down to thinking about what I want to
> do.

> *Adelaide,* We may get into a discussion and I'll get up and
> *describing a* smoke outside the door and still participate. On one
> *meeting with* hand, that could be moving away from the conflict,
> *male colleagues:* but it's not; it's really a power thing. I'll move out
> here, but you have to sit there and listen to me. It's
> changing the dynamic. The one who changes it gets
> the power. The one who is changing gets watched.

14 Indeed, lung cancer, the second most important health effect of cigarette smoking, was assumed to be a male disease as recently as the 1960s. This was because lung cancer takes
twenty-five years to develop and women had not, by 1960, been smoking at significant rates
for twenty-five years. In the 1990s, however, lung cancer will become the leading cancer killer
among women in North America.

The time I would do it is when I want them to listen
to me, to see it my way ... and so I might move, so
they have to listen. I feel in a position of more control, it's useful, it's manipulative, is what it is.

2. Smoking as a means of controlling emotional expression

Vera: I don't want to be miserable, I don't want to bark at
people. Because I like to be nice.

Victoria: If I didn't smoke I would be angry and irritable. I
don't want to be like that ... I don't want to be growl-
ing at everybody, at my daughter, for example, at
my family ... if I didn't smoke I'd be lashing out at
people ... there's so many other things that you have
to control.

Alberta: ... if I'm angry about something, I can have a cigarette and then not have to express it some other way.

3. Smoking as a means of creating a self-image

Alice: I actually think I relate smoking to cheating death
and I relate all my addictions personally as I'm
tough, I cheat. Not that I'm tough to smoke, but I'm
cheating death.

On contemplating
quitting, Alberta said: ... we are the outcasts and we have our own bonding
because of that and I would miss that.

4. Smoking as a means of exhibiting or reflecting dependency

For Carla: My cigarettes have been more consistent than any
people in my life ... a real time marker.

For Judith: I can't rely on somebody to make me feel secure like

I do with a cigarette. I can't rely on people. The only person I can rely on is myself ... and a cigarette.

5. Smoking as a means of problematizing identity and searching for self

Jessie: [I] must [now] assume responsibility for my life and that includes and implies quitting.

Barbara: Cigarettes do control me, I guess, but I control them.

These five themes emerged in both groups of women, with only minor differences in prominence emerging between the two groups. Under each of these themes, further subdivisions were identified.[15] The five themes were regarded as categories, for the purpose of developing theory. The subthemes were viewed as properties, or as elements of the categories. Developing linkages between these categories formed the basis of the theory about the meaning of smoking to women.

After these steps, the themes of "control" and "adaptation" emerged from the data as the dominant threads in all five categories. The data from the women on the theme of "control" focused on both controlling external forces in their lives and controlling their emotional responses. The data on the theme of "adaptation" focused on adapting to both the individual circumstances of their lives and the externally imposed roles.

Various subthemes reflect the interpretation of these women's smoking as an *active* response, intended to *control* some aspect of experience (for example, using smoking to create an image, distinguish oneself from others, and proactively define oneself in relation to others). Other subthemes reflect the *passive* response, intended to *adapt* to some aspect of experience (for example, the use of smoking as comfort, a way to defuse conflict, or as a way to absorb and suppress negative emotions).

However, *all* of these subthemes reveal the utility of smoking as a means of defining the self in relation to the world including one's identity, image, and emotional response to social reality. While this process is often fraught with contradiction and is inconclusive, the respondents often described smoking as an integral component.

15   These are: a) the equalizer, bonding, distancing, and defusing functions; b) independence, difference, symbol and ritual, conformity and approval, and weight control; c) suppression of negative emotions, alleviating emotions, allowing positive emotions, and anesthetizing feelings; d) support, predictability, and malleability; e) guilt, tension about the female identity, contradictions, and self-castigation.

In general, the meaning of smoking to women most often crystallized around searching for self, or problematizing identity. The largest part of the interview material hinged on some aspect of this theme. Inherent in this is considerable contradiction and resulting tension, not only within and between the subgroups of the sample but also often within the same woman. Examples of the issues that emerged here include:

A) the contradictions of smoking (seeking control but being controlled by an addictive substance),
B) self-castigation (the self-aspersions of weakness resulting from being unable to control [quit] smoking),
C) guilt (feeling guilty about the effects on others, but not about themselves),
D) tension about the female identity (are they addicts or rebels, passive or active, feminine or not?).

Smoking is, or has become, at least one mechanism through which women can make and express their identity. Women's smoking, like many other behaviours, is and was, for the women in this study, an activity that is an important component of their self-definition and psychosocial experience in the world. As the definition of women's smoking has undergone, and continues to undergo, social and cultural redefinitions, the woman smoker is continually pushed to change her definition of self in relation to smoking behaviour, and the meaning of smoking with respect to the self. Assessing smoking's meaning in this way involves both exploring the role of smoking for women from the "inside" of the body, as well as exploring its meaning as derived from and applied by external sources. The meaning(s) of smoking for women from both of these viewpoints are multilayered, interactive, variable, and in a constant state of evolution. In deriving a comprehensive theory of the meaning of smoking to women, then, both viewpoints and their interactive, dynamic relationship must be acknowledged and understood.

It is useful to apply Sandra Lee Bartky's concept of "disciplinary practices" to women's smoking behaviour. She suggests that there are three "disciplinary practices" that are carried out on women to create the artifice of femininity and influence the female identity. These are "those that aim to produce a body of a certain size and general configuration; those that bring forth from this body a specific repertoire of gestures, postures, and movements; and those that are directed toward the display of this body as an ornamented surface."[16]

Aspects of these disciplinary practices that encourage certain kinds of deportment or emotional style in women can be linked to some of the data and emerging theory of this study. For example, Bartky suggests that expressions of women's true emotional states are actively discouraged. Examples are measures such as "wearing a fixed smile" despite one's inner state, or eliminating facial wrinkles despite their indication of past emotional experiences.

The use of smoking to suppress negative emotions as described by the women in this study is an example of this type of "disciplinary practice" at work. While the women describe this as a reason for smoking, it can also be understood as a benefit to society of women's smoking, given what Bartky terms "the modernization of patriarchal domination" (p.64). In this sense, smoking's utility is a current phenomenon; there is only a seventy-year history of women smoking cigarettes in Canada. However, society benefits from women's smoking in that women's full expression of discontent, the unscreened response to the realities of oppression, stress, and conformist pressure, is muted and siphoned off through the addiction to and the act of smoking.[17]

In other words, smoking (and other disciplinary practices) may be burdens, but they are also elements of an individual's social competence. Giving up smoking would constitute for these women what Bartky calls "de-skilling" (p.77), a process with losses attached. When the issue is looked at in this way, the women in the study can be seen as demonstrating their agency in part through smoking; and, as they clearly expressed, they would suffer a void in their sense of self and their ability to negotiate social life if they were to give up the behaviour. Responses to the last question "Can you visualize yourself as a non-smoker? What would your life have to be like?" indicate the significance of smoking as part of personal identity. Judith, for example, said:

If I could have my life the way I wanted it, I don't think I would smoke. I wouldn't have to worry about being scared or not, [I'd

16   S. Bartky, "Foucault, Femininity and the Modernization of Patriarchal Power," in I. Diamond and L. Quimby eds., in *Feminism and Foucault: Reflections on Resistance* (Boston, Northeastern University Press, 1988), p.64.

17   In this sense, tobacco is similar to psychotropic drug use in women. Society benefits from prescribing various drugs to women that will act as a buffer between social reality and psychological response. Tobacco and psychotropics differ markedly from other drugs such as alcohol and hallucinogens on this level.

be] at ease with myself. I would be relaxed the whole time. [If] my life was happy, I wouldn't need it. I wouldn't be constantly looking over my shoulder, thinking I've got to defend myself.

Vera, in response to the same question:

I guess if you thought someone really, really cared ... if you're in a really good relationship where there's lots of love. I can't even see myself without a cigarette, like every time I picture myself I have a cigarette going.

And Alberta:

... cigarettes have been with me for most of my life. It's been something that's been really consistent and something that I can rely on.

Finally, Victoria states:

It frightens me, it actually frightens me, to think of not smoking. I'm not sure why, it must be more of a security thing.

CHANGING THEORY

A theory of the meaning of smoking to women, as evidenced by the data in this study, can be stated as:

Smoking is an important means through which women control and adapt to both internal and external circumstances. Smoking is a means of mediating between the world of emotions and outside reality. It is a means of reacting to and/or acting upon social reality and a means of defining the self in relation to lived experience.

As the threads of control and adaptation inhabit all five of the categories of the data, they form the essence of the developing theory. It must be recognized, though, that theorizing about women and smoking is also a dynamic activity, as meaning is constantly evolving in response to changing internal and external definitions of smoking and self. The question of whether smoking is an active or a passive response to the world remains. In some cases, as women, we can only react to the world, our place in it, and our emotional responses to it. In other cases, we may seek the assistance of tobacco and behaviours such as smoking to forge a sense of self. Whatever our circumstances, as women we must continuously struggle to define ourselves in a world that still largely excludes consideration of our experience in forming definitions of female identity.

CHANGING PRACTICE

Implications for policy and program design

To be effective, program development in tobacco control for women must account for the female experience and subjective interpretations of smoking. As long as there are subjectively based meanings of smoking for women and subjective mechanisms for interpreting smoking, straightforward health information programs based on a rational-medical model will not suffice. Also, the specific cultural significance of smoking must underpin appropriate programming.[18]

The limitations of the traditional medical and epidemiological perspective on smoking are being challenged, allowing socio-cultural perspectives to influence tobacco control and policy development. Tobacco control neglected the "possible subjective benefits of smoking" and denied "the existence of an everyday logic which involves factors other than medical criteria."[19]

The research reported here offers a socio-cultural theory of women's smoking that is based on the subjectivity of the woman smoker. It suggests that program and policy development should also acknowledge the important role of women's smoking in the management of the female experience, in which identity is presented, social interaction framed, and emotions tempered. This emphasis on identity definition and development is particularly important in countries like Canada,

18   For example, tobacco use in First Nations communities in North America is extremely complex and deep-rooted in shamanistic, medicinal, and cultural traditions. Separating traditional meanings of tobacco from the relatively recent patterns of smoking cigarettes is an enormous but necessary task best done by First Nations people themselves. In Canada, for example, some Native people feel that, while alcohol was introduced by the "white man," tobacco was originated and owned by Native people. This presents a different context for tobacco education and control messages.

19   A. Wetterer and J. von Troschke, *Smoker Motivation* (Berlin: Springer-Verlag, 1986), p.79.

where the remaining or new female smokers are most likely to come from disadvantaged groups.

Currently, low-income women (and men) and First Nations people are most likely to be smoking, and young women most likely to be taking up smoking. In this context the preservation of self-identity and resistance of stigma will be paramount issues and will presumably continue to inform the meaning of smoking for women and diverse populations.

Similarly, policy development in tobacco control can be reassessed in light of the trends of the data and qualitative material reported here. An example of macro tobacco control policy is legislation to raise the tobacco tax, making cigarettes less easily available. This is an effective macro measure based on a theory of reducing consumption by restricting availability.

Given women's lower average wage, and in light of the increasing concentration of smokers in low-income, unemployed, and Aboriginal groups, the impact of higher taxation is enhanced. No Canadian research yet exists on the effects of price increases on disadvantaged smokers, but a study in the United Kingdom revealed that low-income mothers considered their food budgets to be elastic, but not their cigarette budgets.[20] In short, the regressive and punitive aspects of squeezing smokers through extraordinary price increases have not been considered to be important compared to the public health effects of lowering overall consumption. A woman-sensitive policy would at least investigate the impact of such a policy and recommend that compensatory measures (such as free cessation assistance to low-income smokers) be enacted simultaneously.

The complicated impact on First Nations communities in Canada of high tobacco taxes also became evident in 1994, when border reserves became a focus of cross-border smuggling and resale of cigarettes. The combination of lack of economic opportunity, historical and legal tax-exempt status, and traditional perspectives on tobacco that differ from the health promoters created a situation in which it became essential to understand the tobacco question from an interdisciplinary, multilayered, and historical viewpoint. It also demonstrated that there were limits to increased tobacco taxation among smokers in Canada, who created a ready market for illegal cigarettes.

20   Action on Smoking and Health (ASH, UK), *Her Share of Misfortune: Women, Smoking and Low Income*, London, 1993; and *Expert Report of the ASH Working Group on Women and Smoking*, London, 1993.

Woman-positive prevention and cessation programs

Woman-specific prevention and cessation programs that are also woman-positive are a recent innovation. Worldwide, Canada and Australia have some of the most progressive programs, and the Canadian efforts have been emulated by global tobacco-control networks and authorities such as the World Health Organization. It is anticipated that some of the female-specific approaches from the developed countries may be tried in countries in which there are still negligible female smoking rates, but at much earlier stages in the female smoking epidemic.

In 1983 the Fifth World Conference on Tobacco or Health identified women (for the first time) as a group for "special concern," and women's smoking as an international concern. Following this, some developed countries, notably Canada and Australia, began to consider women a special group in smoking prevention and cessation and to develop some specific woman-focused messages.

The efforts to focus on women's smoking in Canada, Australia, and the United Kingdom were improving in the 1980s, but clearly suffered from a lack of a coherent analysis or theory. Consequently, some campaigns were properly woman-positive, while others in the same country or state were not. The advertising firms hired by government agencies to conceptualize campaigns have provided an additional obstacle. Many enlightened health-promotion workers find themselves arguing with (often male) media experts about effective advertising themes, struggling to create woman-positive campaigns. In the last five years, however, Canada has developed a more coherent framework for woman-positive prevention and cessation programs, due to more activism and research in the area of women's smoking.[21]

Some dissenters claim that since men's smoking rates are still higher than women's, any efforts in program creation and specificity should be focused on men. Others simply see this as evidence of feminist redefinition and overdramatization of a simple problem: that of addiction to a substance through habituated use, and the need for cessation strategies. These critics ignore the impact of inequality or gender on health or on the experience and meaning derived from smoking, and they often insist

21   In Canada, the "Take Control" program emerged as a tobacco initiative and was a collaborative and comprehensive prevention and cessation program aimed at women and girls. In Australia, the "Smoking, Who Needs It?" campaign emerged from the National Campaign against Drug Abuse and was directed at prevention and cessation in young women.

on more recognition of male smokers.

Such backlash and scepticism are predictable when what was considered a relatively straightforward public health problem becomes politicized through the suggestion that non-medical or non-biological factors may have the greatest influences on critical aspects of the problem. This redefinition of smoking as a social issue invokes the involvement of different experts, the influence of different policy, and the presentation of different solutions. In bringing a more generalized social definition to the public health problem of women's smoking, we would be challenging the authority and influence of the traditional experts on smoking prevention and cessation.

Suggested programming for women smokers

Despite recent advances, there is still no widely understood theoretical basis for future woman-specific and positive program development. Applying the theory developed in this study, several approaches can be recommended.

Each of the five theme areas emerging from the data in this study reveals different modes of controlling and adapting to particular life circumstances. The use of smoking to mediate the "paradox" of being female in a misogynist world is legal, logical, and beneficial to the social order and the status quo. To counter this powerful encouragement for women to smoke and/or continue to smoke, we need to define alternative program responses.

This material and message should not be confined to the internal and internalized responses and emotions of females; it should include the externalized emotions and responses of women to our lived reality. Combining these components in prevention and cessation materials and campaigns would help to diffuse the responsibility for preventing and stopping women's smoking. In short, women's smoking would be reframed as a social problem, not an individual problem.

Within each theme in the data in this study there is material that would be useful in potential programs. For example, the use of smoking in the presentation and management of self must be exposed and deconstructed before it can be replaced. Equally important is the identification of the latent benefits of women's smoking to society and the various ways that social institutions at different times and places ascribe meanings to women's smoking as a means of controlling women.

Similarly, the programming can include and expose the impact of social pressure on the development of women's image and the promotion of smoking as a positive adjunct to this image (through fashion magazines, movies, and cigarette advertisements). This addresses, from an external location, the use of smoking for women in creating and projecting an image. Whether smoking is used either to demonstrate active rebellion and resistance or passive capitulation to patriarchal reality, it is making a statement regarding our interactive relationship with our socio-cultural milieu.

The programming also needs to include information about the qualities of tobacco and its effect in comparison to other substances. If smoking can be accurately labelled and understood as a form of self-medication similar to psychotropic drug use, women smokers will see not only the extent to which smoking is controlling in an addictive sense, but also how tobacco is seen as a preferred substance from a social viewpoint. As women, we will understand how our use of smoking to suppress negative emotions, reduce stress, and cope increases our passivity and compliance, enhances our ability to carry out prescribed roles, and reduces the demands we make on others.

Finally, women smokers report a dependable psychosocial source of comfort from smoking. When we derive security, comfort, and friendship from cigarettes, it may preclude us from placing those demands on partners, job superiors, family, or friends. Society is less likely to be concerned about smoking if it assists in maintaining emotional equilibrium in its female members and provides significant social and economic benefit.

To be effective, such programs should have diverse goals and measures of success beyond cessation including the legitimate and measurable goals of reduction of consumption, temporary cessation, or simply a heightened awareness regarding one's smoking behaviour. To de-emphasize and redefine cessation and to allow these other measures of success to be counted for participants are important steps in improving women's programming.

More control efforts should be woman-specific and woman-positive. Women smokers constitute a specific audience who would benefit from special treatment particularly in the face of the practice of tobacco companies, which have long targeted females in their advertising.

Essential to all such efforts is a supportive environment in which women can share their experiences or, in the case of media campaigns, a supportive message in which women are not revictimized, devalued, or blamed. Anything less will impair the development of strong women's identities in contemporary society and increase the level of external pressure upon women smokers.

Tobacco-control programs should be comprehensive to allow observation and inclusion of the many other issues and threads that emerge when women consider their smoking. We should place emphasis on acknowledging the importance of the issues raised and meanings attributed, the uses of smoking that women document, and the ways in which smoking is identified as forging or supporting identity.

If due recognition is made of such material, then serious prevention and treatment programs must address alternative forms of coping and adaptation and, in the case of cessation, replacement of such meanings in the lives of girls and women. Without doubt, comprehensive programs need to empower, educate, and train women through examining the needs to control and adapt to lived realities through smoking. In turn, those who create and promote such programs must learn from women smokers. All too often, programs are applied to people who are perceived to be in need of assistance, whereas this approach would attribute dominant value to the input of the participants in such programs.

In general, a more sensitive, holistic approach is warranted, with particular emphasis on understanding the psychosocial benefits that women receive from smoking and on engaging with this material and replacing these benefits in a humane manner. According to this testimony, women's lives could be improved in significant ways as a direct route to reducing women's smoking.

CONCLUSION

The history of women's cigarette smoking in Canada is only seventy years old. As smoking rates diminish, the most privileged quit first, and the least privileged last. Conversely, as smoking is introduced to developing countries by aggressive multinationals, the most privileged in the population acquire the habit first, and then it is diffused through the population as a symbol of progress and modernity. While only 5-10 per cent of the women in developing countries are current smokers,[22] this proportion is rising steadily, as cigarettes are introduced in countries with less educational facilities, health-care services, or regulation in place.

The problem of smoking is being transferred to the less privileged, particularly in developing countries. Many millions of people, male and female, will die from smoking before this epidemic wanes. In the meantime the tobacco companies are exploiting every possible market with sophisticated advertising and promotion and economic incentives to governments. The companies are using the knowledge gained from understanding the smoking behaviour and the smoking epidemic in developed countries such as Canada to assist in forming strategy for developing countries.

The specific knowledge surrounding women smokers, such as that revealed in the research presented here, is useful for planning ways to counteract the development of women smokers in other countries. It is important to pursue issues regarding class, gender, aboriginal status, and race if the real meaning of smoking is to inform the development of effective action against tobacco in the future. Most importantly, the reflections and analysis of women smokers themselves offer us all the most important guidance and insight. A feminist analysis, an interdisciplinary approach, and qualitative methods are crucial additions to traditional tobacco research.

SUGGESTED READINGS

ASH (Action on Smoking and Health) *Her Share of Misfortune: Women, Smoking and Low Income.* London, 1993.
Claire Chollat-Traquet, *Woman and Tobacco* (also *Les Femmes et le Tabac* and *La Mujer y el Tabaco*), Geneva: World Health Organization, 1992.
Hilary Graham, *When Life's a Drag: Women, Smoking and Disadvantage.* London: Department of Health, 1993. Available from HMSO, PO Box 276, London, England SW8 5DT.

---

22   Claire Chollat-Traquet, *Women and Tobacco* (Geneva: World Health Organization, 1992).

Lorraine Greaves, *Smoke Screen: Women's Experiences of Tobacco*. Halifax: Fernwood Books, 1995.

Lorraine Greaves, *The Background Paper on Women and Tobacco*. Ottawa: Health and Welfare Canada, 1987, and *Update*, 2nd edition, 1990. Available from Health Services and Promotion Branch, 5th Floor, Jeanne Mance Building, Ottawa, Ontario K1A 1B4.

Lorraine Greaves, *Taking Control: An Action Handbook on Women and Tobacco*. Ottawa: Canadian Council on Smoking and Health, 1989.

Bobbie Jacobson, *The Ladykillers: Why Smoking is a Feminist Issue*. London: Eden Press, 1981.

Bobbie Jacobson, *Beating the Ladykillers*. London: Pluto Press, 1986.

Jerie Jordan, ed., "Herstories: How Tobacco Touches Women's Lives," in *World Smoking and Health*, 19, no.2, Atlanta: American Cancer Society, 1994. Available from 1599 Clifton Road NE, Atlanta, Georgia 30329-4251.

Georges Letourneau and Mario Bujold, *Smoking in Groups at Risk: The Francophones of Quebec*. Ottawa: Health and Welfare Canada, 1990. Available from Health Services and Promotion Branch, 5th Floor, Jeanne Mance Building, Ottawa, Ontario K1A 1B4.

Alan Marsh and Stephen McKay, *Poor Smokers*. Poole, Dorset, England: Policy Studies Institute, 1994. Available from BEBC Distribution Ltd., PO Box 1496, Poole, Dorset, England BH12 3YD.

KAREN MESSING

Chapter Nine: Don't Use a Wrench to Peel Potatoes: Biological Science Constructed on Male Model Systems Is a Risk to Women Workers' Health

RECENTLY, RESEARCHERS AT THE CENTRE POUR L'ÉTUDE des interactions biologiques entre la santé et l'environnement (CINBIOSE) applied to a government granting agency for money to study the health problems of women entering non-traditional manual jobs.[1] Our hypothesis was that since these jobs had been designed in relation to the average male body, tools and equipment might be the wrong size and shape for the average woman. Women might get musculo-skeletal problems from trying to perform tasks in awkward positions with badly designed equipment. In collaboration with a sociologist, we would also examine resistance to adapting the jobs so that more

1   I am grateful to the Social Sciences and Humanities Research Council of Canada, the Conseil québécois de recherche sociale, and the Equality Fund of Labour Canada for research support. I thank Lucie Dumais and Serge Daneault for helpful comments. Although I have signed this paper alone, my fellow researchers at CINBIOSE have made major contributions to it. Many of the ideas in the first section were first discussed with Donna Mergler, who was responsible for pointing out the nefarious effects of concentrating on pathology and some of the consequences of adjusting for sex. The second section leans heavily on the work of Nicole Vézina, and the ideas arise from discussions with Nicole as well as Lucie Dumais, Julie Courville, Céline Chatigny, Ana Maria Seifert, Micheline Boucher, and Suzanne DeGuire. The discussion of work and family responsibilities is indebted to conversations with Louise Vandelac and Andrée-Lise Méthot. Parts of this paper were originally published in K. Messing and D. Mergler, "The Rat Couldn't Speak, but We Can: Inhumanity in Occupational Health Research," in R. Hubbard and L. Birke, eds., Re-inventing Biology, Race, Gender and Science Series (Indianapolis: Indiana University Press, forthcoming).

women could do them. This question was part of a larger project on musculo-skeletal problems among workers of both sexes.

Some time after submitting the grant, we received a phone call from the project officer. He said he wanted to help us out. The two scientists who had been asked to comment in writing on the quality of the application had reported favourably on all aspects, but he did not think the peer review committee that they reported to would find the subject relevant. He suggested that we change the project résumé so the word "women" would be eliminated. We could then deal with the "global" problem of tools and equipment ill-adapted to the diversity of the human body. He mentioned that some men from Asiatic countries were quite small and might also have problems with tools and equipment.

After some soul-searching we changed the résumé but not the project description. However, without explanation, funding was refused for the part of the project dealing with women in non-traditional jobs. Some time later I met a member of the peer review committee and asked him why they had cut that part of the project. He explained, "In occupational health, there are central problems and peripheral problems. You were dealing with a peripheral problem." Asked for more examples of each type, he offered "construction workers falling off scaffolding" as central and "stress" as peripheral.

Funny thing: whenever we do educational sessions with women workers, stress is the number one health problem mentioned. We once asked a health and safety representative in a poultry-processing plant for the most important problem of the workers she represented. We expected to hear about cold temperatures (2°C all day long), repetitive movements (one chicken about every ten seconds), or irregular schedules (most workers learn the night before what time they are expected at work the next day, and they learn during the day what time they will be able to go home at night).[2] But she immediately tapped her head and said, "Stress: The most important problem site is the one between the ears."

How does it happen that a problem that is considered central by women workers is considered peripheral by those who decide where research money should be concentrated? Why are women's claims for compensation for physical problems caused by stress (heart attacks, for

2   M-J. Saurel-Cubizolles, M. Bourgine, A. Touranchet, and M. Kaminski, *Enquête dans les abattoirs et les conserveries des régions Bretagne et Pays-de-Loire: Conditions de travail et santé des salariés: Rapport à la Direction Régionale des Affaires Sanitaires et Sociales des Pays-de-Loire*, INSERM, Unité 149 (Villejuif, France, 1991).

example) refused four times as often as men's?[3] In particular, it seems, the further the workers are from scientists in sex, social class, and race, the more easily the scientists can ignore their needs in deciding on research priorities. But these phenomena are not accidents; they are part of the structure of academic research in occupational health.

Indeed, certain rules and standards of occupational health research support the inhumane treatment of workers, particularly women workers: 1) occupational health research is done in a context that opposes the interests of workers to those of employers and governments, where the workers have many fewer resources; 2) to avoid naming these issues, scientists are encouraged to attribute an abstract scientific value to their studies, which disconnects them from the situation under study; 3) standard practices for the conduct of occupational health research and rules for the determination of scientific quality contain hidden biases against the demonstration of occupational health hazards, particularly those affecting women; the emphasis is on well-controlled studies done in situations that bear little resemblance to real life; 4) judgement of the value of scientific research takes place in the dark anonymously, with no confrontation of judge and judged and no recourse by the scientist whose work is rejected; and 5) myths of excellence, relevance, rigour, and responsibility are used to justify the type of research done and the people allowed to do it.

Some mechanisms exist for breaking loose from this vicious circle, and some workers have succeeded in challenging it. The group of researchers with whom I work at CINBIOSE has developed in a context that facilitates collaboration between women workers and researchers; and this collaboration has led to some new ways of looking at health problems.

1. WHY THE SCIENCE OF OCCUPATIONAL HEALTH IS NOT GOOD ENOUGH FOR WOMEN WORKERS

Employers' and Employees' Interests in Occupational Health

In North America, research and practice in occupational health have been conditioned by the workers' compensation system. Accidents and illnesses covered by workers' compensation are not subject to other re-

3   Katherine Lippel, *Le stress au travail* (Cowansville, Que.: Les éditions Yvon Blais, 1993), p.228.

course.[4] The compensation system is an insurance-like set-up paid into by employers. Employers' payments, like other insurance premiums, are affected by their workers' rates of compensation, as well as by the overall level of compensation paid. Thus, employers have a collective and individual interest in limiting the number of compensable conditions.[5]

Research in occupational health has been influenced by pressure to answer the question, "Was this illness caused by an occupational exposure?" (In other words, is this illness compensable?) Problems that could not result in compensation are not considered to be occupational health problems. Research is concentrated on injuries and illnesses that have a clearly defined cause in a bona fide paid occupation, such as accidents to construction workers and miners. So, for example, the effects of women's unpaid work are not considered to be occupational health problems.[6] Occupational AIDS research has concentrated on health-care workers rather than on the much more heavily exposed sex workers, who are not covered by workers' compensation.

The link to compensation is well illustrated by the situation in Quebec, where the research money available from the occupational health granting agency is explicitly tied to the concept of "priority sectors": those occupational sectors with only 25 per cent of workers, but where compensation has been heaviest in previous years.[7] Research and prevention attempts are thus concentrated in mining, construction, and heavy industry; fewer than 10 per cent of workers in the priority sectors are women. This method of determining research priorities ordinarily results in a low scientific interest in women workers.

Women and men have very different jobs,[8] and the study of most traditional men's jobs does not yield information on risks in women's jobs.

4   This is one reason why employers in the United States have been anxious to restrict women's access to non-traditional jobs thought to cause reproductive damage. A foetus cannot be covered by workers' compensation, and a malformed child could potentially sue an employer for millions of dollars.

5   A historical and political treatment of workers' compensation can be found in Katherine Lippel, *Le droit des accidentés du travail à une indemnité: Analyse historique et critique* (Montreal: Thémis, 1986).

6   In fact, women's domestic work overload is often used as a reason for refusing compensation. Recently, the employer presented evidence in a musculo-skeletal injury case purporting to show that the woman had in fact injured herself by carrying heavy loads in her kitchen.

7   Commission de la santé et de la sécurité du travail, *Rapport d'activité 1992* (Quebec: CSST, 1993).

8   See, for example, Pat Armstrong and Hugh Armstrong, *The Double Ghetto* (Toronto: McClelland and Stewart, 1993).

Since their risks have not been thoroughly studied, women's working conditions have not been integrated into the standards for compensation.[9] It is hard to identify new compensable conditions when funding priorities favour finding low-cost engineering solutions to known problems such as noise and the lifting of heavy weights. During the first six years of its creation, 73 per cent of the projects funded by the Quebec Institute for Research in Occupational Health and Safety involved absolutely no women workers.[10]

Thus, many health problems of women workers do not fall within the purview of the workers' compensation system, but are relegated to the general health services. At the same time, policies of the Ministry of Health and Social Services (MHSS) fail to identify women's working conditions as a source of health problems.[11] For example, one part of a major policy paper identifies musculo-skeletal problems such as arthritis and rheumatism and depression as particularly common among women. Another section identifies these same problems as possible effects of workplace conditions. But the link between the two is made nowhere in the discussion or the action proposals. The numerous studies linking women's repetitive and low-control jobs to musculo-skeletal and mental health problems have been ignored.[12]

Occupational health research, then, is not driven primarily by the necessity to provide information leading to the protection of workers' health, but by a financial incentive: to lower compensation costs for employers and governments. The invisibility of women's occupational health problems permits employers to save money by transferring compensation costs to the public health-care sector.

9   Carole Brabant, "Heat Exposure Standards and Women's Work: Equitable or Debatable?" *Women and Health* 18 (1992), pp.119-30; Karen Messing, Lucie Dumais, and Patrizia Romito, "Prostitutes and Chimney Sweeps Both Have Problems: Toward Full Integration of the Two Sexes in the Study of Occupational Health," *Social Science and Medicine* 36 (1992), pp.47-55.

10   Céline Tremblay, "Les particularités et les difficultés de l'intervention préventive dans le domaine de la santé et de la sécurité des femmes en milieu de travail," paper presented at the 58th Annual Meeting of the Association canadienne-française pour l'avancement des sciences, Université Laval, Quebec City, May 14, 1990.

11   Ministère de santé et des services sociaux, *Politique de la santé et du bien-être* (Quebec: Ministère de santé et des services sociaux, 1992).

12   See Karen Messing, *Occupational Health and Safety Concerns of Canadian Women: A Review/Santé et sécurité des travailleuses: un document de base* (Ottawa: Labour Canada, 1991).

Criteria for Receiving Research Funds

Occupational health research grants can be obtained directly from employers in industries in which there is concern about human health. For example, I once attended a presentation at which a representative from Alcan described the pioneering work the company had sponsored on heart disease and cancer among its own workers. For some reason not entirely clear to us Alcan was proud of the exceptional research opportunities provided by the chemical and physical aggressors in its plant. Working for employers has been a source of funds and advancement for occupational health researchers. Successive chairmen of the McGill Medical School's Department of Epidemiology and Biostatistics have received funding from the asbestos mine-owners, the Celanese Corporation, and an explosives plant. An editor of the learned journal *Mutagenesis* has been funded by employers of radiation-exposed workers, and meetings of the Environmental Mutagenesis Society are supported by chemical companies, whose scientists report their studies on genetic damage among their employees. Funds can also be requested from government, private, or university funding agencies, which employ "peer review" (a panel of scientific experts) to determine whose research they will fund. Peer review is also used to judge the quality of research when a scientific paper is presented for publication.

Donna Mergler and I once examined determinants of our own success in getting government grants and found that proposals were more likely to be accepted if the project involved non-humans or human cells in culture rather than in live humans, if the work was done in a laboratory rather than in the field, if there was a woman on the peer review committee, and if there was no visible worker input at any level of the project.[13] Projects refused (and other proposals accepted by the same granting agency) included: a questionnaire-based study of reproductive problems of health-care workers (a study of their cells was accepted); a study of neurotoxic effects suffered by metal-exposed workers (a comparison of different neurotoxic tests of unexposed people was accepted); a study of ergonomic and social difficulties suffered by women in non-traditional jobs (a study of musculo-skeletal problems of men and women in traditional jobs was accepted). Thus, studies were funded in inverse proportion to the likelihood that their results might support

13   Karen Messing and Donna Mergler, *Determinants of Success in Obtaining Grants for Action-Oriented Research in Occupational Health* (Las Vegas, Nevada: Proceedings of the American Public Health Association, 1986).

compensation or social change. In particular, all our proposals dealing with problems specific to women were rejected during that time.

Other feminist researchers also have difficulty finding funds for these aspects of their work. Although women now constitute almost half the workforce, research in women's occupational health is strikingly under-funded. In 1989 the Health and Welfare and Labour ministries asked us to prepare a critical review of women's occupational health studies in Canada,[14] and we found that our federal granting agencies did not have much to offer. According to Health and Welfare Canada, it supported sixty-four projects on women's health, of which only three addressed women's occupational health in any way. Only 3.1 per cent of the small amount of money spent in that year on *women's* health was allocated for research on women's occupational health. Many projects supported by Health and Welfare that should have included the health effects of women's jobs did not appear to do so. For example, no occupational de-terminants were included in studies on premenstrual syndrome, factors associated with outcomes of surgery, risks for development of hyperten-sion during pregnancy, and women and health in the middle years. The situation has not changed dramatically since then.[15]

How does this work? How can supposedly objective committees act with such unanimity to prevent improvement of women's working condi-tions? Part of the answer to these questions lies in the secrets of the peer re-view process. Grant applications are sent for review to experts who know the name of the applicant, but the names of these experts are concealed both from the applicants and from other committee members. Their re-ports are then examined by committees composed of well-established sci-entists, who make the final decisions on funding. This peer review process takes place almost entirely in the dark. Judgements are irreversible; refus-als of grants can never be appealed, even when the grounds for refusal contravene the granting agencies' own published rules for funding.[16] Dis-

14   Messing, *Occupational Health and Safety Concerns*; Karen Messing, *Doing Something about It: Priorities in Women's Occupational Health* (Ottawa: Health Canada, Proceedings of the Round Table on Gender and Occupational Health, 1993), pp.155-61.

15   National Health Research and Development Program, *Research Support to Women's Health Issues* (Supplemented with information supplied by Mme Raymonde Desjardins), 1986-87.

16   We were once refused a grant on the grounds that our work was too applied, insufficiently re-lated to basic science objectives. We replied by quoting sections of the grant agency's own ap-peal for projects, which clearly and emphatically stated that applied work should be funded. We were told to submit our grant proposal again the following year. Our new proposal was rejected on the same grounds. We then submitted the same proposal without the applied part: the request was enthusiastically accepted and funded (and was among the top five pro-posals).

cussion in committee is confidential; participants are asked to disclose nothing of what is said. In some agencies, committee members vote in secret so that not even the members know the final rating of a project. This leaves the (political) heads of the agencies in a powerful position to make decisions that cannot be reviewed.

The veil lifts occasionally to reveal abusive practices. Recently, a medical researcher described the operation of an "old boys' network" at the Medical Research Council of Canada, suggesting that the network acts to discourage projects from "outsiders."[17] The Council approved projects almost automatically when the name of the researcher was well known to the committee, while it examined proposals from unknown applicants more critically. Further, many granting agencies have their peer-review committees name their successors, ensuring continuity in the control of funds.

Following are several examples of the practices in funding occupational health research, drawn from comments on grant proposals, submitted papers, and publications. These practices make it very difficult to find funding for studies of interest to women workers.

"Sufficient Evidence to Justify a Study"

Union women often express surprise and dismay after finding out how little we know about many substances to which women are routinely exposed at their jobs. This ignorance of women's exposures can have a self-reinforcing effect. One factor that weighs heavily in the decision to fund a study is, paradoxically, the demonstration that there is sufficient evidence to show that a given exposure-effect link exists. This tendency is particularly pronounced in Canada, where many researchers expect that scientific questions will be generated first in the United States. Refusals of our grant applications and those of our colleagues on the effects of manganese and styrene on chromosomes were justified on the grounds that evidence was insufficient to link these substances with the effects; the same teams were given large amounts to study the neurotoxic effects of these same substances in the same workers, because some evidence already existed to show these effects. Grants were given to the same teams for studying the exhaustively well-known effects of ionizing radiation on chromosomes, on the basis that well-established systems provided a better chance of studying genetic effects. These acceptances

17   Gilles Ste-Marie, "La recherche scientifique au Canada: Un trafic déloyal," *Le Devoir*, May 23, 1992.

and refusals may also be motivated by the fact that government and employers do not lose money in compensation by re-establishing a known causal link. If so, this would explain the rather puzzling phrase of a member of the scientific council of one of these agencies: "We don't want to spend our money preventing problems that haven't even happened yet!"

"Relevance to Health"

Another important criterion used to assess proposals for occupational health research is that the research should be relevant to human health. The medically trained committees interpret this to mean that the research must deal with pathologies[18] rather than indicators, signs or symptoms of deterioration in physical or mental states. Occupational health professionals generally come from medical faculties, where they have been trained in the diagnosis of pathologies; no part of their education ensures that they have ever studied exposures in a factory. The length and cost of training these professionals ensure that they usually do not come from working-class families. The pathologies can be studied in either humans or animals, but they must concern diseases with clear diagnoses. For example, a recent study of determinants of hand and wrist pain used workers' reports of symptoms as an indicator of health effects. The finding of a high level of pain among grocery cashiers performing repetitive movements was dismissed by other scientists with the comment: "It is highly unlikely that the superficial survey question truly identifies carpal tunnel syndrome."[19]

This requirement for pathology has three consequences. First, the pathology must have been diagnosed. Yet, as Lorraine Code points out in her chapter, the diagnosis of pathologies in women has been slowed by bias and stereotyped assumptions. Second, this requirement forces the researcher to consider events that are rare among populations still at work. Ill people often leave the workplace. They can still be studied, but relating their illnesses to their prior working conditions requires a great deal of extrapolation. Third, researchers must study working populations of enormous size in order to find a few cases of illness. Studies become extremely expensive, restricted to the largest workplaces, the very best-recognized scientists, and the best-defined risks. Thus, funds are

18   The distinction is made here between diseases diagnosed by a physician (pathologies), symptoms perceptible only to the worker herself, and pre-pathological alterations in the body, which can be revealed by researchers (signs or indicators).

19   Philip Harber, Donald Bloswick, Laura Penna, John Beck, Jason Lee, and Dan Baker, "The Ergonomic Challenge of Repetitive Motion with Varying Ergonomic Stresses," *Journal of Occupational Medicine* 34 (1992), pp.518-28.

less available for work on women's occupational health problems, since women tend to work in smaller workplaces and their problems have not interested the best-known scientists.

A still more significant consequence of waiting for pathology to occur is an increase in human suffering. Prevention strategies are most successful before pathology occurs. Symptoms of pain and distress may indicate that musculo-skeletal disease is just around the corner. Women with irregular menstrual cycles caused by variable schedules or men with pesticide-associated low sperm counts may someday have fertility problems. Waiting for the disease to happen is a delaying tactic that gets in the way of improving working conditions that could have been related to physiological or psychological effects.

Is This Health Problem Real?

The question of the "reality" of health problems is an especially important issue in occupational health, because employers' decisions about whether to compensate work-related diseases or to invest money in improved working conditions are often based on a cost-benefit analysis. For example, a ventilation system was installed in one twenty-seven-year-old plant only after workers became sensitized to the results of exposure to circulating radioactive dust.[20] This was long after the company was made aware that the dust was radioactive. With women workers, employers can delay recognition of a problem by invoking sexist denials of women's problems. For example, women workers exposed to toxic solvents or pesticides may find their symptoms of dizziness, nausea, and headaches attributed to hysterical overreaction, described in scientific language as "mass psychogenic illness."[21]

A good example of a problem treated incorrectly because of sexist bias is heat exposure. Men are typically exposed to heat at dramatic levels in foundries; this type of exposure can produce serious disorders or even death. Legal limits for heat exposure are based on studies of dynamic muscular, heat-generating work typical of these kinds of industries. However, women rarely work in this kind of factory, but often work in badly ventilated kitchens or laundries. When laundry workers complained about the difficulty of ironing sheets in thirty-degree temperatures, the employer replied that existing standards permitted thirty-

20   Karen Messing, " Union-Initiated Research in Genetic Effects of Workplace Agents," *Alternatives: Perspectives on Technology, Environment and Society* 15,1, (1988) pp.14-18.

21   Carole Brabant, Donna Mergler, and Karen Messing, "Va te faire soigner, ton usine est malade: La place de l'hystérie de masse dans la problématique de la santé des travailleuses," *Santé mentale au Québec* XV (1990), pp.181-204.

degree exposures and there was therefore no problem. In fact, such low-level heat exposure does not produce specific heat-related illness. However, when it is coupled with postural and gestural constraints involved in lifting wet sheets or moving cooking pans (rapidly moving upper limbs with little displacement of the lower body), heat puts stress on the heart, resulting in non-specific symptoms of discomfort and distress. In response to a request from women workers, Carole Brabant and her colleagues showed that cardiac strain in women laundry workers exceeded recommended levels 40 per cent of the time during warm summer months, and was comparable to levels recorded for miners.[22] Other common problems that scientists and employers have found easy to ascribe to neurosis are cumulative trauma (musculo-skeletal) disorder found among assembly-line workers doing repetitive tasks, solvent-related neurotoxic effects, and menstrual disorders (see below).[23]

Compensation can be refused to women on the basis of a "scientific" judgement that the worker is not "really" ill. I still remember with horror the story told by a woman who worked for twenty years on an assembly line in a cookie factory. She was proud of her job and had never been late or absent from work. However, when the repetitive motions she made while wrapping small cakes finally caused shoulder pain that made her unable to work, the company contested her compensation case with scientific testimony that she was not ill. Her distress was enormous: how could the company for whom she had done honest work for so long call her a liar? Her tiny salary did not make her rich, but she had thought she still had her good name.

The human consequences of scientific "rigour" in defining occupational illnesses are borne by the workers, not the scientists.

---

22   Carole Brabant, Sylvie Bédard, and Donna Mergler, "Cardiac Strain among Women Laundry Workers," *Ergonomics* (1989).

23   Yolande Lucire, "Neurosis in the Workplace," *Medical Journal of Australia* 145 (1986), pp.323-27; N.M. Hadler, "Cumulative Trauma Disorders: An Iatrogenic Concept," editorial, *Journal of Occupational Medicine* 32 (1990), pp.38-41; and Rosemarie Bowler, Donna Mergler, Stephen S. Rauch, and Russell P. Bowler, "Stability of Psychological Impairment: Two-year Follow-up of Former Microelectronics Workers' Affective and Personality Disturbance," *Women and Health* 18 (1992), pp.27-48.

Objectivity: "Some Of These Girls Have Become Rather Anxious"[24]

The type of reasoning that results in restrictive scientific definitions of occupational effects on health can be demonstrated in relation to one of our research areas that has never been specifically funded and for which several grant requests have been refused: the study of workplace effects on menstrual function. Well over half of European and North American women of reproductive age now do paid work, and 30-90 per cent of menstruating women report lower abdominal and lower back pain associated with menstrual periods.[25] It is therefore surprising that the scientific literature on menstruation has rarely concerned itself with the effects of workplace risk factors on menstrual cycle symptoms, and that western occupational health literature has almost never included menstrual symptoms among outcome variables.

One reason could be that sexist researchers have been sceptical about the existence of occupational effects on the menstrual cycle. For example, after reporting that beginning airline hostesses underwent unfavourable changes in the menstrual cycle 3.5 times as often as they underwent favourable changes, researchers commented: "There is not enough information to explain the pathophysiology of dysmenorrhea. The frequent association of dysmenorrhea with other [sic] neurotic symptoms is indicative of its psychological origin."[26] Earlier researchers had been even more frank: "In the course of the discussions which form an integral part of the annual medical examination of Hostesses it has become evident that some of these girls have become rather anxious because of [articles in the lay press on the effects of flying on air hostesses].... Let us consider the assertion that flying, particularly in jets, has a definitely adverse effect on the menstrual function of hostesses.... When the individual tables are studied, it can be seen that the greatest deterioration occurred in regularity, followed by dysmenorrhea. The former is not at all surprising [in view of the known effects of jet lag on biorhythms of men]; the latter, however, is not a measurable entity but is highly subjective and it is just here that the psychological aspect may be of the greatest

24   R.G. Cameron, "Effect of Flying on the Menstrual Function of Air Hostesses," *Aerospace Medicine* (September 1969), pp.1020-23.

25   N.F. Woods, A. Most, and G.K. Dery, "Prevalence of Premenstrual Symptoms," *American Journal of Public Health* 72 (1982), pp.1257-64; G. Sundell, I. Milsom, and Anderson, "Factors Influencing the Prevalence of Dysmenorrhea in Young Women," *British Journal of Obstetrics and Gynaecology* 97 (1990), pp.588-94; and S. Pullon, J. Reinken, and M. Sparrow, "Prevalence of Dysmenorrhea in Wellington Women," *New Zealand Medical Journal* 10 (February 1988), pp.52-54.

26   R.E. Iglesias, A. Terrés, and A. Chavarria, "Disorders of the Menstrual Cycle in Airline Stewardesses," *Aviation, Space and Environmental Medicine* (May 1980), pp.518-20.

importance."[27] In other words, menstrual pain reports are not to be trusted because scientists don't understand them.

When we demonstrated with standard epidemiological techniques that the menstrual cycle could be affected by schedule irregularities, the results were termed "cute" by some occupational health physicians, who nevertheless warned that publicizing the results would injure the scientific credibility of the research team.[28] This contempt for women's suffering was reflected in the tone of the comments we received when our requests for funding of studies of the effects of working conditions on dysmenorrhea were refused. Since well over half of young women experience menstrual pain, these attitudes may be responsible for prolonging a great deal of unnecessary suffering.

"Rigour": The Rules

In the following discussion we present some rules for the standard conduct of occupational health research, drawn from textbooks and comments on grant requests or submissions to learned journals. Although the discussion is technical, we feel it is important to demonstrate that even cold clear rules for statistical significance conceal class- or sex-biased assumptions that increase the suffering of workers. We wish to underline the fact that seemingly arcane debates on control groups and dependent variables are important in decisions to deny compensation to victims of occupational hazards.

"Appropriate Study Design"
Epidemiology textbooks suggest two types of study, both of which divide populations into categories.[29] The case-control study divides people into well and not well, looking at the proportions of exposed and not exposed among them. The cohort study divides workers into exposed and not exposed, looking at the proportions of well and not well among them. The relevant other variables are "adjusted for." (Are the workers and controls the same age? Do they smoke and drink to the same extent?) If the differences are statistically significant, a relationship is established.

27   Cameron, "Effect of Flying," pp.1020-23.

28   Karen Messing, Marie-Josèphe Saurel-Cubizolles, Monique Kaminski, and Madeleine Bourgine, "Menstrual Cycle Characteristics and Working Conditions in Poultry Slaughterhouses and Canneries," *Scandinavian Journal of Work, Environment and Health* 18 (1992), pp. 302-09

29   The following section draws heavily for its examples of orthodoxy on Richard R. Monson, *Occupational Epidemiology* (Boca Raton, Fl.: CRC Press, 1980).

Most peer-review committees will insist that cohort studies include "reference" populations, groups that differ from workers *only* by not being exposed to the agent or condition thought to be associated with a health effect. However, this is an unrealistic requirement. For example, we presented a study in which 720 poultry-processing workers reported their work schedules and their menstrual cycles in detail.[30] We found that those who had variable schedules (about half) had more irregular cycles than those who went to work and left at the same time every day. Workers' menstrual cycles were also affected by the cold temperatures and fast work-speed in this industry. Reviewers criticized the study because we did not compare poultry-processing workers to workers in some other industry: "Menstrual cycle abnormalities were studied retrospectively ... in 726 women working in poultry slaughterhouses or canning factories. The most serious problem with this study is that a control population was not studied."

Such criticisms represent a belief on the part of reviewers that some factory environments involve no risk factors. They wanted us to find a group of women workers in a factory in the same region without exposure to irregular schedules, cold temperatures, or a fast work-speed. But in fact women factory workers are always exposed to some toxic factors. We think that such comments are evidence that the reviewers (supposedly chosen for their proven expertise in the field) have little notion of what most factory jobs are like. It is hard for us to imagine a real control group that would satisfy these referees.

Keeping The Sample Uniform

Requirements can be such as to ensure that study populations represent only a very partial view of reality. Researchers insist that populations examined be as "uniform" as possible, and that uniformity be ensured by eliminating any unusual parts of the population. It is interesting to see which criteria are thought to make populations non-uniform. In cancer research, uniformity might be sought by requiring study subjects to share an urban or rural environment, some nutritional habits, or medical history. But women are more often eliminated to make samples uniform. Shelia Zahm has recently published a bibliography of studies of occupational cancer among women. Of 1,233 cancer studies published in 1971-90 in the eight major occupational health journals, only 14 per cent presented analyses of

30   Messing et al., "Menstrual Cycle Characteristics," pp.302-9.

data on white women and only 10 per cent on non-white women.[31]

In 1988, Gladys Block and her colleagues published a study of cancer among phosphate-exposed workers in a fertilizer plant.[32] Among 3,400 workers, 173 women were eliminated with the sole comment, "Females accounted for only about 5% of the study population, and were not included in these analyses." However, the 38 male workers in the drying and shipping department were not considered too small a population for study; the study noted a significant rise in their death rate.

Another example was a study, paid for with $2 million in public funds, relating cancers to a huge number of occupational exposures. When we asked the researcher why his study excluded women, he replied, "It's a cost-benefit analysis; women don't get many occupational cancers." He did not react when we suggested that his argument was circular, nor when we pointed out that for women taxpayers, the cost-benefit of a study excluding them was infinitely high. The resulting papers, published in peer-reviewed journals, made no attempt to justify the exclusion of women.[33]

In fact, there *are* some well-identified occupational cancers among women. A study of members of the American Chemical Association shows that women members have significantly high rates of ovarian and breast cancer. A Canadian study revealed that hairdressers are especially likely to get leukemia and ovarian cancer.[34] But information is still sadly lacking in this area, because of the "scientific" elimination of women from studies of occupational cancer. Thus, scientists reinforce the notion that women's jobs are safe, that women's concerns about environmental influences on breast cancer (for example) are unfounded, and that it is justifiable to exclude women's jobs from prevention efforts. Is this because scientists feel far removed in sex and/or social class from women factory workers and hairdressers?

31   Shelia Hoar Zahm, *Women's Health: Occupation and Cancer, Selected Bibliography* (Washington, D.C.: National Cancer Institute, 1993); Shelia Hoar Zahm, Linda M. Pottern, Denise Riedel Lewis, Mary H. Ward, and Deborah W. White, "Inclusion of Women and Minorities in Occupational Cancer Epidemiological Research," in *Proceedings of the International Conference on Women's Health: Occupational Cancer* (1993), p.14.

32   Gladys Block, Genevieve Matanoski, Raymond Seltser, and Thomas Mitchell, "Cancer Morbidity and Mortality in Phosphate Workers," *Cancer Research* 48 (1988), pp.7298-303. This is only one of many examples.

33   Jack Siemiatycki, Ron Dewar, Ramzan Lakhani, Louise Nadon, Lesley Richardson, and Michel Gérin, "Cancer Risks Associated with 10 Organic Dusts: Results from a Case-control Study in Montreal," *American Journal of Industrial Medicine* 16 (1989), pp.547-67.

34   J. Walrath, F.P. Li, and S.K. Hoar, "Causes of Death among Female Chemists," *American Journal of Public Health* 75 (1985), pp.883-85; J.J. Spinelli, R.P. Gallagher, Pierre R. Band, and W.J. Threlfall, "Multiple Myeloma Leukemia and Cancer of the Ovary in Cosmetologists and Hairdressers," *American Journal of Industrial Medicine* 6 (1984), pp.97-102.

"Adjustment For Relevant Variables"

"Adjusting" for a variable while analysing data means using a mathematical procedure to eliminate its effect. It is reasonable, for example, to adjust for smoking when examining the relationship of dust exposure to lung damage, because smoking is an independent determinant of lung damage and might confuse the issue if those exposed to dust smoked more or less than those not exposed. We may need to add a correction factor to the lung function of non-smokers before testing the relationship between dust exposure and lung damage.[35] This procedure, called "adjusting for smoking," allows us to determine the effect of dust on the lungs while taking into account the deleterious effects of smoking.

i) Adjusting For Sex:

However, such adjusting has been applied widely and abusively to sex differences. Studies that examine the health of workers often find that women workers report more symptoms of poor health or psychological distress than do their male counterparts. The approach to these differences is to "adjust" for sex, by adding a correction factor to the symptoms of male workers. All the studies of the wrist disease called carpal tunnel syndrome cited in a major review article "adjust" for sex, even though it has been shown repeatedly that sex is not related to carpal tunnel syndrome if anthropometric measurements related to wrist anatomy and physiology are taken into account.[36]

Adjusting would be appropriate only if sex were an independent determinant of poor health reports, for example, if women were weaker or complained more than men. If we think that "sex" is in itself a determinant of health in the same way as tobacco consumption, we will adjust for sex in relating working condition to health effects. If we think that sex is a surrogate for living or working conditions, we will be forced to carry out more complex analyses.[37]

35   By analogy, if smokers were twice as likely to get cancer, the number of cancers among non-smokers could be multiplied by two before analysis.

36   Brabant, Mergler, and Messing, "Va te faire soigner," pp.181-204; Mats Hagberg, Hal Morgenstern, and Michael Kelsh, "Impact of Occupations and Job Tasks on the Prevalence of Carpal Tunnel Syndrome," *Scandinavian Journal of Work Environment and Health* 18 (1992), pp.337-45, Table 2; and Diana S. Stetson, James W. Albers, Barbara A. Silverstein, and Robert A. Wolfe, "Effects of Age, Sex, and Anthropometric Factors on Nerve Conduction Measures," *Muscle and Nerve* 15 (1992), pp.1095-104.

37   Similar errors are often made when people of different races are studied. See, for example, Nancy Krieger, "Social Class and the Black/White Crossover in the Age-specific Incidence of Breast Cancer," *American Journal of Epidemiology* 131 (1990), pp.804-14; and Nancy Krieger and Diane L. Rowley, "Re: 'Race, Family Income and Low Birth Weight,'" *American Journal of Epidemiology* 135 (1992), p.501.

For example, we are in the process of analysing the results of a study by French researchers. In 1987, Marie-Josèphe Saurel-Cubizolles and Monique Kaminski and collaborators collected data from interviews and medical examinations of 878 women and 592 men employed in 17 poultry slaughterhouses and canneries.[38] Among them, women have significantly more leaves for health problems and work accidents than men (43 per cent cf. 33 per cent, p <0.001). Table 1 shows some associations between working conditions and medical leave for respiratory problems for women and men.[39] These associations differ by sex: women workers have more problems when the temperature is variable and when they have young children; men have fewer problems when the temperature is variable, and they do not seem to be affected by the presence of children. As we continue the analysis, we find that the factors statistically associated with respiratory problems differ by sex.

There may be differences between men's and women's bodies that cause them to react differently to the same workplace.[40] For example, women may regulate temperature differently from men. But it is more likely that the disparity is due to the different work activities ascribed to men and women in the home and at work. For example, a large number of studies show that women do most housecleaning, child care, and domestic chores (Table 2). Women in the French study were also more likely to do repetitive work, work quickly, work in the cold, and have a work station poorly adapted to their size, while the men were more likely to lift weights, to work with wet hands, wet feet, and wet clothes, and to have irregular schedules.[41] In short, adjusting for sex may mean adjusting for important working conditions. Thus, the standard techniques can obscure the types of suffering women experience at their jobs and help maintain the illusion that women are physically, mentally, and

38 The methods and many results are presented in Saurel-Cubizolles et al., "Enquête dans les abattoirs."

39 These are from unpublished data collected by Marie-Josèphe Saurel-Cubizolles and Monique Kaminski of INSERM, Unité 149, Paris, which we are analysing in collaboration with them. We are grateful for technical help from France Tissot and Marie-Aude Le Berre.

40 Messing, Occupational Health and Safety Concerns; and Julie Courville, "Les obstacles ergonomiques à l'intégration des femmes dans les postes traditionnellement masculins," M.Sc. thesis, Département des sciences biologiques, Université du Québec à Montréal, 1990.

41 Saurel-Cubizolles et al., Enquête dans les abattoirs; and Marie-Aude Le Berre, "Etude des conditions et des arrêts de travail dans des abattoirs de volaille et des conserveries," Rapport de stage présenté au CINBIOSE et au Département de Statistique, IUT Vannes. This analysis is based on data from Saurel-Cubizolles et al.

TABLE ONE: SICK LEAVE FOR RESPIRATORY PROBLEMS AMONG POULTRY-SLAUGHTERHOUSE AND CANNERY WORKERS

	WOMEN			MEN		
	NO SICK LEAVE DURING THE YEAR	TOOK SICK LEAVE DURING THE YEAR	TOTAL	NO SICK LEAVE DURING THE YEAR	TOOK SICK LEAVE DURING THE YEAR	TOTAL
HAS CHILDREN UNDER SIX	253	56 (18%)	309	173	20 (12%)	193
NO CHILDREN UNDER SIX	514	54 (10%)	568	359	40 (10%)	399
TOTAL	767	110	877	532	60	592
		p<0.001, chi²			n.s., chi²	

	WOMEN			MEN		
	NO SICK LEAVE DURING THE YEAR	TOOK SICK LEAVE DURING THE YEAR	TOTAL	NO SICK LEAVE DURING THE YEAR	TOOK SICK LEAVE DURING THE YEAR	TOTAL
WORK TEMP. CONSTANT	490	60 (11%)	550	217	32 (13%)	249
WORK TEMP. VARIABLE	276	52 (16%)	328	312	27 (8%)	339
TOTAL	766	112	878	532	60	588
		p<0.001, chi²			p<0.001, chi²	

emotionally "the weaker sex."[42] Such analyses reduce the amount of money allocated to prevent occupational disease in women.

ii)Adjusting for Socio-Economic Status (SES)

Epidemiological studies often refer to subjects' socio-economic status or social class, a loose concept that can mean different things, depending on how it is defined operationally. SES can be determined by reference to individuals' income, occupation, or educational level.

However, these determinations are often made according to the husband's occupation or education. In the past women's jobs have been ignored when determining family SES, with women assigned the same status as their husband or father. This method hides women's contribution to family income, although the additional income may improve the health of the family. There has recently been some discussion of how to take changing family situations into account, but standard techniques have not yet evolved, since the social class related to a given family income can vary according to the number of people who contribute to that income.[43] Adjusting for SES when relating work to health may therefore be misleading and diminish the possibility of finding effects among women, men, and families.

Additional problems result from the fact that a job title may not be associated with the same income or education for women as for men. More education may be required of women, and their job content may be different from men's.

Despite the vagueness and difficulties associated with determining SES, income is definitely associated with health status and with the presence/absence of some risk factors in the physical environment. Pregnancy outcome is much worse among the poorest Canadian women than among the richest.[44] The poor do not eat as well as the rich, they

---

42   The appropriate procedure is to analyse the data separately for both sexes, only considering them together if the same relationships appear to be operating in both sexes. See Margrit Eichler, "Nonsexist Research: A Metatheoretical Approach," *Indian Journal of Social Work* 53, 3 (1992), pp.329-41.

43   B.R. Blishen, W.K. Carroll, and C. Moore, "The 1981 Socioeconomic Index for Occupations in Canada," *Revue canadienne de sociologie et anthropologie* 24 (1987), pp.465-88.

44   Russell Wilkins, "Health Expectancy by Local Area in Montreal: A Summary of Findings," *Canadian Journal of Public Health* 77 (1986), pp.216-20; D. Blane, G.D. Smith, and Mel Bartley, "Social Class Differences in Years of Potential Life Lost: Size, Trends and Principal Causes," *British Medical Journal* 301, pp.429-32; and Russell Wilkins, Greg J. Sherman, and P.A.F. Best, "Findings of a New Study Relating Unfavorable Pregnancy Outcomes and Infant Mortality to Income in Canadian Urban Regions in 1986," *Health Reports* 3 (1991), pp.7-31 (Statistics Canada Catalogue 82-003). This study classes SES according to residence.

smoke more, and they are more likely to be exposed to certain environmental pollutants.

In studying workplace effects, it is hard to know how to take all of this into account. People of different social classes also have very different work environments. This may be true of people in the same workplace, and even of those with the same job title. One only has to think of secretaries in large corporations to realize that the work environments of those who hold the same job title can vary with social class. Some epidemiologists adjust for social class when they study the effects of work on health. For example, large and often-cited studies on pregnancy and work or fertility and work[45] have used this technique. However, since job status is an important determinant of social class, adjusting for SES can obscure the real effects of a work environment.[46] In fact, some health effects previously attributed to poverty may in fact be due to poor working conditions. In all these ways, adjusting for social class acts to obscure relationships between exposures and effects, resulting in underestimates of occupational disease, especially for women workers.

Accurate Evaluation Of Exposure

Allocating workers dichotomously to ill and well comparison groups can mask biologically important phenomena that could help identify hazardous situations before pathology occurs, but similar false dichotomies can also occur when classifying workers as exposed or unexposed. Such classification (even into several exposure categories) is prone to error and thus to concealment of important occupational hazards.

Exposure to toxic substances or stressful conditions can be monitored in several ways. Taking measurements in the workplace is recognized as the best method, although it does not always relate well to health effects. Working the Monday night shift may involve different products, concentrations, and methods than does activity during the day shift on Thursday. Workers even a few metres apart can be exposed quite differently. A supervisor may stand back from a tub of solvent

45   Alison D. Macdonald, J. Corbett McDonald, Ben Armstrong, Nicola Cherry, C. Delorme, A. Nolin, and D. Robert, "Occupation and Pregnancy Outcome," *British Journal of Industrial Medicine* 44 (1987), pp.521-26; and P. Rachootin and J. Olsen, "The Risk of Infertility and Delayed Conception Associated with Exposures in the Danish Workplace," *Journal of Occupational Medicine* 25 (1983), pp.394-402.

46   Chantal Brisson, D. Loomis, and N. Pearce, "Is Social Class Standardisation Appropriate in Occupational Studies?" *Journal of Epidemiology and Community Health* 41 (1987), pp.290-94; and Jack Siemiatycki, S. Wacholder, R. Dewar, et al., "Degree of Confounding Bias Related to Smoking, Ethnic Group and Socioeconomic Status in Estimates of the Associations between Occupation and Cancer," *Journal of Occupational Medicine* 30 (1988), pp.617-25.

TABLE 2: HOURS OF WORK IN THE HOME PER WEEK AMONG FRENCH
POULTRY-SLAUGHTERHOUSE AND CANNERY WORKERS

SEX	MEAN	%<5.1 HOURS	%>20.1 HOURS
WOMEN (813)	20.1	3.9	43
MEN (549)	5.1	54	0.5

Data from Saurel-Cubizolles and Kaminski, compiled by Le Berre.

FIGURE ONE: DISTRIBUTION OF GENETICALLY DETERMINED
CHARACTERISTICS BY SEX

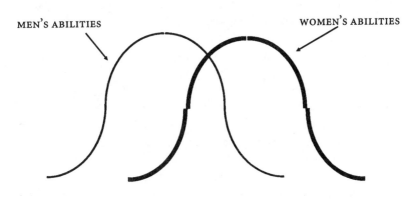

FIGURE TWO: ADAPTED FROM GUÉRIN ET AL., P59 BY ADDITION OF
FAMILY RESPONSIBILITIES

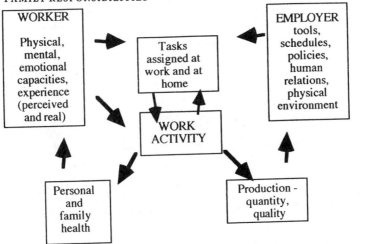

while a worker holds her face directly over it. Cold drafts may play on the neck of one worker but not another. Studies that sample at one time or one site per department may in fact produce very inaccurate results.

Since women and men with the same job title are often assigned very different tasks, they may have different exposures. For example, we recently studied municipal workers' jobs by pairing women and men hired for the same job as near as possible to the same date. At the time of the interview (about six years after hiring), thirty-four of the fifty-three pairs of men and women were assigned to the same jobs. But even among these thirty-four "true" pairs, only half gave similar job descriptions.

Over half (27/52) of the women interviewed reported that they did not do the same tasks as their male colleagues. According to interviews with both women and men gardeners reporting a sexual division of labour, women were more likely to do weeding and planting and pruning bushes. Men were more likely to do "heavier" tasks such as pushing loaded wheelbarrows uphill, pruning trees, and using forks and picks. Men were also more likely to use machines such as the cultivator.

Another example of inaccuracy in studies that do not directly measure exposure involves using job title as a measure of exposure. It is common to compute standardized death ratios by profession, comparing causes of death with respect to professional categories. This information is usually sought from death certificates, where information is notoriously inaccurate.[47] Since women are often classed as housewives unless they currently hold jobs outside the home,[48] women's professional categorization after retirement age is even less valid than men's and their death certificates can be less accurate. The fact that farm women are not classed as farmers but as farmers' wives, for example, has kept them out of large studies of pesticide-induced cancer. Also, the fact that women's job titles are less nuanced than men's makes it harder to describe women's exposures. "Clerical workers," for example, can work in many different industries with concomitant exposure to many different circumstances. When researchers attempt to examine the relation between

47   Irving J. Selikoff, "Death Certificates in Epidemiological Studies including Occupational Hazards: Inaccuracies in Occupational Categories," *American Journal of Industrial Medicine* 22 (1992), pp.493-504. Unfortunately this study appears to have included only white males; although this is not clearly stated, it is implied by the fact that death rates are compared with those of white males.

48   Elizabeth G. Marxhall, Lenore J. Gensburg, Geraldine B. Roth, Georgia K. Davidson, and Lawrence J. Dlugosz, "Comparison of Mother's Occupation and Industry from the Birth Certificate and a Self-administered Questionnaire," *Journal of Occupational Medicine* 34 (1992), pp.1090-96.

work and health, overgrouping can dilute associations of effects with hazardous conditions. In summary, imprecision in estimating exposure blurs relationships between exposures and effects and causes the underestimation of toxic effects of working conditions.[49]

These imprecisions are caused in part by a class- and sex-biased reluctance to believe worker reports. In many cases, workers have a fairly good idea of their exposure levels, but their judgements are not considered to be objective and are discounted by researchers. To relate working conditions to illness, researchers refer to "experts." For example, in a study of respiratory symptoms among 13,568 workers, experts were asked to class certain jobs as exposed or not exposed to dust by using tables relating exposures to job title. The tables had been derived seven years previously in another country, but the researchers offered this justification: "Although [an expert exposure estimate] cannot be considered an ideal reference, it is not biased by misclassifications of exposure according to personal factors as it is based only on job titles and industry sectors."[50] This study went on to correlate reported symptoms of dust exposure (difficulty breathing, asthma) with the ratings of experts. The study also correlated symptoms of dust exposure with the workers' own reports of dust exposure. Not surprisingly, the workers' reports were much better correlated with symptoms than were the experts' reports. In fact, for women workers, the correlation with experts' ratings were quite low. Did the researchers conclude that the experts' estimates were incomplete, wrongly applied to women's jobs, or out of date? Not at all: when self-reported exposure was better related to symptoms than expert-reported exposure, the self-reports of exposures and symptoms were taken to be wrong. If educated men were closer to the experts, the men were said to have made fewer errors than the women or the less-educated. But there is no reason why an "expert" who has never been in a workplace is better able than a worker to describe dust exposure; experts consistently underestimate both women's exposures and women's health problems.

Contempt for non-experts' reports of exposure has a scientific name: *recall bias*, a supposed tendency of ill people to overreport exposures. It is frequently invoked (as it was in the above case) to contest using workers' reports, but its existence has never been satisfactorily demonstrated.[51] This scepticism with regard to the estimates of interested par-

49   N.J. Birkett, "Effect of Nondifferential Misclassification on Estimates of Odds Ratios with Multiple Levels of Exposure," *American Journal of Epidemiology* 136 (1992), pp.356-62.

50   Mohammed Hsairi, Francine Kauffmann, Michel Chavance, and Patrick Brochard, "Personal Factors Related to the Perception of Occupational Exposure: An Application of a Job Exposure Matrix," *International Epidemiology Association Journal* 21 (1992), pp.972-80.

ties might be comprehensible in scientific terms if it were applied to both workers and employers. But data supplied by the company under study are routinely used as sources for exposure estimates. Company management is thus often allowed to choose the time and place of sampling for various exposures.

"Statistical Significance"

Before a drug, cosmetic, or food product can be marketed in North America, it must undergo extensive testing on animals. Although these tests do not guarantee that these substances are safe for humans (or even for animals in their natural environment), they do show a concern for human consumers. Contrary to the situation with regard to drugs and cosmetics, no law requires employers to be sure that a new work-site condition is safe before exposing workers to it. For example, tens of thousands of women worked with video display terminals (VDTs) before the first study of VDT effects on pregnancy. Even now, no one is yet absolutely sure that VDTs do not pose a danger for pregnant women. But pregnant women have not stopped working with VDTs while waiting for the evidence to come in. In this and many other cases, a decision has been made to place the burden of proof on the worker rather than on the employer. That is, an agent or condition must be proved dangerous before being removed from the workplace. Many women must have difficult pregnancies or malformed children before a dangerous chemical is removed from the workplace, although no tests are required before a new procedure is introduced.

This anti-worker bias has been heartily endorsed by scientists in their requirements for statistical tests. There is usually a rather long interval between the first doubts about particular working conditions and the time when the final word is in on the exact level of risk. Initial studies may show a weak relationship between an exposure and an effect, so that scientists have had to set a standard for accepting that a relationship exists. Standard scientific practice is to accept that there is a risk if there is less than one chance in twenty that the observed association was due to happenstance. In other words, in order for scientists to accept the fact that Agent X causes problems for pregnancy (or any other physiological state), a study must establish the toxic effects with "95 per cent cer-

51   Michael Joffe, "Male- and Female-mediated Reproductive Effects on Occupation: The Use of
     Questionnaire Methods," *Journal of Occupational Medicine* 31 (1989), pp.974-79; Michael
     Joffe, "Validity of Exposure Data Derived from Interviews with Workers," *Proceedings of the
     23rd International Congress on Occupational Health*, Montreal, 1990, p.61; and Susan MacK-
     enzie and Abby Lippman, "An Investigation of Report Bias in a Case-control Study of Preg-
     nancy Outcome," *American Journal of Epidemiology* 129 (1989), pp.65-75.

tainty." This means that if the researcher would have eighteen chances in twenty of being right in concluding that there is a risk, the study is considered to be "negative," that is, no risk has been demonstrated. This is true even if the group being studied is so small that there is virtually no chance of demonstrating an effect with 95 per cent certainty.[52]

Furthermore, for scientists to be really sure of their conclusions, more than one study must show the same relationship. Given the small numbers of workers in most women's workplaces and the large numbers of potential hazards, it is no wonder that very few dangers for pregnancy or fertility have been established.[53] The burden of proof in these statistical tests is on the side of minimizing the costs of improvements in hygiene rather than on minimizing questionable exposures. This is a political decision, but in the scientific literature it is presented as a scientific decision about "the standard level of statistical significance," and is never justified or explained.

"Lack of Bias"

Probably the most frequent question we hear from other scientists is about our relationship with unions.[54] Our colleagues express concern that we might be forced to falsify our findings in order to support union demands, or that our results may be misrepresented. We have often heard rumours that discussion of our grant applications during peer review is fraught with references to our close relationship with trade unions. The fact that our studies are often initiated by workers is thought to lead to bias.

Our colleagues seem to think that when workers are involved in efforts to improve their working conditions, they will fake symptoms to gain their point. Our work has been criticized on these grounds, even when elaborate study designs are used to take this possibility into account and even when the patterns of physiological change are so specific to the toxic effect that the worker would have to be a specialist in order

52   H.L. Needleman, "What Can the Study of Lead Teach us about Other Toxicants?" *Environmental Health Perspectives* 86 (1990), pp.183-89; and Karen Messing, "Environnement et santé: La santé au travail et le choix des scientifiques," in *L'avenir d'un monde fini: Jalons pour une éthique du développement durable*, Cahiers de recherche éthique, no.15 (Montreal: Editions Fides, 1991), pp.107-10.

53   Not only pregnant women are affected. Any powerless group (among which workers and women are well represented) may have the burden of proof placed on it without explicit justification.

54   The second-most frequent refers to our feminism. A critique of one of our articles on feminist perspectives in occupational health began, "This emotional article ..." We think the emotion was the reviewer's!

to produce them.

Many studies are published that have been initiated or inspired by employers, and the major granting agencies have put forward programs for university-industry collaborative research. One is forced to conclude that bias is only perceived when it acts in opposition to the prejudices of "mainstream" scientists. When bias is shared by most scientists, it is invisible and unremarkable.

A recent scientific paper illustrates some of the bias in interpretation that passes peer review when the employers' perspectives are supported.[55] In a study of 2,342 Quebec workers who had been compensated in 1981 for a spinal injury, records for the following three years were examined to see whether the workers were compensated for any other occupational spinal injury. The authors adjusted for sex and age without presenting any information on whether sex and age were related to working conditions, and without justifying these choices. They offered exposure information: we have no idea what job the worker was doing during the three years of follow-up.

The authors found that the workers whose initial absence from work was short were less likely to receive compensation for a recurrence. They mention that 70 per cent of those going back to work still feel pain and infer that symptoms are not a major factor in determining when an injured worker returns to work. Their interpretation: "A longer duration of the initial episode *resulted in* [our emphasis] more absence from work in the three year study period, both in terms of total cumulative duration of absence and risk of recurrence." The authors suggest that physicians should return injured workers rapidly to the workplace in order to lower the likelihood of recurrence.

Our interpretation would have been different: that workers who return quickly are less severely injured and thus less likely to suffer a relapse or re-injury. We would explain the fact that 70 per cent of workers feel pain but return to work anyway by the difficulties of dealing with the compensation system (no information was sought on the reason for return to work) or to machismo (sex differences were not presented, they were "adjusted for," so we cannot consider this hypothesis). This image of workers as lazy malingerers coddled by their colluding physicians was published in the clinical literature, where it can be cited to block compensation to injured workers who stay out "too long." Thus, human suf-

55   Michel Rossignol, Samy Suissa, and Lucien Abenahaim, "The Evolution of Compensated Occupational Spinal Injuries," *Spine* 17,9 (1992), pp.1043-47.

fering can be justified by a class-biased view of workers presented in the guise of "objective" scientific research.

The Supporting Myths: Responsibility and Excellence

The myths of rigour and objectivity justify scientists who conceal life-threatening risks to exposed workers, especially to women and minority workers. But two other myths also act to maintain this system in place: "responsibility" and "excellence."

"Responsibility" is a name often given to concealing risks. Our colleagues criticize any scientist who releases information outside refereed journals, because they believe unvetted information should be kept out of the public domain. Several of us at CINBIOSE have been criticized and threatened with legal action for giving information to workers about their own cells. A grant request was refused on the grounds that examining sperm counts of metal-exposed workers would be "irresponsible," since it would give them information they "didn't need" (because a low sperm count does not necessarily prevent conception and does not affect the well-being of workers who are not trying to conceive) and would needlessly upset them. Such "responsibility" keeps workers from being able to organize to prevent biological damage.

Lately there has been a lot of pressure from university administrators to hire "excellent" researchers for academic positions. Excellence of candidates is judged by proven grant-getting ability and the ability to publish in peer-reviewed journals with high impact factors.[56] Thus, the ability to accept the biases of the dominant culture in occupational health is a bona fide occupational qualification for a career in research. In addition, academics in occupational health have already been subjected to a selection process for membership in a privileged class, quite distant from that of the workers they will be studying. Much has been written about the racial, sex, and class composition of the medical and academic professions.[57] Similarly racism, sexism, and class bias can directly block

56   The guesswork has now been taken out of the task of evaluating candidates' curriculum vitaes by the use of impact factors for the journals in which a candidate has published; the impact factor is calculated as the average number of times an article in the given journal is cited in articles published during the current year.

57   J.L. Weaver and Sharon D. Garrett, "Sexism and Racism in the American Health Care Industry: A Comparative Analysis," in Elizabeth Fee, ed., Women and Health (Farmingdale, N.Y.: Baywood, 1983), pp.79-104; Claudia Sanmartin and Lisa Snidel, "Profile of Canadian Physicians: Results of the 1990 Physician Resource Questionnaire," Canadian Medical Association Journal 149 (1993), pp.977-84; and Anne Innis Dagg, "Women in Science: Are Conditions Improving?" in Marianne G. Ainley, ed., Despite the Odds: Essays on Canadian Women and Science (Montreal: Véhicule Press, 1990), pp.337-47.

access to university positions. In North America, government affirmative action policies provide the only serious force for including women and ethnic minorities as members of the occupational health establishment; no ways have yet been developed to facilitate the access of working-class people to university positions. But even these minor pressures towards demographic diversity in scientific institutions have recently been opposed by a discourse on "excellence" that suggests "quality" should be the only criterion for hiring.

However, scientists may be perceived as non-excellent for reasons related to their sex, class, or colour.[58] Working-class people or people of colour may express themselves in language somewhat different from that of middle-class professionals, language that may be misperceived as inaccurate or sloppy. Women students who combine childrearing with scientific training, or those who need to earn money while studying, may be misperceived as being not serious about science. (We were once told by the director of a granting agency to get rid of one of our researchers, who had trouble meeting deadlines. When we pointed out that she worked over forty hours a week despite the fact that her children's ages were three months, eighteen months, and six and eight years, he repeated that she was not serious about her work.) Thus, "excellence" can be a name given to exclusionary practices that keep women, working-class people, and minorities out of university departments and thus maintain social distance between researchers and the workers they study. Bias that makes it difficult to perceive the excellence of certain researchers can only be compensated by efforts to recruit and maintain a broader spectrum of scientists.

Forces for Change

How is it that we at CINBIOSE have survived the pressures that have forced many other scientists to use standard methods and approaches? We think that our success is due to the existence of several different structures that have been put in place in Quebec after struggles by working people and progressive scientists: 1) agreements between our university and the three major Quebec labour unions; and 2) provincial granting agencies or programs that include representation from the groups being studied.

58   Karen Messing, "Sois mâle et tais-toi: l'excellence et les chercheures universitaires," *Women's/Education/des femmes* 9 (Autumn 1991), pp.49-51.

Agreements Between the University and Community Groups

The Université du Québec à Montréal was founded in 1969 with a mandate to serve the Quebec community, including "those sectors of the community not usually served by universities." It has signed agreements with the three major Quebec unions, the Confédération des syndicats nationaux (CSN), the Fédération des travailleuses et travailleurs du Québec (FTQ), and the Centrale de l'enseignement du Québec (CEQ), providing resources for responding to union requests (such as release time for professors who participate in educational activities, university seed money for research).[59] These agreements have given us the opportunity to participate in union-organized workshops on work and health, to produce information on noise, radiation, and solvents, to work with the unions' women's committees to write brochures on the protection of pregnant women, women's occupational health, and health risks for women in non-traditional jobs, to carry out research in response to needs expressed by workers, and to provide expert testimony in litigation involving occupational health.[60]

During the 1970s, professors at the Université du Québec à Montréal joined the CSN. We negotiated clauses in our collective agreement to recognize work done in the context of the university-union agreements.

59   The Confédération des syndicats nationaux has 200,000 members, about half of them women; the Fédération des travailleuses et travailleurs du Québec has 350,000 members, about 30 per cent of them women; the Centrale de l'enseignement du Québec represents all of Quebec's primary and secondary school teachers, as well as some junior college and university lecturers and professors, and some support staff, with a large majority of women members. See also Comité conjoint UQAM-CSN-FTQ, *Le protocole d'entente UQAM-CSN-FTQ: sur la formation syndicale* (1977), Services à la collectivité, Université du Québec à Montréal, CP 8888, Succ. A, Montreal, Quebec H3C 3P8; Comité conjoint UQAM-CSN-FTQ, *Le protocole UQAM-CSN-FTQ: 1976-1986, Bilan et perspectives* (1988), Services à la collectivité, Université du Québec à Montréal; and Karen Messing, "Putting Our Two Heads Together: A Mainly Women's Research Group Looks at Women's Occupational Health," in J. Wine and J. Ristock, eds., *Feminist Activism in Canada: Bridging Academe and the Community* (Toronto: James Lorimer, 1991), reprinted in *National Women's Studies Association Journal* 3 (1991), pp.355-67.

60   The university also has an analogous agreement with women's groups called Relais-femmes. For information on this agreement, see Université du Québec à Montréal, *Le protocole UQAM-Relais-femmes*, Services à la collectivité (1982); and Marie-Hélène Côté, *Bilan des activités 1987-88 et perspectives pour la prochaine année*, Services à la collectivité (1988). In this context, we have furnished some expertise to the local women's health centre (Centre de santé des femmes) and to some groups involved with employment access such as Action-Travail des Femmes. We also work with some predominantly male unions. These experiences are outside the scope of this chapter, and are described in two papers: Donna Mergler, "Worker Participation in Occupational Health Research: Theory and Practice," *International Journal of Health Services* 17 (1987), pp.151-67; and Messing, "Union-initiated Research on Genetic Effects of Workplace Agents," *Alternatives: Perspectives on Technology, Environment and Society* 15 (1987), pp.15-18.

Because our work in occupational health is carried on as part of our regular workload (for forty-five hours of teaching in unions we can be released from forty-five hours of university teaching), many professors have been available to work with unions. The unions gain access to university services and grants. Union-initiated research, which is often received with hostility by the scientific community, *must* be recognized by our employer, at the risk of grievance procedures in the context of our collective agreement. Scientists gain access to interesting and provocative research questions and useful information on working conditions and their effects.[61]

Several features of the university-union agreement have been important in making it productive: explicit recognition of the power imbalance between career researchers and community groups, with structures in place to guarantee that the needs of both are recognized throughout the entire project and guarantees of scientific credibility through peer review. Although peer review committees need to be sensitized to the specific difficulties of community-based research, they provide an important guarantee of quality for the community group and help to maintain the scientific credibility of the researchers. Title to the research results is held by the researcher and by the initiating organization. Seed money is available for feasibility studies, which are often necessary given the radically new questions posed by community groups.

Input From The Community In Granting Agencies

Two Quebec granting agencies include representatives from labour or community groups in the committees that give out funding. The Quebec Institute for Research in Occupational Health and Safety includes representatives from labour and management on its scientific council; the two sides explicitly and openly negotiate to fund research they consider important. This process paradoxically appears to allow for *less* bias in funding, because the practical consequences of the projects are put on the table from the outset. Thus the committee identifies projects that have been initiated by unions or by employers, and the opposing parties are able to state their objections and insist on appropriate guarantees of balance and objectivity in the research design.

During the early 1980s, one of the labour representatives was in charge of women's affairs for her union and we were able to get funding

---

61   Karen Messing and Donna Mergler, "Unions and Women's Occupational Health in Quebec," in L. Briskin and P. McDermott, eds., *Women Challenging Unions* (Toronto: University of Toronto Press, 1993).

for some feminist studies. However, since her departure no such studies have been funded. We (and the union women's committees) have turned to the Quebec Council for Social Research, which incorporates community representatives in its decision-making processes. The Council is currently funding a study of the impacts and consequences of methods used to reconcile family and professional responsibility, initiated by the FTQ women's committee, as well as a study of ways to make women's work more visible, in partnership with women's committees from all three unions.

Through these institutions we have been able to build relationships with women workers. Over the years, we have been able to count on support, information, and guidance from union members, from health and safety committees, and from the very active women's committees of the three major trade unions in Quebec. With them, we have been able to come to a better understanding of the needs of women in the labour force and provide information that has been helpful to them. Their solidarity has been a source of strength to us over many years, and their insights have been invaluable. From the cleaner who explained to us why "light work" was heavier than "heavy work," to the technicians who told us why time-and-motion studies were not a good way to organize radiotherapy treatments, to the factory workers who made us understand why being able to go to the bathroom when you need to is an important health practice,[62] workers have constantly put us in touch with real occupational health problems. If our colleagues had similar opportunities and information, perhaps they would change the rules for occupational health research. They might find it easier to believe workers' accounts of risks and symptoms and put a higher priority on protecting workers' health.

2. PRACTICAL IMPLICATIONS OF DOING WOMEN-BASED RESEARCH

Since 1978 CINBIOSE scientists have been doing research in collaboration with women workers. Due to the constraints on us and on them, we cannot say that our research agenda is entirely driven by women's questions; rather, it represents a compromise between the needs of women and other workers and the requirements of academia and unions. Still, if we define feminist research as research that responds to questions asked

---

62   Doctors testified otherwise, but the workers won their case, thanks to a report prepared by Donna Mergler.

by women and proposes to improve the status of women in society, we have been engaged in feminist research for fifteen years.[63] Through these experiences we have been forced to think and act differently from the ways we had been taught during our scientific training.

We present several examples of this evolution, still in progress: 1) we have learned to think differently from other biologists about male-female biological differences in relation to fitness for specific jobs; 2) We have learned to redefine work activity in studies of occupational health and ergonomics; 3) and we are rethinking questions of expertise and knowledge.

We are not sure whether we have developed specifically feminist methodologies. Feminist studies share the necessity of challenging disciplinary and methodological barriers with other community-oriented research. Community members want answers to their questions, which are not confined to single disciplines or schools of thought. We have therefore had to take seriously the painful task of integrating inputs from social scientists, ergonomists, and biologists. We have been forced to explore combinations of qualitative and quantitative research methods, and interactions between the two.

Some writers consider that feminist methodologies require researcher subjectivity to be explicitly put to use. We in the natural sciences are not yet in a political position from which we could question the official stance of objectivity in our published papers.[64] We are already marginal in our approach to occupational health, because we are women, we work with unions, and we are not doctors. When we question established research methods, other scientists tend to think we haven't understood them properly due to our weird background. Most of our studies have therefore employed existing methods. However, many of the questions we have asked have ensured that the methods had to be applied in a new context or in a different situation. We are therefore not proposing new feminist methodologies for biological research, but just demonstrating the new insights we receive when our research is guided by a feminist agenda.

63   Shulamit Reinharz, *Feminist Methods in Social Research* (New York: Oxford University Press, 1992).

64   Patrizia Romito describes with wry humour the fate of one of her medical research papers, which did not appear sufficiently detached for the U.S. journal that she submitted it to: P. Romito, *Lavoro e salute in gravidanza* (Milan: Franco Angeli, 1990), pp.13-23.

Male/Female Biological Differences from the Point of View of Women Workers

One area in which our collaboration with women's committees has stimulated us to new ways of thinking has been in the area of research on the relative physical strength of women and men. Much current research around women and work has been motivated by questions of equality/inequality and fitness. Can women lift heavy loads?[65] Should pregnant women be exposed to chemicals? However, women workers phrase things differently. How can I get to rest when I'm tired? Whom can I get to help me when a job is too heavy? What is perceived as an equality question by scientists is experienced as a health and safety issue by workers. These two ways of thinking affect research on occupational injuries and illnesses as well as on examinations of the sexual division of labour.

Does The Sexual Division Of Labour Protect Women's Health?
In many manual occupations there is a rigid sexual division of labour. Women and men are assigned to very different jobs, whose requirements are often quite dissimilar. Although the actual jobs may be assigned to one sex in one place and time but to the other sex a few miles away or a few years later, the division of labour by sex persists.[66] One of the explanations often given is that women are biologically different from men and therefore cannot do the same jobs. Jobs held by men are more difficult, and women are not able to do them. Many women workers share this point of view. For example, Dumais and other CINBIOSE researchers found that women workers in a cookie factory resisted doing jobs assigned to men because they are "too hard."[67] Table 3 shows that work done by women and men has very different requirements. The men lift heavy weights from time to time, and the women manipulate smaller objects at high speed.

We have examined some data relevant to the relative safety of women's jobs. The classic way to compare health risks of men's and women's jobs is by looking at the likelihood of the workers sustaining

65 Evidence on this point has been reviewed by Courville, "Les obstacles ergonomiques à l'intégration des femmes"; and summarized in Messing, *Occupational Health and Safety Concerns.*

66 See, for example, Harriet Bradley, *Men's Work, Women's Work* (Minneapolis: University of Minnesota Press, 1989).

67 L. Dumais, K. Messing, A.M. Seifert, J. Courville, and N. Vézina, "Make Me a Cake as Fast as You Can: Determinants of Inertia and Change in the Sexual Division of Labour of an Industrial Bakery," *Work, Employment and Society* 7, 3, (1993), pp.363-82.

occupational injuries and illnesses by sex.[68] In Quebec, men are compensated three times as often as women. Information from other jurisdictions gives even higher ratios. The interpretation is that women's jobs are safer, due to the fact that women are unfit to be assigned to heavy work.[69] However, one of the reasons why women's traditional work appears to be a safe refuge for them is that its workload and risks have not been characterized. Only recently have ergonomists begun developing ways to represent the extraordinary demands made on women in factories and services. Most of the costs of repetitive work have been borne by women workers, and the struggle for recognition of cumulative trauma disorders has been largely waged by feminist researchers.[70]

We have studied a cleaning service assigned to suburban trains in France and employing nineteen men and seventeen women.[71] There was a rigid sexual division of labour, with the task of toilet cleaning assigned exclusively to women. Interviews and observations revealed a number of physical constraints associated with the work, and particularly with toilet cleaning, which involved trajectories of over twenty kilometres a day and work in uncomfortable postures. Some 25 per cent of cleaning time

68 We have described this phenomenon in K Messing, J. Courville, M. Boucher, L. Dumais, and A.M. Seifert, "Use of Interview Data to Complement Occupational Accident Reports When Comparing Health and Safety Risks of Blue-collar Jobs by Gender," *Safety Science* 18 (1995). Note that "work accidents" include injuries and illnesses attributable to paid work.

69 G. Laurin, *Féminisation de la main d'oeuvre: Impact sur la santé et la sécurité du travail* (Montreal: Commission de la santé et de la sécurité du Québec, 1992), p.52; C.A. Bell, N.A. Stout, T.R. Bender, C.S. Conroy, W.E. Crouse, and J.R. Myers, "Fatal Occupational Injuries in the United States, 1980 through 1985" *JAMA* 263 (1990), pp.3047-50; J.E. Cone, D. Makofsky, and R.J. Harrison, "Fatal Injuries at Work in California," *Journal of Occupational Medicine* 33 (1991), pp.813-817; A. Hough, "Comparison of Losses due to Accidents Reported by Males and Females," *Journal of Occupational Health and Safety Australia and New Zealand* 5 (1989), pp.237-42; Laurin, *Féminisation de la main d'oeuvre*; J.C. Robinson, "Trends in Racial Equality and Inequality and Exposure to Work-related Hazards," *AAOHN Journal* 37 (1989), pp.56-63; and Norman Root and Judy R. Daley, "Are Women Safer Workers?" *Monthly Labor Review*, September 1980, pp.3-10.

70 L. Punnett, J.M. Robins, D.H. Wegman, and W.M. Keyserling, "Soft Tissue Disorders in the Upper Limbs of Female Garment Workers," *Scandinavian Journal of Work, Environment and Health* 11 (1985), pp.417-25; Barbara A. Silverstein, L.J. Fine, and T.J. Armstrong, "Occupational Factors and Carpal Tunnel Syndrome," *American Journal of Industrial Medicine* 11 (1987), pp.343-58; and Susan Stock, "Workplace Ergonomic Factors and the Development of Musculoskeletal Disorders of the Neck and Upper Limbs: A Meta-analysis," *American Journal of Industrial Medicine* 19 (1991), pp.87-107.

71 K. Messing, C. Haëntjens, and G. Doniol-Shaw, "L'invisible nécessaire: l'activité de nettoyage des toilettes sur les trains de voyageurs en gare," *Le travail humain* 55 (1992), pp.353-70; and K. Messing, G. Doniol-Shaw, and C. Haëntjens, "Sugar and Spice: Health Effects of the Sexual Division of Labour among Train Cleaners," *International Journal of Health Services* 23 (1993), pp.133-46.

was spent in a crouched position. Women employees suffered from many musculo-skeletal problems. One woman over sixty was unable to stand up straight, probably due to the fact that she had swept under train seats with a tiny broom for over twenty-five years. Another, aged forty-five, had persistent back pain, but even a letter from her doctor explaining that she should not bend over did not succeed in excusing her from cleaning toilets. By contrast, men's jobs involved occasional to very occasional lifting of heavy weights, and some work accidents had occurred. Older men, however, were assigned to a job (chrome polishing) that required little energy expenditure or force. Thus, men and women did specific jobs, but only the risks associated with the men's jobs were recognized.

We have also observed hospital cleaning. Light work, done primarily by women, involves dusting, cleaning toilets, and disinfecting beds. Lifting the end of a bed during disinfection is very difficult; the end weighs twenty-five kilograms and tends to block. The number of disinfections varies according to the ward and the hospital, but it can be up to three or four a day. No other especially heavy manipulation is involved, but other constraints involve cramped, bent postures, prolonged scrubbing, and high reaching. In several hospitals women have to dust in very awkward positions due to a rule that (as one supervisor put it) "Women are not allowed to climb stepladders. If a woman climbs a stepladder the hospital's liability insurance no longer applies." The insurance policy may be fictional, but the rule is in effect in several hospitals. Men's cleaning jobs involve mopping floors, operating floor polishers and vacuum cleaners, and sometimes washing windows and emptying garbage cans. Most of this work is done while walking, and it usually does not involve scrubbing. In the hospital under study workers of both sexes and supervisors agreed that "light" work was more difficult than "heavy" work. Still, women workers by and large refused to do "heavy work," on the grounds that they did not like to climb ladders, that the mops were too heavy, or that the men were hostile to the idea. Both sexes suffered from a relatively high rate of work illnesses and injuries (one worker in four per year is compensated).

We are now selecting dimensions on which to analyse "light" and "heavy" cleaning systematically. Our major problem is that none of the grids currently available in ergonomics can be applied, since the task components that make women's jobs difficult have been unrecognized. For example, we are looking for "objective" correlatives of meticulousness, which hospital cleaners and municipal cleaners alike mentioned as an important characteristic of women's work in cleaning. We will observe the amplitude of movements and the number of times the same surface is cleaned. We will record rubbing and scrubbing incidents as indicators of precision requirements. We hope that these methods can be applied to a variety of women's traditional jobs, in order to represent effectively the difficulties of these jobs. At the same time, it has been necessary to discuss these findings with women workers, because we are suggesting that they redefine their notions of hard work and safe work.

Are Women Wrong When They Say Men's Jobs Are Riskier?

If the sexual division of labour does not prevent women from doing hard jobs, we must ask what purpose it serves. One of the purposes may be to justify health risks by reference to sexual stereotyping. Since work injuries and illnesses occur when the worker's capacity is exceeded by the job requirements, we must consider in this light the fact that men have many more work injuries and illnesses than women. At face value (discounting for the moment the fact that women's occupational health problems have been underreported) the data suggest that men are more apt than women to be in jobs that are ill fitted to their capacities. In other words, risk of injury is an occupational health problem for men, but a reason for exclusion of women.

Our experiences in union training sessions suggest that, although many women accept pain and suffering as chronic components of their jobs,[72] men are in fact more likely to accept acute risk. We observed this in an educational session with textile workers. Sex-typed jobs in their factory, with a 90 per cent male workforce, were eliminated following the enactment of human rights legislation. Changes in the collective agreement abolished seniority by sex and made all jobs accessible to all workers. A single seniority list replaced the separate male and female lists, and all workers were asked to follow the same career path. These changes coincided with heavy cuts in employment due to automation. Since many of the women's jobs on an assembly line were cut, they found themselves "bumped" to entry-level jobs. One of those jobs involved driving a motorized cart with ten 300-pound rolls of fabric. The

---

72 Julie Courville and Nicole Vézina found, in a study of poultry-slaughterhouse workers, that 71 per cent of the women doing a repetitive cutting job had experienced neck and shoulder pain during the previous week and one in five regularly experienced pain during work.

rolls had to be manipulated onto the cart, and the back end of the cart had to be directed manually, with a lever placed in an awkward position. Many women objected to doing this job because they were afraid they might hurt their backs, and they were laid off, one by one, until 90 per cent of the layoff list was female. The women demanded restoration of the segregated seniority lists. The union women's committee and the company pointed out in vain that the man who had done this job successfully for the previous two years was five feet three inches tall and weighed 130 pounds. The women retorted that they would not accept the risk of back problems.

Hospital workers have told us similar stories. A woman fought to gain access to a kitchen worker's job, then laid a grievance against lifting the heavy kitchen pots, which the male workers had lifted for years. In many hospital departments, the hospital sets informal guidelines so that a given number of men are on duty at one time. A male orderly told of being the only "official" man on duty when a patient had a seizure. He was called from the other end of the hospital to control the patient alone while being watched by four women with the same job title and the same official duties as he had. In the past, the higher pay men received for this job compensated them for the risk of injury. When the pay differential was abolished after union struggles, men like this worker ask, "Why should I take extra risks?" We conclude that women are not wrong in thinking that it is safer to relegate certain aspects of jobs to men. But we must ask whether this is the best tactic that can be used to minimize health risks to women. For example, would it not be better to train all workers to handle psychiatric emergencies using less physical strength?

Physical strength may in fact be invoked when a health and safety problem should be addressed for all workers. Strength is only mentioned when there is an underlying message that women are not "fit" for some task. But it is erroneous to pose the question of strength just in terms of women's capacities. We do not know whether there would be excess health costs if the "average" woman persisted in doing the manual tasks done by men; women in non-traditional jobs are a small, highly selected group. But we also do not know whether men would be "strong enough" to do the high-speed repetitive tasks done by women, followed by evenings and weekends occupied by domestic tasks. The concept of strength has been limited to women's attempts to enter non-traditional fields and has not included men's intolerance of the physical requirements of women's work.[73] The concept of physical strength, for example, usually includes weight-lifting rather than work-speed. Endurance may be a requirement for women who combine a long paid work day with long hours of child care and domestic work, but this has not been included in the image of strength that emerges from the ergonomics literature.

One anecdote may illustrate these issues. In a poultry-processing plant, both women workers and the employer objected when we suggested that the women could do some of the heavier jobs assigned to men. They agreed that the women could do the jobs, but pointed out that the jobs assigned to women would also have to be desegregated. All present agreed that men would not be able to do the inspecting and sorting jobs quickly and carefully enough and that the women would just have to do them over again. Talk of integrating women into men's jobs was abandoned.

Using Sexual Stereotyping To Justify Exploitation Precludes Adequate Methods For Health Protection

These reactions of workers have led us to understand that sexual stereotypes can be used to justify extreme physical exploitation. The sexual division of manual jobs may result from the fact that some jobs are at the limits of human capacity. The dexterity required to wrap 7,800 cookie packages per day kept men from applying for "women's jobs" in the cookie factory, while the women refused to lift the 40-kilogram bags of sugar up to the top of the mixing machine. In a package-sorting job, handling 12,000 kilograms per day of packages was too heavy for most women, particularly given the fact that work-site arrangements made the job harder for shorter workers. Women were eliminated de facto from this job.[74]

These excessive job requirements may be motivated by economic interest. Employers may save money by keeping working conditions close to the human limit. One plant installed soundproofing only until the legal limit of 90dbA was attained and then stopped, although only half the conveyor belts were soundproofed and the plant was still uncomfortably

73 Perhaps because job applications have been lacking, no attention has been paid to the capacity of men to do women's traditional work. This situation appears to be changing with the rise in unemployment among young men. Women's committees complain that men are moving into assembly-line jobs usually held by women.

74 J. Courville, N. Vézina, and K. Messing, "Analyse des facteurs ergonomiques pouvant entraîner l'exclusion des femmes du tri des colis postaux," *Le travail humain* 55 (1992), pp.119-34.

noisy.[75] We were consulted by a group of cleaners who were forced to carry their vacuum cleaners in a harness on their backs while cleaning stairs and hallways on the night shift. The company felt that time would be saved and the workers could cover a larger territory. However, the weight of 11 pounds, the 40°C temperature of the exhaust expelled onto the back, and the noise of 79.6 dbA were all within the limits of legality even though the cumulative effect was exhaustion.[76]

In fact, it may be that some jobs are so close to the limit of human capacity that they exceed the capacities of almost all members of one sex. In our study of women in non-traditional municipal jobs, only the largest (male) workers were able to do gardening without suffering pain or excessive fatigue. Requirements that exclude all but the tallest, heaviest workers or exclude those with family responsibilities will be hard for women; those that require a very high degree of dexterity and patience will not be tolerated by most men. In biological terms, men and women are distributed along overlapping normal curves of height, weight, ability to lift weights, endurance, patience, and dexterity (Figure 1). The degree of overlap varies with the characteristic: there is more overlap in the strength required to push weights than to lift them, for example. However, the degree of overlap can be changed by changing the job characteristics. Use of appropriate equipment can transform lifting motions into pushing, and using different tools can permit smaller workers to take advantage of their greater flexibility. Changing the types of tools and equipment or adjusting the working level can make all the difference in whether a job can be done safely and easily by members of both sexes.

Thus, there is no job that can be done by all men and no women, or by all women and no men (with some trivial exceptions such as sperm donor or surrogate mother). However, some jobs have extreme requirements, such that they are situated at or near the non-overlapping portions of the curves of male and female abilities. These jobs nevertheless involve health risks for both sexes, because when constraints are sufficient to exclude one sex, they are often at the limit of the capacity of the other. In hospitals men complain that the jobs women escape by virtue of their sex pose just as many problems for men. In fact, the requirements of jobs traditionally assigned to men make them more likely to be injured, whereas women's jobs make them more likely to contract ill-

75   At 90 dbA, 30 per cent of workers will be deaf at retirement.

76   Report submitted by a consulting firm to the Quebec Health and Safety Commission, 1992.

nesses such as repetitive strain injuries.[77]

We have learned from workers that biological differences between women and men should not be studied in isolation. Health is protected when the job is appropriate for workers' capacity, which is affected by their physical abilities and personal and social situations, as well as the tools and equipment available in the workplace. These relationships are presented schematically in Figure 2 (adapted and made gender-inclusive from a similar figure in an ergonomics textbook).[78] It can be seen from this representation that attributing male-female differences in work performance to chromosomes is a vast oversimplification.

Thus, we have been led by interactions with workers from a static view of the fitness of women's bodies for their jobs to a dynamic view of job-biology interaction. We therefore are suggesting to the workers as well as to occupational health specialists that questions they are asking about fitness for work be recast as questions about the ability of the work situation to accommodate human diversity and different techniques. We no longer look at the accidents of men and the pain of women as a necessary part of jobs that are appropriate for each sex. This change in perspective has impelled us to search for methods to understand real job requirements and their interactions with workers' bodies. We now do detailed observations of the work situation, in order to discover which aspects of the jobs will impact differentially on the characteristics of the average woman and the average man, and to suggest changes in techniques, tools, or equipment to make jobs safer and more accessible.[79]

Questioning the Home/Work Dichotomy

As occupational health researchers, we have tended in the past to accept current definitions of "occupations" as including only paid work. One of our current projects is leading us to question this definition. The

77   R. Andersson, K. Kemmlert, and A. Kilbom, "Etiological Differences Between Accidental and Non-accidental Occupational Overexertion Injuries," *Journal of Occupational Accidents* 12 (1990), pp.177-86.

78   F. Guérin, A. Laville, F. Daniellou, J. Duraffourg, and A. Kerguelen, *Comprendre le travail pour le transformer* (Montrouge, France: Editions de l'ANACT, 1991).

79   See, for example, J. Courville, N. Vézina, and K. Messing, "Analysis of Work Activity of a Job in a Machine Shop Held by Ten Men and One Woman," *International Journal of Industrial Ergonomics*, 7 (1991), pp.163-74. The carpenter Kate Braid covers this point poetically in "These Hips," in *Covering Rough Ground* (Vancouver: Polestar Book publisher, 1991). See also K. Messing, J. Courville, and N. Vézina, "Minimizing Health Risks for Women Who Enter Jobs Traditionally Assigned to Men," *New Solutions: A Journal of Environmental and Occupational Health Policy* 1,4 (1991), pp.66-71.

women's committee of the Fédération des travailleurs et des travailleuses du Québec asked CINBIOSE to do a study of how men and women with young children balance family responsibilities. In an exploratory study, Louise Vandelac and Andrée-Lise Méthot interviewed twenty-three women and four men about techniques used to balance professional and family responsibilities.[80] During the interviews we realized that current work organization segments human existence into two non-interpenetrating spheres. Workers are expected to leave their desires and needs at the door of the workplace. Their home life is not supposed to affect their capacity to work. In occupational health jurisprudence, a domestic determinant of a health problem is an accepted reason for denial of compensation.[81] The workplace, however, is allowed to impinge on all areas of the workers' lives by requiring shift work, overtime, and schedule irregularities and by inducing fatigue and health symptoms that follow the worker home. Since in theory workers come to the office without their families, the workplace is organized as if workers had no life outside.[82] Only 15 per cent of a very large sample of French slaughterhouse workers know at the beginning of work the time when they will finish.[83]

The organizational components of tasks may exclude workers with family responsibilities, particularly women. Thus, women may be eliminated from some jobs due to the impossibility of reconciling them with family responsibilities, or women may choose to restrict their family lives to keep their jobs. Barrère-Maurisson reports that within a large company, family responsibilities appeared to be a factor in job allocation: certain functions were always carried out by young, single men, others by married women, still others by older men with non-working wives.[84]

80   L. Vandelac and A-L. Méthot, *Concilier l'inconciliable* (Montreal: Fédération des travailleuses du Québec, 1993).

81   We were involved in the case of a woman with shoulder problems that were attributed not to her repetitive task but to the fact that her cupboard shelves at home were too high. Industrial deafness cases invoke the worker's Ski-Doo or presence at a discothèque as reasons to deny compensation.

82   Workers are not compensated for loss of quality of life due to symptoms, only for illnesses and injuries. The unequal separation of domestic responsibilities within families may have been a response to the extreme demands of the workplace. This point has been recently reviewed in P. Armstrong and H. Armstrong, *Theorizing Women's Work* (Toronto: Garamond Press, 1991), ch.5.

83   Marie-Aude Le Berre, "Etude des conditions et des arrêts de travail dans des abattoirs de volaille et des conserveries," report of a project done with CINBIOSE and INSERM, Unité 149 and presented to Département de Statistique, IUT Vannes (1993).

84   M-A. Barrère-Maurisson, *La division familiale du travail: La vie en double* (Paris: PUF, 1992).

Preliminary results from our twenty-three interviews suggested that, at the birth of a child, company policies and pay differentials make it desirable for women to reduce their paid hours or take unpaid leave while men work extra hours to make up the difference in pay.[85] In another CINBIOSE study, municipal workers (90 per cent of them men) do not know where they will be working from one week to the next. Women entering these jobs were significantly less likely than men to be living with children, possibly due to the difficulty of reconciling women's family responsibilities with extremely irregular work hours.[86]

When the workplace is organized in this way, there are heavy consequences for those who attempt to fulfil their obligations to their families. Women may go through great difficulties just to ensure that the day-care centre can reach them in an emergency, or to be able to talk to their school-age children during that critical period between the end of the school day and the mother's arrival. For example, telephone operators are not allowed to make or receive telephone calls while working. If a school or babysitter calls to say that a child is ill, the message is posted on the bulletin board, where it can be picked up at break time. Under these circumstances, women with children may be unable to continue at these jobs, or at best they must spend enormous time and effort trying to devise methods of communication, contingency plans, and fall-back scenarios.

Our contacts with workers have led us to suggest that employers include family role requirements in their occupational health programs. It is already recognized that workers have physiological lives that go beyond the immediate requirements of the workplace. For example, employers usually provide lunchrooms, water fountains, and bathrooms. A logical extension of this realization is that workers have families, so they need appropriate shifts, access to telephones, and provision for family illness. We are now trying to induce occupational health specialists to include interactions with family responsibilities in their conceptions of workplace norms and standards. For example, exposure standards for many working conditions suppose an eight-hour working day followed by sixteen hours of rest, a condition not available for many workers or for most women workers. We have also proposed in the scientific litera-

85   Vandelac and Méthot, *Concilier l'inconciliable.*

86   Karen Messing, Lucie Dumais, Julie Courville, Ana Maria Seifert, Nicole Vézina, "Comment ajuster le 'col bleu' à 'Madame Tout l'Monde': Les obstacles d'ordre physique à l'intégration des femmes dans des postes non-traditionnels," in M. des Rivières, M. de Koninck, and K. Messing, eds. *Dépasser les obstacles et les résistances,* Conseil du statut de la femme du Québec (1994).

ture on ergonomics that family responsibilities be included in a dynamic conception of worker-job interaction.[87]

Using Knowledge of Workers and Professors

We are also exploring issues relating to expertise. Questions of knowledge versus experience are central to the development of feminist research.[88] Respect for women's experiences and perceptions has been proposed as a central element of feminist research methodologies. Incorporating worker knowledge in the data-gathering process poses a specific problem in occupational health, where an immediate money value is attached to credibility. If the worker is believed, she will be paid for her work accident or pregnancy leave (for dangerous work). If not, the employer and government will profit financially. The financial stakes may explain why we have been threatened with lawsuits and prosecution for illegal medical practice for merely reporting to workers what they themselves have told us in questionnaires.

However, our expertise is also critical in assisting workers to gain recognition for their health risks. Any de-emphasizing of our qualifications has proved risky in situations opposing us to employer-paid experts. Both because we are women and because we use non-traditional language about workers, we may be treated with less respect by both workers and employers. For example, we are called by our first names while other experts are referred to by their titles. We have not yet successfully resolved the contradiction between insisting on respect for our expertise and pressures to mystify that expertise.

Much of our work has been done with the hospital workers' unions, where the problem of credibility is compounded by authoritative statements from employer representatives who are doctors. We once gave an information session in a hospital radiology department. Halfway through the session, the room was so hot and humid it was hard to continue (the temperature was 26°). When we raised this point, workers laughed at us and said it was always like that in their department. They had raised the point with the department head, who had explained to them that it was because they were women that they felt hot, since the men did not feel uncomfortable. The women's biology was making

---

87   See Messing, Lucie, and Romito, "Prostitutes and Chimney Sweeps Both Have Problems," pp.47-55; and Messing, Méthot, and Vandelac, (submitted) "Comment inclure dans l'analyse du travail l'activité qui consiste à concilier les tâches professionnelles et domestiques?"

88   Lorraine Code, *What Can She Know? Feminist Theory and the Construction of Knowledge* (Ithaca, N.Y.: Cornell University Press, 1991), ch.6.

them react abnormally to comfortable temperatures. We tried explaining to the workers that a whole sex could not be abnormal, but they did not react. We suggested that they ask the doctors for scientific references, but this made them uneasy. We suggested that one reason might be that the doctors did not perform the extensive physical manipulation of patients, almost all of whom had to be transferred manually from stretchers to radiography tables and back. This suggestion seemed quite reasonable to the workers, but they were sure that it was useless to try to reason with the doctors; the doctors knew they were right and had medical degrees to prove it.

It is sometimes tempting for us to try to oppose the doctors' assertions with our own, in negotiations or during tribunals. After all, we do have some claims to expertise, and it is fun to show how much smarter we are. However, we have learned repeatedly that in occupational health hearings power is knowledge, not the reverse. Although our "expert" testimony has helped gain some rights for women workers, time after time we have seen our work defeated not by being proven false, but by groundless assertions from other "experts" with closer links to employers, or by simple statements from employers that allowing the worker's claim would lead to others and result in enormous costs.[89] These experiences have led us to the conclusion that a transfer of power from us to the women workers is a necessary step in improving working conditions. The transfer of power will be attempted through characterization and valorization of the workload of three groups of women: bank tellers, primary school teachers, and office clerks. We are combining our knowledge of biology and ergonomics with women's knowledge about their own jobs to characterize their workload and its effects.

The aim of the project is to create a worker-university partnership that will pool information about the workload in a context that will allow workers to systematize and validate their own experience of their workload. Because the project is being co-ordinated by the union women's committees, results can be used to focus suggestions for change in the workplace. For example, in the public service sector, women tell us that they no longer take their mid-morning and mid-afternoon breaks. "We don't have enough replacement people, we can't leave a helpless patient alone, saying 'Sorry, it's break time.'" Taking breaks is an important health determinant; in the French abattoir study,

---

89   For example, our article on the heavy workload of sewing machine operators was used to justify paid early leave ("*retrait préventif*") for pregnant operators. However, employers soon challenged this practice, asserting that discomfort was not danger and that there was no risk to a foetus from the mother's discomfort. The issue of the heavy workload was drowned in semantics and the worker lost her case, setting a dangerous precedent.

the strongest predictor of mental and physical health limits was the number of breaks per day.

During our project, workers will keep records of the number of breaks they take and what they do on their breaks. We anticipate that this procedure will demonstrate that they are paying with their bodies and minds for the cuts in public sector employment. Needless to say, many scientists will not consider the results of this study to represent an objective estimate of workload. Our project is, rather, intended to give the workers tools that will enable them to recognize and promote recognition of this workload, so they will feel entitled to create conditions for better health. This approach is analogous to those that have been used to support higher salaries for women's work by documenting women's hidden competence.[90] In an analogous way, we are trying to demonstrate the extent and importance of women's hidden workload. We are finding grids developed in employment equity struggles to be helpful, although these are intended to assess skills rather than effort. But, as I have pointed out above, indicators of workload have not usually been available for traditional women's work. The project should also help us to develop new tools to evaluate workload, particularly mental and emotional workload.

CONCLUSION

Recently the Medical Research Council of Canada invited several researchers to participate in an all-day discussion of a "Women's Health Agenda." It was interesting to hear the dialogue between feminist scientists who recommended "listening to women's voices" and other biomedical experts pleading for "data-driven research priorities" and "measurable outcomes." The latter sounded very reasonable. At a time of pressure on public funds, it is hard to justify working on problems with no measurable effects. Women particularly have a hard time saying outright that money should be invested in an area because we say so. At the same time it seemed absurd to many of us to demand that research be oriented by available data, when in fact few reliable data are available on women's health.

90   Jane Gaskell, "What Counts as Skill? Reflections on Pay Equity," in Judy Fudge and Patricia McDermott, eds., *Just Wages: A Feminist Assessment of Pay Equity* (Toronto: University of Toronto Press, 1991); see also Catherine Teiger and Colette Bernier, "Ergonomic Analysis of Work Activity of Data Entry Clerks in the Computerized Service Sector Can Reveal Unrecognized Skills," *Woman and Health* 18,3 (1992), pp.67-78.

At the end of the day, feeling wounded and uncertain after many compromises and some raised voices, we were not sure that the Council would change its priorities. But the dialogue had made us dream of the day scientists will be given money for sufficient women-oriented data collection to create a new gender-inclusive science of occupational health, including adequate measurement techniques and rules for people-based validation. We do not know whether this process will lead to new methods or new applications of old methods, because it is only just beginning.

TABLE 3. PHYSICAL CHARACTERISTICS OF 10 JOBS OBSERVED ON THE VARIETY LINE IN A COOKIE FACTORY

JOB	Type of weights: weight per item (kg)	Type of manipulation	Frequency/hour
USUALLY MALE			
MIXER OPERATOR	sacks (flour, sugar): 40	lift, carry, cut empty	4
	big bags (pastry ingredients): 11-12	lift, carry, cut empty	2
	small bags (other ingredients):0.4	lift, carry, cut empty	1
	buckets (eggs liquid sugar): 11 or 22	open valve, fill in, lift, carry, pour over	4
LAYER OPERATIOR	machine parts (plastic and metal)	carry and fix/screw	if new production
	baking pans (empty): 4	lift/carry	variable
OVEN ATTENDANT	baking pans (empty) 4	push/pull (3-4 at a time) lift/put on trays/push	480 if conveyor stops
ICER OPERATOR	machine parts (plastic)	fix/unscrew/carry	if new production
	tank of icing (on wheels): 213	push/pull, shovel icing	2
BIG BOX STACKER	small boxes: 285 g	pick up, carry (6 at a time)	432
	big boxes: 12.4	lift, put down/up	54
BOX FOLDER	dies: 8.3. 15.4, 2.0, or 4.0	lift, carry, hold & screw	if new production
	unfolded boxes: 1.0 or 1.5	lift, carry, place	variable
BOTH SEXES			
CONVEYOR ATTENDANT	baked cakes: 20g	turn over, check/discard	3600
ALL WOMEN			
WRAPPER OPERATOR	decorated baked cakes: 34g	pick up, place in line, lift, check/discard	7920
PACKER	wrapped cakes: 34g	press, push in (4 at a time)	2640

SUGGESTED READINGS

Pat Armstrong and Hugh Armstrong, *Theorizing Women's Work*. Toronto: Garamond Press, 1991.

Ruth Bleier, ed., *Feminist Approaches to Science*. New York: Pergamon Press, 1985.

Harriet Bradley, *Men's Work, Women's Work*. Minneapolis: University of Minnesota Press, 1989.

Wendy Chavkin, ed., *Double Exposure: Women's Health Hazards on the Job and at Home*. New York: Monthly Review Press, 1984.

Ann Fausto-Sterling, *Myths of Gender*. New York: Basic Books, 2nd ed., 1992.

Office of the Senior Advisor, Status of Women, Health and Welfare Canada, *Proceedings of the Research Round Table on Gender and Workplace Health*. Ottawa: Health Canada, 1992.

Ruth Hubbard, *The Politics of Women's Biology*. New Brunswick, N.J.: Rutgers University Press, 1990.

Karen Messing, Donna Mergler, and Carole Brabant, eds., *Women and Health* 18,3 (1992).

Karen Messing, *Occupational Health and Safety Concerns of Canadian Women*. Ottawa: Labour Canada, 1991.

Jeanne Stellman and Mary Sue Henefin, *Office Work Is Dangerous for your Health*. New York: Pantheon Books, 1983.

Lisa Vogel, "Debating Difference: Feminism, Pregnancy and the Workplace," *Feminist Studies* 16 (1990).

M. ANN HALL

Chapter Ten: Women and Sport: From Liberal Activism to Radical Cultural Struggle

As a sport feminist, I see my task as advocating for the inclusion of sport on the feminist agenda and ensuring that feminism is part of the sports agenda. Since the early 1970s my academic work has proceeded on basically two fronts. On the one hand, I have been involved in studies and conducted surveys that fall under the broader rubric of social policy research, and more specifically gender equity research. This research has been directed primarily at documenting and explaining the underrepresentation of women in all aspects of sport, from participation to leadership; for example: the place of sport and physical activity in the everyday lives of Canadian women; the meaning of sex equality in Canadian sport; the participation of adolescent girls in physical activity; the career patterns of former women Olympians; the gender structuring of national sport organizations; and most recently, a comparative study of women's sport advocacy organizations.[1] Certainly

1   M. Ann Hall, "Sport and Physical Activity in the Lives of Canadian Women," in Richard S. Gruneau and John G. Albinson, eds., *Canadian Sport: Sociological Perspectives* (Don Mills, Ont.: Addison-Wesley, 1976), pp.170-99; M. Ann Hall and Dorothy A. Richardson, *Fair Ball: Towards Sex Equality in Canadian Sport* (Ottawa: Canadian Advisory Council on the Status of Women, 1982); M. Ann Hall and Janice Butcher, "Adolescent Girls' Participation in Physical Activity," Report of a Five-year Longitudinal Study, Planning Services Branch, Alberta Education, 1983; M. Ann Hall, "Women Olympians in the Canadian Sport Bureaucracy," in Trevor Slack and Bob Hinings, eds., *The Organization and Administration of Sport* (London: Sport Dynamics Publishers, 1987), pp.101-26; M. Ann Hall, Dallas Cullen, and Trevor Slack, "Organizational Elites Recreating Themselves: The Gender Structure of National Sport Organizations," *Quest: The Journal of the National Association for Physical Education in Higher Education* 41, 1 (1989), pp.28-45; M. Ann Hall, Dallas Cullen, and Trevor Slack, "The Gender Structure of National Sport Organizations," *Sport Canada Occasional Papers* 2, 1 (1990); M. Ann Hall, "Feminist Activism in Sport: A Comparative Study of Women's Sport Advocacy Organizations," in Alan Tomlinson, ed., *Gender, Leisure and Cultural Forms*, CSRC Topic Report 4 (Chelsea School Research Centre, University of Brighton, 1995).

other feminist scholars have contributed significantly to the documentation and analysis of gender inequity in Canadian sport, most notably
Helen Lenskyj at O.I.S.E. and Nancy Theberge at the University of Waterloo.[2]

The other side of my academic work has been more theoretical. Until
recently "women in sport" research was dominated by a psychological
and individualistic bias often called "categoric" because it focused on
the differences between men and women and attempted to explain those
differences through biology or socialization. The problem with categoric
research is that it cannot account for the complexities of social structure
and power relations. Similarly, distributive research, which attempts to
identify the barriers to equality, never confronts the power relations that
constitute sexism (or other inequalities). Over the past decade there has
been a discernible shift from traditional categoric and distributive research to a clearer understanding of what constitutes more theoretically
informed analyses of social relations of power in sport and leisure. What
this recognizes is that gender, class, and race relations are characterized
by unequal relationships between dominant and subordinate groups,
that sport plays a role in their construction and persistence, and that
they take specific forms in particular times. There is now general agreement that our scholarship must provide a critical analysis of the cultural
and ideological practices determining these relations.[3]

The development of a radical theoretical critique of sport, and specifically of gender relations, has not seen a parallel in sport activism.
Feminist activism in sport in Canada, and elsewhere in the world, has
been predominantly liberal in nature, and its primary focus has been on
ensuring girls and women equal access to sport and recreation opportunities long available to boys and men. The reasons for this are complex,
although, as Helen Lenskyj argues, the structure of amateur sport in
Canada, which is highly state-subsidized and not likely to produce individuals with a radical critique, has been a contributing factor. At the
same time, there has been little support from the grassroots women's
movement because politically engaged feminists tend to marginalize or

2   For comprehensive summaries of this research and scholarship, see Helen Lenskyj, *Women,
     Sport and Physical Activity: Research and Bibliography*, 2nd ed. (Ottawa: Minister of Supply
     and Services Canada, 1991), and Helen Lenskyj, *Women, Sport and Physical Activity: Selected
     Research Themes* (Gloucester, Ont.: Sport Information Resource Centre, 1994).

3   For a more complete discussion of these developments, see M. Ann Hall, "Gender and Sport
     in the 1990s: Feminism, Culture, and Politics," *Sport Science Review* 2,1 (1993), pp.48-68; Al-
     ison M. Dewar, "Incorporation or Resistance? Towards an Analysis of Women's Responses
     to Sexual Oppression in Sport," *International Review for the Sociology of Sport* 26,1 (1991),
     pp.15-23; Jennifer A. Hargreaves, "Gender on the Sports Agenda," *International Review for
     the Sociology of Sport* 25,4 (1990), pp.285-308.

dismiss sport as unimportant to the real struggles over sexual equality.[4]

The problem, therefore, is that there is still not only a noticeable gap between theory and practice but also minimal analysis about *how* to make women's sport political. There are literally millions of participants, athletes, coaches, administrators, officials, educators, and volunteers all working towards the betterment of women's sport, and towards gender equity, for whom this theorizing is as foreign as another language. In the past I have argued that those working in academe, who focus on research and scholarship, should be working hand in hand with those on the front line — be they participants, competitors, teachers, coaches, professional and volunteer leaders, policy-makers, or activists. Feminists, I have also argued, are concerned about the unification of theory and practice, the personal and the political, and it should be no different in sport. Unfortunately, the theory is becoming more and more inaccessible, the language increasingly obtuse, and some of the research less and less applicable to the everyday world of women's sport.

Here, I address two central questions: first, why is there an increasing gap between theory and practice in women's sport; and second, what can (or should) we do about it? On the one hand, using Canada as an example, I will show how and why feminist activism around sport has been almost exclusively liberal in philosophy and strategy. Attempts to push the agenda to a more radical feminist approach have not met with much success. On the other hand, the scholarship about gender (and sport) is becoming increasingly more radical in its critique, yet little of this research is actually used (or read I assume) by those working towards sex equality and gender equity in Canadian sport. How then to bring the world of academe/theory and the everyday world of women's sport (men's sport too) closer together? As one pro-feminist male colleague working in the same area puts it: the key question is not should our research be engaged with the real world, but rather, whose interests should our research serve?[5]

4   Helen J. Lenskyj, "Good Sports: Feminists Organizing on Sport Issues in the 1970s and
        1980s," *Resources for Feminist Research/Documentation sur la recherche féministe* 20,3/4
        (1991), pp.130-35.

5   Michael A. Messner, "White Men Misbehaving: Feminism, Afrocentrism and the Promise
        of a Critical Standpoint," *Journal of Sport and Social Issues* 16,2 (1992), pp.136-44.

6   Jennifer Hargreaves, *Sporting Females: Critical Issues in the History and Sociology of Women's
        Sports* (New York and London: Routledge, 1994), pp.237-42; *Women and Sport: Policy and
        Frameworks for Action* (London: The Sports Council, 1993).

LIBERAL VERSUS RADICAL FEMINIST AGENDAS IN SPORT

Over the past decade there has been a subtle shift in the discourse of human rights in Canada and elsewhere from "equality" to "equity." This
has occurred in most areas of organizational life, including sport. Equality generally meant "equality of opportunity," and women (along with
other disadvantaged groups) were identified as target groups. In sport,
equal opportunity programs were designed to increase women's overall
participation by opening up opportunities for them to enjoy equal access. The shift to equity signals a more comprehensive view, where the
focus is no longer exclusively on women (or any other group) but on a
system, in this case sport, that needs to change to accommodate them.[6]
As long-time sport activist Bruce Kidd puts it, "Equality focuses on creating the same starting line for everyone; equity has the goal of providing everyone with the same finish line."[7] It was stated even more clearly
in a report on gender equity from the Department of Athletics and Recreation at the University of Toronto: "An athletics program is gender
equitable when the men's program would be pleased to accept as its own
the overall participation, opportunities and resources currently allocated to the women's program and vice versa."[8] For many sport organizations, and certainly university athletic programs, this would be seen as
a "radical" departure from the past.

Whether the focus is on equality or equity, the fundamental philosophy underlying both is best described as liberal reformism. Sport feminists have worked hard, especially over the last decade, to ensure that
more sports are now more accessible to more women than ever before.
They have fought for, and sometimes won, "easier access and better facilities for women in sports, improved funding and rewards, equal rights
with men under the law, top quality coaching on par with men, and an
equivalent voice with men in decision-making."[9]

While liberal approaches to sport equity often seek to provide girls
and women with the same opportunities and resources as boys and men,
and to remove the barriers and constraints to their participation, they
do not always see as problematic the fundamental nature of male-

7   Bruce Kidd in *Towards Gender Equity for Women in Sport: A Handbook for National Sport
     Organizations* (Ottawa: Canadian Association for the Advancement of Women and Sport
     and Physical Activity, 1993), p.4.

8   "Task Force on Gender Equity," Final Report to the Council of the Department of Athletics
     and Recreation, University of Toronto, December 31, 1993. The actual statement was from
     Athletics Administration, April 1993, p.22.

9   Hargreaves, *Sporting Females*, p.27.

defined sport, with its emphasis on hierarchy, competitiveness, and aggression. Liberal feminism in sport also tends to treat women as a homogeneous category, not recognizing that there are enormous differences among us in background, class, race, ethnicity, age, disability, and sexual preference, all of which lead to very different expectations and experiences of sport.

A more radical feminist approach would adopt an unequivocal women-centred perspective that recognizes and celebrates differences among women, and at the same time seriously questions male-dominated and male-defined sport. It also recognizes the centrality of issues around sexuality in women's experiences of oppression. In practice, radical feminists in Canadian sport have, as Helen Lenskyj suggests, "worked towards establishing autonomous clubs and leagues that are completely outside state-controlled amateur sport systems."[10] These include the many women-only clubs and leagues, some openly lesbian or lesbian-positive, which are free to modify the rules and organize their play along explicitly feminist principles of participation, recreation, fun, and friendship. Examples in Canada include the Notso Amazon Softball League in Toronto and an outdoor group called Women of Outdoor Pleasure in Edmonton. Jennifer Hargreaves, a British sport sociologist, describes a netball club called Queens of the Castle, which is situated in an inner-urban area of London with a predominantly working-class and black membership. Defying the strait-laced, schoolgirl image of British netball, the Queens of the Castle have created their own sport culture by encouraging non-conformist and flamboyant playing clothes, the open discussion and negotiation of all values and practices, a truly caring ethos and support network, and opposition to all forms of racial harassment. They have become successful at attracting young, urban, working-class women to a sport not noted for its egalitarianism.[11]

Women involved in sport advocacy work often fail to take up issues raised by their more radical feminist counterparts outside sport, issues such as sexual harassment and abuse, male violence against women, lesbian visibility, and the politics of difference. Any radical feminist critique of sport must deal with these important issues.

10   Lenskyj, "Good Sports," p.32.

11   Hargreaves, *Sporting Females*, pp.250-51.

HOW ARE WE DOING? INCHING TOWARDS GENDER EQUITY IN
CANADIAN SPORT

A glance through the sports pages of Canadian newspapers might lead
one to conclude that women are striding into the world of sport as never
before. Take for example women's ice hockey, which has emerged from
obscurity with a remarkable upsurge in participation. The Canadian
team won their third World Championships in Lake Placid in 1994, and
they will be in medal contention when women's ice hockey becomes an
Olympic sport in 1998. Manon Rhéaume, a Canadian from Quebec City,
made hockey history when she played in a 1992 National Hockey League
exhibition game. Women's judo was included in the 1992 Barcelona
Olympics, the first time in the history of the Olympics that women have
competed in a purely combative sport. Women's soccer was a medal
sport at the World University Games in 1993, and it will be added to the
women's events at the Atlanta Olympics in 1996. The executive doors
are now open wider for women in professional sports, with women
owning teams and working in the front office of every league. The All-
American Girls Professional Baseball League, which included many Canadian players in the 1940s, is at last receiving its due through the popular film *A League of Their Own* and a continuing spate of books, articles,
and documentaries.[12] Who can forget the sheer grit of rower Silken Lau-
mann, who won a bronze medal at Barcelona despite a devastating leg
injury, and of lesser known basketball player Tracy MacLeod, who came
back to play college ball at Brandon University only a few months after
having part of her leg amputated? Canada's Paralympic team, which
competes in an Olympic-style competition for athletes with disabilities,
has traditionally won its fair share of medals. In the 1992 Summer Para-
lympics in Barcelona, Canadian women track and field athletes won six
gold medals, the wheelchair basketball team also won the gold, and
swimmer Joanne Mucz distinguished herself by winning five gold medals in the swimming events. Calgary skier Lana Spreeman, who as a child
lost a leg in a farm accident and was competing in her fifth winter Para-
lympics, brought back one silver and three bronze medals from Lillehammer in 1994.

In *Fair Ball: Towards Sex Equality in Canadian Sport*, written for the
Canadian Advisory Council on the Status of Women in 1982, we asked

12   See, for example, Lois Browne, *Girls of Summer* (Toronto: HarperCollins, 1992); Susan E.
     Johnson, *When Women Played Hardball* (Washington: Seal Press, 1994); and Gai Ingham
     Berlage, *Women in Baseball: The Forgotten History* (Westport, Conn.: Praeger, 1994).

whether equality existed in three major areas: participation at both the recreational and competitive levels, leadership in coaching and administration, and in school and university physical education. Not surprisingly, the answer was no, although we did acknowledge that there had been some progress towards removing many of the institutional and legal barriers to sex equality. We noted that increasing numbers of girls and women participated in sport for both recreation and competition, but that women were underrepresented (indeed declining) in leadership positions whether as coaches, administrators, executives, or as members of the physical education and recreation professions.[13]

Where are we in the 1990s, over a decade later? While sport systems are inching towards gender equity, there is still a very long way to go. The latest national surveys of the sport and leisure patterns of adult Canadians show that women and men are now equally active in low-intensity exercise activities, and women are considerably more active in some activities like walking, social dancing, and home exercise.[14] Women's involvement in physical activity is far more likely to take the form of individual fitness activities than organized sports; however, there are significantly more barriers to their activity and leisure than for men. Domestic and family responsibilities, time constraints, lower incomes, and lack of programs still restrict women's involvement.[15] These problems are compounded for women with disabilities, whose rate of participation is lower than that of able-bodied women due to inaccessible facilities, transportation problems, and lack of program information.[16]

When it comes to participation in competitive sport activities, major sex differences still persist. Except for bowling and volleyball, which are often more social than competitive, the majority of the small percentage who do compete are male. One statistic that has remained fairly constant over the last decade is that girls and women make up about one-third of

13   Hall and Richardson, *Fair Ball*, pp.51-73.

14   Ann Hall, Trevor Slack, Garry Smith, and David Whitson, *Sport in Canadian Society* (Toronto: McClelland & Stewart, 1991), pp.156-57.

15   There is now a considerable body of research and scholarship around the topic of "women and leisure." Those interested in pursuing some of this work should peruse books and articles by key researchers in the area such as Rosemary Deem, Karla Henderson, Susan Shaw, Erica Wimbush, and Margaret Talbot. Two recent Canadian studies that would be good starting points are: Maureen A. Harrington, "Time after Work: Constraints on the Leisure of Working Women," *Loisir et société/Society and Leisure* 14,1 (1991), pp.115-32; Patricia L. Hunter and David J. Whitson, "Women, Leisure and Familism: Relationships and Isolation in Small Town Canada," *Leisure Studies* 10,3 (1991), pp.219-33.

16   E. Jane Watkinson and Karen Calzonetti, "Physical Activity Patterns of Physically Disabled Women in Canada," *CAHPER Journal* 55,6, 1989, pp.21-26.

the registered participants in competitive sport. For example, in Edmonton recent statistics show that 32.6 per cent of the total community sport registrants are female, with girls favouring figure skating, ringette, softball, gymnastics, and equestrian sports; whereas boys prefer hockey, soccer, baseball, and downhill skiing.[17]

At the other end of the competitive scale, the 1992 Summer Olympics in Barcelona offered 159 events for men, 86 for women, and 12 open to both women and men. Therefore men had double the chances to compete for a medal. The ratio of events at the Winter Olympics is somewhat better: in 1994 in Lillehammer there were 34 events for men, 25 for women, and two mixed. Canadian Olympic teams, although they have fewer women, do have an appropriate gender balance given the existing events, and women will have more opportunity to compete as their Olympic programs continue to grow.[18] However, many countries participating in the Olympics send no women at all. In the 1988 Seoul Olympics, with 160 countries participating, 42 sent no women; these were mainly Asian and African nations, which are predominantly Muslim. What is even more significant is that most of the Olympic winners come from a tiny proportion of these countries. For instance, of the 160 competing countries in 1988 in Seoul, only 18 per cent of them won medals in the women's events, and only seven countries (East Germany, Soviet Union, United States, Romania, Bulgaria, China, West Germany) won eight out of ten (79 per cent) of all women's medals.[19] These same countries accounted for fewer of the women's medals (58 per cent) in the 1992 Barcelona Olympics due to the political changes in Eastern Europe, which have reunited the two Germanies but severely curtailed the sport systems in the state-socialist countries of Romania, Bulgaria, and Russia. Regardless, Olympic success for women (and men too) is highly concentrated among select countries, which means there is a long way to go to expand women's Olympic involvement.

Women are still vastly underrepresented as sport leaders in Canada just as they are everywhere else in the world. Starting at the top, only

17   City of Edmonton statistics supplied by Kim Sanderson of the Parks and Recreation Department.

18   For detailed gender statistics on the Olympics, see Rob Beamish, "Towards a Socio-Cultural Profile of Canada's High Performance Athletes," *International Review for the Sociology of Sport* 27,4 (1992), pp.279-88; and Sandra Kirby and Amanda Le Rougetel, "Games Analysis," *CAAWS Issue Papers* 1,2 (1993).

19   Mary A. Boutilier and Lucinda F. San Giovanni, "Ideology, Public Policy and Female Olympic Achievement: A Cross-National Analysis of the Seoul Olympic Games," in Fernand Landry, Marc Landry, and Magdeleine Yerlès, eds., *Sport: The Third Millennium* (Sainte-Foy, Que.: Les Presses de l'Université Laval, 1991), pp.397-409.

seven of the 94-member International Olympic Committee are women. Among the presidents of the 174 national Olympic committees world-wide, six are women, one of whom is Carol Anne Letheren, the President of the Canadian Olympic Association. In Canada, among the national sport organizations, 28 per cent of senior executives in paid positions are women, as are 23 per cent of the technical directors. Among the volunteer sector, about 25 per cent of boards of directors, committee members, and provincial representatives are women, although this number does vary by sport. Women are significantly under-represented in coaching, especially at the elite levels. For example, in 1992, only 16 per cent of university head coaches were women, and a little over half of all women's teams were coached by women. At the very elite level, women occupied a mere 3 per cent of all national team head-coaching positions and 18 per cent of all national coaching staff positions.[20]

How do we explain this female underrepresentation? Based on a good deal of research that focuses on the gender structuring of sport organizations, the organizational processes and dynamics that structure gender, and the relations of power between women and men within an organizational context, the reasons are fairly clear:

1   women face stereotypical notions about their competence, despite their formal qualifications, organizational resources, and technical expertise;

2   women are assumed (in actuality or in the perception of themselves and others) to lack the proper training, motivation, and skills to succeed;

3   women must prove themselves and work their way up the sport hierarchy, whereas men's competence is taken for granted;

4   women who choose to enter a primarily man's world must learn the language, symbols, myths, beliefs, and values of that male culture, sometimes becoming "honorary" men;

20   See *Towards Gender Equity for Women in Sport: A Handbook for National Sport Organizations* (CAAWS).

5   women's family responsibilities are a "given" and beyond the control of the organization; child-care facilities and arrangements, for example, are generally of no interest to the organization;

6   a strong and informal male network (and a weak female network) exists that enhances men's (and discourages women's) opportunities;

7   male elites ensure the maintenance of the status quo, and their own power, by selecting individuals most like themselves;

8   women both perceive and experience discrimination in greater numbers than do men;

9   most sport organizations usually see no need to initiate any sort of affirmative action program or structure to address the needs of women, although some organizations do and have.[21]

Women's sport at all levels still has serious difficulties attracting corporate sponsorship from the private sector. Even though the "marketability" of some of Canada's top women athletes has improved considerably, especially if they do well, male athletes on average earn more. Winners in low-profile, often obscure sports (a good example is double gold medal winner and biathlete Myriam Bédard) have a tougher time finding significant national sponsors and do not earn nearly as much as those in the top earning sports, such as figure skating.[22] Professional

---

21   This material has been taken from Hall et al., *Sport in Canadian Society*, p.170. For good representation of the research studies from which this summary is made, see: David Whitson and Donald Macintosh, "Gender and Power: Explanations of Gender Inequality in Canadian National Sport Organizations," *International Review for the Sociology of Sport* 24,2 (1989), pp.137-50; Hall et al., "Organizational Elites Reproducing Themselves"; Hall et al., "Gender Structure of National Sport Organizations"; Annelies Knoppers, "Explaining Male Dominance and Sex Segregation in Coaching: Three Approaches," *Quest* 44 (1992), pp.210-27; Suzanne Laberge, "Employment Situation of High Performance Coaches in Canada," *Sport Canada Occasional Papers*, 3,1 (1992); Nancy Theberge, "The Construction of Gender in Sport: Women, Coaching, and the Naturalization of Difference," *Social Problems* 40, 3 (1993), pp.401-13.

22   Marina Strauss, "Quest for Gold Doesn't End with Games," *The Globe and Mail*, February 24, 1994, p.B7; André Picard, "The Synchronized Life of Sylvie Fréchette, *The Globe and Mail*, December 17, 1993, p.A14; Steve Keating, "Row, Row, Row Your Boat, Gently into Cash," *The Globe and Mail*, September 2, 1993, p.A14; James Christie, "All That's Gold May Not Glitter," *The Globe and Mail*, December 19, 1992, p.A22; Mary Jollimore, "No Gold for Olympic Heroes," *The Globe and Mail*, July 25, 1992, pp.D1,D4.

sport remains largely a male preserve, because career opportunities for women athletes are concentrated in a few sports, notably golf, tennis, and figure skating. There are still large differences in earnings and endorsement incomes among male and female professional athletes even in the same sport.

The media coverage of women's sport, except around the time of an Olympics, is continually dismal. In their third annual survey of the coverage by Canada's largest daily newspapers (twenty-one in total), the Canadian Association for the Advancement of Women and Sport and Physical Activity found the average space devoted to women's sport was 8.8 per cent, up from 2.8 per cent in 1991.[23] Television coverage is about the same, with a heavy focus on individual sports such as golf, tennis, figure skating, and gymnastics. Women athletes are often trivialized by media representations (a preoccupation with their appearance, for example), which serves to undercut and denigrate their efforts. Media sport also offers a prime site for the ideological construction of gender differences, which forces people to make comparisons between men and women and establishes male performance as the yardstick for *all* sport, including women's. Nonetheless, as Mary Jollimore, a Canadian sports journalist who contributes frequently to *The Globe and Mail*, has observed: "While the balance of power in the sports world remains tipped against them, female athletes rose time and time again with performances that captured the public's attention."[24]

There has been progress towards gender equity in the last decade. But there are continual reminders of just how male-dominated sport in Canada really is. For example, one of the small towns featured in Stuart McLean's best-selling *Welcome Home* is Foxwarren, Manitoba, where hockey still matters. A student at my university grew up in that town not so long ago and remembers with considerable bitterness the trivialization of women's lives and how their work, compared to playing hockey and producing grain, is only a side-show:

> Women and girls come second in the whole community to hockey
> and keeping the area alive. Girls spend hours at the rink, waiting
> for something to happen, waiting for the game to be over. My
> family, like most others, organized the budget and time around
> hockey games, hockey tournaments, hockey equipment for my

23   "Expanded Survey Reveals a Modest Upsurge in Coverage of Women's Sports," CAAWS
      News Release, February 8, 1994. The survey covered a two-week period from November 22
      to December 6, 1993 and is therefore a reflection of the coverage of winter sports.

24   Mary Jollimore, "It Was an Impressive Year for Women Athletes," *The Globe and Mail*, December 22, 1992, p.A12.

brothers, food and transportation to the games. Boys get all the benefits of hockey: they get the attention, the adulation of family and friends, and the actual physical joy of doing.... Women learn from hockey who is important in patriarchy: who actually plays the game. They learn that they are only spectators and supporters and should wait around and watch.[25]

FEMINIST ACTIVISM IN SPORT: THE CANADIAN CASE

Feminist organizing and activism around sport issues in Canada have been shaped by the structure of the Canadian sport system, which has a high degree of government involvement. The federal government alone invests over $75 million annually into sport, for several important reasons: sport is part of human nature; sport is part of our national identity and an expression of our culture; sport is about pursuing excellence; sport is healthy; and sport is a means to ensure certain social benefits such as bilingualism, gender equity, regional access, and ethical conduct.[26] Since the passage of Bill C-131, An Act to Encourage Fitness and Amateur Sport, over thirty years ago, the direct and ongoing intervention of the state has resulted in the rationalization of the Canadian sport system, with the creation of a professional bureaucracy with a more corporate style of management. The control of amateur sport has been largely removed from the hands of volunteers and is now directed by a new professional elite.

Canadian sprinter Ben Johnson tested positive for anabolic steroids at the Seoul Olympics in 1988, provoking an unprecedented examination of sport in Canada. The 1990 report of the Dubin Inquiry into the Illegal Use of Drugs and Banned Practices Intended to Increase Athletic Performance was followed by more reports, sport forums, and intergovernmental workshops. In 1992 the Federal Minister's Task Force on Federal Sport Policy published Sport: The Way Ahead, which offered over one hundred recommendations to advance and enhance sport at all levels across the country. The federal government is responding to these recommendations primarily through the development of a "sport plan" for Canada. Organizationally, the Fitness and Amateur Sport Directorate, which has had its own minister since 1976, was split in 1993, with

25   Tanis Talbot, "Hockey as a Symbol of Patriarchy: Welcome Home," Femspeak, University of Alberta Women's Law Forum Newsletter, January 1993; see also Richard Gruneau and David Whitson, Hockey Night in Canada: Sport, Identities and Cultural Politics (Toronto: Garamond Press, 1993).

26   Fitness and Amateur Sport, Toward 2000: Building Canada's Sport System, the Report of the Task Force on National Sport Policy (Ottawa: Government of Canada, 1988), pp.16-17.

Sport Canada going to Canadian Heritage, and Fitness Canada going to
Health Canada.

Pressing for Change: Lobbying Government

From the time of Bill C-131 in 1961 until the publication of the *Report of
the Royal Commission on the Status of Women* in 1970, governments at
all levels paid little attention to the plight of women's sport.[27] There were
two specific recommendations in the *Report* directed at the lack of equal
opportunity for girls in school sport programs.[28] The federal government responded (none too willingly) to these recommendations by hiring a women's consultant, Marion Lay, within the Fitness and Amateur
Sport Branch. Her duties included, among other things, "defining the
problems facing women in sport, and establishing programs to alleviate
these problems." *Fair Ball* contains a detailed description of those early
years at the Branch when one person, assisted by a few others hired on
contract (including Abby Hoffman and myself), were attempting to
convince senior officials that the needs of women in sport were not adequately met through existing policies, programs, and structures.[29] There
was strong resistance to the suggestion that the administration of Canadian sport should be restructured to accommodate the needs of women.
I think back on those days and shake my head. We were trying to find
solutions to what we believed were relatively simple problems, not realizing that the changes we naively "demanded" attacked the system at its
core, and that men do not give up power willingly.

There were some successes throughout those years due to the perse-

27   This section relies on a variety of sources: my own recollections and observations; docu-
     mented sources where noted; and other accounts, most notably Mary Keyes, "Feminist Lob-
     bying and Decision-Making Power in Fitness and Amateur Sport National Policies, Pro-
     grams and Services: The Case of Canada," in Landry, Landry, and Yerlès, *Sport: The Third
     Millennium*, pp.419-30; Lenskyj, "Good Sports"; Donald Macintosh and David Whitson,
     The Game Planners: Transforming Canada's Sport System (Montreal & Kingston: McGill-
     Queen's University Press, 1990), pp.59-91; and Hall et al., *Sport in Canadian Society*, pp.90-
     101.

28   *Recommendation 77*: We recommend that the provinces and territories (a) review their poli-
     cies and practices to ensure that school programmes provide girls with equal opportunities
     with boys to participate in athletic and sports activities, and (b) establish policies and prac-
     tices that will motivate and encourage girls to engage in athletic and sport activities. *Recom-
     mendation 78*: We recommend that, pursuant to section 3(d) of the federal Fitness and Ama-
     teur Sport Act, a research project be undertaken to (a) determine why fewer girls than boys
     participate in sport programmes at the school level and (b) recommend remedial action. *Re-
     port of the Royal Commission on the Status of Women* (Ottawa: Information Canada, 1970),
     pp.185-87.

29   See Hall and Richardson, *Fair Ball*, pp.84-90.

verance of a small number of women located in government, in universities, and in the national sport organizations. They included:

1   two national conferences on women in sport, one in 1974 and one in 1980, both of which helped to focus the issues, provide a measure of progress, and mobilize action among various sectors of the sport system;

2   the establishment in 1980 of the Fitness and Amateur Sport Women's Program with a mandate and budget that meant the federal government was willing to commit resources and personnel to the issues and to encourage national sport organizations to do the same;

3   the founding in 1981 of a national advocacy organization, the Canadian Association for the Advancement of Women and Sport (CAAWS);

4   the 1982 publication of *Fair Ball: Towards Sex Equality in Canadian Sport* by the Canadian Advisory Council on the Status of Women, which provided a wider audience for discussion of the issues;

5   the 1986 publication by Fitness and Amateur Sport of *Policy on Women in Sport*, which set out the official goal of equality of opportunity for women at all levels of the sport system;

6   the establishment in 1987 of the National Coaching School for Women, an annual week-long residential school, supported by various partnerships of national sport organizations and operating on explicitly feminist principles;

7   the 1993 incorporation of gender equity into the guiding principles of the Canadian Sport Council, the new collective voice of Canada's sport community.

However, in its examination of "equity and access," the Minister's Task Force on Federal Sport Policy concluded that even with an advocacy organization, a federal equity policy, and staffing guidelines to encourage fuller participation, little change had occurred over the past ten years:

> In accountability for public funding, national sport organizations must understand the legal definition and intent of gender equity and implement it through legislation, constitutions and policies. NSOs must work toward equality by removing systemic barriers and discrimination.
>
> It is the considered view of the Task Force that the pace of involving and advancing girls and women across the sport continuum, and in all levels of sport organizations, must be significantly accelerated in order to display fair and equitable treatment of 50 per cent of the Canadian population.[30]

Legal Challenges to Inequality: The Separate-versus-Integrated Debate

Until the institution of provincial human rights commissions in the mid-1970s, there was little or no recourse for Canadian girls and women who complained of sex discrimination in sport. Over seventeen years have passed since the first sport-related complaints of sex discrimination were filed, and the majority of cases involve girls wishing to play on exclusively male soccer, softball, or ice-hockey teams. Other complaints have been directed at the restriction of women from playing at private golf clubs during prime hours; pregnancy testing and the reduction of funding to high-performance athletes because of pregnancy; female reporters being banned from male team locker rooms; or in one case about employment discrimination, a male physical education teacher wanting to teach girls' physical education. Most complaints are resolved without resorting to a formal board of inquiry (or tribunal), or eventually to the courts. In fact, there have been only about twelve such "formal" cases altogether.[31]

The most famous of these cases was that of Justine Blainey, who in 1985 was chosen to play on a boys' hockey team in the Metro Toronto Hockey League but was barred from playing by the Ontario Hockey Association. She wanted to play boys' hockey because of the bodychecking and slapshot, neither of which were allowed in the girls' league. The Blainey case is important because legally it helped strike down a discriminatory clause in the Ontario Human Rights Code that specifically

---

30 *Sport: The Way Ahead*, the Report of the Minister's Task Force on Federal Sport Policy (Ottawa: Minister of Supply and Services Canada, 1992), p.151.

31 For a summary and analysis of these cases, see Hall and Richardson, *Fair Ball*, pp.18-28; and Cathy Meade, "The Efficacy of Canadian Human Rights Legislation in Dealing with Sex Discrimination and Gender Inequality in Sport," unpublished paper, University of Alberta, 1993.

exempted membership in athletic organizations, participation in athletic activities, and access to the services and facilities of recreational
clubs from its sex equality provisions.[32] Through the precedence set by
the Blainey case, many sport organizations simply changed their policies
and began to allow girls to participate.

The Blainey saga is also important because it helped to focus debate
around an issue that has forever split the women's sport community: sex-
separated versus sex-integrated sports and organizations. On one side of
the debate are those who argue that only through separate (but equal)
programs for girls and boys will equality be achieved, and that if girls are
allowed to integrate on boys' teams, then so must boys be allowed to play
on girls' teams, which would, in their view, be extremely harmful to girls'
and women's sport. The integrationists, on the other side, argue either
that ability and not sex should be the criterion for forming athletic teams,
or that where girls do not have the opportunity to participate in a particular sport except through an all-male team or league, they should be
permitted to play with boys if they have the necessary skills. They also argue that the "disadvantaged" individual (in this case girls) should be allowed to move up to boys' competition; whereas boys, who are considered "advantaged," should not be allowed to move down. Finally, they
argue that because resources are often not available for a parallel girls'
structure, one league would be more efficient and less costly.

In Canada, and primarily in Ontario, ice hockey has been the main
battleground on which the complexity of these debates becomes evident. Although most feminists saw the Blainey case as a victory for human rights, there were some women who argued vehemently against her
right to play boys' hockey, notably those involved with girls' and
women's hockey. They did so for primarily two reasons. Because they
support the separate-but-equal philosophy, they argued that the admission of girls to boys' hockey would spell the end of girls' hockey. In this
they were clearly wrong, as witnessed by the tremendous growth of "female hockey" in the last decade, both at the recreational and highly
competitive levels; and there have been no legions of boys clambering to
play in girls' leagues. Second, those who advocate separate programs
continue to reject the assertion that the developmental and competitive
needs of girls and women cannot be met within their own programs, and

32 In April 1986, because of an appeal by Blainey, the Ontario Court of Appeal struck down sub-
    section 19(2) of the Ontario Human Rights Code, ruling that it contravened the equality pro-
    visions (section 15) in the Canadian Charter of Rights and Freedoms. Blainey then took her
    original complaint against the Ontario Hockey Association back to an Ontario Board of In-
    quiry, which eventually ordered that the OHA be prohibited from refusing any female the
    opportunity to compete for a position on a hockey team on the same basis as males.

they challenge the notion that boys' hockey is a better and more legitimate version of their own game.[33] The women's game does not permit intentional bodychecking, and there is virtually no fighting, both of which are the mainstay of the men's professional game, although there are boys' minor hockey programs and men's recreational leagues that ban them too. Women's hockey and also ringette (played almost exclusively by girls and women) are good examples of sports that are kept fervently "separate" by their leaders and organizers because they believe the real question is not the ability of females to play with males, but the legitimacy and recognition of women's sports.

For integrationists, the issues surrounding the separate-versus-integrated debate are complex, and it is highly unlikely that a single approach will serve the interests of all girls and women in all sport contexts. Helen Lenskyj argues convincingly that certain factors must be taken into consideration before policies and programs intended to address the problem of sex inequality in sport will achieve their goal: age of the female athlete (pre- or postpubertal); context of the sport (school, community, university); level of competition (from recreational to highly competitive); history of the sport (traditionally male, female, or both); and the nature of the sport (team, individual, contact).[34]

Feminist Organizing and Sexual Politics: CAAWS

The Canadian Association for the Advancement of Women and Sport and Physical Activity (CAAWS) was founded in 1981 at a workshop funded by the Women's Program in Fitness and Amateur Sport and attended by a small group of sport administrators, federal government representatives, athletes, coaches, university-based physical educators, and representatives from the major national feminist organizations. From the very beginning, CAAWS saw itself as a feminist organization. Its first mission statement read: "CAAWS seeks to advance the position of women by defining, promoting and supporting a feminist perspective on sport and to improve the status of women in sport."[35] The fact that

---

33   I am grateful to Nancy Theberge at the University of Waterloo for this information; she is engaged in an important and interesting study of women's hockey in Canada.

34   See Helen Lenskyj, "A Discussion Paper: Female Participation in Sport," report prepared for CAAWS and Sport Canada Joint Steering Committee, April 1984.

35   CAAWS Annual General Meeting Kit, 1982. CAAWS has now drifted away from its original feminist mission. In the latest promotional material there is no mention of feminism, and in 1992 a new vision for the organization was created. Their mission statement now reads: "To ensure that girls and women in sport and physical activity have access to a complete range of opportunities and choices and have equity as participants and leaders."

CAAWS was at the same time openly feminist and government funded was not at all unusual given the politics of the state and the Canadian women's movement at the time. As Canadian political scientist Jill Vickers has pointed out, an operational code of the second-wave women's movement in Canada is the belief that change is possible and that state action is an acceptable way of achieving it. "Most Canadian feminists," she argues, "perceive the state more as a provider of services, including the service of regulation, than a reinforcer of patriarchal norms, and most seem to believe that services, whether child care or medicare, will help."[36] The founders of CAAWS and its subsequent leaders struggled hard to work out its relationship with the larger Canadian women's movement, and the feminist perspective that was the basis of its organizational philosophy. Also, because the women's sport network in Canada is relatively small, a few key individuals, all with a strong sense of feminism, have remained influential in CAAWS since its inception or have returned at various points to provide leadership and energy.

The structure of the amateur sport system in Canada—primarily state-funded through national sport bodies—has in large measure been responsible for the liberal path taken by most feminist organizing. Lenskyj also argues that "given the tightly structured, hierarchical nature of Canadian sport systems, there are limited points of entry for feminist activists."[37] The male sport community is the most vocal exponent of sport as a politically neutral activity, and the high degree of government involvement in sport (and in groups like CAAWS) means that it is sometimes difficult for these groups to criticize the hand that feeds them. Therefore, the focus of CAAWS, aside from trying to survive as an organization, has been primarily on bringing about gender equity within the sport system.[38] The organi-

---

36   Jill Vickers, "The Intellectual Origins of the Women's Movement in Canada," in Constance Backhouse and David H. Flaherty, eds., *Challenging Times: The Women's Movement in Canada and the United States* (Montreal & Kingston: McGill-Queen's University Press, 1992), pp.44-45.

37   Lenskyj, "Good Sports," p.131.

38   There are now a number of studies of CAAWS that provide useful background material and analysis. See, for example, Janis Lawrence-Harper, "The Herstory of the Canadian Association for the Advancement of Women and Sport," a report prepared for CAAWS, November 1991; Samantha Scott-Pawson, "The Canadian Association for the Advancement of Women and Sport (1981-1991): An Organizational Case Analysis of a Feminist Organization," M.A. thesis, School of Physical and Health Education, Queen's University, 1991; Janis Lawrence-Harper, "Change in a Feminist Organization: The Canadian Association for the Advancement of Women and Sport and Physical Activity 1981-1991," M.A. thesis, Department of Physical Education and Sport Studies, University of Alberta, 1993; Susan L. Forbes, "Government and Interest Group Relations: An Analysis of the Canadian Association for the Advancement of Women and Sport," M.A. thesis, Department of Political Science, Wilfrid Laurier University, 1993.

zation's information package states:

> Today, CAAWS has positioned itself as an agent of change, using cooperation, collaboration and consultation to bring gender equity for girls and women to the sport community. Our activities are wide-ranging. We commission and publish issue papers on topics of critical significance to gender equity. We work to increase media and public awareness of the importance of our issues. We share news of important developments with our cross-country network through *Action Bulletin*, our quarterly newsletter. We are partners in a grassroots program called Community Initiatives that is running in 13 communities across Canada. We celebrate outstanding achievement at our annual Breakthrough Awards ceremony. We sponsor informal get-togethers for the people who work at the Canadian Sport and Fitness Administration Centre, where CAAWS is housed. And we participate in decision-making at all levels of the sport community.[39]

Even though organizations like CAAWS are expressly liberal feminist, there are still struggles within them around differing ideological positions. The difference has primarily been between those who proclaim a liberal approach versus those who seek a more radical feminist approach, and for the most part the struggle has been around sexual politics. Throughout its existence, CAAWS has made a serious effort to be both anti-homophobic and lesbian-positive. In the mid-1980s, resolutions were passed at various annual general meetings: "CAAWS endorses the inclusion of sexual orientation in the Canadian Human Rights Code"; "CAAWS is opposed to discrimination against lesbians in sport and physical activity; CAAWS undertakes to support advocacy efforts to ensure lesbian equality of rights"; and "Given that there are lesbians with CAAWS, and homophobia within CAAWS, the Association needs to address these internal concerns." However, despite these well-meaning resolutions and the workshops that produced them, lesbians in CAAWS have experienced difficulty in keeping the lesbian visibility and homophobia issues on the agenda.[40] The membership and leadership have always been split between those who see sexuality as a private and personal concern versus those who see it as a political issue.

39   "CAAWS the Driving Force Towards Equity for Girls and Women," backgrounder sheet in CAAWS information kit.

40   See Helen Lenskyj, "Combating Homophobia in Sport and Physical Education," *Sociology of Sport Journal* 8,1 (1991), pp.61-69; Lenskyj, "Good Sports"; and Lawrence-Harper, "Change in a Feminist Organization."

For some, the organization was perceived to have an "image problem," as expressed through letters of concern to the CAAWS newsletter, whenever the lesbians in CAAWS became too visible. For others, and certainly those taking a more radical stance, the human rights and education strategies were insufficient because they were too liberal and they depoliticized sexuality. There has been relative silence on the issue for the past few years, and to some extent the state has played a role in enforcing this silence with the 1987 directive from the Secretary of State Women's Program (which was at the time a major source of funding for CAAWS) that it would no longer fund proposals and groups whose primary purpose was "to promote a view on sexual orientation."

In 1990 CAAWS was one of several national women's organizations that lost all its operational funding from the Secretary of State Women's Program, and although it had some project money from the Women's Program in Sport Canada, it was forced to downsize drastically and rely on volunteer assistance. The organization struggled to survive, only to be saved a year later by an agreement to move it into the mainstream of sport by establishing an office in the Canadian Sport, Fitness and Administration Centre in Ottawa, where all national and multisport organizations are located, and to provide it with substantial core and project funding through Sport Canada's Women's Program. There is an important distinction to be made here between an organization that promotes *sport for women* versus one that advocates for *women in sport*. The former denotes a more radical feminist perspective in the sense that CAAWS is a women's organization that promotes its aims through sport; the latter represents a distinctly liberal approach, which seeks to improve the lot of women already in sport through a sports organization for women. As an organization, CAAWS has struggled between these two visions for its entire existence. Its current focus on gender equity, its physical presence at the Centre, its visibility and work in the Canadian Sport Council, and its willingness to work with other national sport organizations mean that its path is even more decidedly liberal now than ever before. CAAWS, however, is not unlike other women's sport advocacy organizations around the world, such as the Women's Sports Foundation in the United States, Womensport Australia, and the Women's Sports Foundation in the United Kingdom. These organizations, if they see themselves as feminist at all, are overwhelmingly liberal in their approach.[41]

41   For more information, see Hall, "Feminist Activism in Sport."

Sport itself has been stubbornly resistant to feminism, liberal or otherwise, and it remains a highly conservative institution. Although there has been some improvement in recent years, attempts to institute gender equity in the sports world have by and large been unsuccessful. Those who study and promote these attempts have been open to criticism and ridicule. From a research perspective it is important to understand how difficult it is to conduct even gender equity research in sport, and with sport organizations, let alone deal with more radical feminist issues around sexuality and difference.

THE PERILS OF DOING GENDER EQUITY RESEARCH IN SPORT

If one is willing to take risks, grab opportunities, and make the sacrifices required (just as *all* previous successful people who started near the bottom have) then gender is *virtually a non-issue* in terms of climbing the *chosen* ladder of success. (emphasis in original)

This statement was made by a male respondent who took part in a large study concerning the gender structure of national sport organizations that I conducted with two colleagues.[42] What this particular individual identified was the considerable difficulty most of our respondents (65 per cent were male) had in accepting that there is a problem in the first place. Most firmly believe either that women are represented in their organization in proportion to their numbers as participants (although in none of the twelve sports we studied was this actually the case), or that their sport is wide open to anyone of either sex providing they are qualified and willing to work. Although women in these organizations see the problem differently, gender issues are mostly *non-issues* for almost all people, both male and female, in these organizations. Even though the women in our study saw many problems that are organizationally based (for example, unconscious discrimination, the success of male networks, women's lack of awareness of positions), they, along with men, were generally opposed to the idea of a gender equity policy or program in their organization, on the grounds that equal opportunity already exists. In fact, other researchers have found that all issues of equity, such as those related to francophones, regional disparities, socio-economic

---

42   See Hall et al., "Organizational Elites Recreating Themselves"; and Hall et al., "Gender Structure of National Sport Organizations."

privilege, ethnicity, athletes' rights, or gender, are basically ignored.[43] The only way this will change in any significant way is to tie the funding of national sport organizations through public money to their commitment to equity and accessibility.[44]

There are two central issues here. One is the problem of convincing sport organizations of the need for gender equity policies and programs, something that CAAWS has made a major priority. The organization has produced a comprehensive handbook directed specifically at national sport organizations, and packed with tools, analyses, questionnaires, and guidelines designed to make the process clear and manageable.[45] They intend to work directly with national sport organizations in helping them develop gender equity policies and programs.

The second issue concerns the role of academic researchers in gender equity policy research, specifically sport-related. In our study of the gender structure of national sport organizations, which was commissioned and sanctioned by Sport Canada, the federal government department responsible for sport and which also funds the Applied Sport Research Program, we encountered open hostility to our research. This antipathy came not from Sport Canada, which was enormously supportive of our efforts, but from individuals within the national sport organizations we studied. It took the form of refusing to be interviewed, or declining to return our questionnaire (59 per cent of the men and 28 per cent of the women refused); or, if they did reply, a few took the opportunity to tell us precisely what they thought of this sort of research. There were also clearly expressed anti-feminist sentiments. For example, only 6.5 per cent of men, compared to 22 per cent of women, agreed that their sport organization needed more feminists. We interpreted these comments as a reflection of very real struggles among men and women over who will have power and who will control, and as a result they have aroused considerable emotion and tension.

43   See Macintosh and Whitson, *Game Planners*, ch.5-8.

44   The federal government has contemplated a "core sports" system whereby only certain sports would continue to receive funding provided they meet certain criteria. One of these was a "commitment to gender equity" as well as targets and strategies for improving gender equity. (See J.C. Best, *Report of the Core Sport Commissioner*, Report to the Hon. Michel Dupuy, Minister of Canadian Heritage, May 1994.) However, this report (which reportedly cost $325,000) has now been shelved, and the government is working on yet another financing system for amateur sport.

45   See *Towards Gender Equity for Women in Sport: A Handbook for National Sport Organizations* (CAAWS, 1993). It comes in two parts: Part One explains the importance of gender equity in sport, outlines the goals of an ideal gender equity organization, highlights practical ways to achieve these goals, and provides an assessment tool to guide the development of goals and policies. Part Two (forthcoming) will provide more detail, tools, and working examples to guide an organization through the process.

Other academic researchers have experienced similar problems, but rarely are there concrete accounts of tensions between the academics who conduct gender equity research and the organizations that fund and implement it. A colleague in Australia has recently done precisely this through an account of his experience with the Australian Sports Commission, the federal authority responsible for sport in Australia.[46] Jim McKay, who teaches in the Department of Sociology and Anthropology at the University of Queensland, received a research grant in 1991 from the Australian Sports Commission to "identify why there were so few women administrators in sporting organizations, with specific emphasis on the barriers to women's access and advancement." In fact, he consulted with me and my colleagues, and his project replicated and extended our study as well as similar work in Britain, Scandinavia, and the United States. He also found that men's and women's perceptions of their sport organizations were highly polarized:

> Whereas most men perceived their organisations to be gender-neutral and governed by merit, most women believed that they were systematically disadvantaged by the following factors: sexual harassment; physical intimidation; having to balance work and family responsibilities; informal male networks; patronage; masculine biases in recruitment, interviewing, selection, development and promotion; inadequate grievance procedures; gender stereotyping; glass ceilings; lack of women role models and mentors; exclusion and isolation; lesbian-baiting; executive inaction regarding GE [gender equity] issues; and the particularly masculine ambience of sport.[47]

None of this came as any surprise to us in that all of these studies have found that women function in organizational cultures in which they are devalued, isolated, and excluded. However, what was unique about Jim McKay's study was that the funding body for his research, the Australian Sports Commission, was the target of unsolicited negative criticism from the respondents in his study as to its own handling of gender equity. In his report to the Commission, *Why So Few? Women Executives in Australian Sport*, McKay included a sample of these negative comments, recommending that "the Commission should have important

46   Jim McKay, "Masculine Hegemony, the State and the Politics of Gender Equity Policy Research," *Culture and Policy* 5 (1993), pp.223-40.

47   Ibid., pp.227-28.

educative, funding and steering functions in ensuring that GE principles were comprehensively integrated into its own organisation and all ASC-funded organisations." What happened subsequently is a disturbing story of how the Commission questioned respondents' perceptions, especially if they were female, and required McKay to make changes in the report. It eventually released an "improved" revised version. The Australian media played a crucial role in affirming the Commission's concerns by claiming that there was no evidence to support the researcher's conclusions and "highly emotive" tone. The lesson to be drawn from McKay's account, one he suggests himself, is that attempting to criticize the very body that funds the research often produces a response that is a "sober reminder of some men's formidable capacity to contain and resist women's experiences of gender."

GENDER RELATIONS AND SPORT: RADICAL CRITIQUES

I will now discuss some of the theoretical work that has been done to develop a radical critique of sport and specifically of gender relations. Here I am addressing the second major question of the chapter: why and how the scholarship about gender and sport is becoming increasingly radical in its critique, and why it is problematic that so little of this research is actually used by those working towards gender equity in sport.

Sport as a Site of Cultural Struggle

The history of modern sport, as in all areas of popular culture, is a history of cultural struggle. There have been numerous and often bitter conflicts in Canada over which sporting practices, styles, beliefs, and bureaucratic forms should predominate. For instance, some traditional sporting practices (such as lacrosse) were marginalized or incorporated into more "respectable" and "useful" ways of playing as the colonizers (primarily the British) imposed their particular sports on the colonized. The class-based struggles of the late nineteenth and early twentieth centuries over the meaning of amateurism and its alternative, professionalism, led eventually to the emergence of commercialized sport. Marginalized groups, such as women and racial and ethnic minorities, have struggled to preserve their values and their ways of playing. Privileged groups — seemingly by consent — have been able to establish their own cultural practices as the most valued and legitimate, whereas subordinate groups (such as women) have to struggle and fight to gain and maintain control over their own sport experience, or in some cases to have their alternative practices and activities incorporated into the dominant sporting culture. Sport in our culture is still viewed by many as a "masculinizing project," a cultural practice in which boys learn to be men and male solidarity is forged. Sport remains a prime site for the maintenance of masculine hegemony. It is for this reason that when women actively participate in the symbols, practices, and institutions of sport, what they do there is often not considered "real" sport, nor in some cases are they viewed as real women.[48]

What follows from this notion of sport as a site of cultural struggle is that the history of women in sport is a history of cultural resistance. In fact the very presence of women in the male preserve of sport is evidence of "leaky hegemony."[49] The women in Victorian Canada who ignored medical warnings regarding athletic activity were challenging the primacy of the uterus, and when they rode defiantly about on their "safety bicycles" (bikes with rubber tires) in their fashionable bloomers, they broke tradition and asserted their independence. Although the school games and sports that girls began to play at the end of the century were intended to make them healthier, and so fitter for academic toil and ultimately motherhood, they nonetheless challenged the notion of the "weaker sex." Revelling in their new-found physical freedom of the 1920s, Canadian women were quite spectacular in the new era of women's competitive sport and excelled in athletics, basketball, speed skating, and swimming. Yet newly trained women physical educators fought to keep women's sport as unlike men's and as far removed from male control as possible by advocating separate programs, teachers, coaches, and officials. They campaigned against all championships (including the Olympics), tournaments, and interscholastic competitions, branding them "unwholesome." Others decried their efforts as reactionary and a step backwards. Resistance, therefore, is never wholly success-

48   For useful articles discussing these ideas in more depth, see: Lois Bryson, "Sport and the Maintenance of Masculine Hegemony," *Women's Studies International Forum* 10,4 (1987), pp.349-60; Iris M. Young, "The Exclusion of Women from Sport: Conceptual and Existential Dimensions," *Philosophy in Context* 9 (1979), pp.44-53; Jennifer Hargreaves, "The Promise and Problems of Women's Leisure and Sport," in Chris Rojek, ed., *Leisure for Leisure: Critical Essays* (New York: Routledge, 1989), pp.130-49.

49   Susan J. Birrell and Nancy Theberge, "Feminist Resistance and Transformation in Sport," in D. Margaret Costa and Sharon R. Guthrie, eds., *Women and Sport: Interdisciplinary Perspectives* (Champaign, Ill.: Human Kinetics, 1994), pp.361-76.

ful, and it often does not result in a transformed cultural practice. It is impossible here to revisit the struggles and resistance of Canadian women in sport over the past 50 years to negotiate a place for themselves in the repressive social relations of their time, or to explore moments of escape and autonomy when they took pleasure in themselves, when they had fun.[50] The point is that sport is an important, though often over-looked or underestimated site, which helps us to understand the repro-duction of (and resistance to) gender relations.

Theorizing Gender Relations and Sport

Sport studies scholars have consistently called for more theoretically in-formed relational analyses of class, gender, race, and ethnic issues in sport,[51] and the past few years have seen a distinct shift from traditional categoric and distributive research to a much clearer understanding of what should constitute a more theoretically informed analysis of the so-cial relations of power in sport and leisure. Although the work is rela-tively new, there is now a substantial body of research and scholarship.

Most sport scholars and theorists now accept that the significance of sport in modern/postmodern life can only be grasped through an analy-sis of culture. Among feminist sport scholars, there is some consensus that the theoretical underpinnings of a truly radical, gendered (and non-racist) theory of sport lie in the combination of feminism and cultural studies, or more succinctly feminist cultural studies. What is reflected here are two primary movements within the broader framework known as the "radical" critiques of modern sport. One is the claim by feminists writing about sport that these critiques rely exclusively on *malestream* theorists, foreground class relations at the expense of other power rela-tions (race, for instance), and take little or no account of feminist theo-rizing and scholarship.

The second theme reflects the rapidly shifting intellectual ground un-der feminism in the 1990s. There is now a confusing array (to me at least) of theoretical positions within feminist discourse and politics, in-

---

50 We do not have a comprehensive and coherent history of women's sport in Canada, al-though certainly there are bits and pieces in the form of theses, dissertations, articles, and book chapters. Most of the material is highly descriptive, thus providing useful chronologies of various aspects of Canadian women's sporting heritage, but very little by way of analysis. The only book-length treatment of the subject so far available is Helen Lenskyj, *Out of Bounds: Women, Sport and Sexuality* (Toronto: Women's Press, 1986).

51 I have developed the ideas and material in this section much more extensively in Hall, "Gen-der and Sport in the 1990s"; and in M. Ann Hall, "Feminism, Theory and the Body: A Re-sponse to Cole," *Journal of Sport and Social Issues* 17,2 (1993), pp.98-105.

cluding cultural hegemony, discourse theory, revisionary psychoanalysis, theories of representation, and, of course, postmodernism and post-
structuralism. In fact, some would argue that there is a perception of crisis in feminism fuelled by identity politics and irreconcilable differences
that have shattered an illusory solidarity.[52] Others argue that over the
past decade there has been a significant "turn to culture" in feminism,
and that the marked interest in analysing processes of symbolization
and representation rather than an interest in models of social structure
indicates a disciplinary shift from the social sciences to the arts, humanities, and philosophy.[53] This transformation has probably been less evident in North America than it has been in Britain and Europe.

Feminism has also played an important role in reasserting the centrality of the body within social theory and sociology, and the body itself
is being re-theorized within an increasingly sophisticated "corporeal"
feminism. Within sport studies there is at least a growing awareness of
the importance of these intellectual movements and debates.

In fact, some of the most exciting and theoretically informed work on
gender and sport uses a feminist cultural studies perspective.[54] Even
though the work is very new, there are some identifiable themes. First,
there is a recognition of the importance of women's sport history that
moves away from a "compensatory and contribution" approach to history to one that fully incorporates gender relations as an analytical category of historical research, and, as well, redefines and expands concepts
such as sport, competition, and women's culture.[55]

Second, there is an increasing sensitivity to "difference" as a notion
both of *sexual difference* and of *differences among women*. In sport studies
scholars have placed more emphasis on sexual difference and have not
taken enough account of differences among women. Categoric research

52   Carla Kaplan, "The Language of Crisis in Feminist Theory," in Glynis Carr, ed., *Turning the
     Century: Feminist Theory in the 1990s* (Lewisburg, Penn.: Bucknell University Press, 1992),
     pp.68-89.

53   Michèle Barrett, "Feminism's Turn to Culture," *Women: A Cultural Review* 1,1 (1990), pp.22-
     24; Michèle Barrett, "Words and Things: Materialism and Method in Contemporary Femi-
     nist Analysis," in Michèle Barrett and Anne Phillips, eds., *Destabilizing Theory: Contempo-
     rary Feminist Debates* (Stanford, Cal.: Stanford University Press, 1992), pp.201-19.

54   See Hall, "Gender and Sport in the 1990s"; see also Susan Birrell and Cheryl L. Cole, eds.,
     Women, Sport, and Culture (Champaign, Ill.: Human Kinetics, 1994).

55   Catriona Parratt, "From the History of Women in Sport to Women's Sport History: A Re-
     search Agenda," in D. Margaret Costa and Sharon R. Guthrie, eds., *Women and Sport: Inter-
     disciplinary Perspectives* (Champaign, Ill.: Human Kinetics, 1994), pp.5-14. One of the best ex-
     amples of this new historical work is Susan Cahn, *Coming On Strong: Gender and Sexuality
     in Twentieth-Century Women's Sport* (New York: The Free Press, 1994).

conducted primarily by psychologists has focused on the gender differences in sport and leisure, explaining these differences through biology or
socialization. Sociologists have identified gender and gender difference as
a social construction and have begun to investigate how sport is used to
construct and promote an ideology of natural difference and inferiority.[56]
More specific research has focused on how the media organize their
(re)presentations of women's sport and make their particular claims to
common sense through trivialization and marginalization, sexualization,
and the construction of "natural" sexual difference. The best of this work
uses critical media and cultural theory and examines the complex relationship between the "text" (newspaper account, television production,
novel), how ideologies are encoded in the text, and how these texts are
"read" by those who consume them (audiences).[57]

With regard to the other meaning of difference, differences among
women, there have been critiques of the exclusionary practices of white
women sport scholars, of theory that treats women of colour as invisible,
rightly insisting on the necessity of critical, relational analyses of the in-
tersections of gender, race, and class.[58] Despite these pleas, the discourse
and research have remained very white dominated. Incorporating even
some of the racial and ethnic differences in women's sporting experiences is difficult, because so much remains to be researched and written,
but as more scholarship accumulates it will become even more difficult
unless we confront some of the problems of integration now. Merely
adding in minority women's experience is not good enough; we must

56   See, for example: Susan J. Birrell and Cheryl L. Cole, "Double Fault: Renee Richards and the
     Construction and Naturalization of Difference," *Sociology of Sport Journal* 7,1 (1990), pp.1-21;
     Susan J. Birrell and Nancy Theberge, "Ideological Control of Women in Sport," in D. Mar-
     garet Costa and Sharon R. Guthrie, eds., *Women and Sport: Interdisciplinary Perspectives*
     (Champaign, Ill.: Human Kinetics, 1994), pp.341-59; Lois Bryson, "Challenges to Male He-
     gemony in Sport," in Michael A. Messner and Donald F. Sabo, eds., *Sport, Men, and the Gen-
     der Order: Critical Feminist Perspectives* (Champaign, Ill.: Human Kinetics, 1990), pp.173-84;
     Nancy Theberge, "Construction of Gender in Sport."

57   Representative and recent examples of this research are: Jim McKay and Debbie Huber, "An-
     choring Media Images of Technology and Sport," *Women's Studies International Forum* 15,2
     (1992), pp.205-18; Margaret C. Duncan, "Sport Photographs and Sexual Difference: Images
     of Women and Men in the 1984 and 1988 Olympic Games," *Sociology of Sport Journal* 7,1
     (1990), pp.22-43; Margaret MacNeill, "Active Women, Media Representations, and Ideol-
     ogy," in Jean Harvey and Hart Cantelon, eds., *Not Just a Game* (Ottawa: University of
     Ottawa Press, 1988), pp.195-211.

58   Alison Dewar, "Will All the Generic Women in Sport Please Stand Up? Challenges Facing
     Feminist Sport Sociology," *Quest* 45 (1993), pp.211-29; Yvonne R. Smith, "Women of Color
     in Society and Sport," *Quest* 44 (1992), pp.228-50; Susan J. Birrell, "Women of Color, Critical
     Autobiography, and Sport," in Michael A. Messner and Donald F. Sabo, eds., *Sport, Men,
     and the Gender Order: Critical Feminist Perspectives* (Champaign, Ill.: Human Kinetics,
     1990), pp.185-99.

pay attention to relations among women and re-theorize at the same time.[59] Sport scholars are only beginning to pay special attention to the developing minority discourse in feminist theory as represented by writers such as Barbara Christian, Patricia Hill Collins, Sneja Gunew, Trinh T. Minh-Ha, bell hooks, Gayatri Spivak, and others.

A third theme is the growing body of work on masculinity and sport. Increasingly, this work uses feminism, cultural studies, psychoanalysis, and postmodernism to theorize what is seen as a problematic relationship between sport and masculinity (more accurately, masculinities). Topics include masculinity and violence in men's sport, homosexuality and homophobia, male bonding in the locker room, the media and sports violence, and black male expression and sport. The men (primarily) who do this research recognize that they need to begin their analyses from explicitly feminist standpoints, avoid the universalization of men's experiences, and critically examine intermale dominance hierarchies (for example, gay and non-gay, blacks and whites).[60]

A final theme, which is only beginning to emerge, is scholarship that will help us to understand the historical and social construction of women's bodily oppression in movement, which I would specifically characterize as the subordination of our physicality. What are needed are concrete, material analyses of the female body (and specific body practices) as a locus of practical cultural control. Interestingly enough, women's bodybuilding has been the subject of cultural analysis from a variety of perspectives. Although I recognize the excellent work done, for example, on the preoccupation with dieting and slenderness among women in some cultures, on the alarming rise of cosmetic surgery particularly among women, on so-called female "diseases" such as hysteria, agoraphobia, and especially anorexia nervosa, and on reproductive issues, what is still missing is a similar analysis of more "positive" body practices associated with physicality among women (in sport, exercise, fitness, movement).

A Political Agenda for Research

Why do we need this "theoretically informed" scholarship anyway? How is it going to help us change the sporting world for the betterment of women (and presumably men too)? Nancy Fraser, a U.S. feminist

59   Linda Gordon, "On Difference," *Genders* 10 (1991), pp.91-111.

60   Three recent books that illustrate this work are: Michael Messner, *Power at Play: Sports and the Problem of Masculinity* (Boston: Beacon Press, 1992); Brian Pronger, *The Arena of Masculinity: Sports, Homosexuality, and the Meaning of Sex* (New York: St. Martin's Press, 1990); and Messner and Sabo, *Sport, Men, and the Gender Order.*

philosopher, suggests at least four reasons why feminists would want and need theory.[61] First, it can help us understand how people's social realities are fashioned and altered over time. This is why sport scholars have stressed the importance of an historical understanding of the gendering of sport, and in particular women's struggle to negotiate their contested place in the sports world. Social identities are also complex and plural, which is why we must pay much more attention to diversity among women based on differences in class, race, and ethnicity as we reconstruct the historical record.

Second, theory can help us understand how, under conditions of inequality, people come together, form collective identities, and constitute themselves as collective social agents. Again, we need to reconstruct the struggles of women in sport, both among ourselves and against others, as we have tried either to resist the dominant sporting culture by providing separate alternatives for girls and women, or to incorporate ourselves and women's sport into the structures of power. Closely connected to this is Fraser's third reason for theory, which is to understand how the cultural hegemony of dominant groups in society is secured and contested. There is now a substantial body of theoretically nuanced scholarship on the ways, for example, in which sport is used to construct and promote an ideology of natural difference and inferiority, how these ideologies are imbedded in media representations of gender, how bodies are gendered through various sporting practices, and how the relationship between sport and masculinity is increasingly problematic.

Lastly, theory should shed some light on the prospects for emancipatory social change and political practice. Theory will not be able to tell us what to do (whether to advocate for separation or integration, for example), but it should help us to understand our culture a lot better than we do now, to pick apart how it functions, and to unravel the various interconnections that keep it together. In the end, theory raises our consciousness level and helps us to provide an ongoing critique of our culture, in this case, our sporting culture.

The trouble with a good deal of feminist theory is that it is not written in clear, precise, and accessible language. This is a problem because sometimes only the theorists understand and read the theory. It seems so far removed from the everyday struggles of women on the "battlefield" of sport. Yet it is vitally important for those same women to un-

---

61   Nancy Fraser, "The Uses and Abuses of French Discourse Theory for Feminist Politics," *Theory, Culture & Society* 9,1 (1992), pp.51-71.

derstand (and read) what is being said by the scholars and theorists. Today we are in a different theoretical era, notably unlike the past when
theoretical concepts like gender stereotyping, role conflict, socialization,
role models, and mentors made sense. Now we need to focus on sport as
a site for relations of domination and subordination (gender, race, class,
and others) and how sport also serves as a site of resistance and transformation.

Gender equity issues need to be tackled from a more radical (and less
liberal) perspective. This means that far more attention needs to be paid
to issues of sexuality: lesbianism and homophobia, sexual harassment
and abuse, sexual violence and sport, and the troubling "gender verification" insisted upon by the International Olympic Committee. A colleague in the United States, Pat Griffin, has for many years argued persuasively for open and serious dialogue about lesbianism and
homophobia in sport and physical education.[62] The difficult topic of
sexual harassment, particularly of female athletes, is beginning to be discussed openly through newspaper stories, television programs, and
some serious scholarship. In Canada, Helen Lenskyj (and CAAWS) are
the leading voices, insisting that the issues be discussed as problems of
sport institutions and organizations rather than of aberrant individuals.[63] Useful social commentary and research around sport and sexual
violence are beginning to appear. Professional male athletes on trial
(with some convicted) for rape, assault, and spousal abuse; women
sportswriters reporting sexual harassment in male locker rooms; and a
plausible relationship between an upsurge in domestic violence and tele-
vised professional football all attest to a growing interest and concern in
this area, certainly on the part of the media.[64] There is also a tremendous
need for research around the threat of sexual violence as a real barrier to
women's leisure and physical freedom, especially in public spaces. Fi-

62   See, for example: Pat Griffin and James Genasci, "Addressing Homophobia in Physical Edu-
      cation: Responsibilities for Teachers and Researchers," in Messner and Sabo, Sport, Men,
      and the Gender Order, pp.211-21; Pat Griffin, "Changing the Game: Homophobia, Sexism,
      and Lesbians in Sport," Quest 44 (1992), pp.251-65; Pat Griffin, "Homophobia in Women's
      Sports: The Fear That Divides Us," in Greta L. Cohen, ed., Women in Sport: Issues and Con-
      troversies (Newbury Park, Cal.: Sage, 1993), pp.193-203. See also Lenskyj, "Combating Homo-
      phobia in Sport and Physical Education."

63   Helen Lenskyj, "Sexual Harassment: Female Athletes' Experiences and Coaches' Responsi-
      bilities," Sports (Coaching Association of Canada) 12,6 (1992); Helen Lenskyj, "Unsafe at
      Home Base: Women's Experiences of Sexual Harassment in University Sport and Physical
      Education," Women and Sport and Physical Activity Journal 1,1 (1992), pp.19-33. See also Har-
      assment in Sport: A Guide to Policies, Procedures and Resources (Ottawa: CAAWS, 1994).

64   See Mariah Burton Nelson, The Stronger Women Get, the More Men Love Football: Sexism
      and the American Culture of Sports (New York: Harcourt Brace, 1994).

nally, through the efforts of committed women, including Abby Hoffman in Canada, the International Amateur Athletic Federation has defied the International Olympic Committee and abandoned the controversial "gender verification" (also known as femininity control) whereby females wishing to compete as "women" at the Olympics must undergo a chromosomal test to prove that they are, in fact, genetically female. The scientific and medical communities have long criticized this practice because it is degrading and potentially psychologically damaging to females, and those with chromosomal abnormalities are disadvantaged athletically rather than advantaged by their condition. Men simply do not masquerade as women at these competitions, and the very rare superficial masculinization of female athletes may, in fact, be due to the crude use of anabolizing doping substances. However, there is still much work to be done to convince the IOC and other international sport bodies to abolish this controversial sex testing and to concentrate instead on improving the opportunities for women around the world to compete at the highest levels.

What I have suggested here is just a small sample of the research that needs to be done so that the gender and sport research agenda becomes more political and more radical. I return in the concluding section to a central theme of the chapter: the noticeable gap between theory and practice, which can only be addressed in any significant way by politicizing both women's sport and women in sport.

POLITICIZING WOMEN'S SPORT (AND WOMEN IN SPORT): RADICAL
CULTURAL STRUGGLE

The politicization of women's sports is unusual. For the most part, sportswomen see sports in an insular way and claim that there is no connection between participation and politics. As a result discrimination goes unchallenged: a deaf ear is turned towards people who make sexist and racist remarks, and nothing is done to change the practices of clubs that (often unintentionally) discriminate against certain groups so that they remain marginalized, alienated and powerless. Dominant structures and discourses are exclusionary; they are the basis of institutionalized discrimination which is hard to shift. There have been few organized initiatives in

women's sports which look beyond the struggle for greater equality with men, and which relate the gender dimension to wider social and political issues as a part of the everyday life experiences of
participation.[65]

As Jennifer Hargreaves suggests here, sportswomen have generally been
resistant to taking an overtly political stance on women's issues and issues of discrimination. The politics and practice of feminism have not
always been recognized as particularly important or relevant. By politics
we mean the struggle to define and to control women's sport: its meanings and values, the structures required, and the debates over policy.
Feminist practice in sport, when it does occur, varies between liberal reformism to a more controversial radicalism, thus producing the inevitable tensions between the two approaches. When governments have
made women's sport a priority, their programs and policies have been
overwhelmingly liberal, but with a welcome shift from a focus on equality to equity over the past decade. When women's sport advocacy
groups, such as CAAWS in Canada and other similar organizations
around the world, become more dependent for funding on either the
state or the private sector, they focus more on a liberal gender equity
framework for change and are less willing, often resistant, to engage in
radical cultural politics.[66] This effectively depoliticizes the issues surrounding women in sport (homophobia is a good example) and makes
it difficult for those interested in pursuing more radically defined issues
and change to be effective. Male-defined sport can be, and often is, challenged and resisted, but especially at the local level, where it is far removed from state-controlled amateur sport systems.

There is a very long road ahead before any form of radical cultural
politics is recognized as being both viable and necessary to future
change in women's sport. As I was finishing this chapter, I attended an
international conference on women's sport organized by the British
Sports Council and supported by the International Olympic Committee. At the conference were some three hundred delegates from over
eighty-five countries representing governmental and non-governmental
organizations, national Olympic Committees, international and national sport federations, and educational and research institutions. The
conference specifically addressed the issue of "how to accelerate the

65   Hargreaves, *Sporting Females*, p.254.

66   See Hall, "Feminist Activism in Sport."

process of change that would redress the imbalances women face in their participation and involvement in sport," and it approved a declaration with an overriding aim: "to develop a sporting culture that enables and values full involvement of women in every aspect of sport."[67] Thematic workshops addressed the continuing problems that plague women's sport: the lack of women in sports administration, development of women coaches, and gender bias in physical education and research. Issues seminars focused on the usual topics: equal opportunity legislation, integration versus separation, cross-cultural differences, challenging sexism, marketing strategies, working in a male environment, and admittedly a few more controversial topics such as women's sport in Muslim cultures, sexual harassment, homophobia, and integrating women athletes with disabilities. Skills seminars provided information on mentoring, networking, advocacy and lobbying, community sports leadership, dealing with the media, and gender awareness training. Delegates agreed to establish and develop an International Women in Sport Strategy, which they hope will be endorsed and supported by governmental and non-governmental organizations involved in sport development on all continents, and enable model programs and successful developments to be shared among nations and sporting federations.

Very few researchers and scholars whose work relates to women and sport attended the conference, which points again to the gap between theory and practice. Indeed, very little of the research and scholarship readily available was incorporated into the conference program, although several recommendations vaguely addressed the need for more research. There was general agreement that strong, international women and sport networks are needed for mutual support, for exchanging knowledge, skills, and "good practice," and for sharing resources. A new organization, Womensport International, was announced at the conference. It aspires to be an umbrella group that will seek positive change for girls and women in sport and physical activity by facilitating global networking and communication. Given the fact that the founders of Womensport International want the organization to be global in scope and outlook, and to connect a vast array of differing cultures, it is no wonder that notions of politicization and radical cultural struggle are absent from its vision. However, it must take on board this more radical perspective, or otherwise it will become just like every other women's

67   The Brighton Declaration on Women and Sport, Women Sport and the Challenge of
       Change International Conference, Brighton, England, May 5-8, 1994.

sport advocacy association. Although some of those associations have made significant gains in bringing more girls and women into sport, sport itself remains as male-dominated and male-defined as always. This is not meaningful progress.

SUGGESTED READINGS

Susan Birrell and Cheryl L. Cole, eds., *Women, Sport and Culture.* Champaign, Ill.: Human Kinetics, 1994.

Adrianne Blue, *Grace Under Pressure: The Emergence of Women in Sport.* London: Sidgwick & Jackson, 1987.

Susan K. Cahn, *Coming On Strong: Gender and Sexuality in Twentieth-Century Women's Sport.* New York: The Free Press, 1994.

Greta L. Cohen, ed., *Women in Sport: Issues and Controversies.* Newbury Park, N.J.: Sage Publications, 1993.

D. Margaret Costa and Sharon R. Guthrie, eds., *Women and Sport: Interdisciplinary Perspectives.* Champaign, Ill.: Human Kinetics, 1994.

Jennifer Hargreaves, *Sporting Females: Critical Issues in the History and Sociology of Women's Sports.* London and New York: Routledge, 1994.

Helen Lenskyj, *Out of Bounds: Women, Sport and Sexuality.* Toronto: Women's Press, 1986.

Michael M. Messner and Donald F. Sabo, eds., *Sport, Men, and the Gender Order: Critical Feminist Perspectives.* Champaign, Ill.: Human Kinetics, 1990.

Mariah Burton Nelson, *Are We Winning Yet: How Women Are Changing Sports and Sports Are Changing Women.* New York: Randon House, 1991.

Mariah Burton Nelson, *The Stronger Women Get, The More Men Love Football: Sexism and the American Culture of Sports.* New York: Harcourt Brace, 1994.

Yvonne Zipter, *Diamonds Are a Dyke's Best Friend.* Ithaca, N.Y.: Firebrand Books, 1988.

LORRAINE GREAVES & ALISON WYLIE,
AND THE STAFF OF THE BATTERED WOMEN'S ADVOCACY
CENTRE: CHERYL CHAMPAGNE, LOUISE KARCH, RUTH
LAPP, JULIE LEE, & BINA OSTHOFF

Chapter Eleven: Women and Violence: Feminist Practice and Quantitative Method

THE BATTERED WOMEN'S ADVOCACY CENTRE (BWAC) IN London, Ontario, is a unique non-crisis, non-residential counselling service for battered women. It was established in 1982, at a time when the primary response to battered women in Canada consisted of emergency housing in the form of shelters and transition houses. These services were largely feminist-run and committed to the provision of crisis support for abused women and their children.

As important as shelters have been and continue to be, they are primarily oriented to providing short-term crisis-intervention services and are usually not in a position to provide continuing support and advocacy for the women who make use of their services. The process of breaking the "pattern of violence"—of seeking redress, of reshaping a violent relationship, of starting a new life—is often lengthy and requires a range of supports. Typically this process has legal and economic, as well as social and psychological dimensions. Just finding a route through the criminal justice system can be a long and difficult process that can benefit from advocacy, and often the sustained support of counselling (not only around issues of abuse but also, for example, on questions of employment) can be crucial in helping an abused woman successfully make changes in her life.

Inspired by a considerable body of North American research and practice that had begun to make clear the need for expanded advocacy and support, the founders of BWAC resolved to establish an agency that would provide integrated, non-crisis, non-residential counselling services. These were designed to provide battered women with more sustained emotional support, legal information, and assistance in gaining access to a range of community services.

The founders also expected that such an agency would attract a range of women who had never made use of emergency housing or seen police intervention, two of the main contexts in which battered women had previously made contact with service agencies and/or the legal system. At the time BWAC was established, almost all estimates of the prevalence of woman abuse and profiles of battered women were based on shelter and police statistics, often reinforcing classist and racist presuppositions about battered women and their partners. A number of those working in the area suspected that battering was more widespread than these statistics suggested and that the factors shaping the realities of this violence were much more complex than typically acknowledged (for example, given extant "learning" and "structure of power" models).[1] When BWAC was established, it was one of a very few non-crisis agencies existing in North America that were potentially in a position to provide a broader picture of woman abuse: of those who suffer and, indirectly, those who perpetrate this abuse; of the circumstances under which the abuse occurs; and of women's responses to violence at the hands of their partners.

From its inception, given this rationale for creating a different kind of service for battered women, BWAC has had a twofold mandate. It provides services to battered women in the London area, and in this its commitment is to advocacy and counselling on behalf of individual women. It is also committed to advocacy on behalf of battered women more generally. A complementary goal of the agency has been to collect information relevant for (re)assessing extant models of abuse and of battered women and, more specifically, for helping to develop services that better meet the needs of battered women. (MacLeod describes how such findings have changed our understanding of woman abuse and the services available to them.)[2] Given this understanding of what feminist

1   See MacLeod's summary: Linda MacLeod, *Battered but Not Beaten: Preventing Wife Battering in Canada* (Ottawa: Canadian Advisory Council on the Status of Women, 1987), pp.39-40.

2   MacLeod, *Battered but Not Beaten*, pp.14-16,19-21.

advocacy involves where it is understood to operate at both an individual and a collective level BWAC has always incorporated data collection
and research into its provision of service, beginning at the intake stage.
In this chapter we consider the interplay between advocacy at these levels, between service provision and research.

In particular, we will explore and critically assess the evolution of the
intake protocol at BWAC from the introduction of a highly structured intake form to the point at which the BWAC staff felt they should reassess its
use. In doing this we hope to identify both the benefits and liabilities of using such a form in the context of an agency devoted to the dual mandate of
advocacy at both individual and collective (social/political) levels.

THE RESEARCH PROGRAM AT BWAC

i) Research objectives and results

From the time BWAC's mandate was established, both staff and Board
members have collaborated in its research program. This has included
the collection of information (primarily by staff members) and its analysis (by both staff and Board members appointed to the BWAC Research
Committee), and also various collaborative ventures designed to make
the results of our research as widely accessible as possible. Under the
general rubric of seeking information relevant for reassessing entrenched assumptions about battering and battered women, our specific
aims in these ventures have been to broaden our understanding of who
endures woman abuse (a demographic analysis), of the forms that this
violence takes, and of the factors that shape women's decisions to stay or
to leave a violent relationship and make changes in their lives. We first
describe briefly some of the results of the BWAC research program related to these questions, and then provide an overview of how they were
realized and of the role that the original quantitative intake form played
in the research process.

Perhaps the most important result of the BWAC research program is
the support it provides for those who have long suspected that standard
estimates of the prevalence of woman abuse systematically miss a very
large number of abused women; this was, in essence, the answer we gave
to the first, essentially demographic question identified above. A high

proportion of women who make use of BWAC's services are not in crisis, they have never made use of shelters, and they have never come to the attention of the police or justice system. Consequently, they would never appear in the records that most estimates and characterizations of abuse are based on, as well as most policies for response to woman abuse.[3] Our analysis of the demographic information collected by BWAC staff also makes it clear that battering very substantially cross-cuts the range of socio-economic categories that we were able to acquire comparative (provincial or federal) statistics for—a finding that undermines classist stereotypes that characterize the victims of battering as low-income, under-educated, working-class, or welfare mothers, whose lives are often complicated by drug or alcohol abuse.[4] Overall, we found that the demographic profile of BWAC users closely paralleled that of women in the general Canadian population.[5]

In addition, we were able to document some of the complexity of women's responses to abuse. This was possible because just under 44 per cent of women attending BWAC up to 1988 were still living with their abusive partner at the time of their intake interview, and many reported that they hoped not to leave but to change these relationships. Our preliminary results strongly reinforced the emerging view that, as

3   The profile of women attending BWAC has been described elsewhere: Lorraine Greaves, Nelson Heapy, and Alison Wylie, "Advocacy Services: Reassessing the Profile and Needs of Battered Women," *Canadian Journal of Community Mental Health* 7,2 (1988), pp.39-51; Greaves, Heapy, and Wylie, "The Value of Advocacy Services for Battered Women" (London, Ont.: London Battered Women's Advocacy Clinic and the Ontario Women's Directorate, 1988). By way of summary of these results, we found that altogether 89 per cent of women making use of BWAC services had never made use of, and felt no need for, emergency housing; 82 per cent had never spoken to lawyers, doctors, or transition-home personnel; and 63 per cent had not previously laid charges against the batterer. The information on which these summary statistics are based was collected in intake interviews with 524 women who visited BWAC between February 1983 and March 1986.

4   The statistical analysis published in 1988 (Greaves, Heapy, and Wylie, "Advocacy Services") did not include information about race or ethnicity. The advocates did make the point, however, that the experiences and responses of women attending BWAC also counter racist stereotypes on many levels, and we incorporated this into the "composites" we developed for a more popular brochure designed to challenge stereotypes about woman abuse; Greaves and Wylie, "Wife Battering: Challenging the Stereotypes" (London, Ont.: London Battered Women's Advocacy Clinic and the Ontario Women's Directorate, 1990).

5   For example, with respect to educational level, 86 per cent of the women attending BWAC between 1983 and 1986 had either completed high school or had some postsecondary education; the figure reported for the 1986 census was 87 per cent. More specifically, 29 per cent of BWAC women have a postsecondary education, while 35 per cent of Canadian women report such a background. Approximately 45 per cent of the women attending BWAC were employed, 54 per cent of them full-time, compared to 52 per cent of Canadian women in 1986. Roughly half those employed were clustered in clerical, sales, and service occupations, also closely approximating the occupational distribution of women nationally.

articulated by Linda MacLeod, "battered women do not fit one psycho-logical or socio-economic mould," and they have very few "common characteristics which are not the direct result of battering."[6] The deci-sion-making processes described by women attending BWAC indicate not only that women typically weigh their options on many dimensions at once, but also that they consider *relative* gains or losses, for example, in determining whether to stay or leave a violent relationship.[7]

These results indicated not only the enormity of the problem of woman abuse, drawing attention to features of its distribution that had not been widely recognized, but also testified to its complexity. They reaffirmed the need to ensure that the services provided battered women are flexible and responsive to their (very diverse) needs. In collecting this information the research program wanted to ensure, as its most immediate objective, that BWAC could provide the services needed by battered women in the Lon-don area and could offer women attending BWAC the best understanding possible of how their experiences fit into the larger patterns of woman abuse emerging in our own research and that of related agencies. But be-yond this, BWAC has always been committed to providing support for ac-tivism on violence issues in the wider community.[8] As a feminist agency en-gaged in *advocacy*, BWAC has a mandate to help reshape the response of service providers to battered women and to lobby for expanding and re-structuring the funding available to agencies that provide services for abused women. Given this, the Research Committee of BWAC has sought to communicate the results of the research program to as wide a range of audiences as possible. These include the women making use of BWAC's services, the larger (local and regional) communities through public edu-cation, other service providers, and policy-makers, researchers, and legis-lators working in the area. Reports on our research program have been pre-sented in a number of different formats: in a relatively academic report (1988); through an extensive public education program undertaken by BWAC staff; in "plain language" brochures that provide composite sketches of some of the kinds of situations and experiences described by women attending BWAC;[9] and, finally, in the content and format of the in-

6   MacLeod, *Battered but Not Beaten*, pp.38,44.

7   Greaves, Heapy, and Wylie, "Advocacy Services."

8   See MacLeod's use of BWAC data in this connection. MacLeod, *Battered but Not Beaten*, p.21.

9   Greaves, Heapy, and Wylie, "The Value of Advocacy Services"; Greaves and Wylie, "Wife Battering: Challenging the Stereotypes" (London, Ont.: London Battered Advocacy Clinic and the Ontario Women's Directorate, 1990).

take interviews at BWAC, through which most of the information reported above was collected.

ii) The Research Process and the Use of a Structured Intake Form

The information that supported the analyses and results sketched above was drawn primarily from a highly structured intake form that BWAC advocates used in their initial interview(s) with women between 1982 and 1991. This form was first developed, and continuously modified, by BWAC staff in collaboration, at various junctures, with members of the Board's Research Committee.[10] It was conceived primarily as a tool to collect information that might assist abused women in the process of understanding their lives and potential choices and, secondly, to underpin program development and delivery. As it evolved, it was a long and detailed form consisting mainly of specific questions designed to elicit short answers that could be entered in structured (check-off) categories of response. Through much of this period it consisted of five sections. The first was organized around questions about the woman's personal history and socio-economic status, as well as that of the abuser and any children involved. A later section included questions about past relationships and family of origin. Finally, several sections asked for detailed information about the type, frequency, and patterns and ramifications of previous abuse. The form was used as the basis for the intake interview and was usually filled out during two sessions.

As a research tool, the intake form provided systematic, readily analysable data on a wide range of factors relevant for understanding woman abuse, including the demographic profiles of those involved, the history of abuse, and the considerations that inform decision-making around response to this abuse. As such, this form has been essential to BWAC's mandate to address issues of violence against women on a social and political level, as well as on the individual client level.

10 Through most of the period when the intake form was developed and used, BWAC employed one part-time staff member who was a research assistant, responsible for coding intake reports, managing the database, and assisting with revision of the intake form itself. While the activities of the research staff person changed over time, the presence of a researcher in the agency (that is, not just on the Board Research Committee) meant that the service and research agendas of the agency were always closely integrated. The main impetus for development of a structured intake form, and certainly most of the specifics of its content (the questions asked and the structure of the form), came from those directly involved in service provision. The Research Committee (made up of Board members working with the research assistant and the counselling/advocacy staff) was involved at various junctures in review and consultation as the form was revised, but its interests were not the catalyst for the development of this form. In fact, the research projects the Committee took up were largely responsive to the sorts of information the staff was collecting through use of the intake form.

As a quantitative instrument, however, the BWAC intake form was unusual in some respects. Most importantly, it was subject to continuous scrutiny and revision in light of what advocates and research assistants learned from the women who had made use of BWAC's services. Although this meant that earlier data sets were not fully comparable with later ones, it ensured that the form was responsive to, and reflected, women's experience. For example, as new forms of abuse and new factors shaping patterns of abuse were reported to counsellor/advocates, the BWAC advocates and research staff added new questions to the sections dealing with women's experiences of violence; and they added questions about the use of pornography as an accompaniment to battering when reports of such practice emerged in a number of intake interviews. In this process of revision, considerations of service and the needs of the women using BWAC's services played a central role. BWAC always expected the intake form not just to generate information useful for research purposes, but to crystallize, in the very questions asked, an emerging (experience-responsive) understanding of the diversity of women who suffer violence, the sorts of violence involved, and, most importantly, the patterns of violence that were emerging within women's individual lives and for women collectively. Thus, BWAC used the intake form both in a therapeutic setting, with a focus on individual women's needs, and as a research instrument.

METHODOLOGICAL AND POLITICAL ISSUES

i) Critiques of Quantitative Methodologies: Objectifying Women's Experience

The use of a highly structured intake form, indeed, of any such "instrument," in the context of a feminist agency committed to providing support and services to women suffering violence runs directly counter not only to the ethos of the shelter movement and other feminist support groups/agencies, but also to much feminist research practice. In the case of feminist agencies and activists working to stop violence against women, the articulation and legitimation of women's experience have been an absolutely central objective; in these contexts the rejection of coercive objectification indeed, of any aggregative, structure-imposing methodology (either of inquiry or of intervention) has often been explicit.

In feminist research more generally, however, there is a strong tradition of resistance to the "objectifying" stance of much mainstream/malestream social science that has systematically silenced women and made them responsible for their own victimization. Dorothy Smith has developed one of the most comprehensive and compelling analyses available of how the conditions of knowledge production in the social sciences both serve and mediate institutional control over our lives.[11] A great many discussions of feminist research methodology and practice take this general line of argument as their point of departure and draw more specific lessons for feminist research that target particular research practices as inherently objectifying—as practices that turn those studied "into objects of scrutiny and manipulation."[12] The objection is that such practices serve to reproduce, in the relationship between the "subject" and the researcher (and the knowledge produced), precisely the hierarchical power structures and inequities that we, as feminists, should be subverting.

Ann Oakley has developed a detailed critique of interview techniques that articulates this concern in particularly compelling terms.[13] She urges that feminist researchers give up the attempt to create (and/or maintain) the "illusion" of a sharp separation of researcher (qua "knower") from the objects of study; we should expect "no intimacy without reciprocity" and should work to systematically counteract the power differences constituting standard hierarchical relationships between researcher and subject.[14] In a similar vein, Stanley and Wise argue for a general proscription against ever "going beyond" women's experience.[15] Any research practice that

11   Dorothy E. Smith, *The Everyday World as Problematic: A Feminist Sociology* (Toronto: University of Toronto Press, 1987); "A Women's Perspective as a Radical Critique of Sociology," in Sandra Harding, ed., *Feminism and Methodology: Social Science Issues* (Bloomington: University of Indiana Press, 1987), pp.84-96 (originally published in *Sociological Inquiry* 44,1 (1974), pp.7-13); *The Conceptual Practices of Power: A Feminist Sociology of Knowledge* (Toronto: University of Toronto Press, 1990).

12   Joan Acker, Kate Barry, and Joke Esseveld, "Objectivity and Truth: Problems in Doing Feminist Research," *Women's Studies International Forum* 6,4 (1983), pp.423-35.

13   Ann Oakley, "Interviewing Women: A Contradiction in Terms," in Helen Roberts, ed., *Doing Feminist Research* (London: Routledge and Kegan Paul, 1981), pp.30-61.

14   Oakley, "Interviewing Women," p.41.

15   Liz Stanley and Sue Wise, "Feminist Research, Feminist Consciousness, and Experiences of Sexism," *Women's Studies International Quarterly* 2 (1979), pp.359-74; *Breaking Out: Feminist Consciousness and Feminist Research* (London: Routledge and Kegan Paul, 1983); "'Back into the Personal' or: Our Attempt to Construct 'Feminist Research,'" in Gloria Bowles and Renate Duelli Klein, eds., *Theories of Women's Studies* (London: Routledge and Kegan Paul, 1983), pp.192-209.

counters or questions a woman's reported experience—including practices that generalize or otherwise decontextualize this experience—par-
ticipates in disempowering regimes of control and imposes interpretation
in ways that are inimical to feminist politics. The (ethnomethodological)
principle at work here is that feminist researchers cannot justify special
privilege according to their own standpoint or insights, over against those
of the people whose lives and practices are under study. Because all realities are constructed, there can never be grounds for judging a subject
"wrong" in what she claims about *her* reality. In one instance, particularly
relevant here, Stanley and Wise observe, "If a housebound, depressed,
battered mother of six with an errant spouse says she's *not* oppressed,
there's little point in us telling her she's got it wrong because of the objective reality of her situation";[16] her account is "*truth* for her," and there can
be no justification for "attempting to impose our reality."[17]

Elsewhere in their discussion of feminist research practice, Stanley
and Wise consider quantitative (generalizing, aggregative) methodologies specifically, reiterating their general argument against "going beyond" experience with special reference to how quantitative methods
exemplify the privileging and objectifying stance of traditional sociology
that they reject. In this Stanley and Wise capture, in particularly uncom-
promising terms, a number of themes that figure in feminist discussions
of research practice when the focus is on quantitative methodologies.
Such methodologies are characterized as a family of practices that are especially prone to objectify those studied, are inherently coercive, and
systematically enforce (or create and reinforce) a hierarchical relationship between "subject" and research. Others argue that these difficulties
are not unique to quantitative methodologies and are not avoided simply by shifting to alternative (ethnographic, for example) modes of inquiry (for instance, Judith Stacey),[18] but in this they reinforce the point
that the dangers of objectification and coercion are ubiquitous to social

16   Stanley and Wise, *Breaking Out*, p.112.

17   Stanley and Wise, *Breaking Out*, p. 113. Stanley and Wise conclude this statement with the
      qualification that interference or imposition is unjustifiable "when they [the subjects] don't
      want us to" suggesting that sometimes one might be justified in imposing an external reality
      on another if this gives some indication that she does "want us" to make such an imposition.
      But what could count as an indication that an imposed definition of reality is invited or ac-
      cepted, particularly in cases in which an individual's sense of self may have been so systemati-
      cally undermined she has internalized the judgement that she doesn't know what she wants,
      so that she is unlikely to resist such an imposition? See also Marilyn Frye, "In and Out of
      Harm's Way: Arrogance and Love," in Frye *The Politics of Reality: Essays in Feminist Theory*
      (Trumansburg, N.Y.: The Crossing Press, 1983), pp. 52-83.)

18   Judith Stacey, "Can There Be a Feminist Ethnography?" *Women's Studies International Fo-
      rum* 11 (1988), pp.21-27.

science and must be addressed by feminist practitioners.

The fundamental concern articulated in these critical discussions is that quantitative methodologies reinforce the privileging of a standpoint "outside" the subjectivity of the women themselves. They serve as a medium by which the structure of dominant malestream expectations are imposed on the experiences of women (among other "subdominant" research subjects), systematically obscuring any aspects of these experiences that do not fit the mould of the scripted questions. It is for these reasons that the use of a quantitative instrument in the context of an agency like BWAC is for many puzzling, if not straightforwardly inconsistent with its feminist mandate and in direct conflict with its commitment to integrate advocacy and service. It threatens to objectify the women who come to BWAC, creating a separation of counsellor/advocate and "client" and imposing a predetermined structure on the recounting of a woman's experience. All of these criticisms are serious and have had to be addressed in the context of feminist practice at BWAC.

ii) Some Possible (Cautious) Feminist Uses for Quantitative Methodologies

In addition to these strong criticisms of quantitative methodologies, a number of feminists urge a more qualified response to the shortcomings, suggesting that the methodologies can be used in non-coercive ways and that they are crucial, in some contexts, to the goals of developing a *political* analysis of women's experience of violence. They are a powerful tool for setting women's experiences in a larger context, grasping the commonalities as well as the differences in our experiences as women, breaking down our isolation, and combatting the forces that construct so much of our experience as idiosyncratic. That is to say, aggregative and otherwise quantifying approaches can be invaluable in moving from the personal to the political; they offer a very powerful set of tools for developing an understanding of how encompassing gender structures (differentially) shape our opportunities and experiences, and how we can most effectively change the conditions that disempower us in these contexts.

Pat Armstrong and Hugh Armstrong, among others, have addressed the first (practice-oriented) component of this argument that quantitative methodologies are not inherently or necessarily coercive in application.[19] They argue that while many quantitative methods and instruments are

19   Pat Armstrong and Hugh Armstrong, "Beyond Numbers: Problems with Quantitative Data,"
      in Greta Hofmann Nemiroff, ed., *Women and Men: Interdisciplinary Readings on Gender*
      (Montreal: Fitzhenry and Whiteside, 1987), pp.54-79. See also Ann Oakley and Robin Oakley, "Sexism in Official Statistics," in John Irvine, Ian Miles, and Jeff Evans, eds., *Demystifying Social Statistics* (London: Pluto Press, 1979), pp.172-89.

badly flawed in standard use, the possibility of designing quantitative studies well, and for feminist purposes, does exist. These studies can be made
sensitive to the nuances and anomalies of our diverse experiences. Their
recommendation is that survey instruments, like those used as the framework for intake interviews at BWAC, should be systematically grounded
in, and developed in response to, detailed qualitative inquiry. On the "garbage in:garbage out" principle, it is crucial that the content and structure of
these instruments should embody (and be made responsive to) a sophisticated qualitative understanding of the variability and complexity of the social phenomena they are used to investigate.

As to the second (principled) element of these critiques, even Stanley
and Wise are not entirely consistent in their strong rejection of practices
that objectify in the sense of "going beyond" women's experience. They
do allow, in cases when the battered woman's "objective reality" seemed
to belie her experiential testimony, that it is sometimes appropriate to
ask "how and why people construct realities in the way that they do."[20]
In this case, it would seem that when you identify what Stanley and Wise
describe as a "reality disjuncture"—incongruities in self-accounting like
the one described above—it may be justified to "go beyond" the experience in question, at least for the purpose of inquiring into conditions
that shape it, both private and public, of which the woman herself may
not be conscious. It may be possible to discover (or conclude) that a
woman's interpretation of her own experience is problematic, at least in
the qualified sense that its internal inconsistencies can alert both her and
the researcher/advocate to some overdetermining conditions that structure her perceptions and self-understanding (and systematic self-mis-
understanding). Where just such a process of mutual and collective in-
terrogation of experience is, in fact, a central part of feminist
consciousness-raising practices of "speaking out"—these practices do
not leave experience where they find it[21]—perhaps the possibility of
critically rethinking and reinterpreting experience is an essential part of
a feminist program of research and advocacy.[22]

20   Stanley and Wise, *Breaking Out*, p.112.

21   See, for example, editorial, "Women's Body, Women's Mind: A Guide to Consciousness
      Raising," *Ms.* 1 (July 1972), pp.18-23; Joan Cassell, *A Group Called Women: Sisterhood and
      Symbolism in the Feminist Movement* (New York: David McKay Co., 1977).

22   These points, and the discussion that follows, are developed in more detail in a paper by Al-
      ison Wylie that describes more generally the debates over "objectification"; "Reasoning
      about Ourselves: Feminist Methodology in the Social Sciences," in Elizabeth Harvey and
      Kathleen Okruhlik, eds., *Women and Reason* (Ann Arbor: University of Michigan Press,
      1992), pp.225-44.

QUANTITATIVE TOOLS AND FEMINIST PRACTICE AT BWAC

These questions about the appropriateness of quantitative instruments for feminist practice played a central role in the process of developing and changing the intake protocol at BWAC over the decade of its use. The pivotal issue was always that of whether such a highly structured intake interview was useful in providing battered women the services they needed, both individually and collectively, not so much that of whether it was, in some abstract sense, consistent with feminist ideals. While the structured intake interview form was in use, it was clear that there were at least three ways in which it was seen to serve the individual women who came to BWAC for support in understanding and changing the conditions of their lives.

i) Confronting Denial

Women often survive in violent relationships by denying or minimizing the systemic nature of the violence they endure. The detailed questions about frequency and patterns of the violence, which were a large part of the structured BWAC intake form, frequently served as a powerful tool in helping women come to terms with the extent and seriousness of abuse they had been suffering when they were prepared to address these issues. Some of the women who seek help at BWAC are resolute in resisting the label of "battered woman," or they systematically minimize the extent of the violence in their lives. When asked in a structured intake interview for details about her experience of violence, however, a woman may give significantly different answers, from a general estimate in response to the question "how many times has the violence occurred?" (for example, "only occasionally;" "maybe half a dozen times") to the picture that emerges when she specifies when the violence began and how often it occurs (for example, "in the first year of our marriage, twenty years ago"; "every month or two ..."). The process of eliciting and juxtaposing specific details of this sort can throw into sharp relief the extent and other significant features of the abuse that women may have forgotten or may systematically overlook in framing their own self-understanding.

The power of such a tool requires advocate/counsellors to make continual judgements about when and how to draw attention to discrepancies in the understanding and experience of abuse presented to them by battered women. Often, such denial or strategies of self-deception are crucial to survival, and provoking disclosures that are self-challenging in a context of intervention raises a whole range of difficult ethical and therapeutic questions. This problem is not unique to an interview process that is organized around a systematic questionnaire; such disclosures can arise in any process of articulating and reflecting on experience. But it is perhaps exacerbated by the use of a highly structured interview format, a process that can powerfully expose and challenge the violence and contradictions we live with.

ii) Moving beyond the Personal

The aims of research and service reinforced one another through the use of a structured intake form in another way as well. Along with information drawn from other sources, the experiences described by women attending BWAC provide a detailed understanding of the forms that battering takes and the conditions under which it occurs, and about the ways women protect themselves and the strategies they adopt to stop the violence in their lives. This information allowed us to draw a larger, comparative picture of the experiences of abused women. This, in turn, provided the basis for formulating questions that could help draw attention to patterns in the abuse and to interconnections between different kinds and aspects of abuse, which women suffering violence may initially see as entirely separate.

To take a concrete example, often women identify "battering" exclusively with physical abuse. When asked if they also experience various (specific) forms of psychological abuse, and/or social and economic control, they may begin to see in their experience a pattern of interconnecting factors and power dynamics that the physical abuse itself serves to obscure; for example, when psychological abuse so undermines a woman's self-esteem and confidence in her own judgement that she may blame herself for increasing social isolation. In this way, the questions built into the intake form, and the very structure of the form its inclusion of sections on physical, sexual, psychological, social, and economic abuse—embody the experiences of a very wide range of women and open the possibility of them recognizing systematic patterns that can only become visible with the benefit of a comparative perspective. The details elicited by highly specific questions also sometimes help women come to terms with a range of less clearly defined kinds of abuse, such as persistent belittling and insults; it allows them to recognize these *as* abusive and as embedded in a framework of systemic violence.

iii) Reducing Isolation

Finally, a third function of the intake form, which is closely related to that of helping women see emerging patterns in their experience, arose from its capacity of helping women set their own experience in a larger context, thus reducing their sense of isolation—often a critical component of the abuse itself. The questions and check-off categories of answers built into the form over several years often illustrated to an abused woman, more powerfully than any amount of educational literature could do, that they were not alone in their experience of violence. However bizarre or idiosyncratic, intimate, and personal a particular experience may seem, when the intake form included a question about *that specific* form of abuse, it was immediately set in a broader context of violent practice; it became clear that similar instances or types of abuse had occurred before, to other women. For example, one of the descriptors of abuse included in the section on the "most recent violent episode" had to do with spitting as a component of violent attacks. In the process of an intake interview, when a woman finished describing the violence she had experienced in her own terms, the counsellor/advocate would ask if she had also experienced any of the other types of violence listed on the form (that is, forms of violence reported by other women in intake interviews, or in the literature on battering). BWAC staff noted that, when asked these sorts of questions, women sometimes remembered or acknowledged a range of violent acts they had suffered but had never described to anyone. It was often a revelation to women that others had suffered from a particularly demeaning type of behaviour, and the question itself established for such a woman the understanding that she was not alone in her experience.

In these ways, then, BWAC counsellor/advocates found that the structured intake form could help a woman face and articulate her own experience, see its patterns, and recognize that it was not isolated or unique to her. It was effective in this, however, only insofar as, and only because, it embodied in condensed form the accumulated experience of all the women who had visited BWAC and those whose experience had otherwise informed the work of BWAC advocates (for example, as reported in the literature on battering). At its best, a structured questionnaire of this sort can crystallize some of the general contours of women's experiences and facilitate a move from the particulars of a personal situation to a systemic, political analysis. It can help to communicate to individual women the experiences and insights of a great many other women who have broken the silence and spoken out about issues of violence in their lives, at the same time as it elicits an account of their own experience. In this way a structured intake form can be useful not just (or even primarily) for research purposes, but as a tool for intervention and counselling in the context of a feminist service agency.

THE PROCESS OF REVIEWING THE INTAKE FORM

Why, then, did the BWAC staff decide to reassess the structured form in late 1991, partially suspending its use and exploring other kinds of intake procedures? Several questions began to emerge regarding the collection, storage, and use of the information collected by BWAC staff through intake interviews. For one thing, there was a sense that the original objectives of the research program had largely been met; did we need ever more detailed information about the demographic profile of women who sought counselling and advocacy outside the framework of residential shelters and the legal system? The information we had collected did serve to undermine many influential stereotypes about who gets battered, and we had had some success communicating this to policy-makers and other service providers.[23] It was not clear that BWAC's further goals of understanding in more detail the needs of battered women and their processes of decision-making would be served by the kind of large-scale aggregative analysis we had originally undertaken. At the same time, the mandate of the agency had shifted; the work of BWAC counsellor/advocates (and of the agency as a whole) was now being conceived less in terms of a mental health model (which had informed the original structure of the intake interview and form), and more in terms

---

23   See, for example, MacLeod's use of BWAC data in *Battered but Not Beaten.*

of a model of education and social change. This was reflected in a decision (partly enforced by funding limitations) to limit the number of individual counselling sessions BWAC could provide women seeking its
services and to dedicate more resources to activities designed to promote public education and bring about social change. As priorities
shifted, and as the need to do more with less grew more pressing (where
funding was concerned), it seemed less and less justifiable to commit as
much as a third of the time a counsellor/advocate could spend with a
woman working through the lengthy intake form. Finally, the backlash
against initiatives in the area of violence against women created an external environment in which the information collected by BWAC was
increasingly liable to be used against BWAC clients. There was a very
real threat that this information could be used in court cases, either
through direct subpoena of BWAC files, or as evidence that BWAC staff
could be required to provide as witnesses.[24] Under the circumstances, it
seemed the better part of wisdom to suspend the use of the existing intake form until the agency had consolidated strategies for protecting clients and established a research agenda appropriate to its new orientation.

As the advocates themselves describe these various concerns, one
central issue was the length of the form and the priorities it enforced. In
particular, as a tool of psychoeducational practice, it tended to deflect
attention from the immediate concerns of safety planning, and given the
point at which it was used there was some concern that women would
minimize the realities of abuse, foreclosing rather than encouraging an
exploration of them. One advocate described these concerns:

> First, logistically, the Intake package is extremely long ... to go
> through the entire package would in fact take the entire initial ap-
> pointment. As a result, the package cannot be filled in in its en-
> tirety during the initial appointment without sacrificing the time
> necessary to spend with a woman doing safety planning.... [Also,]
> at the time of the initial appointment, it is not unusual for a
> woman to minimize or deny that certain tactics of control have
> been used against her. There is a risk, therefore, that what infor-
> mation we gather [at this point] may not accurately reflect [a]
> woman's realities, although it may accurately reflect their social

24   This backlash against battered women and public action on violence issues very effectively
     subverts the work of counsellor/advocates and of women's agencies. Counsellor/advocates
     describe a range of practices that systematically isolate and marginalize them, trivializing or
     otherwise undermining their work on violence and echoing the treatment of abused women
     in general.

conditioning to minimize the abuse, or blame themselves.

With the move to less emphasis on counselling and more on social change and advocacy, BWAC raised a number of quite fundamental questions about the whole purpose and nature of the "intake" process. Another advocate/counsellor described this process:

> BWAC [had] shifted its focus from a mental health model to a radical educational model; however the data collection package did not reflect this change. It became somewhat contradictory to be discussing issues with a woman from an educational point of view and then asking her data collection questions that reflected a mental health paradigm. Also, with BWAC's shift in service, the intent behind the initial meeting with the woman changed. It became a vital piece of safety planning and referral to resources. Given the length of the data collection package, it would have taken the whole first session to complete the package. It became more and more apparent that the woman's need was to have her questions addressed and her safety needs attended to and not the data collection.

A more specific question, reflecting this shift in mandate, had to do with the efficacy of asking for extensive detail about the woman's family of origin and, indeed, that of the batterer. This presupposed and reinforced precisely the generational "cycle of violence" model that the staff at BWAC, and many others working in the area of woman abuse, had come to question. A third advocate/counsellor put this point in particularly compelling terms:

> A difficulty related to the synonymous nature of intake and research is the whole issue of family of origin abuse.... We no longer provide counselling with that focus. Therefore I am concerned that when we ask the question in terms of intake, there will be the expectation that we are able to assist ... in this area. For many women it might also be something that they are not prepared to deal with at the present time and we are imposing that. And as we have already discussed, gathering this information reinforces the

cycle of violence theory as passed from generation to generation and misses the big picture. I guess the other thing ... is that I especially don't care to gather information about the abuser's history and family of origin—it too, I think, further reinforces the dysfunctional family theory and abdicates responsibility. It is often hard enough to get women to focus on themselves without spending this time on the abusers. The only rationale that makes sense to me, re gathering information about abusers, is the woman's safety.

By extension of this last observation, several advocate/counsellors say that they do continue to make partial use of the intake form when it assists with problem-solving and helps introduce the discussion of abuse. Another BWAC staff member said:

I use the sections of the form for basic information and problem-solving: who is she in the world, what does she have access to or need, i.e., money, a counsellor in her faith, legal representation, a police complaint laid? I have found some women welcome the form to guide discussion because they don't know where to begin or what to say.

One particular woman comes to mind.... Filling out the history of abuse form was a powerful experience. She came to BWAC because she recently realized that she had been emotionally abused. When we filled out the physical abuse section of the form she realized that she had also been repeatedly physically abused. For her this included: being spit on, pinched, pushed, shoved, confined, having her hair pulled, shaken, thrown to the floor. She realized that her internal definition of [physical] abuse has been successive blows that left bruising. We were able then to acknowledge the extent of his abuse, its impact, and the limitations of the cultural and criminal definitions of woman abuse.

The power and politics of this interaction lay in her ability to see how our culture defines woman abuse, how other women had defined it, and how their definition (the form) helped her to understand the breadth and impact of his abuse.

By way of summary, another advocate/counsellor specified the questions she thought crucial to address in an intake interview:

> For the purposes of intake, I believe that the information I require from a woman is related to 1) assessing that she is abused by our definition and therefore meets our mandate, 2) determining her current situation and level of danger, 3) ensuring that she is aware of community resources to assist with her safety, 4) gaining an understanding of her connections and resources in the community, and 5) determining which community institutions she has already come into contact with and possible need for advocacy.

This advocate/counsellor went on to reaffirm the importance of research for BWAC, but to consider the implications of a changed mandate for integrating these interests with those now central to the intake process.

> What I feel strongly about is the need to gather information that could be used as a catalyst for institutional change. The current package includes questions about medical attention and police intervention only. I believe that we could be more systematic in tracking all institutions and at different levels, i.e., from police and lawyers up to judges. We could ask women how they were responded to and whether the response increased accountability of the abuser or put them at greater risk.
>
> A very large issue that women with children face is custody and access, and the ways that the court system does not acknowledge woman abuse as relevant in contrast with the father's rights. We know that there are few resources for women facing the hostile court system while trying to protect their children. Gaining more information in this area could lead to the development of new programs and hopefully changes in the court system.

The executive director of BWAC, Julie Lee, commented further on this issue of research priorities:

> On a day-to-day basis the Battered Women's Advocacy Centre cannot possibly do its work without learning as much as possible

about the situations and needs of the women we serve. On an individual basis we need the information in order to do the best that we can to support and advocate for our clients. On a collective basis, we need information that will instruct us, and those that we lobby and confront, about the patterns, dynamics, and structural barriers faced by assaulted women. In this context, then, we cannot pretend that research is not an integral piece of the front-line work that we do with battered women.

Where the specifics of this mandate are concerned, the BWAC staff identified a number of new areas in which there was a pressing need for more detailed understanding about the experiences and needs of battered women, and for information specifically relevant to the agency's goals of advocacy designed to realize social change. Several different advocate/counsellors made a number of suggestions.

It would also be valuable to add/develop a section on HIV/AIDS as I found that many women report sexual abuse that would be seen as "high risk" and/or that they believe their partners have had affairs and the women are unsure how "safe" they were. Given the power dynamics inherent in abusive relationships, negotiating for safe sex potentially puts the woman at risk, or is simply not a possibility. Also, transmitting HIV has been reported as an intentional act of violence. It is important to acknowledge this reality.

It is imperative, to me, to expand the form to include methods of tracking institution's responses to women who have experienced abuse. Those institutions being: the criminal and civil justice system, churches, welfare, victim witness, legal aid, family mediators, custody, support, and access.

For our purposes, we assess personal safety (i.e. her immediate safety in relation to a violent partner), as well as a woman's safety in relation to various institutions and agencies with which she must interact (i.e., is she being oppressed in the criminal justice system, civil legal matters, income support?).

While collecting information about the legal system, we could also look towards civil legal advisors and the use of lawyers and legal aid. We have struggled and continue to struggle with providing women referrals to lawyers who will be knowledgeable about woman abuse and the barriers intrinsic to the legal system. If we gathered enough information about lawyers' poor responses and what women are needing we could lobby the Bar Association and perhaps seek funding to provide education to them, or at least be on an advisory committee, if this is not getting too big for our wee staff!

As the BWAC staff describe the agency, its combined mandate of service, advocacy, and research are necessarily and continuously organic; it must be responsive to changes both internally and externally, in the needs of battered women and in the environments and institutions they must negotiate when they seek to end the violence in their lives. Consistent with the original commitment to ensure that the structured intake form would be responsive to the needs of women attending BWAC and what BWAC learned of their experiences, the decision to re-evaluate its use reflects changes in the contexts of BWAC practice. Parts of the original form (in its final incarnation) are still being used when they fit with the current goals of the agency and particular counselling situations. There is every expectation that this process of review will result in a renewed and transformed set of research goals that will build on and build well beyond the foundations laid in earlier years.

DISCUSSION AND CONCLUSIONS

i) Lessons Learned: Accountable Practice

Instruments like the structured intake form must be used with care. The key, we believe, is rooting the use of such a form in a context of feminist consciousness and feminist practice. The requirements for turning these tools to *feminist* use that emerge in BWAC's practice are: a) they must embody women's experience; b) they must continuously evolve in response to this experience; and c) they must be used in a supportive, woman-focused, non-coercive way. Above all else, such tools must never become an end in themselves, defining the research and advocacy agendas of those who use them.

To take the third condition first, it is crucial that such an instrument is not allowed to create the kind of false objectifying distance Oakley criticizes. There is always the potential for an interview relationship structured by a rigid research agenda to become coercive and constraining; just as the organization and content of the instrument can open up new possibilities for understanding experience, it can also pre-empt the telling of stories that challenge the wisdom and knowledge embedded in the intake form. It is crucial, then, that as *feminist* service providers, those using such a form should see it as a tool; the advocate/counsellor's judgement about how to use it and, most especially, when to set it aside must take precedence over any ritualistic "application" of such a tool.

Reified, such an instrument quickly becomes a straightjacket: the first two conditions address this issue. Holding the BWAC intake form open to continuous revision ensured that a research interest in maintaining "comparability" did foreclose the possibility of recognizing new forms of abuse and response as women reported them to BWAC counsellor/advocates. In short, a dialectical, action-oriented methodology in the use of these instruments is crucial, if they are to embody and facilitate the growth of collective understanding.

This experience-responsive use of a quantitative instrument illustrates the constructive potential that lies behind the point made by Armstrong and Armstrong (1987); quantitative methods and instruments are only as good as the background knowledge brought to bear in designing them. That is, they will be non-coercive and productive of new understanding only to the extent that their organization and content reflect a sophisticated, *qualitative* understanding of the experiences they are meant to capture. The main lesson to be drawn from the BWAC experience is that qualitative and quantitative insights must be continuously integrated in an ongoing research process. As in the context of consciousness-raising practice,[25] the dialectical movement between a systemic and an individual level of understanding experience is crucial not only to feminist research but also to feminist advocacy and service practice. Speaking experience *together*, collectively, is useful precisely because it allows us to see our experiences in a wider, different context. But collective speaking is only a reliable guide for understanding individual experience and for concrete action if it is held accountable to the differences within and between the experiences of diverse women; these experiences are always located at the intersection of many different systems

---

25   See, for example, Catharine A. MacKinnon, "Feminism, Marxism, Method, and the State: An Agenda for Theory," in N.O. Keohane, M. Rosaldo and B.C. Gelpi, eds., *Feminist Theory: A Critique of Ideology* (Chicago: University of Chicago Press, 1982), pp.1-30. This point is discussed in more detail in Wylie, "Reasoning about Ourselves."

of oppression and privilege, operating simultaneously along lines of race, class, sexual orientation, ethno-cultural and religious affiliation, age, and ability—to name just a few of the differentiations that are immediately relevant to women in a Canadian context.

ii) Balancing the Political and the Personal

Significant limitations counterbalance the power of the quantitative analysis made possible by use of a structured intake form. Its very strength is, in a sense, its greatest liability. The power of the "political" insight realized by articulating the systemic nature and complexity of the violence women face from their partners is achieved precisely by washing out the "personal." The texture and the immediacy of women's experiences are lost in aggregative statistics that summarize the demographic profile and decision-making practices of women attending BWAC. It was out of a concern with these limitations, and a commitment to make the results of our analysis meaningful to as wide an audience as possible, that we undertook to develop several "plain language" brochures.[26] These provide a series of fictionalized accounts of particular women and their experience of battering; they are composites designed to challenge stereotypes, illustrating the diversity of the experience and situations that battered women had described to BWAC counsellor/advocates over the years. Most importantly, these materials help to capture and communicate some of the rich complexity of women's experience of abuse. This was not just important for ensuring that the results of the BWAC research program were accessible to a wide range of audiences, but it was also considered to be part of the dialectic by which experience is brought into critical dialogue with the generalizing constructs built into the entire intake process.

iii) The Complexity of "Subjects" and the Aims of Feminist Research

Although the use of a structured intake questionnaire has been discontinued, it was for many years an important tool for collecting information that served the goals of advocacy at both a personal/individual level and a broader social/political level. As such, it supported the mission of BWAC as a feminist agency committed to making systemic change in

26   Greaves and Wylie, "Challenging the Stereotypes."

the way we understand and respond to woman abuse, as well as to supporting individuals dealing with issues of violence in their own lives. Taken out of a context of practice that is committed to feminist principles of empowerment, such tools have enormous potential to be used in ways that are objectifying and oppressive. We suggest, however, that while some methodologies for research and intervention hold greater potential for abuse than others, none is necessarily or inherently pernicious.[27] Rather than advocating any one methodology as "best" for feminist purposes, we urge a reflective and situated pragmatism. It is crucial that we recognize, in practice as well as in theory, the enormous complexity of women's lives and of our activist aims. And with this, we must be prepared to use as wide a range of methods in our research as we do in service and advocacy, always vigilant that, as tools, they should serve our purposes rather than define them.

At BWAC this reflexive process has been ongoing and illustrates the complexity of balancing multiple agendas, each of them organic and responsive to the changing needs of the women served both individually and collectively. Above all else, what the experience at BWAC teaches is that fundamental questions about what it means to do research and advocacy as a feminist can never be set aside; these questions can never be considered closed. The very process of learning about women's experiences, and of acting as advocates for women, necessarily transforms the questions we must ask and the methods we use to address them.

27   See Stacey, "Can There Be a Feminist Ethnography?"

SUGGESTED READINGS

Kathleen Barry, *Female Sexual Slavery*. New York: Avon Books, 1979.

Changing the Landscape: Ending Violence, Achieving Equality. Final report of the Canadian Panel on Violence against Women. Ottawa: Ministry of Supply and Service Canada, 1993.

Family Violence in Canada. Ottawa: Statistics Canada, Canadian Centre for Justice Statistics, June 1994.

Linda Gordon, *Heroes of Their Own Lives: The Politics and History of Family Violence*. New York: Penguin Books, 1988.

Judith Lewis Herman, *Trauma and Recovery*. New York: Basic Books, 1992.

Kerry Lobel, ed., *Naming the Violence: Speaking Out about Lesbian Battering*. Seattle: Seal Press, 1986.

Linda MacLeod, *Battered but Not Beaten: Preventing Wife Battering in Canada*. Ottawa: Canadian Advisory Council on the Status of Women, 1987.

Linda MacLeod, *Wife Battering in Canada: The Vicious Circle*. Ottawa: The Canadian Advisory Council on the Status of Women, 1980.

Diana Russell, *Rape in Marriage*. New York: Macmillan, 1982.

Violence against Women Survey: Survey Highlights. Ottawa: Statistics Canada, 1993.

Kersti Yllo and Michele Bograd, eds., *Feminist Perspectives on Wife Abuse*. Newbury Park, Cal.: Sage, 1988.

BRENDA O'NEILL

Chapter Twelve: The Gender Gap: Re-evaluating Theory and Method

FEMINIST RESEARCHERS USE A MULTIPLICITY OF METHODS. Shulamit Reinharz, in her recent book *Feminist Methods in Social Research*, reviews some of these many methods and concludes, "Social research has many feminist voices. Clearly, there is no single 'feminist way' to do research."[1] In this chapter I argue for including quantitative methods in this diverse set because they present a unique opportunity for conducting research on women in general and their political behaviour in particular. One quantitative method of data gathering, survey research, makes possible the study of samples of individuals in numbers not feasible with other research methods. These large samples allow for the statistical analysis of relationships within the data set and for generalizations about the population they are drawn from. Such generalizations are virtually impossible to make on the basis of small numbers. This information is necessary for arriving at any conclusions about the political behaviour of women as a group and about the forces that shape their political attitudes and beliefs.

It is also true that the surveys employed to conduct much of this research have numerous limitations. Pat Armstrong and Hugh Armstrong list some of the limitations of aggregative statistics such as those collected by Statistics Canada.[2] In this chapter, I evaluate the 1988 Canadian

<hr />

1   Shulamit Reinharz, *Feminist Methods in Social Research* (New York: Oxford University Press, 1992), p.243.

2   Pat Armstrong and Hugh Armstrong, "Beyond Numbers: Problems with Quantitative Data," in Greta Hofmann Nemiroff, ed., *Women and Men: Interdisciplinary Readings on Gender* (Montreal: Fitzhenry and Whiteside, 1987).

National Election Study, a large-scale survey of the sort often used to study political phenomena, and outline some of the limitations encountered in adapting it to the study of women's political behaviour.[3] Pointing out these limitations may result in better surveys in the future. It also demonstrates the complexity of adapting available data sets for the study of women and issues of concern to them.

Despite these shortcomings, large-scale surveys do provide important research possibilities. Research on the gender gap presents one such possibility. Much of the work on this subject illustrates thoughtful feminist research devoted to studying the political attitudes of women and including their experiences in theories on attitude formation.[4] For example, Pamela Johnston Conover examines the relative importance of feminist beliefs in shaping women's opinions and Pippa Norris looks at the degree to which the gender gap in attitudes is a cross-cultural phenomenon.[5] Both of these researchers employ quantitative methods and survey data in their work and in so doing provide illustrations of their value.

SURVEY INSTRUMENTS

To assess the limitations of surveys and survey methodology it is first necessary to briefly outline the method itself and the techniques and standards involved.[6] The description that follows is simplified and may mask the complexity of this technique. Survey methodology has become increasingly precise and complex as added attention to and greater use of the method increases the research undertaken on it. As a result, "It is no longer true that 'anyone can do a survey'.... To do a good survey re-

---

3   The 1988 CNES was not chosen as an example because of any methodological problems with the survey; instead it is presented as an example of the type of quantitative survey currently available for studying women and thus represents the standard survey instrument likely to be encountered.

4   I define gender gap research as feminist since it seeks to expand empirical knowledge, critique existing theory, and reconceptualize core concepts to include the experiences of women. This definition is borrowed from Kay Boals, "Political Science," *Signs: Journal of Women in Culture and Society* 1,1 (1975), p.161.

5   Pamela Johnston Conover, "Feminists and the Gender Gap," *Journal of Politics* 50,4 (1988), pp.985-1010; Pippa Norris, "The Gender Gap: A Cross-National Trend?" in Carol Mueller, ed., *The Politics of the Gender Gap* (Beverly Hills, Cal.: Sage Publications, 1988).

6   More detailed information on the survey process is available in a number of texts, including Floyd J. Fowler Jr., *Survey Research Methods*, 2nd ed. (Newbury Park, Cal.: Sage Publications, 1993) and Charles H. Backstrom and Gerald Hursh-César, *Survey Research*, 2nd ed. (New York: Wiley, 1981).

quires expertise and professionalism at every stage: design, sampling, questionnaire development, interviewing, analysis and reporting, based on an extensive theoretical framework well grounded in practice and methodological research."[7] Unfortunately, this call for precision and complexity has not guaranteed that all surveys are "good" surveys.

Quantitative survey data are collected in a highly structured format from a large sample selected in such a manner as to allow for inferences to be made about the population from which the sample was drawn. Sampling, a process with its own set of technical considerations and statistical requirements, is necessary because surveying a large population, for example all Canadians, would be too costly and time-consuming.

An important consideration in any survey is cost: interviewing a large sample of respondents about a selection of their attitudes and opinions is an expensive undertaking. Time is also an important consideration: the sample should be surveyed in as short a time frame as possible to limit the possibility of intervening events affecting some responses; and there are limits to the number of questions that can be included on survey instruments. Researchers must balance these two considerations with the desire for comprehensiveness. Comprehensiveness relates to both the information gathered in the survey and the sample selected for inclusion in the study. A survey that fails to gather information relevant for examining the research hypothesis, or uses a sample that is not representative of the population, is not one upon which strong conclusions can be based.

The average survey asks the preselected sample a large number of closed questions. Closed questions limit the number of possible responses to a preselected few in order to allow for aggregation of the responses. Surveys can also include open-ended questions, which are less structured and do not force the respondent to answer the question within the preset response categories. These questions are generally less common than closed ones; they are difficult to code into the small number of categories required for aggregation.

Surveys can gather various types of information, but usually include questions on socio-demographic data, such as education and age, questions regarding attitudes and opinions on a broad range of topics, and questions on some elements of behaviour. Behavioural questions in election studies address such topics as voting behaviour and other kinds

7 Jean Morton-Williams, *Interviewer Approaches* (Brookfield, Vt.: Dartmouth Publishing, 1993), p.2.

of political activity. The responses given to such questions are numbered into a small set of categories, which allows them to be treated arithmetically and thus allows for statistical examination of the gathered data. Generalizing from a sample to the population means the loss of some information.

The questions included in a survey instrument are determined by the underlying research questions driving the analysis. Surveys and election studies have at their core a particular research hypothesis, selected by the research team. The hypothesis provides direction on the information to be gathered.

Surveys employ two main methods of data collection. The first is the interview, often conducted by telephone. Standard interviewing manuals recommend that the interviewer remain somewhat distant from the interviewee to minimize the likelihood of directing the respondent's answers. This recommendation is based on research noting that a warm and friendly interview style is likely to increase response bias when compared with a task-oriented and businesslike interview style. An interviewer is to behave as a "professional and impartial collector of important information for a serious and interesting purpose."[8] Ideally the interviewer's presence should in no way influence a respondent's perception of the questions or answers in the survey—the interviewer should be a "neutral medium through which questions and answers are transmitted"[9] — since any bias introduced into the data as a result of the interviewer could be interpreted as a characteristic of the data. Feminist researchers have offered a strong resistance to this interview style.

The second method of data collection is the mailed questionnaire, which respondents complete at their convenience without the help of an interviewer and then return by mail. In contrast to personal interviews, these questionnaires minimize the likelihood of respondents giving what they perceive to be "socially acceptable answers," because the forms are completed in private, and thus may be good vehicles for eliciting information on highly personal issues such as abortion.

The 1988 Canadian National Election Study (CNES) is an example of a large-scale survey, and it can be examined to gauge the degree to which it allows for an effective investigation of women's political behaviour and the gender gap in particular.[10] The survey instrument was designed

8   Morton-Williams, *Interviewer Approaches*, p.124. For examples of this research see Eleanor Singer and Stanley Presser, eds., *Survey Research Methods: A Reader* (Chicago: The University of Chicago Press, 1989).

9   Earl Babbie, *The Practice of Social Research*, 5th ed. (Belmont, Cal.: Wadsworth Publishing, 1989), p.245.

by four male political scientists who wanted to examine the campaign dynamics and the effects of issue and leader traits on voting behaviour during the election. The survey itself was administered in three parts: a campaign period telephone survey; a post election telephone survey; and a self-administered mailback survey. Interviews were conducted with a sample of 3,609 Canadians over the course of the election campaign, and thus the study represents one of a limited number of large-scale surveys available in Canada today.

Telephone interviews were conducted with the help of the CATI (computer-assisted telephone interview) system: the interviewer sits in front of a computer screen and is prompted by the computer to ask certain questions of the respondent in a specific order. The interviewer has only to key in the responses. The system is efficient: many questions can be answered in a relatively short interview period, and human error in the recording of the responses is minimized. Moreover, this interview method makes it easy to experiment with the survey questionnaire, more so than with the traditional pencil and paper interview method.

Given its research focus, the 1988 CNES included questions dealing with voting behaviour, socio-demographic information, and opinions on a number of issues that the principal investigators believed to be particularly relevant in the 1988 campaign. The mailback portion of the survey included the greatest share of questions dealing with opinions on a large number of public policies and issues: fiscal priorities, the economy and economic conditions, capitalism and socialism, reform, various groups in Canadian society, and rights and liberties. The research team made an effort to include questions allowing for time-series comparison with previous CNES surveys (a very limited number exist) and to solicit suggestions from colleagues on possible additions to the survey instrument.[11]

FEMINIST CRITIQUES OF SURVEY METHODS

The most common critiques of these methods address claims to objectivity, the interview techniques employed in quantitative surveys, the failure to research questions of direct concern to women, the methodo-

10   The 1988 CNES was directed by Richard Johnston, André Blais, Henry Brady, and Jean Crête, and funded by the Social Sciences and Humanities Research Council of Canada. The data were collected by the Institute for Social Research at York University. Technical information on the study was taken from David Northrup and Anne Oram, *The 1988 National Election Study: Technical Documentation* (North York, Ont.: York University, Institute for Social Research, 1988).

11   They received two responses to their canvassing, both from male colleagues.

logical problems with surveys, and the unquestioned authority granted to quantitative data.[12]

At the most abstract level, feminist critiques of quantitative methods reject the claim of objectivity and value neutrality driving the mainstream pursuit of knowledge, a pursuit critically evaluated in Lorraine Code's chapter in this book. The use of quantitative methods, including survey methods, for studying social phenomena is said to deviate from these claimed attributes in a number of respects: the research question itself is likely to be driven by what researchers and funding institutions, dominated by male academics, interpret as being important and relevant research questions; the questions researchers select to include in the instrument necessarily limit and often distort the picture that is interpreted in the data; and the limiting of responses to those preset in the survey instrument is likely to silence pertinent voices if they are not seen as such by the researchers. The values of researchers enter into every decision made in the research undertaking and influence the information they generate. The authority granted to statistics and surveys makes it particularly important to question their objectivity, given their potential for bias. Researchers who support the use of quantitative methods of data collection in studies of women also challenge the notion that quantitative methods are objective and value free. The "many reinterpretations, reconstructions, and reanalyses of existing data from the new perspective" serve to highlight both the limited focus of previous research and its value-laden conclusions.[13] In Canada examples of this work include Janine Brodie's research on women's rates of participation in political institutions and Sylvia Bashevkin's reviews of women within political parties. Work by Americans Virginia Sapiro and Sandra Baxter and Marjorie Lansing perform a similar function.[14] Any criticisms of the

12   For excellent reviews of feminist critiques of quantitative methods and some responses to them, see: Toby Epstein Jayaratne, "The Value of Quantitative Methodology for Feminist Research," in Gloria Bowles and Renate Duelli Klein, eds., *Theories of Women's Studies* (Boston: Routledge & Kegan Paul, 1983); Vicky Randall, "Feminism and Political Analysis," in M. Githens, P. Norris, and J. Lovenduski, eds., *Different Roles, Different Voices* (New York: Harper Collins, 1994); and Reinharz, *Feminist Methods*, ch. 4.

13   Joyce McCarl Nielson, "Introduction," in Joyce McCarl Nielson, ed., *Feminist Research Methods* (San Francisco: Westview Press, 1990), p.20.

14   For Canada, see Sylvia Bashevkin, *Toeing the Lines: Women and Party Politics in English Canada*, 2nd ed. (Toronto: Oxford University Press, 1993); and Janine Brodie, with the assistance of Celia Chandler, "Women and the Electoral Process in Canada," in *Women in Canadian Politics*, Kathy Megyery, ed., Lortie Royal Commission of Electoral Reform and Party Financing, vol.6 (Toronto: Dundurn Press, 1992). For the United States, see Sandra Baxter and Marjorie Lansing, *Women and Politics: The Visible Majority* (Ann Arbor: The University of Michigan Press, 1983); and Virginia Sapiro, *The Political Integration of Women* (Urbana: University of Illinois Press, 1983).

method rendered by these researchers are directed at its application in mainstream research rather than the method itself. Thus while some feminists see the problems with the objectivity claimed in quantitative research as reason for abandoning the method altogether, other academics, myself included, believe that complete objectivity is merely an ideal. The method can be salvaged and adapted through working to ensure that quantitative analysis is as close to the ideal as possible.

Previous claims to objectivity have been critically re-evaluated so that feminist research now gathers and includes information relevant to analyses of women. This "new objectivity" embraces more modest claims than those often caricatured by feminist critiques of the method. As Vicky Randall puts it, "A social science that really did believe that how a research topic emerges is irrelevant, that fact and value can ever be entirely disentangled and which insisted religiously that every piece of social analysis involved identifying a question, generating a hypothesis to answer that question, devising a method of testing the hypothesis and so on, emulating laboratory-style techniques of the natural sciences, would certainly be out of touch with reality."[15]

Thus scientific claims to objectivity no longer imply treating the subjects of research as objects or accepting research and researchers as value free; rather, feminist researchers accepting of the value of quantitative methods have modified such claims to include a "commitment to look at contrary evidence; a determination to aim at maximum replicability of any study; a commitment to 'truth-finding'; and a clarification and classification of values underlying the research."[16]

A main target of feminist criticisms is the interview method employed in large-sample surveying. These feminists see the task-oriented method of collecting data as a one-sided exchange of information in which respondents are treated as commodities to be discarded once the information has been gathered. They argue that the survey instrument directing the interview silences important voices.

Many of these critics dismiss the use of quantitative methods altogether. Ann Oakley's critique of traditional interviewing methods exemplifies the body of feminist work advocating more qualitative methods of interviewing and data collection.[17] Her work on motherhood involved interviewing women, and it soon became apparent that the task-

15   Randall, "Feminism and Political Analysis," p.13.

16   Margrit Eichler, *Nonsexist Research Methods: A Practical Guide* (Boston: Allen and Unwin, 1988), pp.13-14.

17   Ann Oakley, "Interviewing Women: A Contradiction in Terms," in Helen Roberts, ed., *Doing Feminist Research* (London: Routledge and Kegan Paul, 1981).

oriented and businesslike style of interviewing recommended by traditional methods did not allow her to elicit the intimate personal knowledge required for her research. Instead of maintaining the more distant
interview stance, she chose to become involved with the subjects. She
answered their questions and allowed the interview process to flow both
to and from the subject. She chose, in other words, to develop friendships with her research subjects. For Oakley, the only responsible and
realistic method of gathering data was to become personally involved
with the research participants in order to fully understand their situations.

Like Oakley, many feminist researchers advocate the use of more
qualitative methods of data collection.[18] Qualitative research seeks information that need not conform to the requirements of quantification. Its
techniques are not driven by the ability to quantify the results obtained
in order to make specific generalizations, but rather allow for the collection of data that reveal the meanings that respondents associate with
events, and that allow respondents to present their perspectives in their
own words without any imposed limits. Qualitative research is thus
more concerned with individual subtleties that cannot be captured by
quantitative methods and is, as a result, more closely involved with its
subjects. Such methods seek the "view from below," rather than the
"view from above" generated by what are argued to be more hierarchical
and coercive interviewing techniques.[19]

But qualitative interview methods also have limitations, most notably
when information must be gathered from a large sample. Large samples
are necessary if researchers wish to identify patterns and processes that
may not be apparent at the individual level. The more involved method
of interviewing of the qualitative approach can place substantial limits
on the number of individuals who can be studied.

Employing qualitative research methods also reduces the likelihood
of agreement on the interpretation of the results obtained, more so than
with research employing quantitative methods. The step of generalizing
from the sample to the population requires the researcher to make value
judgements regarding the relative importance that respondents attached
to each of their statements, as well as on the degree of similarity across
the responses, for purposes of aggregation. Such judgements are not as

18   There are a number of qualitative research methods including ethnography and oral history.
      See Reinharz, *Feminist Methods,* for a detailed look at the many qualitative methods em-
      ployed by feminist academics.

19   This phrase is borrowed from M. Mies, "Towards a Methodology for Feminist Research," in
      Bowles and Duelli Klein, *Theories of Women's Studies,* p.123.

likely under closed questions, where the coding of responses occurs within explicit, systematic, and comprehensive rules. Thus while qualitative techniques are most likely to provide the researcher with a clearer and deeper understanding of the meaning attached to each response and of the interpretation given to specific questions, the method is limited in the degree to which its results can be said to exist in the population at large, at least with the degree of statistical accuracy afforded to large samples.

Survey methods allow the researcher to generalize from a sample to the population, but this ability comes at the cost of limited information. Methodological and technical considerations constrain survey interviewing, and the statistical analysis of a large number of responses demands data that are standardized and can be generalized. Such requirements necessitate the use of an interview process that is strictly controlled to ensure comparability. Because of these requirements, the information generated by this method will be less comprehensive than that generated by more qualitative approaches.

Nevertheless, the requirements of quantitative interview methods do not restrict or hinder the gathering of *some* types of information. Surveying respondents for their opinions on general public issues and topics, such as the deficit and welfare spending, is unlikely to present the same difficulties as gathering opinions and data on such highly personal issues as motherhood, rape, incest, or woman abuse. These personal subjects require an interview process that is less structured and more sensitive to the respondent than the telephone interview directed by a structured questionnaire. An element of trust must exist in the relationship between researcher and researched to elicit the desired information.

The nature of the more general issues suggests that a qualitative interview method is unlikely to generate information at variance with that generated by more quantitative approaches. Many public policy attitudes and ideological questions address topics that respondents might not have thought much about prior to the actual interview, and the interview process is likely to be the first time they attempt to crystallize their thoughts in any form. An element of trust is not essential for conducting interviews on such issues. Moreover, Alison Wylie and Lorraine Greaves, in this book, suggest that with care quantitative interview methods can be employed successfully, by feminist standards, to study even such highly personal and emotional topics as woman abuse. But, as they suggest, success in this area depends on ensuring that the survey instrument evolves as information on the topic is gathered, and that the instrument does not become coercive.

Feminist critics also point out that mainstream quantitative research is not often driven by questions and hypotheses that are of concern to women. This is becoming less true, however, as attested by a glance at recent issues of mainstream social science journals and at the many newer journals directed specifically at issues of concern to women. Much of this change has been initiated by women academics, and it is hoped that the changes will continue.

The complaint has greater validity when it is directed specifically at the research questions that have driven large-scale Canadian surveys. Quantitative research on women has generally had to rely on government-sponsored statistics or the analysis of secondary surveys such as the CNES. The analysis of secondary data sources is a problem that plagues all researchers. Employing surveys designed to study political phenomena other than those which are the focus of one's research limits analysis to the questions asked and the information gathered by those surveys, limits that are often significant because surveys reflect and are shaped by their central research question.

Relying on secondary data sources is unavoidable, for the most part due to the prohibitive costs of conducting independent large-scale surveys. Recent cuts to funding in general, and the fact that researchers proposing projects of concern to women must approach funding institutions that have their own set of priorities, suggest that it may be some time before a large-scale survey project devoted exclusively to the study of an issue or phenomenon of concern to women is undertaken.

But the limits accompanying the analysis of secondary data should not be overstated. There exists a large amount of quality work in Canadian political science that is based on secondary data sources. And Canadian surveys have increasingly included information relevant to the study of women despite the fact that the central research questions are not specifically targeted to women. For example, past CNES studies have neglected to include some rather basic questions relating to women, but recent studies have made efforts to improve the instrument. The 1965 and 1974 CNES surveys failed both to ask respondents if they had children at home and to ask women about their employment outside of the home. The 1984 CNES was somewhat improved, since it included questions on the number and ages of children in the household.[20]

It is heartening to know that the principal investigators of the 1988 CNES were aware of their limited perspective when designing the survey instrument. In a conversation, one of the principal investigators of the survey mentioned that the group was very much aware that they were "four Catholic men" sitting around the room trying to decide the important policy components of the 1988 election campaign. Their values and the questions of importance to their study directed the survey instrument. Ideally, secondary surveys would include information allowing for comprehensive examinations of women's political behaviour. The reality is that feminist research is limited by the information available in secondary data sources. This is unlikely to change until surveys are undertaken specifically to study the relevant forces in women's lives and the questions of importance to them.

Some of the concerns raised by feminists have also been stressed by other critics of quantitative methods. Question wording, question order, the data collection method chosen, and interview style are all factors that directly determine response validity. But the increased use of the survey method in past years by academics, political parties, and other organizations and the attention that surveys have received outside academia have meant that the method itself has been the subject of much research and examination, and as a result the method has been greatly refined. *Public Opinion Quarterly* is a journal devoted exclusively to publishing articles analysing survey methods, and it reports on research designed to improve them. Examples of "bad" surveys conducted without regard for the standards of the method should not be used as illustrations of the method's inherent shortcomings. But neither should the results of surveys be uncritically accepted as legitimate. The decision to either accept or reject the interpretation of the results advanced should be made after careful examination of the survey questionnaire and the assumptions upon which it and the results rest, a responsibility not often taken seriously.

Many feminists are also sceptical of the potential to turn "hard" scientific data (read male data) into "female" data. Results and conclusions based on biased or incomplete information, or collected in a for-

---

20   The earlier omissions are reported in Jerome H. Black and Nancy E. McGlen, "Male-Female Political Involvement Differentials in Canada," *Canadian Journal of Political Science* 12,3 (1979), pp.471-97. The improvement is noted in B.J. Kay, R.D. Lambert, S.D. Brown, and J.E. Curtis, "Gender and Political Activity in Canada," *Canadian Journal of Political Science* 20,4 (1987), pp.851-63.

mat that renders their reliability and validity questionable, are often taken as fact because of the authority granted to the method.

I argue that by analysing the values that enter into research and the research method itself, "hard" quantitative data can be made into unbiased data. Advocating the abandonment of survey analysis in feminist research would be to disregard a unique and relevant technique for hearing women's voices. Armstrong and Armstrong similarly advocate "theoretically informed and sceptical caution in the use of data"[21] because the assumptions underlying the data determine the degree to which the data provide a realistic picture. Their work, and this chapter, in highlighting some of the problems with quantitative data, implicitly accept the value of quantitative data but suggest that there is room for improvement.

THE BENEFITS OF QUANTITATIVE METHODS

Survey methodology allows for the gathering of a significant amount of reliable information from a large sample of respondents based on consistently conducted interviews. Inferences about the population from which the sample was drawn and generalizations can be made from the aggregated data. In order for research to build upon itself and for the search for knowledge to be cumulative, the method employed in that research must be structured to facilitate such goals as intersubjective transmissibility (different observers of the same data reaching similar conclusions), testability, and replicability.[22] Quantitative methods allow for these goals to be approached.

Gender gap research is an example of how quantitative methods can expand our understanding of women's political behaviour, although it can be limited in its investigative power due to the employment of secondary data sources. But the benefits of this research—not limited to the re-evaluations of previously held theories and conclusions—should not be overlooked because of these limitations. Previously held "hard" facts about the political behaviour of women are being re-evaluated, and the faulty reasoning and assumptions that led to them are being pinpointed. Jane Jaquette points out that defining politics in terms of male experience, notably war and defence, necessitates concluding that women are less interested and more apolitical because they are less supportive of

---

21   Armstrong and Armstrong, "Beyond Numbers," p.59.

22   Jill Vickers, "Memoirs of an Ontological Exile: The Methodological Rebellions of Feminist Research," in Angela Miles and Geraldine Finn, eds., *Feminism in Canada: From Pressure to Politics* (Montreal: Black Rose, 1982).

these experiences.[23] Such re-evaluations are the first steps towards gender-free theories of political science.

Surveys allow feminist researchers to measure women's attitudes, often with a view to overturning misplaced beliefs about those views, and to force changes in the political agenda because of this information. They can also provide insight into generational changes taking place in attitudes, brought about in part by the feminist movement, women's increasing education levels, and changes in their employment positions outside of the home.

Nonetheless, as feminist researchers, we must be careful that these goals do not blind us to the potential for misuse of any of the methods we employ, quantitative and qualitative alike. The survey method can be employed in an objectifying manner, but it is not inherently objectifying. Like all methods, the precision and sophistication required for the proper application of survey methodology must be respected and its use restricted to research topics appropriate to survey research.

THE GENDER GAP: APPLYING THE 1988 CNES

The concept of the gender gap in political attitudes offers an important example of the application of quantitative methods to feminist research. The increasing evidence suggesting that gender, in combination with other social forces, is an important factor in political behaviour in many countries has served to increase the attention directed towards the notion of the gender gap in the media and in academic circles.[24] Much of this evidence is based on survey data similar to that found in the 1988 CNES, and thus its evaluation serves as an important exercise.

The gender gap as a social phenomenon is deserving of attention for two main reasons. First, the gender gap phenomenon is linked to the larger question of whether women and men differ politically as a result

23   Jaquette looks at some of these re-evaluations in her examination of the impact of modern feminism on political science in "Political Science-Whose Common Good?" in Cheris Kramarae and Dale Spender, eds., *The Knowledge Explosion* (New York: Teachers College Press, 1992).

24   For European evidence on the gender gap, see Norris, "The Gender Gap"; for the United States see Baxter and Lansing, *Women and Politics*, Keith T. Poole and L. Harmon Zeigler, *Women, Public Opinion and Politics* (New York: Longman, 1985), and Robert Shapiro and Harpreet Mahajan, "Gender Differences in Policy Preferences: A Summary of Trends from the 1960s to the 1980s," *Public Opinion Quarterly* 50 (1986), pp.42-61; and for Canadian evidence see Kathryn Kopinak, "Gender Differences in Political Ideology in Canada," *Canadian Review of Sociology and Anthropology* 24,1 (1987), pp.23-38, and John Terry, "The Gender Gap: Women's Political Power," *Current Issues Review* (Ottawa: Library of Parliament, 1984).

of differences in their nature, in the values they hold, or in the socially constructed definitions of their "proper" roles. This question is one that is not limited to the discipline of political science. But as it relates to political issues, research on the gender gap presents an interesting opportunity for studying those factors that directly influence opinions about political issues and beliefs. Thus it helps build an understanding of not only whether women and men differ politically, but also whether women act as a cohesive political group. Second, the phenomenon highlights the degree to which mainstream politics and political science have rested on male definitions of politics. Analysis of the gender gap has provided a focus on the degree to which issues of importance to women have generally been ignored by the media and political institutions. Whether the gender gap exists or not, focusing on it in the development of a questionnaire may provide the impetus for moving these issues onto the political agenda.

The notion of a gender gap first appeared in the literature examining U.S. elections in the early 1980s. A study of Reagan's bid for the presidency revealed that women were more supportive of Democratic candidates than were men. In 1980 women were 4 per cent less likely to support Reagan as a presidential candidate than were men, and by 1984 that figure had grown to 9 per cent.[25] The discovery of and discussion surrounding this voting margin were significant, for they signalled a recognition of the potential women held as a powerful voting bloc.

This significance was underscored by the discovery of voting gender gaps in other countries. In Canadian elections between 1974 and 1988 women's support for the Liberal Party ranged from 3.4 percentage points to 9.1 percentage points higher than the support of men for that party, and in 1984 British women abandoned the Conservative Party despite having supported it in greater numbers than men since the 1960s.[26] This evidence suggested that the gender gap was not simply a North American phenomenon, but rather a general tendency in voting behaviour across developed countries.

The discovery of the voting gender gap was followed by research noting that voting differences were matched by gender gaps in political attitudes. Since 1980 election studies and survey research have documented

---

25   Henry C. Kenski, "The Gender Factor in a Changing Electorate," in Mueller, *The Politics of the Gender Gap*, p.44.

26   Peter Wearing and Joseph Wearing, "Does Gender Make a Difference in Voting Behaviour?" in Joseph Wearing, ed., *The Ballot and Its Message: Voting in Canada* (Toronto: Copp Clark Pitman, 1991), p.344; Pippa Norris, "Conservative Attitudes in Recent British Elections: An Emerging Gender Gap?" *Political Studies* 34 (1986), p.120.

such gaps in a number of countries, including the United States, Canada, and Britain. Conventional wisdom on the gender gap in political attitudes holds that women are more likely than men to oppose the use of nuclear energy and military force, give more support to compassion issues, and reveal more conservative tendencies on "traditional" issues.

Women's opinions reveal a consistent and strong trend away from men's opinions on the issues of defence and force. Robert Shapiro and Harpreet Mahajan report that in U.S. surveys conducted between 1952 and 1983 the average gender percentage-point difference on questions dealing with the issue of force was 8.1, with men selecting the more violent options. In Canada, evidence presented by John Terry suggests even larger differences: in Gallup survey data gathered in 1983 and 1984, gender differences ranged from 12 to 18 percentage points on questions dealing with the issues of cruise missile testing and the chances of nuclear war.[27] The gender differences on questions dealing with these issues have been consistent across surveys, and they are statistically reliable: their size usually exceeds the margin of error for the samples on which they are based.

Men also consistently reveal opinions on compassion issues that are less liberal than women's: women tend to endorse a strong role for government on issues concerned with welfare policies, aid to the poor, the unemployed, and others in need. But these differences are not as large as those reported for the issues of force and defence. In their research, Shapiro and Mahajan report that U.S. survey data showed the average gender percentage-point difference on 'compassion' issues to be 3.3, while it was 5.8 for questions dealing with support for regulation and protection. Comparable Canadian data, as reported by Terry, show that women are more likely to support expanding social welfare programs by a 6 percentage-point difference.[28] Using survey data other than those employed by Terry, Kathryn Kopinak found that Canadian women "ideologically favour a redistribution of power in the workplace as well as a redistribution of valued goods and services by government."[29] Unfortunately the attitude scales employed in her research are not directly comparable to the other results reported above. But consistent differences recorded in various surveys in both the United States and Canada support a conclusion that the gap on compassion issues exists, even if smaller in size than differences on defence issues.

27   Terry, "The Gender Gap," p.12. The U.S. surveys examined included the General Social Survey, Gallup and Harris data, and the American National Election Studies; Shapiro and Mahajan, "Trends in Gender Differences," p.49.

28   Shapiro and Mahajan, "Trends in Gender Differences," p.50; Terry, "The Gender Gap," p.11.

29   Kopinak, "Gender Differences," p.29; her analysis examines the 1979 Quality of Life Survey.

TABLE 1: GENDER DIFFERENCES IN SUPPORT OF SELECTED ISSUES

| | MEN | WOMEN | DIFFERENCE |
	%	%	%
Support free trade (L2)	48.1	29.1	19.0
Purchase nuclear submarines (L9)	42.6	29.1	13.5
Reduce welfare payments (BQ6)	37.2	33.1	4.1
Support farmers/fishermen (QA5)	52.2	64.1	-11.9
Support profit system (QC2)	68.7	61.9	6.8
Individual over community (QE4)	18.7	14.6	4.1
Religion important (QF4)	55.8	67.5	-11.7
Prevent buying pornography (QA10)	20.1	37.4	-17.3
Women have careers (QE1)	40.2	39.8	0.4
Abortion personal choice (L6)	48.9	47.2	1.7

Note: A positive difference indicates men support the issue more than women; a negative difference indicates women are the stronger supporters. The sample included 1,075 men and 1,024 women, but these numbers vary across variables as a result of missing data. The corresponding CNES variable name appears in brackets and the exact wording of issue questions can be found in Appendix 1.

There is also evidence that women hold more conservative opinions than men: they score higher on religious fundamentalism scales, are more likely to endorse school prayer and support traditional definitions of the family, and support the censorship of TV programming and a rise in the legal drinking age. Support for the existence of gaps on these "traditional" issues is less conclusive, however, as results are usually smaller than those recorded in the defence and compassion issues, and contradictory evidence does exist.[30]

The gender gap evidence is compelling, at least for attitudes on compassion and defence issues, for two main reasons: first, the difference in attitudes on these questions has appeared over time; and second, the difference is consistent despite survey effects, particularly question wording. Alternative measures of attitudes employed to survey different

30 For example, Cook and Wilcox found no significant difference in support for school prayer; see Elizabeth Addell Cook and Clyde Wilcox, "Feminism and the Gender Gap: A Second Look," *Journal of Politics* 53,4 (1991), pp.1111-22. See also Pamela Johnston Conover, "Feminists and the Gender Gap," p.995; Shapiro and Mahajan, "Trends in Gender Differences," p.52; and Terry, "The Gender Gap," p.13.

samples are providing consistent and hence reliable conclusions.

The 1988 CNES includes a large number of attitudinal questions that allow for an examination of the degree to which the above patterns existed in Canada at the time of the 1988 election. I selected several of these questions, one from each of the areas of the gender gap discussed, as well as a few issues of specific concern to women, to examine the potential of as well as the problems associated with survey data like those available in the CNES. The gender gaps that appear in these variables are reported in Table 1.[31] Appendix 1 gives the exact wording of these questions as they appeared in the 1988 CNES questionnaire.

The evidence presented in Table 1 suggests that in 1988 there were substantial gender differences in several political attitudes. The largest difference in attitudes, 19 percentage points, appears in support for the Free Trade Agreement, a particularly salient issue during the 1988 election campaign. Similarly large differences appear in those areas that previous research has highlighted as gender gap issues: on support for the purchase of nuclear submarines, support for government intervention in declining industries such as agriculture, the importance of religion in one's life, and support for restrictions on the sale of pornographic books and movies. This evidence adds to previous research and supports the existence of the gender gap in Canada and as a larger attitudinal phenomenon.

On some issues there is little difference in attitude by gender. Interestingly, women and men show little difference in their attitudes on abortion and on women having careers, despite the common assumption that these issues separate them. On one element of the compassion issue, women and men think alike in terms of using cuts to welfare payments as a means of eliminating the deficit. Only a 4 percentage-point difference separates women and men on this issue. The emphasis on difference, then, should not be made at the expense of sameness: women and men think alike on a number of issues, and this point should not be overlooked.

The research potential of quantitative analysis is not limited to the simple recording of differences in attitudes. By assessing the strength of relationships between variables, the method also allows for the discovery of patterns and for predictive statements regarding the relative influence of various factors in the shaping of attitudes. Socio-demographic infor-

31 Although a limited number of variables are examined here, the 1988 CNES includes several questions that each tap one dimension of a particular attitude or belief. For instance, I report the difference in attitudes on the purchase of nuclear submarines as an example of the gender gap on the issue of defence. I could have examined other attitudes on defence spending more generally or on Canada's membership in NATO. This is one of the strengths of a survey instrument this lengthy: it allows researchers to examine a policy issue with a number of questions, a practice that lends greater support to their conclusions.

TABLE 2: EFFECTS OF SOCIO-DEMOGRAPHIC VARIABLES ON SUPPORT
FOR THE FREE TRADE AGREEMENT

	MEN %	WOMEN %	DIFFERENCE %
FAMILY INCOME			
$29,000 or less	44.3	23.9	20.4
$30,000 to $59,000	45.0	32.5	12.5
$60,000 or more	60.3	45.3	15.0
EMPLOYMENT STATUS			
Working	49.7	29.3	20.4
Unemployed/Laid Off	41.4	19.6	21.8
Retired	47.3	26.5	20.8
Student	39.2	38.2	1.0
Disabled	**	**	**
Homemaker	**	31.2	**
MARITAL STATUS			
Married/Partnered	49.5	32.2	17.3
Divorced/Separated	53.0	24.5	28.5
Widowed	50.0	20.2	29.8
Never Married	41.4	25.0	16.4
CHILDREN AT HOME			
No Children	48.2	48.0	0.2
One child or more	30.7	27.1	3.6
EDUCATION			
Less than Postsecondary	46.1	26.3	19.8
Postsecondary	50.5	32.4	18.1
AGE			
34 and under	44.1	28.2	15.9
35-54	52.3	29.8	22.5
55 and over	47.1	29.6	17.5

Note: Entries are the share of respondents in that category supporting the
Free Trade Agreement. The ** indicates the number of respondents in
the category is too small to be meaningful. Some of the original categories have been collapsed.

mation is often used for this purpose. Socio-demographic characteristics have been shown to correlate strongly with political attitudes,[32] and thus this information is an important component of surveys.

Table 2 provides a brief and by no means exhaustive example of analysis on the gender gap using the information included in the 1988 CNES. This example is limited to opinion on the Free Trade Agreement, mainly due to constraints of space and time. Comparison of similar analyses on the many opinions tapped by the survey would allow for generalizations that are not possible with a single example.

As Table 2 shows, the gender gap on the free trade issue is consistent in that women in all categories are less supportive of the agreement than men. But the gap varies in size across the categories of some variables. For instance, the percentage-point difference in support for free trade stands at 22.5 among the thirty-five to fifty-four age group. It drops among the other two age groups, which reveals age as a modifier of the gender gap. The difference exists because support for the agreement varies with age in the men's sample; women's attitudes do not reveal a similar variation across the age categories.

Similar variation in the size of the gap occurs across the categories of family income, but in this instance support varies with income for both women and men. Both show increased support for the agreement with increases in income, yet the greatest level of support shown by women is just equal to the weakest support level given by men: 45 per cent. This emphasizes the distance between men and women in attitudes on this issue. Note also that support varies by a greater amount in women's opinions, suggesting that income plays a greater role in the determination of their opinions on this issue.

Each of these two variables "explains" some part of women's and men's attitudes: differences across age suggest that generational (or cohort) effects are at work; and differences across income suggest that self-interest may play an important part in determining attitudes. Support for the Free Trade Agreement was in part determined by whether one felt it would be economically harmful or helpful; and for men at least, support was also determined by some factors, social and otherwise, important to a particular age category. This information is key to determining the causes of the gap: both cohort effects and the effects of self-interests differ in some respects between the women and men.

---

32   The gender gap research examined in this chapter, with the exception of the research by Shapiro and Mahajan, analyses patterns underlying the gender gap in attitudes.

This limited example suggests the information available through analyses of surveys. The 1988 CNES survey reveals that women and men think alike on some issues. On others, they do not. A further point illustrated by this examination is that gender alone does not provide a sufficient explanation for the gender gap. Differences in support for the agreement vary across the categories of some socio-demographic variables, suggesting that other factors are relevant determinants of the gender gap. Social forces and structural factors are important shapers of attitudes, and their effects are unique to each gender.

EVALUATING THE 1988 CNES: ATTITUDE MEASUREMENT

An important step in feminist research is to look beyond results and evaluate the variables employed in quantitative analyses. Laying bare the assumptions that underlie research directs attention towards misleading information and invalid conclusions and serves to reduce their appearance in subsequent research.

The level of confidence placed in any survey should be based on the degree to which it was conducted following defensible principles and standards of survey research. The 1988 CNES is a methodologically sound example of survey analysis conducted accorded to established principles. Nonetheless, as feminist researchers employing survey data, we need to think about how the framing of questions in the survey instrument directs the responses given to them. As employers of secondary data we must be clear on just what the original question was designed to measure.

Attitude measurement is neither straightforward nor simplistic. Unlike socio-demographic characteristics, attitudes are not fixed: they vary with a number of factors, including question wording, question order, and question format. The survey question as posed and the survey environment are important determinants of response, and experimental research on survey construction and design is beginning to investigate the nature of that variation.[33] This research is still in its infancy, but there are a number of general principles guiding attitude measurement in surveys.

To justify aggregating attitude responses, employers of survey data must impute the same intent to all respondents. To ensure this is the

---

33   While previous research attempted to minimize this variation, current research is analysing it in the hopes of explaining its sources. The 1988 CNES is part of this new research, because it included experiments designed to measure the effects of sourcing on attitudes. An excellent summary of the state of public opinion research can be found in Paul Sniderman, "The New Look in Public Opinion Research," in Ada Finifter, ed., *Political Science: The State of the Discipline* (Washington, D.C.: American Political Science Association, 1993).

case, survey researchers attempt to phrase questions in unambiguous terms to make the issue or question clear to respondents. It is also important that respondents are given the opportunity to admit they have no knowledge of an issue or topic. Despite this effort, there is no guarantee that respondents will not interpret questions incorrectly or provide answers despite little or no knowledge of the topic. Properly conducted surveys cannot eliminate these possibilities, but they can minimize them.

Some of the questions selected from the 1988 CNES for examination can serve as illustrations. For example, the free trade question specifically mentions that the deal is with the United States, but despite the wording some respondents may answer the question as a statement of their support for all and any ties with the United States, rather than as a statement of their support for the opening up of specific trade ties. Some respondents may also choose to answer the free trade question despite having no knowledge of the free trade deal itself. The inclusion of the "don't know" response does not eliminate this possibility, but it reduces the likelihood.

The question on pornography — "Should adults be prevented from buying pornographic books and movies?" — allows four responses: "Yes, because pornography degrades women"; "No, because it is impossible to define what is pornographic"; "Neither"; and "Undecided." A respondent may believe that the distribution of such material should be limited to prevent children from having access to it, or that distribution should be in keeping with community standards, or both. In any event, respondents must decide between giving a "yes" answer that might not accurately correspond to their beliefs, and a "neither" or "undecided" response.

The decision to provide survey respondents with explicit alternatives mitigates the likelihood that they will answer the question based on different criteria. Attitudes on limiting access to pornographic material do not exist in a vacuum; they are grounded in and directly related to other issues, such as women's and civil rights. As worded, the question forces respondents to choose between the two competing sets of rights. Had the question merely allowed for a "yes/no" response, respondents would have supplied their own alternatives, and these would be invisible to the researcher. Variation in question interpretation remains a possibility, but, "Specification of alternatives by the researcher standardizes the question for respondents and indicates specifically the alternatives against which they wish to report their opinions."[34]

Certainly, any attitudinal questions from the CNES employed in subsequent research should be examined to determine how the wording shapes the responses given to them and to reveal the meaning of those responses.

EVALUATING THE 1988 CNES: SOCIO-DEMOGRAPHIC DATA

Socio-demographic information is rarely assumed to be anything but a straightforward reporting of characteristics such as age and income, and the fact that these characteristics can vary by gender is often overlooked. Table 3 shows the gender differences in some socio-demographic characteristics to highlight this variance. As these differences increase, so does their relevance to the gender gap. For instance, low-income women are generally more supportive of welfare policies than low-income men. The gender gap in opinion on welfare issues will be larger as the share of low-income women becomes greater than the share of low-income men. A comparison of the shares of women and men in the categories of the age variable (which have been collapsed to a smaller number of categories than in the original survey data) also emphasizes the reality that women live longer than men. This accounts for the greater number of widows among them, a fact that merits greater attention than it has been afforded in the past.

Employment status similarly varies by gender. A large share of women designate their employment status as "homemaker," a share not matched among the men. Thus work is interpreted differently by each gender and should be evaluated differently. The questions surrounding employment status and the homemaker category merit increased attention.

How can the survey researcher evaluate the meaning of homemaker status? There are several possibilities. For example, homemaker status may reflect a woman's temporary departure from the workplace due to the presence of children in the home. In such cases, her attitudes might reflect her earlier connections with the paid labour force. If this is the case, her opinions are not likely to be greatly influenced by the short time spent as homemaker. Alternatively, some of the women who do hold the traditional, conservative beliefs associated with the homemaker role may not be included in this indicator because they have entered the

---

34   Seymour Sudman and Norman M. Bradburn, *Asking Questions* (San Francisco: Jossey-Bass Publishers, 1987), p.140.

workforce out of financial need rather than free choice. Women working outside of the home are being included in the working category, even though for purposes of measuring adopted adult sex roles they should be grouped into the homemaker category.

Comparing women who report themselves as homemakers in the work status variable to other women can provide some insight. In Table 4, I compare homemakers and other women in the 1988 survey based on a number of categories. Homemakers have more children living at home than other women, are more likely to be married (90.3 per cent of homemakers are married), are less likely to have a postsecondary education, and are more likely to attend religious services. They are less likely to support abortion and more likely than other women to think women should stay home and have families rather than careers. These findings suggest that homemakers are different from other women and illustrate the problems with examining women as a single category. Women are not a homogeneous group, and treating them as such masks important differences within the group.

Another variable often employed in social research but rarely scrutinized is the socio-economic index. The effects of socio-economic status are often analysed using the Blishen Socio-economic Index, and this measure is included in the 1988 survey. But the index itself is a less than perfect measure of the occupational status hierarchy.[35] There exists a number of problems in socio-economic status indices based on income and education levels associated with occupational titles, particularly in their application to women. As Bernard Blishen, William Carroll, and Catherine Moore point out, women and men in the same occupational category are likely to have different incomes, but by definition the Blishen index equalizes their occupational status because it is based in part on pooled median income levels for every occupational category.[36] Others have pointed out that job content is also likely to vary for women and men in similarly titled occupations, which undermines one of the basic assumptions in the construction of such indices. The exclusion of homemaker from such indices weakens them further and reveals the status accorded to the work itself.[37]

35   I am grateful to Karen Messing for pointing out the problems associated with the Blishen index.

36   Bernard Blishen, William Carroll, and Catherine Moore, "The 1981 Socioeconomic Index For Canada," in *Canadian Review of Sociology and Anthropology* 24 (1987), p.472.

37   K. Messing, L. Dumais, J. Courville, A.M. Siefert, and M. Boucher, "Evaluation of Exposure Data from Women and Men with the Same Job Title," *Journal of Occupational Medicine* (forthcoming); and Pat Armstrong and Hugh Armstrong, *The Double Ghetto*, rev. ed. (Toronto: McClelland and Stewart, 1984).

TABLE 3: SELECTED SOCIO-DEMOGRAPHIC DATA BY GENDER

	MEN %	WOMEN %
FAMILY INCOME		
$29,000 or less	34.9	46.3
$30,000 to $59,000	41.9	39.5
$60,000 or more	23.6	14.3
EMPLOYMENT STATUS		
Working	74.0	49.1
Unemployed/Laid Off	5.6	5.3
Retired	13.8	16.4
Student	4.8	6.7
Disabled	0.9	1.0
Homemaker	0.7	21.4
MARITAL STATUS		
Married/Partnered	69.9	63.4
Divorced/Separated	7.7	9.6
Widowed	2.2	9.7
Never Married	20.1	9.6
CHILDREN AT HOME		
No Children	55.2	56.5
One child or more	44.8	43.5
EDUCATION		
Less than Postsecondary	53.2	54.8
Postsecondary	46.8	45.2
AGE		
34 and under	37.1	36.1
35-54	40.7	35.5
55 and over	22.3	28.5

Note: Some percentages do not add up to 100 due to rounding. Some of the original categories have been collapsed.

TABLE 4: COMPARISON OF HOMEMAKERS AND NON-HOMEMAKERS

I - DEMOGRAPHIC VARIABLES	HOMEMAKERS (N—218)	NON-HOMEMAKERS (N—806)
CHILDREN LIVING AT HOME (Mean Value)	1.19	0.73
MARITAL STATUS	%	%
Married/Partnered	90.3	56.1
Divorced/Separated	2.8	11.5
Widowed	5.5	10.8
Never Married	1.4	21.6
EDUCATION		
Less than Postsecondary	69.7	50.7
Postsecondary	30.3	49.3
RELIGIOUS ATTENDANCE (N12)		
Never	7.0	11.8
Less Than Weekly	44.5	51.2
Weekly or More	48.5	37.0

II - ATTITUDES		
ABORTION (L6)		
Never Permit	17.5	9.0
Permit After Need Established	47.9	40.2
Woman's Personal Choice	34.6	50.8
EGALITARIANISM (QE1) Everyone would be better off if more women:		
Were satisfied to stay home and have families	38.1	19.8
Were encouraged to have careers of their own	24.1	44.1
Neither/Undecided	37.7	36.1

Note: Some of the original categories have been collapsed.

Other variables in this survey are categorized in a manner that precludes the examination of certain relationships. For example, mainstream quantitative research often uses income as a measure of material self-interest. This survey uses family income as its income measure. A measure that treats everyone within the family unit equally in terms of income presents problems. This measure groups single-parent family income together with the income level of two-parent families and single adults. By ignoring these important differences, the measure assumes a limited definition of the "family." Equal income levels in these groups do not imply similar material interests. Thus family income distorts reality when it alone is used as a measure of material self-interest.

The marital status variable is also problematic. The combination of married and partnered couples into a single category assumes a similarity that may be misleading. Married couples, most likely heterosexual, and partnered couples, more likely to be lesbian, gay, or couples that eschew the traditional marriage union and the titles that accompany it, are likely to differ in their attitudes, values, and interests, and thus should be allowed to appear as individual categories of marital status. The problem increases with the number of partnered couples in the category. Including two distinct groups within the same category eliminates the possibility of examining the effects of all variants of marital status on opinion formation.

To assess the degree to which biological rather than social forces are the underlying reasons for differences in attitudes between women and men, a survey requires information on fertility and the number of dependent children living at home. The 1988 CNES limits this information to the number of children under eighteen who live in the household. As Armstrong and Armstrong point out, this measure fails to take into account divorced or separated offspring who may have returned home, an increasingly likely occurrence given rising divorce rates.[38] It also fails to provide a means of distinguishing between those women who have given birth and those who have not. As a result, the relevance of motherhood on opinion formation and the complete effects of dependent children in the home cannot be fully examined.

Also important, and particularly for examining the gender gap, is information that allows for the measurement of gender group consciousness. Gender group consciousness "embodies an identification with

---

38   Armstrong and Armstrong, "Beyond Numbers," p.58.

similar others, positive affect towards them, and a feeling of interdependence with the group's fortunes."[39] It has been argued to be of central importance in the determination of women's issue positions and in the relative salience women assign to various issues, and a necessary component of feminist identity.

The only variable in the survey that assesses the degree to which respondents consciously identify with women as a group is a thermometer scale variable that measures how "positively" one feels towards feminist groups. This does not directly correspond to identification with women. Question wording is also of importance, because the word "feminist," rather than "women," can invoke negative connotations among some respondents. Indicators of group consciousness are more often measured in terms of how "close" (rather than the negative/positive thermometer measure) the respondent feels towards women, and whether the respondent chooses women as the group she feels the closest to. This measure captures identification with a group more adequately than our less reliable "positive" question. Furthermore, it escapes the problem involved in asking respondents about feminists, and the negative connotations that accompany the term, by asking about women in general. Researchers can employ the thermometer question as a measure of group consciousness, but they must also address these important issues in order to determine their impact on the research questions under examination.

CONCLUSION

Feminist critiques of quantitative and survey methods have resulted in an important re-evaluation of the application of the method to studies of women and politics. These critiques have played some part in initiating the gradual revision of survey instruments to include questions that allow for a more comprehensive investigation of women's political behaviour. Feminist research on the gender gap is helping to improve our understanding of women's attitudes and some of their sources. However, as this examination of the 1988 CNES and its application to gender gap research has shown, there is still much work to be done.

This chapter presents examples of the methodological challenges facing feminist researchers employing secondary data sources. Some of the problems outlined are technical: the omission of information from the

39   Sue Tolleson Rinehart, *Gender Consciousness and Politics* (New York: Routledge, 1992), p.14.

survey, and improper categorizations of response. Others are less easily resolved. This lack of perfection should not be seen as a ground for abandoning the method and the investigation; as surveys and measures improve, our understanding of the nature and sources of the gender gap improves along with them.

Examples of clearly biased and objectifying survey research are easily found. These examples tell us much about how the method has been used in the past. Yet they tell us very little about the possibilities that the method presents to feminist researchers. To paraphrase Virginia Sapiro, we must look to the method as a choice, rather than a trap.[40]

APPENDIX 1

(L2) As you know, (Canada/the Mulroney government) has reached a Free Trade Agreement with the United States. All things considered, do you support the agreement or do you oppose it?

(L6) Of the following three positions, which is closest to your opinion: one, abortion should never be permitted; two, should be permitted only after a need has been established by a doctor; or three, should be a matter of the woman's personal choice?

(L9) As you may know, the (government/Conservative government) intends to buy 8 or more nuclear submarines for the Navy to assert government sovereignty in the Canadian North. All things considered, do you support or oppose buying nuclear submarines?

(XH9) Now let's talk about your feelings about some groups. How do you feel about feminist groups? (The thermometer runs from 0 to 100 degrees, where 0 represents a very negative feeling and 100 a very positive feeling.)

(QA5) Farmers or fishermen who cannot make a living should shift into another line of work just like any other small business has to do OR get government help because their skills and way of life are essential for Canada.

40　Virginia Sapiro, "Reflections on Reflections: Personal Ruminations," *Women & Politics* 7,4 (1987), p.26.

(QA10) Should adults be prevented from buying pornographic books and movies? No, because it is impossible to define what is pornographic OR yes, because pornography degrades women.

(QB6) To cut their deficits, governments should reduce welfare payments. (strongly approve to strongly disapprove)

(QC2) The profit system brings out the worst in human nature OR teaches people the value of hard work and success.

(QE1) Everyone would be better off if more women were satisfied to stay home and have families OR were encouraged to have careers of their own.

(QE4) In our society today, too much emphasis is placed on: individual freedom at the expense of the community interest OR conformity and obedience to the community.

(QF4) Religion is an important part of my life. (mainly agree or mainly disagree)

Note: Variable names beginning with an X were part of the postelection telephone survey, and those beginning with a Q were part of the self-administered mailback survey.

SUGGESTED READINGS

Bella Abzug and M. Kelber. *Gender Gap*. Boston: Houghton Mifflin, 1984.

Pat Armstrong and Hugh Armstrong, "Beyond Numbers: Problems with Quantitative Data," in Greta Hofmann Nemiroff, ed., *Women and Men: Interdisciplinary Readings on Gender*. Montreal: Fitzhenry and Whiteside, 1987.

Sandra Baxter and Marjorie Lansing, *Women and Politics: The Visible Majority*, 2nd ed. Ann Arbor: University of Michigan Press, 1983.

Pamela Johnston Conover, "Feminists and the Gender Gap," *Journal of Politics* 50,4 (1988).

Margrit Eichler, *Nonsexist Research Methods: A Practical Guide*. Boston: Allen and Unwin, 1988.

Floyd J. Fowler, Jr., *Survey Research Methods*, 2nd ed. Newbury Park, Cal.: Sage Publications, 1993.

Kathryn Kopinak, "Gender Differences in Political Ideology in Canada," *Canadian Review of Sociology and Anthropology* 24 (1987).

Carol Mueller ed., *The Politics of the Gender Gap*. Beverly Hills, Cal.: Sage Publications, 1988.

Ann Oakley, "Interviewing Women: A Contradiction in Terms," in Helen Roberts, ed., *Doing Feminist Research*. London: Routledge and Kegan Paul, 1981.

Shulamit Reinharz, *Feminist Methods in Social Research*. New York: Oxford University Press, 1992.

Sue Tolleson Rinehart, *Gender Consciousness and Politics*. New York: Routledge, 1992.

Virginia Sapiro, *The Political Integration of Women*. Urbana: University of Illinois Press, 1983.

SANDRA BURT

Chapter Thirteen: The Several Worlds of Policy Analysis: Traditional Approaches and Feminist Critiques

In its broadest sense, public policy consists of actions that governments choose to take, as well as actions that they choose not to take; and policy analysts have sought to explain and evaluate these decisions. As these analyses have evolved, most obviously since the emergence of the western welfare state, they have largely excluded women's interests. To some extent this exclusion can be explained by the relative absence of women from policy-making circles until the early 1980s. But a more powerful and enduring factor was the early adoption of rational, self-interested man as the reference point for both policy development and policy studies.

Since the early 1970s feminist scholars have gradually challenged this exclusion of women from policy inquiry. Initially they framed the challenge as a problem of numbers, and more recently as a conceptual problem grounded in the notion of rational man as the ideal citizen. Increasingly feminist scholars have contributed new and varied approaches to public policy analysis, informed variously by their concern for inclusive, socially responsible, and socially responsive research. Their contributions have been significant but still largely invisible within the policy analysis field. The result has been an emerging tension between feminist alternatives and traditional main/malestream policy studies.

For the most part feminist approaches have involved frame-shifting rather than the adoption of new research methodologies. In their attempt to explore the implications of existing public policies such as welfare delivery or employment equity, feminist policy analysts have sought to include women's interests and perspectives. Increasingly they have sought as well to contextualize women's interests, beginning with the assumption that women themselves should be the reference point for analysis. This process of challenging traditional policy perspectives has been ongoing since the early 1970s, with the earliest efforts limited to adding women's experiences and concerns to existing research agendas. But in the face of difficulties they encountered with incorporating domestic violence, for example, on a list dominated by concerns for national integration, the economy, and the constitution, feminist policy researchers increasingly have challenged the prevailing guidelines for policy research and sought to integrate, first, gender considerations and, later, class, race and other specificities into more inclusive frameworks for analysis. Over time feminists also have concerned themselves with giving voice to the various members of the policy communities they study. Their efforts have met with surprising resistance from traditional researchers, who have dismissed the new work as irrelevant, subjective, or poor scholarship.

In this chapter I look at the development of feminist discourse in Canada, reflecting on the various ways in which feminists have tried to carry out gender-inclusive research on policy. I also look at the traditional responses to that discourse, considering how and why traditional researchers have often resisted these efforts.

CONFRONTING THE PROBLEM OF EXCLUSION

In the early 1970s a few women working within the social sciences began to question the exclusion of women from writings about life in the public sphere as it was then understood. Susan Bourque and Jean Grossholtz, writing and working in the United States, were among the first to argue that traditional malestream writings about public life were based on the incorrect assumption that women had not taken part in the political process. They wanted to count women in — to show how women had engaged in political decision-making. They were concerned as well with exploring the structural, situational, and socialization obstacles that had historically restricted women's access to formal political activity and resulted in a persistent and disquieting gap between the proportion of women in the population and women's representation on policy-making bodies.

This early feminist critique went beyond the need to study women as members of political élites. But the interest in learning more about women in legislatures provided a starting point for a feminist research agenda. For some it seemed to be a straightforward goal easily incorporated into existing research strategies. Even this apparently simple process of counting the numbers of women involved at various levels of a political hierarchy was carried out almost exclusively by women. In the United States Jeane Kirkpatrick led the way in 1972 with her open-ended interviews with forty-six women members of U.S. state legislatures.[1] She found that these women had absorbed the existing male culture of the policy-making world, and concluded that they were far removed from a politics of gender difference. Kirkpatrick rejoiced in her discovery of these "normal" women (her term), who were, just like their male counterparts, driven by the quest for power.

In Canada Sylvia Bashevkin was one of the first social scientists to search for women's presence in political life. She began her analysis of women and politics by reviewing the existing literature on political participation. Her examination of U.S. electoral studies in particular led her to conclude that the conventional wisdom — that women and men behaved quite differently in the public sphere — was incorrect with reference to voting behaviour. She suggested, "Turnout, partisan preferences, and other characteristics of American and Western European women became increasingly similar over the approximately forty year period from the end of World War I through the late 1950s."[2] In her later work on Canadian political parties Bashevkin continued her examination of the numerical representation of women among party elites and focused on affirmative action measures that could produce gender parity on the decision-making bodies of political parties.

These works were representative of an emerging consensus among both male and female scholars in North America: that women were catching up to men in political participation. Carole Pateman labels this

---

1   Jeane J. Kirkpatrick, *Political Woman* (New York: Basic Books, 1974).

2   Sylvia Bashevkin, "Women and Politics: Perspectives on the Past, Present, and Future," paper presented at the Annual Meeting, Canadian Political Science Association, 1979.

catching up phenomenon "domesticated feminism," an idea based on the assumption that existing political structures can accommodate feminist demands.[3] Domesticated feminism, either as a program of action or as a guiding framework for research, has served to maintain the invisibility of women by merging their frequently distinctive political claims with men's actions in the political process.[4] This may explain why it has become the most popular approach among those traditional policy analysts who have sought to demonstrate their sensitivity to gender issues while at the same time maintaining their old categories. The consequences have been significant for publication possibilities and dominant research guidelines, with most support directed to research programs in which scholars have evaluated women in terms of male standards.[5]

The possibility of demonstrating the existence of gender differences was popularized in 1982 with the publication of Carol Gilligan's work on moral reasoning.[6] In a conceptually rich discussion of the reasoning of U.S. college students and women seeking abortions, Gilligan explored the possible existence of a gender gap in morality. In spite of some methodological problems (in particular her selection of a gender-specific issue such as abortion), Gilligan's analysis contributed to the intellectual richness of feminist research. Subsequent feminist research on women's political activism moved away from the earlier depiction of public woman as a reflection of public man to the contemplation of difference. In the United States, Virginia Sapiro's examination of the political integration of women into public life provided evidence that feminist attitudes and reactions to feminism are an important part of contemporary U.S. political culture. In Canada, by 1983 Bashevkin had moved beyond a study of the numerical representation of women in politics to a consideration of the relationship between women's partisan support patterns and their treatment by the political parties.[7]

3   Carole Pateman, "Introduction: The Theoretical Subversiveness of Feminism," in Carole Pateman and Elizabeth Gross, eds., *Feminist Challenges* (Sydney: Allen and Unwin, 1986).

4   Thus, for example, political interest was treated as a single variable in quantitative analyses of political behaviour. Qualitative research has shown some gender differences in the interpretation of interest. Men were more likely to view interest as partisan activity, while women often interpreted it as concern for social and political issues.

5   Karen Messing makes a similar point in her chapter about funding for studies of women's occupational health and safety.

6   Carol Gilligan, *In a Different Voice: Psychological Theory and Women's Development* (Cambridge, Mass.: Harvard University Press, 1982).

7   Sylvia Bashevkin, "Social Change and Political Partisanship: The Development of Women's Attitudes in Quebec," *Comparative Political Studies* 16,2 (July 1983), pp.147-72.

In my work at that time I explored the possibility that women and men inhabit different political worlds, that the similar behaviours of women and men (or of racial groups or social classes) at the polls or during political campaigns could mask significant attitudinal differences. While the same proportions of women and men might go to the polls on election day and make similar choices among available candidates, the reasons for their actions could be quite different. With the use of qualitative interviewing techniques I concluded that this was indeed the case for the women and men in the study. And while the short-term consequences for the political system might be similar, the long-term consequences for political change could be very different. The editors and reviewers of traditional social science journals were unsympathetic both to this argument and to the qualitative research methods I employed. The article was published in *Women and Politics* a journal committed to feminist research in the social sciences.[8]

Given that main/malestream political science generally was becoming more inclined to accept the proposition of similarity — that women were becoming "good men" as they moved into the public sphere — researchers could contemplate women's concerns within the existing frameworks for policy research without making any changes in their traditional assumptions about the qualities necessary for, or the priorities established in, political life. The consequences for evaluating women's needs were disastrous. When she reviewed the Canadian politics literature in 1987, Naomi Black found "the continued absence of women plus a limited attempt to explain their lesser level of participation." She also noted the absence of any "reflection of feminist critiques that women 'lag' behind men."[9]

The same pattern is apparent in the policy field. The record of Canada's leading academic journal of policy analysis is a case in point. *Canadian Public Policy* was first published in 1975. Between 1975 and 1993 the journal editors published 509 articles, of which 6 were concerned with women's issues narrowly defined as child care, affirmative action, male violence, or prostitution. A search for references to women's interests in areas beyond those artificially limited boundaries yielded 10 additional articles (see Table 1). Policies that could affect women and men differently, such as free trade or the delivery of social services, were usually examined without regard for such a possibility. Typical is a recent

8   Sandra Burt, "Different Democracies? A Preliminary Examination of the Political Worlds of Canadian Men and Women," *Women and Politics* 6,4 (Winter 1986), pp.57-79.

9   Naomi Black, "The Child Is Father to the Man: The Impact of Feminism on Canadian Political Science," in Winnie Tomm, ed., *The Effects of Feminist Approaches on Research Methodologies* (Waterloo, Ont.: Wilfrid Laurier University Press, 1989), p.231.

TABLE ONE: SOME SUBJECTS COVERED IN *CANADIAN PUBLIC POLICY*, 1975-93

ARTICLE THEMES	FREQUENCY
	%
monetary policies	20
natural resources	6
energy	6
federal/provincial relations	4
employment policies	4
economic development	4
trade	4
health	4
transportation	4
social services	2
environment	2
"women's issues"	1

analysis of the economic costs of AIDS in Canada, in which Jon Harkness assesses "the reduction in Canada's current human capital stock as the result of AIDS."[10] Harkness proposes that the "principal cost of AIDS is indirect, being the loss of human capital (or potential output) as a result of the premature death or disability of AIDS victims."[11] The human capital cost includes an individual's lifetime contribution to both market and non-market output. For ease of calculation Harkness categorizes the typical AIDS sufferer as a childless working man: "The data will not permit one to compute the human capital embodied in each and every PWA [person with AIDS]."[12] He calculates the average potential labour income of AIDS sufferers using 1988 data from Statistics Canada. In spite of the fact that women have lower earning potential than men, one could argue that the gender difference in labour-market value is not

10   Jon Harkness, "The Economic Cost of AIDS in Canada," *Canadian Public Policy* XV,4 (December 1989), p.405.

11   Ibid., p.406.

12   Ibid., p.408.

statistically significant[13] for this calculation, given that the vast majority (2,166 of 2,323 cases recorded in 1988) of sufferers were men. But the gender difference in human capital cost becomes more pronounced and potentially significant when nonmarket output (for example, housework, and child care) is taken into account. And future projections of a dramatic increase in the number of women with AIDS also cast doubt on the reliability of Harkness's male model.

Women are also largely absent from *How Ottawa Spends*, an annual review of federal government priorities and policy initiatives prepared for academics and policy practitioners. The editors have always been interested in social policy issues, but gender is almost invisible in the collections, even when the authors are concerned with issues that obviously affect women's lives. For example, in the 1990/91 edition Allan Moscovitch reviews the child benefits program, conceptualizing it as a child and/or family benefits issue and avoiding discussion of the contribution of eroding child-support funds to the increasing feminization of poverty.[14] There are some exceptions to this pattern, but only in the contributions authored by women. For example, in 1989 Susan Phillips assessed the Conservatives' child-care strategy,[15] and in 1991 she examined changes in Conservative support for women's and multicultural groups.[16]

One of the newest contributions to the public policy literature is a 1993 collection edited by Michael Atkinson. For *Governing Canada*, Atkinson and his contributors selected four policy areas for consideration: macroeconomic policy, trade and industrial policy, social policy, and environmental policy. These areas all clearly have an impact on the lives of both women and men, and often in significantly different ways. Yet the contributors generally treat women and men as one category of analysis, ignoring as well the implications of racial differences. For example, Ian Greene reviews Canadian courts and court policy, but seems

13   Donna S. Lero and Karen Johnson, "110 Canadian Statistics on Work and Family," background paper prepared for the Canadian Advisory Council on the Status of Women (Ottawa: April 1994), p.6.

14   Allan Moscovitch, "The Social Sector and Child Benefits Reform," in Katherine A. Graham, ed., *How Ottawa Spends, 1990-91: Tracking the Second Agenda* (Ottawa: Carleton University Press, 1990), pp.171-218.

15   Susan Phillips, "Rock-a-Bye, Brian: The National Strategy on Child Care," in Katherine A. Graham, ed., *How Ottawa Spends, 1989-90: The Buck Stops Where?* (Ottawa: Carleton University Press, 1989), pp.165-208.

16   Susan D. Phillips, "How Ottawa Blends: Shifting Government Relationships With Interest Groups," in Frances Abele, ed., *How Ottawa Spends, 1991-2: The Politics of Fragmentation* (Ottawa: Carleton University Press, 1991), pp.183-227.

unaware that some of the most significant legal decisions in the interpretation of the Charter of Rights and Freedoms have been responses to arguments developed by feminist lawyers. For instance, the Legal Education and Action Fund (LEAF), formed in 1984 by a group of feminist lawyers and legal advisers, has worked to engage in equality rights cases in the courts and set the agenda of many groups that are part of the women's movement.[17] LEAF's arguments for substantive rather than exclusively legal equality as well as its concern with placing women's legal battles in an appropriate social and/or economic context have been groundbreaking. But in his review Greene omitted any reference to LEAF or to the cases affecting women's status. The omission is significant, because the arguments of feminist lawyers have been strikingly different from those presented by their male colleagues in Charter-based cases. In the same collection Carolyn Tuohy discusses what she calls the two worlds of social policy: "a relatively niggardly set of policies directed at income security," and "a system of national health insurance that is both generous and outstandingly popular."[18] Women are invisible in her analysis as well, in spite of the obvious connections between health care and reproductive issues. The list of major income maintenance, medical, and hospital-insurance programs does not include maternity leave payments. Finally, the extensive bibliography at the end of the book does not include any of the major feminist policy analyses undertaken in the past few years.[19]

One possible explanation for women's near invisibility in traditional policy analysis is gender bias, or selective exclusion. Over the years, successive governments' decisions to facilitate women's employment opportunities, legislate voluntary affirmative action measures, or accept some responsibility through the unemployment insurance program for maternity leave protection for women have been part of an industrial strategy. The early work of the Women's Bureau of the federal Department of Labour brought the stories of women in the labour force first to the attention of successive ministers of labour and subsequently to the federal government. All of the issues listed by women's groups in two surveys I conducted in 1984 and 1993 have at some point been presented

---

17   I develop this is the argument in "What's Fair? Changing Feminist Perceptions of Justice in English Canada," *Windsor Yearbook of Access to Justice* 12 (1992), pp.337-55.

18   Carolyn Tuohy, "Social Policy: Two Worlds," in Michael Atkinson, ed., *Governing Canada: Institutions and Policy* (Toronto: Harcourt, Brace, Jovanovich, 1993), p.273.

19   For instance, among the most important policy studies are Judy Fudge and Patricia McDermott's feminist assessment of pay equity, the excellent feminist analyses of charter cases, and Janine Brodie and Jane Jenson's work on abortion policy.

to government officials or elected representatives for consideration. Women's groups and feminist members of the House of Commons have represented women's interests to governments. The repeated failure of these governments to address the central concerns of these feminist activists constitutes public policy.

Another explanation is gender blindness, or the common belief among traditional policy analysts that women and men, as they appear in public life, are essentially interchangeable. Both Carole Pateman and Iris Young, among others, suggest ways in which western liberal-democratic societies have excluded women by adopting a set of principles developed by and for men and offered to the polity as universal. For Pateman the problem originates in the social contract, which masquerades as a contract of freedom while containing within it a sexual contract that encodes men's domination over women. In the social contract, women as differentiated beings are "excluded from the central category of the individual" and given access to the public sphere only when they take on the characteristics of the individual as man.[20] Pateman argues that accepting the public sphere as it is means accepting a set of "male attributes, capacities and modes of activity."[21]

Iris Young's point is more specifically addressed to policy analysis. She exposes the problem as "accepting as given institutional structures that ought to be brought under normative evaluation." These institutional structures have been created within a distributive politics that suppresses "difference by conceiving the polity as universal and unified."[22] Policy analysts have historically limited their research to the study of these existing structures, to the study of what governments do. In a recent review of approaches, Leslie Pal challenges the old boundaries, defining public policy as "a course of action or inaction chosen by authorities to address a given problem or interrelated set of problems."[23] Stephen Brooks adopts this definition in his text on public policy in Canada, but neither Pal nor Brooks evaluates a full "range of matters which are subject to public choice and in which governments are involved."[24]

20   Carole Pateman, *The Sexual Contract* (Cambridge: Polity Press 1988), p.6.

21   Carole Pateman, "Introduction," in Carole Pateman and Elizabeth Gross, eds., *Feminist Challenges: Social and Political Theory* (Sydney: Allen and Unwin, 1986), p.7.

22   Iris Marion Young, *Justice and the Politics of Difference* (Princeton: Princeton University Press, 1990), p.10.

23   Leslie A. Pal, *Public Policy Analysis, An Introduction*, 2nd ed. (Scarborough, Ont.: Nelson, 1992), p.2.

24   Richard Simeon, "Studying Public Policy," *Canadian Journal of Political Science* IX,4 (December 1976), p.559.

Brooks insists upon the researcher's ability to demonstrate what he calls the intentional exclusion of demands. Brooks concludes, "The 'blindness' of policy-makers to gender inequality did not constitute a policy of maintaining inequality but was due to the systematic exclusion of what today are called 'women's issues' by a dominant culture that did not perceive gender inequality in problematic terms."[25] Pal repeated this theme in 1992, noting that policy implies deliberation. If an idea hasn't entered the minds of most policy-makers, "It is inappropriate to designate their inaction as policy."[26] Patriarchal assumptions may form the backdrop for policy exclusions, but they can't be considered policy without evidence of "deliberate" intent. And so, even with a reformed outlook on the field, policy analysts often fail to allow themselves the conceptual space to take gender into account.

These working definitions of policy restrict the scope of traditional analysis to the agenda established by political elites. In Canada, where consistently fewer than 10 per cent of elected representatives at either the provincial or federal level of government have been women, research has been devoted almost exclusively to priorities set by men. With few exceptions these priorities have reflected men's interests and have been concerned with life in the so-called private sphere only as it relates to (provides support for or facilitates) life in the public sphere. Yet the women who have been members of Canadian legislatures have frequently adopted feminist positions in parliament. Best known are women such as Agnes Macphail or Grace MacInnes, who struggled to convince their male colleagues in the House of Commons that they must address policy questions with a view to women's best interests.

Manon Tremblay notes the present-day tendency for women sitting in the Quebec National Assembly to express their feminism in debates. Linda Trimble documents the willingness of women in the Alberta legislature to experiment with new ways of exchanging information about issues across party lines, particularly when they are in opposition.[27] However, two important constraints limit the scope of impact of these initiatives. First, at least during the past twenty years, the perspectives of women in

25 Stephen Brooks, *Public Policy in Canada: An Introduction* (Toronto: McClelland and Stewart, 1989), pp.16-17.

26 Pal, *Public Policy Analysis*, p.7.

27 Manon Tremblay, "Quand les femmes se distinguent: feminisme et represéntation politique au Québec," *Canadian Journal of Political Science* XXV,1 (1992), pp.55-68; Linda Trimble, "A Few Good Women: Female Legislators in Alberta, 1972-1991," in Randi Warne and Cathy Cavanaugh, eds., *Standing on New Ground: Women in Alberta* (Edmonton: University of Alberta Press, 1994).

elected office have been largely contained within the liberal-feminist insistence on women's right to compete equally with men for the same jobs in an unchanged public sphere. Only recently, and primarily in the context of growing concern with the problem of violent acts committed by men against women, has there been some consideration of problems with current gender constructions. Second, there have been too few women in legislative offices to form a "critical mass" for policy reforms. Women's legislative influence has been moderated by the operation of structural constraints on policy, including the concentration of significant power in the hands of the prime minister and the division of feminists along party lines in the legislatures. Even in those rare situations in which women sit as cabinet members, their actions are restricted by the principles of cabinet solidarity and responsible government.

Kim Campbell's political journey provides a good example of such constraints. As a new member of the House in the 1980s she was prepared to affirm her feminist position and on occasion provide funding for public forums at which feminist voices, rarely heard in policy-making circles, could find public expression. In 1991 Campbell, as minister of justice, convened a symposium on "Women, Law, and the Administration of Justice." Using public funding Campbell encouraged groups outside the traditional limits of public policy to attend that symposium, including Native women's associations and groups representing immigrant and racial minority women, as well as disabled women and sexual assault organizations. Some of the participants saw this as an opportunity to give public voice to their transformative feminist positions and engage in a dialogue with some of the professional, more traditional liberal-feminist organizations also represented at the symposium.[28]

These feminist voices could be heard in some of the recommendations worked out by the delegates. While for the most part the resolutions were framed within the discourse of equal opportunities for women, some did acknowledge the politics of difference. The delegates recommended better representation of women on judicial bodies; a maternity leave policy for women engaged in the delivery of justice; the development of a code of ethics for judges; and guarantees to ensure that women would have more say in the decisions of the Supreme Court of Canada. The list also included demands for a separate Aboriginal justice system and for "recognition that gender identity is predetermined by

28   Interview with Lee Lakeman, Canadian Association of Sexual Assault Centres, October 1992.

many factors and cannot be determined exclusive of race, culture, ethnicity, class, sexual orientation, ability, language, etc."[29]

In 1993 the federal government published its response to the recommendations of the symposium. The response was formulated within an
equal rights agenda that excluded the symposium endorsement of gender difference, consistent with Carole Pateman's claim "that individuals
are feminine and masculine, that individuality is not a unitary abstraction but an embodied and sexually differentiated expression of the unity
of humankind."[30] Excluded as well was recognition of race and class distinctions, and their implications. The new minister of justice, Pierre
Blais, rejected any suggestion emerging from the symposium that
women's needs were special needs. Instead he reaffirmed the principle
that had become government policy in the 1970s, that women should be
treated just like men. The government was sympathetic to the need to
inform judges and law enforcement officials about sexual equality, but
did not agree to programs explaining positions of gender difference.[31]

Government policies for women in Canada have been framed within
the boundaries of equal opportunity since the early 1970s, when there
was growing legislative awareness of the movement of women into public life, especially the labour force. In successive government documents
and policies, justice and fairness for women have been defined as equal
access to federal programs, services, and employment. Even the issue of
male violence, which has little if anything to do with equal opportunity
and much to do with the consequences of patriarchal social arrangements, has been absorbed by governments into the equality framework
as a problem of public safety (protection of private property and the
person). It therefore seems unlikely that, in the near future at least, recognition of gender difference will be encoded in legislators' chosen
courses of action. Consequently, policy analysts interested only in investigating "what is" have no reason to concern themselves with a feminist
agenda that in many respects looks considerably different from the government's agenda. Policy analysts may take a look at "women's issues,"
but only in the restricted framework of equality rights.

29   "Recommendations from Delegates from Organizations Dedicated to Women's Equality to
     the Symposium on Women, Law and the Administration of Justice," Vancouver B.C., June
     10-12, 1991, unpublished document.

30   Pateman, "Introduction," p.9.

31   Canada, Department of Justice, *Department of Justice Response to the Recommendations from
     the Symposium* (Ottawa: Supply and Services, 1993).

THE CONSEQUENCES OF ADDING ON

There have been some exceptions in recent years to the overwhelming pattern of excluding women from policy analysis. Some edited collections on the political process in Canada have taken women as a group into account, although Native, Inuit, and racial minority women have been largely ignored. Some authors and editors have been prepared to add a set of "women's issues" to the list of relevant concerns, or include a separate chapter on women in their collections.[32] This add-on process is problematic for several reasons. In the first place, it is not at all clear what counts as "women's issues." The issue of child care illustrates this point well. While historically women have assumed the major responsibility for caring for children, their rights and duties as child-care providers have shifted over time. At the time of Confederation, Canadian fathers had absolute guardianship rights over their children. The process of reducing this right did not begin until 1887, and even then only in Ontario, where a mother could apply to the courts for guardianship. Currently the leadership of the national child-care coalition prefers to label child care as a parental issue, in an attempt to encourage both parents to share the responsibility. But the major share of childrearing is still in practice the mother's responsibility. So the identification of child care as a women's issue is in some dispute. At the very least, men who are fathers have a vested interest in policy outcomes on this issue.

At the same time, issues that appear to be gender-free often have different consequences for women and men. This was one of my findings in a recent study of the organic farm movement in Ontario.[33] I examined the emergence of producer groups that call themselves organic or ecological and evaluated their struggle with Agcare (a federation of conventional producers) to control the environmental farm-policy agenda in Ontario. At one level the contest between the organic and conventional groups was over the use of herbicides and pesticides in commodity production. In the context of heightened consumer awareness of food safety issues, the election of an NDP government committed to sustainable agriculture, and discussions about secure funding for farm organizations, there was stiff competition for control over environmental farm issues.

32   See, for example, James P. Bickerton and Alain-G. Gagnon, eds., *Canadian Politics*, 2nd ed. (Peterborough, Ont.: Broadview Press, 1994) or Robert M. Krause and R.H. Wagenberg, eds., *Canadian Government and Politics*, 2nd ed. (Mississauga, Ont.: Copp Clark Pitman, 1995).

33   Sandra Burt, "The Greening of Ontario Agriculture," unpublished manuscript.

At another level the contest was between the proponents of traditional, relatively small, mixed-production family farms and agribusiness. Within this context the outcome of the struggle between community and commercially based agriculture has special significance for women. The organic movement, represented by groups such as the Ecological Farmers Association and the Organic Crop Improvement Association, is committed to sustainable, ecologically sound agriculture. This means diversity in production, small-scale livestock operations, and sensitivity to soil needs and food safety. The members of these ecological/organic organizations meet with each other frequently, speaking at one another's meetings and sharing expertise. They are bound together by a common love for the land and a commitment to working with nature, to stressing self and community development in their programs. This sense of community, combined with a call for sustainable farm practices, has resulted in the establishment of a network of family farms in southern Ontario, farms modelled on the traditional, turn-of-the-century pattern that Nettie Wiebe describes in her chapter in this book. The extended-family and community-based support services for women and children in such a network are significantly different from the market-driven resources servicing the more conventional, larger, monoculture farms that have become the norm in the 1990s. Agcare was successful in capturing the policy space of environmental agriculture in Ontario, and this will have significant implications for family structure and for the lives of Ontario farm women in the future.

There are other examples of feminist attempts to engender public policy analysis by explaining the consequences for women of what are commonly viewed as gender-neutral issues. Free trade is one such issue, which has been examined by Marjorie Cohen for its impact on women's work.[34] More recently the Ontario Women's Directorate published its analysis of Canada's movement into the North American Free Trade Association and the implications of the deal for women. The authors of the report conclude, "Women are over-represented in many industries that are gender-sensitive and, therefore, women's jobs are at risk."[35] Sylvia Bashevkin extended this analysis in her study of the involvement of the National Action Committee (NAC) on the Status of Women in the free trade issue.[36] She

34   Marjorie Griffin Cohen, *Free Trade and the Future of Women's Work* (Ottawa: Can Centre for Policy Alternatives, 1987).

35   Ontario Women's Directorate, *The North American Free Trade Agreement* (Ontario: 1993), p.1.

36   Sylvia Bashevkin, "Free Trade and Canadian Feminism: The Case of the National Action Committee on the Status of Women," *Canadian Public Policy* XV,4 (December 1989), p.363-75

examined NAC's decision to integrate its earlier social policy and abortion concerns with a feminist critique of free trade. Bashevkin argues that NAC "obtained an unprecedented economic policy profile during the free trade debate,"[37] and suggests that NAC's subsequent federal funding cuts were related to its confrontational stance on the issue. Unfortunately, some readers have interpreted this work as an indication that women's groups have "come of age" with their move away from "second-order" women's issues to "first-order" economic issues. Rather than accepting the proposition that NAC brought gender concerns to free trade, they have concluded that free trade brought NAC to "normal" politics.[38]

In addition to this problem of artificially constructing a category of "women's issues," the process of adding on usually results in the segregation of women's concerns as a special topic with minority status, thereby perpetuating women's invisibility. The decision to condense the woman question into one chapter of a book leaves the remaining authors free to work within traditional paradigms, thereby minimizing their discussion of women's concerns. And since the editors retain control of the manuscripts published within their collections, they can limit the opportunities for feminist discourse.

Finally, the selection of a "women's issue" for analysis does not guarantee a sensitivity to women's concerns. A recent example from the policy literature is the issue of abortion, which obviously affects women's lives. Throughout Canadian history abortion has also been a matter of public concern; it was included, for instance, as a prohibited act in the Criminal Code in 1892.[39] It was not until 1969 that an amendment to the Code (section 251) legalized abortions sanctioned by a therapeutic abortion committee consisting of three people, one of them a physician. In 1988 the Supreme Court of Canada declared section 251 unconstitutional, thus removing abortion from the Criminal Code's confines.

Canadian women's history is replete with accounts of how the movement of abortion from an illegal to a restricted legal act has played a central role in women's lives and in the various waves of the women's movement. For example, in the nineteenth century some women experimented with various unsafe abortion techniques, including ingesting boric acid and turpentine.[40] By the mid-twentieth century the issue was

---

37   Ibid., p.363.

38   My students offered this interpretation in a third-year course in research methods.

39   Alison Prentice et al., *Canadian Women: A History* (Toronto: Harcourt, Brace, Jovanovich, 1988), p.165.

40   Ibid., p.164.

still alive, eventually giving rise to the 1970 Abortion Caravan, which "ended in Ottawa on Mother's Day with a demonstration that closed up Parliament, as women chained themselves to the Visitor's Gallery."[41] The demand for reproductive freedom runs through all strains of contemporary feminist thought and practice, as either a central or a necessary part of women's quest for greater understanding of their past and an engagement in their future.

In 1991 Pal included the abortion policy saga as a case study in a text on Canadian public policies designed for use in undergraduate Canadian politics and public policy courses.[42] In his review of abortion, Pal describes some of the events that took place between October 3, 1967 (when the House of Commons Standing Committee began hearings on three private members' abortion bills), and January 31, 1991, when the Senate defeated Bill C-43 in a free vote. Bill C-43 was sponsored by Kim Campbell, then minister of justice, and would have returned abortion to the Criminal Code following the 1988 decision of the Supreme Court that struck down section 251. Pal examines the Commons debates on the issue and describes the court cases that occurred between 1969 and 1989.

In spite of the obvious involvement of women in the abortion process, as well as published accounts documenting the centrality of this issue in the second wave of feminist activity in Canada, Pal's account gives little space to women and women's interests. Instead he focuses on the story of one man, Henry Morgentaler (the physician seeking the legal right to perform abortions), and his contest with the media, legislatures, and courts. The exploration of Morgentaler's private life and political convictions personalizes abortion as a man's issue. Women are counted into the analysis only occasionally and peripherally, as members of a "minority political movement."[43] The description of feminist activism on the abortion issue understates the involvement of groups such as the Canadian Abortion Rights Action League and fails to take into account the impact of this policy issue on women's lives. Pal confuses the pro-choice side of the debate with a pro-abortion position, although he explains his use of pro-abortion rights in an endnote. After his review Pal offers ten discussion questions for students. They are good questions,

41   Naomi Black, "The Canadian Women's Movement: The Second Wave," in Sandra Burt, Lorraine Code and Lindsay Dorney, eds., *Changing Patterns: Women in Canada, 2nd ed.*, (Toronto: McClelland and Stewart, 1993), p.152.

42   Leslie A. Pal, "Courts, Politics and Morality: Canada's Abortion Saga," in Leslie A. Pal and Robert Campbell, eds., *The Real Worlds of Canadian Politics* (Peterborough, Ont.: Broadview Press, 1991), pp.1-70. A slightly revised version of the study also appeared in the 1991/92 edition of the Public Policy Series, *How Ottawa Spends* (Ottawa: Carleton University Press).

43   Pal, "Courts, Politics and Morality," p.3.

ones that lead students to consider the constraints affecting policy decisions and the new interaction developing between the courts and the
legislatures in Canada. But they do not encourage students to think
about women's health issues as they relate to abortion. Nor do they lead
them to consider the appropriate relationship between public policies
and private lives. Finally, they don't suggest the need to consider in
greater detail how items arrive on the public agenda, or why abortion
became a key issue in the 1960s, while legislators saw other issues, such
as male violence and child care, as much less significant.[44]

In 1985 Susan McDaniel examined Canada's abortion policy from a
feminist perspective, taking as her primary concern the impact of legislative decisions and anti-abortion activities on women's access to abortion.[45] Like Pal, she provides readers with a review of abortion law and
policy in Canada. Unlike Pal, she investigates the implications of abortion policies for women's lives, concluding that the therapeutic abortion
committees set up by the 1969 abortion law, the courts, and the legislatures have assumed that "women should be mothers and impediments
of every kind are put in the way of those seeking to end unwanted pregnancies."[46] McDaniel also investigates the opposing worldviews of the
pro-choice and anti-abortion activists in order to place their lobbying
activities in a conceptual framework. She is interested in discovering
whether restricting access to abortions results in a greater number of live
births, or fewer safe abortions. She concludes, "Abortion policy as it is
presently [in 1985] implemented in Canada has enormous implications
for women's lives." Further, she notes that it "is a male-dominated system in which women's appropriate roles are defined by men for their
own purposes."[47] Her study conceptualizes abortion as a women's issue
that has been transformed into men's policy, in the legislatures, in the
courts, and in medical circles. The transformation, she argues, has not
adequately served women's interests or needs.

The startling contrast in the perspectives of these two authors helps
to bring the distinctions between traditional and feminist policy-re-
search approaches into focus. Even when an issue that is obviously con-

---

44   I asked students in my graduate seminar on women and politics to read the works by Pal and
McDaniel. Our discussions provided the starting point for my early musings about the nature of public policy research in Canada.

45   Susan A. McDaniel, "Implementation of Abortion Policy in Canada as a Women's Issue,"
Atlantis 10,2 (Spring 1985), pp.75-91.

46   Ibid., p.81.

47   Ibid., p.89.

nected to women's lives is the subject of analysis, the traditional approach can result in the near exclusion of women from consideration. In this example, Pal's overriding concern for the role of the courts in the setting of Canadian policy agendas made it possible for him to completely avoid a consideration of the consequences of abortion policies for women. This in turn may account for his failure to take into account the role of feminist activists in the policy-making process. This failure has several sources, one of which is the traditional domination of men and men's interests in a state modelled on the male contract. Current policy-analysis frameworks feed into this tradition, accepting only "deliberate" actions as appropriate for study. Underlying, unstated assumptions — among which preconceived notions of gender roles are prevalent and pervasive — are beyond the range of legitimate concerns. Another source is the invisibility of much of the work produced by feminist scholars. Pal does not list McDaniel's article as a reference, probably because it was published in *Atlantis*, a journal well known by other feminists but generally ignored by traditional academics.

THE SEARCH FOR NEW APPROACHES

Many feminist scholars have reacted to traditional policy research by seeking new publication avenues. This research segregation has been fuelled by the continued resistance of traditional researchers to feminist approaches (and in particular to the proposition that gender inclusiveness does not necessarily imply gender sameness), expressed in publication decisions, advice to graduate students, and teaching curricula. The commitment to publishing in feminist outlets has been liberating in many ways, allowing researchers the space to explore new research methods and challenge traditional values. But for both academics and policy-makers it has also resulted in the academic invisibility of much good feminist research. This feminist invisibility in academic circles, apparent in some of the examples given here, has been accompanied by an invisibility in policy-making circles as well.

In the 1970s, when the federal government established the agencies charged with investigating or improving the status of women in Canada, it institutionalized feminist invisibility by segregating women's issues and according them minority status. This process of institutionalization had some positive, primarily short-term consequences for women. For the first time women could obtain public funds for activist projects as well as for research. They could even publish their work through government agencies. But in most cases the agencies were firmly within government control. Researchers working for Status of Women Canada, for example, could have no illusions that they were operating as independent consultants. And although the directors of some of these programs (in particular the Women's Program in the Secretary of State) were able to initiate changes in women's lives through their provision of funds to women's groups, these funds eventually became part of the federal government's equal opportunity program.

The Advisory Council on the Status of Women seemed to be an exception to a government-controlled pattern. The Council was set up by the Liberal government of Pierre Trudeau in 1973 with a mandate to bring issues of interest to women to the attention of the federal government.[48] From the outset it was given some freedom to act independently, with the authority to investigate such matters "as the Council may deem appropriate."[49] This principle of independent action was reaffirmed in 1976, when the Council's mandate was renewed. In her final annual report Katie Cooke, the first chair of the Council, noted approvingly that "the Government has re-affirmed the mandate of ACSW as an independent council with the power to determine its own priorities and make its own recommendations simultaneously to the Government and to the public."[50] Between 1973 and 1982 the Council did indeed operate as an independent feminist research agency. Throughout that period it published research reports on child care, women in unions, and labour strategies that were critical of patriarchal structures, and it repeatedly challenged the prevailing pattern of government policy.[51]

In 1982 Doris Anderson, president of the Council since 1979, resigned in the context of controversy over her decision to hold a conference on women and the constitution. This was the first public indication that the independence of the Council was in jeopardy. The events that followed

48   The Council published a review of its twenty-year history in 1993. See Canadian Advisory Council on the Status of Women, *Expanding Our Horizons* (Ottawa: CACSW, 1993).

49   Ibid., p.5.

50   Katie Cooke, *Annual Report 1975-1976* (Ottawa: Canadian Advisory Council on the Status of Women), p.5.

51   See, for example, Julie White, *Women and Unions* (Ottawa: CACSW, 1980).

illustrate the fragility of feminist visibility in policy-making circles. One of the first indications of a shift in the Advisory Council's mandate came in 1987, when the Council (then led by Sylvia Gold) published *Integration and Participation*, an analysis of women's work in the home and labour force.

Several researchers had been hired on contract to write the various chapters in the publication, on the understanding that they would be acknowledged as the authors of their work. The process of writing and revision took several years. The authors submitted their work to the Council, completed the required revisions, and resubmitted. They understood that the final versions they submitted would be published as written, but the published accounts contained significant changes. In one case a critique of employers' unwillingness to do more than the absolute minimum to safeguard women's health on the job was rewritten as a commendation of employers' commitment to health concerns.[52] The author's draft presents a hard-hitting critique of employers' unwillingness to control workplace hazards that place women at risk for reproductive or genetic damage. In the published version the Council softened this critique with an employer-friendly commendation of programs for substance abuse and fitness: "Employers are also aware of the issue and are designing policies and programs to address these concerns. These include providing fitness programs, developing preventive measures on smoking and cardiovascular disease, and designing programs to curb alcohol abuse."[53] Even when confronted with the possibility of a law suit by the author, Gold refused to remove the altered phrases from the publication, arguing that the Council retained the right to make editorial changes in its publications. The author eventually dropped the suit when faced with rising legal costs.

In 1988 the Council again exercised its newly defined mandate to alter the conclusions of its researchers. Nicole Morgan wrote an assessment for the Council of the status of women in the federal public service between 1908 and 1987, reporting some progress for women in the service.[54] For example, in 1987 the federal public service had about 90,000 female workers, an increase of 15 per cent from 1976; in that same period the proportion of female managers had increased threefold. Morgan also reported some problems. There are, she notes, several ways to cal-

---

52   Interview with Karen Stotsky, Ottawa, July 1994.

53   Canadian Advisory Council on the Status of Women, *Integration and Participation* (Ottawa: CACSW, 1987), pp.87-88.

54   Nicole Morgan, *The Equality Game: Women in the Federal Public Service (1908-1987)* (Ottawa: CACSW, 1988).

culate women's advancement. One can calculate the proportion of women compared to men in senior jobs; or one can compare "the manner in which hierarchical levels evolve in the respective populations."[55] Using the first technique one can argue that women progressed substantially between 1976 and 1987. Female executives were only 2.4 per cent of the total in 1976, and they reached 8.7 per cent in 1987. But, as Morgan points out, the male pyramid shifted in this same period, with more men moving into middle management positions as women climbed the executive ladder. "The fundamental issue that this ... trend raises is the speed at which both groups have advanced. Because women have lagged behind in the past, they will never catch up to men unless their advancement is more rapid, which does not seem to be the case."[56]

The Advisory Council's communique/press release on Morgan's book tells a different story. The Council announced that nearly 40 per cent of executive and senior management appointments between 1976 and 1985 went to women. In a response to the Council, Morgan protested that these data were incorrect. She noted: "This would not matter at all if the percentage were not seriously wrong. For the years when this information is available ... we find that in 1986, for example, only 14.9% of the Executive and senior management appointments went to women as recently as two years ago."[57] Morgan continued in her letter to list misleading quotations and figures used by the Council in its communique. The matter was never resolved.

FURTHER REFLECTIONS ON PRACTICE

Traditional male/mainstream academics have long been engaged in the pursuit of policy changes. They became heavily involved in the business of advising governments in the 1970s in Canada. For J. Vanderkamp, the first editor of Canadian Public Policy, this means providing governments "with new perspectives and alternatives, and groups and individuals with a basis for making more informed contributions."[58] In his reflections on the first eight years of his journal's life, he writes that the publication "was designed to deepen our understanding, to strengthen

---

55   Ibid., p.54.

56   Ibid., p.54.

57   Personal communication from Nicole Morgan to Sylvia Gold, President of the Advisory Council on the Status of Women, December 12, 1988.

58   J. Vanderkamp, "Canadian Public Policy: The First Eight Years," Canadian Public Policy, VIII,4 (August 1982), p.518.

the dialogue between practical scholars and scholarly practitioners and to help make the analysis of policy an acceptable scholarly activity."[59] Somewhat later Leslie Pal, in a contribution to an international journal "devoted to the improvement of policy-making," argued that academic policy analysts could be hired by governments as "consulting critics" in order to integrate the social sciences more closely with government policy-making.[60]

Feminist policy researchers are well equipped to offer alternative policy advice that takes women into account. Most apparently, during the past twenty years they have developed the skills needed to listen to women's needs, perspectives, and experiences as they are articulated in different racial, class, and situational positions. To date the voices they hear have not reached the policy-making community. A separatist approach to feminist research has provided the space for developing these new skills. But feminist methods also require that these skills be used to transform political practice.[61]

SUGGESTED READINGS

Judy Fudge and Patricia McDermott, eds., *Just Wages: A Feminist Assessment of Pay Equity*. Toronto: University of Toronto Press, 1991.

Kathleen P. Jones and Anna G. Jonasdottir, eds. *The Political Interests of Gender*. London: Sage, 1985.

Elizabeth Meehan and Selma Sevenhuijsen, eds., *Equality Politics and Gender*. London: Sage, 1991.

Carole Pateman and Elizabeth Gross, eds., *Feminist Challenges* Sydney: Allen and Unwin, 1986.

Anne Phillips, *Democracy and Difference*. University Park, Pennsylvania: Penn. State University Press, 1993.

Richard Simeon, "Studying Public Policy," *Canadian Journal of Political Science* IX,4, (December 1976), pp.548-80.

59   Vanderkamp, "Canadian Public Policy," p.518.

60   Leslie A. Pal, "Consulting Critics: A New Role for Academic Policy Analysts," *Policy Sciences*, 18 (1985), pp.357-69.

61   I wish to thank Lorraine Code, Terry Downey, and Leslie Pal for their comments on an earlier draft of this chapter. The Social Sciences and Humanities Research Council of Canada supported some of the work I report here.

Contributors

Linda Archibald is a social policy consultant in Ottawa. She has been working on various projects with Pauktuutit since 1988.

Sandra Burt is associate professor of political science at the University of Waterloo, where she was the first co-ordinator of Women's Studies and is now the advisor on Academic Human Resources. In her research she has examined different forms of political participation, as well as the methods used traditionally by social scientists to measure that participation. Her work has been published in *Canadian Public Policy*, the *Windsor Yearbook of Access to Justice*, and *Women and Politics*. She is now examining the changing relationship between national and local women's groups in Canada, as well as between women's groups and the state.

Lorraine Code is professor of philosophy and director of the Graduate Programme in Philosophy at York University in Toronto, and a member of the Graduate Faculty in Social and Political Thought and in Women's Studies. She is the author of *Epistemic Responsibility* (UPNE, 1987), *What Can She Know? Feminist Theory and the Construction of Knowledge* (Cornell, 1991), and *Rhetorical Spaces: Essays on (Gendered) Locations* (Routledge, 1995). She is co-editor of *Feminist Perspectives: Philosophical Essays on Methods and Morals* (1988) and *Changing Patterns: Women in Canada* (1988; second edition, 1993). She is working, as general editor, on a one-volume *Encyclopedia of Feminist Theories*, to be published by Routledge UK.

Mary Crnkovich is a lawyer working with Pauktuutit on its Justice project. She is the editor of *Gossip: A Spoken History of Women in the North*.

Kristin Colwell teaches in the Early Childhood Education program at St. Lawrence College in Kingston, Ontario. In 1984-85 she taught at Croydon College in London, England, on an exchange arrangement, and in 1988-90 she was at Arctic College in Iqaluit, Northwest Territories, where she set up an early childhood education program.

Susan Ehrlich is an associate professor of linguistics and chair of the Department of Languages, Literature and Linguistics at York University. She is the author of *Point of View: A Linguistic Analysis of Literary Style* (Routledge, 1990), and co-author with Peter Avery of *Teaching American English Pronunciation* (Oxford University Press, 1992). Her forthcoming book on language, power, and ideology will be published by Blackwell Publishers, Oxford.

Lorraine Greaves is a sociologist, activist, speaker and researcher on issues of violence against women, and women and addictions. She has a B.A. and M.A. from the University of Western Ontario and a Ph.D. from Monash University, Australia. She is the director of the Centre for Research on Violence Against Women and Children in London, Ontario, and is on the faculty of Fanshawe College. The centre is devoted to creating and encouraging action research in a partnership with community service agencies, community colleges and universities. She is a co-founder of the London Status of Women Action Group, the Battered Women's Advocacy Centre, the London Women's Monument Project, and the Centre for Research on Violence Against Women and Children. She has served several national and international women's organizations, including the National Action Committee on the Status of Women and the International Network of Women Against Tobacco. She has authored papers, book chapters, and articles on issues of violence against women, women's tobacco use, and the women's movement, and a book, *Smoke Screen*, about women's tobacco use.

Ann Hall is a professor in the Faculty of Physical Education and Recreation at the University of

Alberta, where she has taught since 1968. She is also a former chair of the Women's Studies Program in the Faculty of Arts at that university. Engaged in "speaking feminism" to the sport and physical education world for over twenty years, she is the author of several books, numerous articles, chapters, and papers. She is at work on a history of women's sport in Canada since 1920.

Karen Messing has been a professor of biological sciences at the University of Quebec in Montreal since 1976. She started her career as a geneticist and became involved in occupational health through an agreement between the University of Quebec and Quebec trade unions. Since 1990 she has directed CINBIOSE (Centre pour l'étude des interactions biologiques entre la santé et l'environnement). She is the author of *Occupational Health and Safety Concerns of Canadian Women*.

Arun Prab Mukherjee was born in 1946 in Lahore, India. After the partition of the country in 1947, her parents fled to India and she was raised and educated in Tikamgarh, Madhya Pradesh. She did her graduate work in English at the University of Saugar, India, and came to Canada as a Commonwealth Scholar to do graduate work at the University of Toronto. She is associate professor in the Department of English at York University, Toronto, and teaches courses in postcolonial literature and women's studies. The mother of a seventeen-year-old son, Gautam, she is also the author of *The Gospel of Wealth in the American Novel: The Rhetoric of Dreiser and His Contemporaries* (1987), and *Towards an Aesthetic of Opposition: Essays on Literature, Criticism and Cultural Imperialism* (1988). She has edited and written the Introduction of *Sharing Our Experience* (1993), an anthology of autobiographical writings by Aboriginal women and women of colour. *Oppositional Aesthetics: Readings from a Hyphenated Space* (TSAR publications, Toronto) is in press.

Brenda O'Neill is completing her doctorate in political science at the University of British Columbia. In her research she focuses on public opinion and gender in Canada. She teaches part-time at Red Deer College, Alberta.

Randi R. Warne is Director of Women's Studies and assistant professor of religious studies at the University of Wisconsin, Oshkosh. She is past-president of the Canadian Society of Church History and is serving a second term on the executive of the Canadian Society for Studies in Religion.

Nettie Wiebe farms with her husband and four children near Laura, Saskatchewan. They grow grains, oilseeds, and pulse crops as well as raising cattle. A community activist, she has worked on agricultural, environmental, and women's issues - particularly farm women's issues. She holds a Ph.D in philosophy from the University of Calgary.

Alison Wylie was trained in the "History and Philosophy of the Social and Behavioral Sciences" (at SUNY-Binghamton) and is interested in feminist critiques of science and feminist research methodologies in the social sciences. In her recent work she examines gender research in archaeology, using this as the basis for an account of situated objectivity. Her essays on feminist initiatives in archaeology have appeared as the 1994 Skomp Lecture (Indiana University), in *Engendering Archaeology* (edited by Gero and Conkey, Blackwell, 1991), and *American Antiquity* (1992); she is co-editor of *Equity Issues for Women in Archaeology* (AAZA/AD forthcoming); and her work on feminist theories of science has appeared in *Resources for Feminist Research, Women's Studies International Forum*, and *Women and Reason* (edited by Harvey and Okruhlik, Michigan 1992). As a member of the board of the London Battered Women's Advocacy Centre, she has collaborated in writing several pamphlets and articles on violence against women. She teaches Philosophy and Women's Studies at the University of Western Ontario.